Society, Science, and Problem-Solving Courts

Society, Science, and Problem-Solving Courts

MONICA K. MILLER, MIA A. HOLBROOK, LOGAN A. YELDERMAN, AND KYLIE KULAK

OXFORD
UNIVERSITY PRESS

OXFORD
UNIVERSITY PRESS

Oxford University Press is a department of the University of Oxford. It furthers the University's objective of excellence in research, scholarship, and education by publishing worldwide. Oxford is a registered trade mark of Oxford University Press in the UK and certain other countries.

Published in the United States of America by Oxford University Press
198 Madison Avenue, New York, NY 10016, United States of America.

CIP data is on file at the Library of Congress

ISBN 978-0-19-005980-4

DOI: 10.1093/oso/9780190059804.001.0001

Printed by Marquis Book Printing, Canada

MIX
Paper | Supporting responsible forestry
FSC® C103567
FSC www.fsc.org

To David Wexler and Bruce Winick who inspired me to study ways courts can promote well-being.
—MKM

To my writing cheerleaders, thank you.
—MAH

To Wendy Schiller, Jessica Pearce, Cheri Ely, Shawn Marsh, Martha-Elin Blomquist, Doug Thomas, and the National Council of Juvenile and Family Court Judges for providing me with knowledge, opportunity, and inspiration.
—LAY

To those who believed in me, and even those who did not.
—KK

The authors would like to thank the International Institute for the Sociology of Law in Oñati, Spain, for allowing the first author to access informants in the data provided in Chapters 9 and 10. The authors would also like to thank the following entities for partial funding that made this book possible: University of Nevada, Reno College of Liberal Arts, University of Nevada, Reno's International Activities Grant program, and the Nevada System of Higher Education Board of Regents. Thanks to Annie Clements for research assistance in Chapter 4. Thanks also to Sarah Harrington for her super-human patience in seeing this book from idea to reality.

Contents

SECTION 5: PROBLEM-SOLVING COURTS: LOOKING TO THE FUTURE BY LOOKING AT THE PAST

CONCLUSION

SECTION 1

INTRODUCTION TO PROBLEM-SOLVING COURTS

1
Society, Science, and Problem-Solving Courts in the United States and Abroad

Problem-Solving Courts

The state of the science and the importance of society

As 2024 began, homelessness remained a major social issue in the United States. Lance Valdez had experienced homelessness since his mother died in 2013; subsequently, he was charged for unlawful entry and received a $200 fine. Devita Liest was homeless since 2017, struggled with drug addiction, and was charged with public intoxication and drug possession. Many people in such circumstances do not have the methods of communication (e.g., email or a phone number), drivers' licenses, or social security cards required to gain employment. Some are unable to take care of their hygiene, medical, or nutritional needs. Many have tickets, fines, or outstanding warrants—for offenses often related to their homelessness (e.g., loitering)—and this makes it difficult to find jobs and housing. Judge Ingrid Uhler and her staff developed an innovative way to help people like Valdez and Liest in their journeys to healthier and productive living.

In December 2023, Judge Uhler dismissed Valdez's fine and Liest's outstanding charges. Liest has been sober for four months, and Valdez soon will be able to get a driver's license—steps that will enable them to find jobs and safe housing. Judge Uhler has helped thousands of people as part of the Shelter Court, which is a joint effort between the San Bernardino County Probation Department and the Superior Court in California (Espinal, 2023). This is commonly called a "homelessness court," a type of problem-solving court (PSC) that focuses on helping people who are experiencing homelessness and other social issues (e.g., drug addiction, mental health problems). This court is unique in many ways, including that the judge and other legal officials do not operate in a courthouse; instead, they go to places where people who are experiencing homelessness congregate and often

Society, Science, and Problem-Solving Courts. Monica K. Miller, Mia A. Holbrook, Logan A. Yelderman, and Kylie Kulak, Oxford University Press. © Oxford University Press 2025. DOI: 10.1093/oso/9780190059804.003.0001

hold hearings there. In December 2023, Judge Uhler and her staff went to Redlands Salvation Army with the goal of helping people overcome homelessness by removing their misdemeanor charges, tickets, or fines. During such hearings, the judge provides contact information for places where they can receive services which will help people like Valdez and Leist.

Similarly, the Phoenix Community Court began operating in January 2024 as a result of a $2.3 million investment the city made to reduce homelessness, which had recently increased 72% (Estes, 2024; Reagan, 2024). The court will operate using a "holistic and compassionate" approach to helping the individual person and the community as a whole. This court uses a pre-adjudication model, meaning that the traditional court process is halted while the person is involved in the Phoenix Community Court. The court provides the person with connections to needed social services designed to help them overcome their challenges. If the person is unable to meet the court's requirements (e.g., using the services to gain housing, employment, and medical services), they will be transferred to the traditional court system.

Homelessness courts such as the Shelter Court and Phoenix Community Court are just one of the 18 types of PSCs discussed in Chapter 2 and throughout this book. These include courts for social issues that can relate to criminal offending, such as addiction or mental illness. Some PSCs address special populations such as prostitutes or veterans. Others address specific crimes such as animal abuse or domestic violence. All are intended to help offenders (and sometimes victims), prevent recidivism, protect the community, and reduce courts' overburdened dockets.

PSCs (sometimes called helping courts or specialty courts) in the United States started with the adoption of a drug court in Florida in 1989 (see Chapter 2 for a description and history of each court type). PSCs have expanded to many other countries, yet many countries have not adopted this PSC model (see Chapters 9 and 10). For example, some countries address social issues in *all* of their courts and there is nothing "special" about courts that help offenders. Other countries have different methods to address social issues outside of the court system (e.g., churches or private organizations). These examples illustrate how culture can play a part in PSCs, which are primarily a feature of Western culture and legal systems (Nolan, 2012). The United States applied a liberal orientation toward PSCs, largely due to a cultural belief that these courts were revolutionizing the legal and criminal justice system in America. Although evidence-based implementation of PSCs was a foundational goal in the United States, the proliferation of these courts severely outpaced the scientific research regarding their effectiveness. Other countries, in contrast, took a more conservative and careful approach to implementing PSCs and incorporated them at a much slower rate, reducing the rapid advancement seen in the United States but enhancing the stability of the courts' integration (Nolan, 2012). Courts in both the United States and in other countries were shaped by their cultural and legal structures and were largely implemented, initially, without sound evidence of their effectiveness. Now that several decades have passed, there is more evidence on the effectiveness of these courts and scientific research is slowly catching up. Additionally, other science is needed to operate PSCs, including drug testing. As such, both society (e.g., culture) and science have played roles in how PSCs have been adopted and implemented.

This book is a review of the types, history, and scientific research on PSCs in the United States and many other countries. It provides a unique focus not found in other literature, however: a focus on *science* and *society*. Science refers to the tools needed to operate the courts (e.g., monitoring the location of people under house arrest to ensure they do not leave their home). Science also refers to the scientific methods of testing whether the courts work as intended and the theoretical and philosophical bases of the courts, such as the principles of therapeutic jurisprudence and procedural justice. Society refers to cultural or subcultural influences on whether societies view social phenomena as problems and what could be possible solutions to these problems. In this book, we have adopted the Social Mind-set (SMS) model (see Chapter 8) to help explain the uneven adoption of PSCs across societies. For instance, the social mind-set of one society might be based on the belief that drug use is a *medical condition* that can be addressed in the court system to prevent criminal recidivism. The social mind-set of another country might be based on the belief that drug use is a *personal choice* and thus does not need to be addressed by the courts. Social scientists call these conflicting beliefs (which vary by society) external/situational versus internal/personal attributions (see Chapter 8). As this example suggests, it is sometimes difficult to separate science and society.

The main premise of the book is that science and society together can explain much of the development, expansion, and variety of PSCs in the United States and many other countries across the globe. More broadly, we posit that society and science are important considerations in both the past and the future of PSCs. This chapter gives a brief description of PSCs and definitions of both science and society as relevant to PSCs. Finally, it gives an overview of each of the chapters of the book.

What Are Problem-Solving Courts?

The homelessness courts previously described illustrate one of the many types of PSCs, which vary by society (e.g., a country, state, or region). More broadly, PSCs are a type of specialty court that handles cases involving certain subsets of a population (e.g., veterans) or types of crimes (e.g., prostitution) or social issues (e.g., drug addiction; Miller et al., 2020). These courts are different from other special courts (e.g., bankruptcy courts) in that they attempt to address the social issues contributing to the person's wrongdoing (Gatowski et al., 2013; Winick, 2003). More specifically, these courts treat underlying conditions (e.g., drug addiction, unemployment) by offering services and case plans (see, generally, Wiener & Brank, 2013) and therapy (see, generally, DeMatteo et al., 2019) based on the specific needs of the offender. These courts are also different from traditional courts in that they require judges to take a more active role, often acting as a case manager over many months or years. In addition to deciding guilt or listening to the case facts, judges in PSCs also connect offenders to appropriate services, monitor the offenders' compliance with services, motivate the offender to continue on in the program, and, if needed, assign punishment for failures to comply (Winick, 2003). PSCs have an intricate relationship with both science and society, as discussed next.

The science of problem-solving courts

In this book, we define "science" as data and theory produced by social scientists (e.g., experts in sociology, political science, psychology, criminal justice) or medical scientists (e.g., experts in psychiatric medications and treatments), as well as technology used by PSCs. This science comes in many forms. First, science can help lawmakers recognize that something occurring in society is, in fact, an issue; identify ways that the issue can be addressed; and evaluate whether solutions could be or were actually effective. For instance, science has helped the legal system track the increase in drug-related crimes and determine that drug-related crimes are a growing problem that needs to be addressed. Science has helped determine that drug abuse is an addiction that can be treated through medical and psychological treatment (see, generally, Chapter 2). Such science encouraged the development of drug courts, which are designed to help participants who experience drug addiction. The drug courts require the offender to take steps (e.g., treatment, education) that will help them recover from their addiction—and hopefully refrain from committing more crimes in the future.

Second, science includes justice theories and principles that are the foundation of some PSCs (see Chapter 3). For instance, therapeutic jurisprudence principles ask the legal system to consider the well-being of the people who come into contact with the system—including offenders in PSCs. Instead of only punishing someone for their criminal wrong-doings, PSCs attempt to help offenders address the social issues (e.g., mental illness) related to their offending. This is an approach that addresses the principles of therapeutic jurisprudence. In addition, justice theories are used as foundations to PSCs differently across countries. Some countries place more of an emphasis on restorative justice and others place more of an emphasis on retributive justice (punishment). Although we generally suggest that science and culture shape these courts, it is also the case that different countries have different cultures *of* science that influence PSCs. This is particularly evident in the application of justice principles (see Chapters 3 and 8).

Third, psychological theories underlie PSCs; this is the crux of Chapter 4. For instance, the rational actor model posits that people who have a decision to make have various options from which to choose. The person considers the costs and benefits of each choice and makes a choice that has the most benefits and fewest costs. Much of the legal system assumes that offenders make rational choices in this way. This includes PSCs; it is assumed that offenders will choose to take steps to address the social issues (e.g., homelessness, addiction) that brought them into contact with the law rather than accept a punishment and continue their lifestyle. Cognitive science, behavioral science, social science, and physiology are all key elements in the scientific study of how PSCs work for their participants. It is through the integration of these fields and their application that PSCs begin to form a programmatic structure that is effective, repeatable, and able to be modeled in other jurisdictions.

Next, science can be used to evaluate PSCs to determine whether they are effective. In general, courts track the outcomes of the people who appear in the courts—sometimes comparing these outcomes to similar people who appear in traditional courts. The evaluation of PSCs frequently involves the exploration of diverse principles of justice and psychological concepts, including therapeutic jurisprudence, procedural justice, community sentiment, and social support. The application of theories from the realms of justice and psychology can manifest differently in PSC evaluations. Courts may prioritize distinct theories in shaping their structure and functioning while researchers may adopt specific theoretical frameworks to steer their assessments. These scientific evaluations of PSCs are the focus of Chapters 5 and 6.

Finally, science can also make PSCs possible by providing the technology necessary for monitoring offenders and communication among service providers and judges (e.g., email, online shared databases). For instance, ankle monitoring technology can test a person's alcohol level and send a report to the courts indicating that the person has consumed alcohol. Similar monitoring equipment uses GPS technology to track a person's location to ensure they do not leave home or other approved locations. Medical science can test a person's drug use through urine tests. Psychological testing can determine the extent of a person's mental illness.

In sum, there are many sciences that brought about the development and implementation of PSCs. From medical and social science to technology, PSCs—and the legal system more generally—rely heavily on science. Whether society has access to and believes in science is but one of the ways that society affects the implementation of PSCs, as discussed next.

The society of problem-solving courts

For the purposes of this book, we define "society" as a group of people that share a common set of beliefs and values, laws and social structure, or geographical area. This could be a country, state, or region. Our definition also includes societal factors, such as norms, habits, economics, and politics. Often a society has a shared history and culture which shape both these beliefs, norms, social structures and their legal system.

Indeed, culture and law are reflections of each other; for example, the culture of a populace affects what is considered a crime, what causes crime, and how the legal system should respond to crime (e.g., rehabilitation or punishment). Some cultures are "tight," demonstrating a lower tolerance for crime and higher preference for punishment compared to "loose" cultures (Gelfand et al., 2006). In some cultures, it is common for people to subscribe to the belief that people can change and improve themselves, and a person's actions are a product of their situation (incremental selves). In contrast, in some cultures it is common for people to believe that a person's actions are indicative of their stable personality (entity selves; Dweck et al., 1995) and change is less possible. As such, it is no surprise that societies around the globe have adopted different laws and procedures to address differing social issues. Chapter 7 discusses these cultural theories and offers some examples of how culture and law have a close relationship—one that sometimes causes conflicts (e.g., when someone acts in a way that is normal in their culture but illegal in another)—and how culture and law should work together symbiotically.

The SMS model (Miller & Westbrook, 2021) helps explain the effectiveness and implementation of PSCs through evaluating what certain societies consider to be a crime and how to respond to that crime. A social issue must be recognized as a problem worthy of social action and the consequences of legal action. The SMS model suggests six psychological and social factors that shape the policy processes; these six factors are elaborated in detail and applied to the creation and processes of PSCs in Chapter 8.

Chapters 9 and 10 consolidate findings from document review, observations, and interviews with informants from approximately 20 countries, including Italy, Spain, Canada, Scotland, Cameroon, Ecuador, India, Brazil, and France. Chapter 9 expands on factors proposed by Miller's (2020) typology describing why some countries have PSCs (e.g., a high-profile event prompted the formation of courts to address the social issue). Interviewees elaborate on country-specific values and features that explain why PSCs have been adopted. In a similar fashion, Chapter 10 expands on Miller's (2020) typology to elaborate as to why some countries *do not* have PSCs, with interviewees providing their beliefs and explanations (e.g., the society has non-legal entities to address social issues).

In sum, society plays a role in whether PSCs are adopted, and if so, how they are adopted. This book provides a general overview of how society and law are intertwined. Simply put, society adopts laws and legal systems to fit its beliefs, history, and needs. In turn, the law can evolve to shape society through controlling the behavior of people in that society.

Book Overview

Although the United States has numerous PSCs (e.g., drug courts, mental health courts, gambling courts), other countries do not have such courts, have altered versions of these courts, or have courts for other issues (e.g., Aboriginal courts). Some societies address their social issues through courts in dramatically different fashion than PSCs in the United States. As previously discussed, this book takes a social science approach to explain what societal factors (norms, economics, politics, etc.) brought about the development of the wide variety of PSCs. It also highlights societal factors that prevent the development of PSCs or make them unnecessary. Additionally, the book investigates the role of science and technology in the development of such courts. For example, science can help determine whether a PSC is effective.

One main premise of the book is that science and society together can explain much of the development, expansion, and variety of PSCs in the United States and some other countries. More broadly, society and science are important considerations in both the past and the future of PSCs.

In Section 1, "Introduction to Problem-Solving Courts," we describe the most common types of PSCs in various societies, including the United States and around the world. This introduction chapter, Chapter 1, lays the foundation for understanding what PSCs are, and how society and science play a role in whether a country adopts PSC or some other alternative to address social issues.

Chapter 2 discusses various types of PSCs in the United States and around the world. Courts have increasingly become specialized; some of these courts include problem-solving or specialty courts, which began with the establishment of the drug courts in the state of Florida in 1989. Decades later, PSCs are no longer solely a US phenomenon and are no longer limited to providing alternative resolution to crimes that address the underlying problem of substance abuse. PSCs in the United States have been formed to address domestic violence, mental health issues, prostitution, gambling, animal issues, gun violations, and a variety of other social issues that are related to crime for some offenders. Some courts are specially designed to address multiple issues, such as co-occurring mental health issues and substance abuse. Courts in some countries have been formed for certain groups of offenders as well, such as veterans or Aboriginal peoples. Some countries have courts that the United States does not have; other countries have courts with similar purposes but major differences in procedure and philosophy. Chapter 2 discusses 18 types of PSCs in many parts of the world and focuses on the unique history, societal differences, and the science of each type of PSC.

Section 2 is titled "The Science of Problem-Solving Courts." Although science is one of the main themes of the whole book, this section is the foundation for understanding the science behind PSCs. PSCs took a huge leap toward incorporating many types of science in the courts. Specifically, this book will focus on science related to justice principles, psychology, medical treatment and diagnosis, and evaluations of the outcomes of PSCs. Although clinical interventions (see DeMatteo et al., 2019) are an important part of PSCs, this is beyond the scope of this book.

Chapter 3 discusses the science-based justice principles behind these courts, highlighting the cultural differences in the perceptions and use of these principles (e.g., restorative justice). Many PSCs rely on science-based justice principles, such as the adversarial process, therapeutic jurisprudence, procedural justice, legitimacy, fairness, restorative justice, and community sentiment. Although the formal application of these justice principles often occurred post-hoc rather than providing the initial basis, the spirit of these justice principles was surely the basis of the development of PSCs. For instance, restorative justice is the notion that the community, the offender, and the victim can all be "restored" through certain collaborative and cooperative legal procedures. For instance, an offender can be ordered to clean up the buildings which they painted with graffiti, or a victim might be given the chance to tell the offender how they have been harmed by the crime. Restorative justice effectiveness is likely greater for less severe crimes and requires cooperation from both the offender and victim(s). Chapter 3 discusses restorative justice and many other justice principles that apply to PSCs.

Next, Chapter 4 discusses the psychology of PSCs. Psychologists have long recognized that culture affects the development of social behavior, social structures, and social procedures. Thus, it is no surprise that culture plays a role in shaping whether a society considers something to be a social issue, and whether that society's people choose to address this issue through the court system. Psychology is important to the science of PSCs because it provides theoretical explanations for human behavior in which all PSCs are trying to redirect (e.g., drug use, criminal behavior). These theoretical explanations are foundational to understanding what types of processes and procedures should be included in court programs and how to approach analyzing success in PSCs.

Operant conditioning, social norms, and moral decision-making are all psychological processes at play in the implementation of PSCs, and these can vary by society. This chapter discusses the psychological concepts that relate to PSCs and the research that supports these concepts. As stated earlier, psychology is an important part of PSCs because courts are designed to change human behavior—a core part of psychological science. Psychological constructs, such as anticipated emotion, operant conditioning, and social norms, and social support—as well as psychological models, such as the rational actor model—can help predict offenders' behavior. For instance, someone might be more successful in completing the court's orders (e.g., treatment program) because they have social support from the people in their life. More broadly, judges might encourage compliance with court orders by offering rewards for positive behavior (e.g., receiving a gift card for not missing any court appointments) and threatening punishment for negative behavior (e.g., going to jail for a weekend for failing a drug test) according to operant conditioning principles. The use of psychological principles will, of course, vary by jurisdiction, society, and country, but many of the court models and underlying assumptions of human behavior translate across all PSCs.

Chapter 5 discusses the scientific evaluations of PSCs. It also compares how their scientific evaluations might differ by country. Scientific evaluations of PSCs indicate that many of the justice principles and psychology concepts discussed in the previous chapters might relate to outcomes. The purpose of this chapter is to detail the various ways PSCs are scientifically evaluated and assess whether this varies by country, society, or jurisdiction, and if it varies by the type of PSC. The type of dependent variables used in evaluation varies by type of PSC. For example, most evaluations use "recidivism" as a dependent variable, but the evaluations operationalize "recidivism" differently. This can also vary by country; for example, evaluations done in other countries vary from those in the United States. This chapter encompasses a comprehensive review of PSC evaluations in the United States and beyond, examining the components of the evaluations that help detail the success and shortcomings of each type of PSC.

Chapter 6 assesses whether the scientific evaluations suggest that PSCs are successful. It summarizes the evaluations that have been conducted on each of the 18 types of courts discussed in Chapter 2. Conclusions are made about why some courts might be more successful than others, both nationally and internationally.

The science behind PSCs relies heavily on assessing their effectiveness through evaluations. These assessments commonly gauge outcomes tied to participant behavior, covering areas like substance abuse, mental health, employment, housing stability, and criminal justice involvement. Depending on research goals and resources, PSC evaluations employ methods such as randomized controlled trials, quasi-experimental designs, and process evaluations. The findings guide evidence-based decisions on implementing and expanding PSCs. This chapter explores the parallels and distinctions in evaluating PSCs, delving into factors influencing the success of certain courts.

Section 3, "Society and Problem-Solving Courts," provides a general overview of "society and law" by highlighting social science theories that have been posited about the relationship between the two and offering examples of cultural clashes in the legal system. Two chapters situate the topic of PSCs and society in the larger framework of society and law. Societies have different "problems" and different ways to handle problems through the legal system. This chapter will demonstrate how conflicts in law can arise because of clashing cultures, traditions, and social situations. The chapter also uses the SMS model (Miller & Westbrook, 2021) to explain how and why societies with similar issues choose to address issues differently through policy development, including the adoption of PSCs.

Chapter 7 suggests that culture and the individual person are inseparable. People shape the culture of the society and the society shapes the people's behavior, beliefs, and thought processes. Law is one of many avenues for a society's people to express their norms and morals, to make sense of the world, and to express their identity. As social psychologists have long noted, law is a social construction; that is, it is a symbol of what the society values and considers right or wrong. Changes in law over time represent changes in behavior, beliefs, and way of life. Law also represents some cultural facets, such as current events, social issues, community attitudes, and ways of thinking. Thus, by understanding culture (within various societies of the United States and around the world), it is possible to understand why PSCs exist (or not) and why they differ from one society to the next.

Chapter 7 then situates the current book within the broader topic of culture and law by providing a discussion—and a wide variety of examples—of the difficulties faced by the legal system when a cultural practice is discordant with the law. For instance, immigrants who move to the United States have the challenge of interpreting laws and social norms, which sometimes vary greatly from their own culture. Because laws and norms are socially constructed, what is considered "child abuse" or "domestic violence" in one country is considered "normal" in another. For instance, the American parenting practice of allowing an infant to cry himself to sleep in a small "cage" (crib) in a separate room from his parents is considered abusive by other cultures. Some defendants have been allowed to use a "cultural defense"—a special defense used in countries such as the United States and Canada. Social scientists who conduct relevant research often testify during such trials.

Part of this chapter discusses a variety of subcultures which could contribute to a person's involvement in the legal system. For instance, in the southern United States, there is a "culture of honor" which includes the belief that retribution for perceived offenses is normal and expected, as one has a right to do "pay back" for transgressions and to protect one's property/family. Chapter 7 discusses the intersection between culture and law generally. This lays the foundation for understanding how PSCs might differ by culture.

Using Chapter 7 as a background for understanding cultural differences in the law, Chapter 8 discusses the concept of the "Social Mind-set (SMS) model." The SMS model posits that societies around the world can vary greatly in their responses to some behaviors, often with one considering the behavior to be a crime and another not. Even when societies do agree that a behavior is a crime, they might disagree about the proper response to that crime. The SMS model builds off the frameworks suggested by Blumer (1973) and Kingdon (2003), who offer complementary explanations for how social issues become law. Both discuss how a social issue is recognized as a problem worthy of legal action and the resulting processes that result in legal action. Yet, those models stop short of explaining why the legal actions that are adopted differ from one country to the next. They do, however, acknowledge that the policy process is influenced by social factors (e.g., high-profile cases and social movements), beliefs, and ideologies. These are some of the factors (e.g., psychological attributions, availability of science, social events, economic situation) that comprise what Miller and Westbrook (2021) call the social mind-set. The SMS model proposes that social mind-sets are precursors to the policy processes described by Blumer and Kingdon. Specifically, the model suggests six social and psychological factors that influence the social mind-set of a society, which in turn shapes the policy processes described by Blumer and Kingdon. This chapter is the first application of the SMS model to a specific context: PSCs.

Section 4, "The Development (or Not) of Problem-Solving Courts," includes two chapters addressing cultural differences in PSCs using the scientific method to explore reasons why some countries adopt PSCs, why some do *not* adopt PSCs, and how some *adapt* the traditional US-based model to fit their culture. Many of these explanations relate to scientific or social influences. Chapter 7 of this book discussed the broader body of research on culture and the law *generally* to provide readers with a better understanding of culture and the courts more *specifically* in this section. By understanding the social science related to culture, it is possible to understand why some societies embrace the "helping" nature of PSCs while others do not. This is the main focus of this section.

Using the previous chapters as a foundation, this section delves into the specifics of the impact of society on PSCs. Both chapters compare many countries to each other and to the United States, and they attempt to make some broad conclusions about society's role in the development (or not) of PSCs. The roles of science and technology are highlighted in the development or rejection of PSCs, as well as the role of social issues and community sentiment. These chapters feature interviews from citizens of various countries expressing their beliefs as to why their countries ultimately adopt or reject PSCs.

Chapter 9 considers why some societies do develop PSCs. This chapter uses scientific methods to explore reasons for the surge in specialized courts vary by country. Even when the underlying problem (e.g., overcrowded courts and prisons) is pragmatic, the choice of how to address the problem (e.g., build more prisons, start PSCs) reflects the values and social norms of the society. Miller (2020) indicates that PSCs can arise for many reasons, including: (1) changes in social structure (e.g., less involvement of churches which used to handle such social issues), (2) changes in social issues (e.g., war veterans face many issues that make them at risk for offending), (3) changes in society's view of problems (e.g., feminist movement brought attention to domestic violence), (4) as a response to society's demands (e.g., community sentiment favors addressing an issue), and (5) advances in science and medicine (e.g., findings that social issues contribute to crime, understanding of addiction, advances in technology to monitor offenders). This chapter expands on the Miller (2020) typology of reasons some societies develop PSCs by including more countries and, possibly, more factors.

In contrast to Chapter 9, Chapter 10 is about why some societies do *not* develop PSCs. Social mind-sets (the focus of Chapter 8) are likely to hinder development of courts, including beliefs that (1) it takes too much time/money to address social issues (a reflection of the society's values); (2) a judge's role is not to help offenders overcome their problems; (3) it is not the court's role to address social issues; (4) the country is bound by their laws to provide "rehabilitative" responses for *every* offender, and not just those with "special" circumstances; (5) the country is struggling with "bigger problems," such as drug cartels, and thus do not focus on individual rehabilitation; and (6) some countries are not exposed to scientific research, technology, or advocates who would bring about awareness of social issues. This chapter sets out a typology, initially set forth by Miller (2020), of reasons some societies do *not* develop PSC. This chapter expands on the Miller (2020) typology of reasons some societies develop PSCs by including more countries.

In Section 5, "Problem-Solving Courts: Looking to the Future by Looking at the Past," this book looks both back and forward to make some broad conclusions about PSCs in the United States and abroad. This section looks backward, identifying how courts have expanded as a whole, and identifying what has "worked" and what did not "work" (e.g., pros and cons). The section also looks forward, identifying how and why special courts might expand or contract in the future. By weighing the pros and cons of courts—and assessing whether they have accomplished what was intended—some general commentary is offered as to the future of PSCs (e.g., should they contract or expand?). This discussion also stresses the role of science and society in both the past and future.

Chapter 11 weighs the pros and cons to determine whether PSCs are needed. This discussion essentially revolves around effectiveness and influence. The results from numerous meta-analyses on PSCs, primarily drug courts and mental health courts, promote the benefits of most courts but raise questions regarding the effectiveness of others (see Chapters 5 and 6). In Chapter 11, the effectiveness of courts' abilities to reduce crime and reduce maladaptive behavior is examined for each court that has this level of research. One limitation noted in the chapter is that many of the types of PSCs simply do not have enough research to provide the public with any true conclusions about their effectiveness. This is problematic because the successes of these courts are still being promoted, despite a lack of supporting research. To address this, a collaborative effort between the courts and researchers needs to be made to apply scientific reasoning to court development and tests of court outcomes.

The final chapter of this book provides the reader with concluding remarks regarding the past and future of PSCs—specifically as is relevant to science and society. Chapter 12 relies on the previous chapters in this book to draw conclusions about how science and society have affected the development (or not) of PSCs in the past, resulting in the courts of today. It also makes predictions about how science and society will affect the PSCs of tomorrow. This includes issues of diversity, establishing quality evaluations, ethics, expansion versus contraction, and areas for improvement.

In sum, this book looks both backward to the development and forward to the future of PSCs that have revolutionized court systems around the world. These efforts have been shaped by both science and society. These efforts highlight the changes in legal systems that can, in some ways, be credited to the brave judges in Miami, Florida, in 1989 who dared to start a controversial new drug court.

2

Overview of the Types of Problem-Solving Courts

Mia A. Holbrook and Mary Dhondt

Problem-Solving Courts Around the World

Over the years, the US court system has evolved from what scholars recognize as solely a traditional adversarial process. Courts have increasingly specialized through this progression, incorporating problem-solving or specialty concentrations. Problem-solving courts (PSCs) began with the establishment of the first drug court in the United States, in the state of Florida, in 1989. Since then, many more have spawned across the United States and beyond and they address so many more issues than drugs (see Atkin-Plunk, 2021; DeMatteo et al., 2019).

PSCs in the United States and across the globe intend to address mental health, prostitution, gambling, domestic violence, animal issues, gun violations, and various other social issues related to crime. Some PSCs address multiple problems, such as co-occurring mental health issues and substance abuse. Other courts, such as veterans' treatment courts, elder protection courts, or Aboriginal courts, focus on the group of participants rather than the offense committed. In addition, some countries have PSCs that the United States does not have, while others have PSCs with similar purposes but critical differences in procedure, practice, and philosophy. This chapter discusses 18 different types of PSCs used in various parts of the world by comparing and contrasting the court components. This chapter will also highlight the unique history, societal differences, and science of each type of PSC.

Society, Science, and Problem-Solving Courts. Monica K. Miller, Mia A. Holbrook, Logan A. Yelderman, and Kylie Kulak, Oxford University Press. © Oxford University Press 2025. DOI: 10.1093/oso/9780190059804.003.0002

Types of problem-solving courts

There are many types of PSCs in the United States and around the world. This chapter will overview the most common 18 types: drug courts, driving while impaired/driving under the influence (DWI/DUI) courts, mental health courts (MHCs), community courts, domestic violence courts, human trafficking courts, gambling courts, prostitution courts, veterans' treatment courts (VTCs), Aboriginal courts, child support courts, family dependency treatment courts, reentry courts, animal courts, gun courts, homelessness courts, US tribal courts, and elder protection courts. Each subsection below discusses these types of PSCs.

While the United States is the leader in PSCs, some countries have courts that the United States does not have. Other countries have courts with similar purposes but effective procedures and underlying philosophical differences. This chapter will highlight the cross-cultural differences and adaptations. Further, courts rely on science (e.g., medical advances, technology, philosophical justice), but this can vary based on type and country. The subsections below discuss many PSCs throughout the world, focusing on science and cultural differences.

Drug courts

History

Drug courts were the first PSCs to emerge in the United States. The first drug court was established in 1989 in Miami, Florida (see also Atkin-Plunk, 2021). Drug courts responded to the overwhelming population of drug offenders imprisoned due to the "War on Drugs" campaign advanced by the government of the day (Finn & Newlyn, 1993). The zero-tolerance "War on Drugs" policy of the early 1970s and the subsequent prison population boom is credited as the "driving force" behind the implementation of drug courts (Stinchcomb, 2010). The Miami-Dade Department of Corrections and Rehabilitation had significant fiscal demands from a constantly increasing jail population; they also received a federal court order to reduce overcrowding to acceptable limits (Stinchcomb, 2010). Additionally, local judges were frustrated from sentencing more offenders to probation, only to have them end up in prison after having their community supervision revoked (Drug Strategies, 1997). As a result, the first drug court provided an alternative solution that included a treatment-oriented approach (Stinchcomb, 2010). The Miami Drug Court's early success and support led to a rapid implementation of drug courts across the United States (Listwan et al., 2006). In 2017, the first drug court opened to specifically target opioids; this opioid court in Buffalo, New York, is specifically tailored to the needs of opioid users in response to the opioid crisis (Shannon et al., 2021).

The creation of drug courts was not based on a theoretical model. Instead, drug courts were a practical response to the overwhelming caseloads and frustrations with the current system (Hora, 2002). However, about a decade after the creation of drug courts, a theoretical framework was established (Shaffer, 2011). There are over 3,000 drug courts in the United States; half of these are adult treatment drug courts (US Department of Justice, 2020). Over 70,000 people are receiving services from drug court programs (Huddleston et al., 2008). After introducing the first drug court in 1989 as an alternative solution, drug courts have been established nationwide.

Operations

Drug courts primarily operate under a model called the 10 Key Components. This model, established by the National Association of Drug Court Professionals, is outlined in materials produced by the US Department of Justice Office of Justice Programs (1997). The 10 Key Components are as follows:

1. Drug courts integrate alcohol and other drug treatment services with justice system case processing.
2. Using a non-adversarial approach, prosecution and defense counsel promote public safety while protecting participants' due process rights.
3. Eligible participants are identified early and promptly placed in the drug court program.
4. Drug courts provide access to a continuum of alcohol, drug, and other related treatment and rehabilitation services.
5. Abstinence is monitored by frequent alcohol and other drug testing.
6. A coordinated strategy governs drug court responses to participants' compliance.
7. Ongoing judicial interaction with each drug court participant is essential.
8. Monitoring and evaluation measure the achievement of program goals and gauge effectiveness.

9. Continuing interdisciplinary education promotes effective drug court planning, implementation, and operations.
10. Forging partnerships among drug courts, public agencies, and community-based organizations generates local support and enhances drug court program effectiveness.

Successful drug courts often use standardized risk assessment tools to target specific treatment needs (Mitchell et al., 2012). Subsequently, court participants work with an evidence-based treatment plan that often occurs in stages (Mitchell et al., 2012). Treatment plans include drug testing, participation in social services, maintaining employment, and more. Termination can occur upon failure to comply with the treatment program. After graduation, participants receive follow-ups to ensure proper aftercare (NADCP, 2013). Drug courts aim to promote positive behavioral changes in court participants by using the 10 Key Components model, evidence-based treatment plans, and the promotion of successful graduation.

Scope of adoption/culture

After the successful implementation of drug courts in the United States, jurisdictions worldwide have considered the benefits of implementing drug court models. When drug courts were first created, it was in response to the overwhelming population of drug offenders, often attributed to the laws regulating drugs. What once was zero-tolerance enforcement has shifted to voluntary treatment programs (Andrews & Bonta, 2006). By the early 1990s, studies on drug addiction found it could not be addressed solely with traditional incarceration (Andrews & Bonta, 2006).

Several countries, including Canada, Australia, Scotland, and Ireland, have developed drug treatment courts primarily based on the US model (Harrison & Scarpitti, 2002). In Canada, the first drug court opened in Toronto, Ontario, in December 1998. Unlike the US model, which focuses on a wide range of drugs, this Canadian court focuses primarily on heroin and cocaine offenders (Harrison & Scarpitti, 2002). Other differences from the US model include a heavy emphasis on supportive social services and the harm reduction philosophy (La Prairie et al., 2002). This focus on harm reduction can be attributed to cultural differences in the style of drug court programs (Nolan, 2010). For example, US drug courts focus on "demand reduction" (Bakht, 2005), incentivizing complete abstinence from drug usage.

On the other hand, international drug courts focus on "harm reduction," which emphasizes safe strategies and techniques to reduce the harm caused by the participant's lifestyle (Nolan, 2010).

In Australia, the first drug treatment court opened in Sydney, New South Wales, in 1999. Based on the US model, people who meet eligibility criteria can choose to participate in court-supervised treatment lasting 12 months or accept a traditional sentence (Freeman, 2003). The court-supervised treatment consists of four elements: drug treatment, social support, regular reporting to court, and regular urine tests. Like other international courts, there is a focus on "harm reduction" (Freeman, 2003). Since the first drug court was created in 1999, courts have been established throughout Australia. While drug courts were created considering drug concerns within the United States, their importance to appropriate sentencing has been recognized internationally.

Science

Most drug courts base their operation on the science of therapeutic jurisprudence and effective intervention (Wexler, 2000). Drug courts target criminal actions by addressing the underlying behavior through treatment services and judicial supervision. First introduced by Wexler (2000), therapeutic jurisprudence is implementing the role of the law through a therapeutic approach (see Chapter 3). When using therapeutic jurisprudence, all court processes, including interactions between actors, organization of proceedings, and legal rules/policies, should be implemented or conducted to encourage health and positive growth (Rottman & Casey, 1999). Implementing therapeutic justice principles can produce better outcomes for PSCs (e.g., Hinshaw, 2005; Schepard & Bozzomo, 2003).

While therapeutic jurisprudence was developed independently of drug courts, the drug court model is a natural application (Hora, 2002). Therapeutic jurisprudence within drug courts relies on collaborations for all criminal justice and public health professionals' decisions to balance treatment with change (Lutze & van Wormer, 2007). The collaboration between judges, social service practitioners, and participants, the voluntary nature, and the provision of treatment services are all consistent with the therapeutic jurisprudence approach (Hora, 2002).

A more comprehensive explanation of the drug court model should consider the restorative justice approach and the principles of effective intervention (Gendreau et al., 1996; Shaffer, 2011). Stemming from meta-analytic work (Gendreau et al., 2006), eight principles of effective intervention developed from the literature (Andrews & Bonta, 2006; Gendreau et al., 1996):

1. Services should be intensive and behavioral.
2. Programs should target the criminogenic needs of high-risk court participants.
3. Characteristics of participants, therapists, and programs should be matched accordingly.
4. Program contingencies and strategies should be enforced firmly but fairly.
5. Therapists should relate to court participants interpersonally, sensitively, and constructively (and should be trained/supervised appropriately).
6. Program structure/activities should be designed to disrupt delinquent behavior.
7. Relapse prevention strategies should be provided.
8. High levels of advocacy and brokerage should be attempted.

As with therapeutic jurisprudence, drug courts were not designed with these principles in mind; however, they can help explain the effectiveness of drug courts (Shaffer, 2011). Therapeutic jurisprudence supplies a framework for understanding the legal piece of drug courts. In contrast, effective intervention supplies a framework for understanding the treatment (psychological and medical) piece of drug courts (Shaffer, 2011).

Other science involved in the drug court process includes the processes required for participants to remain drug-free. This includes using technology such as drug tests, urine analysis, ankle monitoring, and email communications. Scientific approaches in drug courts also center around the combination of psychological and medical advancements to assist in the healing process of addiction (Shaffer, 2011).

In sum, drug courts use a variety of philosophical approaches which have been scientifically developed and tested. Using the sciences of therapeutic jurisprudence, restorative justice, and effective intervention, drug courts can produce positive outcomes for participants by addressing the underlying causes of their criminal behavior.

DWI/DUI courts

History

The next PSC to be considered is the DWI/DUI court, created in response to concerns over driving under the influence offenses and the success of drug courts (see also Petrucci, 2021). In 2012, 1.28 million drivers were arrested in the United States for driving under the influence of alcohol or drugs (Federal Bureau of Investigation, 2013), and 10,322 people died due to impaired driving (NHTSA, 2012). In 2010, the estimated cost of accidents involving alcohol impairment was $44 billion (National Center for Statistics and Analysis, 2015). Procedures such as sobriety checkpoints have been critical in deterring and catching drunk drivers (Wallace, 2011). However, 25% of all DWI offenders will become repeat offenders (Warren-Kigenyi & Coleman, 2014). DUI is a complex offense because factors contributing to an arrest could be as severe as an addiction to alcohol or simply a lapse in judgment by the offender about their alcohol consumption (Wallace, 2011).

Offenders commit one-third of all DWI transgressions with a prior DWI conviction (NHTSA, 2007). Repeat DWI offenders are commonly White, male, under the age of 40, single, alcohol dependent, in non-white-collar occupations, and often have a blood alcohol concentration (BAC) of 0.18 or higher during arrest (Wallace, 2011). Those who suffer from alcohol or other substance abuse issues are more likely to recidivate, especially when incarcerated instead of being treated for their addiction. Incarceration alone does not deter repeat offenders, but treatment effectively works toward deterrence by providing tools and support (Hora et al., 1999).

Court actors and practitioners in Arizona, New Mexico, California, Oklahoma, and Indiana formed a DUI/drug court advisory panel in 1998 after the success of drug courts. The goal was to establish a problem-solving program similar to the drug court model but designed to fit the population of repeat DWI offenders (Freeman-Wilson & Huddleston, 1999). DWI courts combine court-ordered sanctions and treatment as the primary solution to change people's behaviors and reduce recidivism (Wallace, 2011). As of 2018, there were 726 DWI courts nationwide (National Association of Drug Court Professionals, 2018).

Operations

DWI courts focus on accountability in their operations, aiming to reduce recidivism rates and establish safer communities effectively (Wallace,

2011). The court team determines which candidates are alcohol dependent, whose behavior can be changed by an intensive program, and which court participants are at greater risk for recidivism (Wallace, 2011).

Because their creation was heavily based on the drug court model, DWI courts follow the 10 Key Components. Intensive supervision, frequent drug testing, a team-based approach, and rewards and sanctions are present in both types of courts. In addition, DWI courts show a heavy focus on intensive, individualized treatment for each participant based on a clinical assessment conducted at program admittance, similar to drug courts (Wallace, 2011). Both the frequency and rigorousness of treatment depend on the participant's assessment and treatment phase (Wallace, 2011).

In the first phase of treatment, participants attend court and treatment frequently. Participants also submit to randomly scheduled drug tests at least once a week, take breath tests regularly, and comply with other court orders, such as attending Alcoholics Anonymous (AA) meetings (Wallace, 2011). After completing the first phase, participants move on to the second phase of treatment. They attend court less frequently while continuing treatment and drug testing. Participants might also obtain employment, work toward a GED, or partake in employment/vocational skills programs and community service. Both phases of treatment aim to encourage participants to move forward to the ultimate goal of sobriety while still addressing underlying issues (Wallace, 2011). Like the drug court model, DWI courts use a method of individualized treatment with intensive supervision and a team-based approach to target the criminogenic needs of court participants.

Scope of adoption/culture

Although DWI courts have had success within the United States, there is no clear evidence that DWI courts have been adopted internationally. However, the problem of driving under the influence of alcohol has been recognized by policymakers throughout Europe (Calinescu & Adminaite, 2018). The European Union is the heaviest alcohol-consuming region globally (WHO Regional Office for Europe, 2017). Many EU countries have implemented rehabilitation programs or other methods to keep alcohol-impaired drivers off the road (Centre for Public Health Excellence NICE, 2010).

Some countries, such as Sweden, Switzerland, Estonia, the United Kingdom, the Netherlands, Finland, and Slovenia, offer driver rehabilitation programs to people with drunk driving offenses (Calinescu & Adminaite, 2018). Austria, Belgium, Finland, France, Sweden, and Poland provide rehabilitation programs, including counseling, alcohol interlock requirements, and close monitoring for DWI offenders (Meesmann & Rossi, 2015). Some countries combine education programming about driving under the influence with treatment programs, while others use penalties, such as fines, driver's license suspensions, and ignition interlocks (ETSC, 2018). Ignition interlocks (Marques & Voas, 2013) use a breath test to measure the operator's blood alcohol level, only allowing the car to start if the operator's level is below the legal limit.

Many EU countries have adopted legislation for alcohol interlocks, including Austria, Belgium, Denmark, Finland, France, Poland, and Sweden. Recognizing that alcohol interlocks offer improvements in cost–benefit savings and road safety, the European Parliament recommended in 2014 that EU countries adopt legislation for mandatory usage of alcohol interlocks in rehabilitation programs within five years (Martino et al., 2014). While strategies to deter re-offending rates among DWI offenders have occurred internationally, DWI courts have only formally existed within the United States.

Science

Because their creation was based on the operations of drug courts, DWI courts operate on the principles of problem-solving and restorative justice approaches. Because people who frequently drive under the influence often struggle with alcohol dependency and addiction, DWI courts attempt to target the critical contributor to their offending behavior in a therapeutic manner. Through cognitive-behavioral therapy, intensive supervision, DUI education, and treatment into the design, courts can reach a wide range of DWI participants (AUDIT, n.d.).

Many jurisdictions implement screenings before program admittance to determine if people are eligible for the court (Martin-Buck, 2016). One example is the Alcohol Use Disorders Identification Test (AUDIT), which has been used worldwide since 1989. The test includes a 10-item screening tool that assesses alcohol consumption and behaviors and alcohol-related problems (AUDIT, n.d.). Other standard screening tools used throughout DWI courts include the Drug Abuse Screening Test (DAST); the Alcohol, Smoking, Substance Involvement Screening Test (ASSIST); and the Cut Down, Annoyed, Guilty, Eye-Opener test (CAGE) (Smith et al., 2010).

Many DWI courts also use universal screenings to ensure needs and risk level are being taken into account (Buck, 2017). Participants with moderate to risky behavior might be referred to brief intervention programs while participants with high-risk behavior are referred to a long-term specialty treatment program (Smith et al., 2010). Overall, DWI courts use intensive supervision, DUI education, interlock systems, and screenings to monitor a participant's success and promote restorative justice within the court.

Mental health courts

History

The next court to be discussed is the MHC, created as a response to the overwhelming number of people with mental illnesses repeatedly cycling through courtrooms, jails, and prisons (Almquist & Dodd, 2009; see also Fanarraga & Koetzle, 2021). Most correctional institutions cannot provide adequate treatment during incarceration or connect people to services after release (Almquist & Dodd, 2009). Between 7–16% of jail inmates experience serious mental illness—four times the rate of the general population for men and eight times the rate for women (Ditton, 1999). Half of all inmates with mental illnesses also have three or more convictions (Ditton, 1999).

Ultimately, a few events led to the creation of MHCs (Reno et al., 2000). The first deinstitutionalization was in the 1960s and 1970s, and the number of mentally ill offenders increased in US jails and prisons (Whitmer, 1979). Second, overcrowding resulted from the "War on Drugs" in the 1980s and a dramatic increase in the homeless population (Reno et al., 2000). Finally, drug courts inspired the creation of all PSCs (Reno et al., 2000).

The first MHC opened in 1997 in Broward County, Florida (Reno et al., 2000). The court was created due to broad concerns over the mentally ill in the correctional population following multiple suicides in local facilities (Reno et al., 2000). The proposal included a court dealing primarily with misdemeanor offenses, intervening early with treatment (Reno et al., 2000). Over 300 MHCs operate in the United States, each serving about 60 to 180 people annually (CSG Justice Center, 2021; Wolff et al., 2011).

Operations

MHCs base their operations on targeting the criminogenic needs of defendants with mental illness (Steadman et al., 2001). Participants for the court are identified through a mental health screening and they voluntarily participate in a treatment plan supervised and developed by court staff and mental health professionals. Overarching goals include improving public safety by reducing criminal recidivism, enhancing the quality of life of those with mental illness, increasing their participation in effective treatment, and reducing court and corrections-related costs through effective alternatives (Almquist & Dodd, 2009).

MHCs vary heavily in their target populations, offenses treated, plea arrangements, intensity of supervision, program duration, and type of available treatment (Council of State Governments Justice Center, 2008). Typically, people are referred to the court through criminal justice actors (Almquist & Dodd, 2009). Overall, the vast majority of participants have a severe mental illness. While this is a general term, typical conditions involve long-term impairment of daily function (Council of State Governments Justice Center, 2008). This could include, but is not limited to, conditions such as schizophrenia, bipolar disorder, severe depression, and anxiety disorders, as well as developmental disabilities (Steadman et al., 2005). It is worth noting, that while substance addiction is considered a mental illness, the diagnosis and treatment of addiction differs from that of mental health treatment (Abram & Teplin, 1991). However, three out of four people in the criminal justice system with mental illness also suffer from a substance use disorder (Abram & Teplin, 1991).

Most courts accept various offenses; some focus on misdemeanors, some on felonies, and many accept both (Almquist & Dodd, 2009). Courts are more likely to admit people with violent crimes if specific conditions are met. However, this varies typically on a case-by-case basis (Almquist & Dodd, 2009). Through mental health screenings and individualized treatment plans, MHCs target the criminogenic needs of court participants to reduce re-offending.

Scope of adoption/culture

After their initial creation and adoption, some countries outside the United States have established their MHCs. Like the United States, Australia noted that people with mental illness are overrepresented in arrests and prison populations (Schneider, 2010). MHCs were first introduced in Australia as a diversion program to decrease recidivism among defendants with mental illness, provide them with treatment, and decrease caseloads in traditional courts (Schneider, 2010). These initial courts have been successful, and currently there is a push in Australia to implement more MHCs throughout the country (Schneider, 2010).

Canada is another country that noted that people with mental illness are overrepresented in their arrests and prison populations (Baba, 2018). While MHCs are not as widespread in Canada as in the United States, they are being implemented to address mental health issues. MHCs have been implemented and practiced in Australia and Canada, with both countries aiming to treat mentally ill defendants and reduce recidivism.

Science

Similar to other PSCs, MHCs base their operations on the sciences of therapeutic jurisprudence and problem-solving principles. When MHCs use therapeutic jurisprudence principles, they promote better insight into the beneficial and harmful consequences of the law (Palermo, 2010). Scientifically, mental disorders are "neurobiological diseases of the brain" and are not controlled by the person; it is believed that they are caused by biological, psychological, and social factors (Council of State Governments Justice Center, 2008). If MHCs consider this idea, then the assumption is that the criminal behavior of people with mental illness stems from criminogenic needs related to their illness (Johnston, 2012). Therefore, through therapeutic justice and problem-solving principles, MHCs seek to understand a participant's behavior and apply appropriate treatment.

Community courts

History

Another PSC in operation is the community court, first created in the early 1990s to respond to the rise in community-related crimes (Lang, 2011; see also Connor, 2021). The first community court was established in 1993 in the Midtown Manhattan area of New York. Ultimately born out of a frustration at crimes that hurt the neighborhood and local community, the Midtown Community Court addressed the prostitution, vandalism, and minor drug possessions overriding the court system (Berman, 2000).

In the 1960s, New York closed a network of magistrate courts, causing caseloads to exponentially back-up within the court system (Berman, 2011). Many cases included quality-of-life offenses involving transient populations, such as prostitution, vandalism, and minor drug possession (Berman, 2011). These offenses continued to rise in the 1970s and 1980s, causing lawmakers to recognize the need for change (Berman, 2011). The idea of a neighborhood-based court devoted specifically to handling minor offenses emerged with the establishment of the Midtown Community Court in 1993 (Berman & Feinblatt, 2001).

Soon after, the Red Hook Community Court in Brooklyn was implemented in 2000. Red Hook follows the same basic model as the Midtown Community Court. However, Red Hook is not located in a transient area; as a result, its victims and court participants are typically residents (Berman & Fox, 2005). The Red Hook Community Court was created in response to the neighborhood facing a crack epidemic. However, the community court did not just handle quality-of-life offenses; juvenile delinquency cases and landlord–tenant disputes were also handled (Berman & Fox, 2005).

Since the implementation of the Midtown Community Court in 1990, over 50 community courts have been implemented. These courts primarily exist in larger cities and communities, such as San Diego, Denver, Atlanta, Portland, and Dallas (Karafin, 2008). Community courts continue to reduce community-related crime through a neighborhood-based approach.

Operations

Community courts operate with a focus on responding to the concerns of an individual community, which is shaped by its economic, political, and social landscapes (Lang, 2011). The majority of community courts hear primarily adult, low-level criminal cases. However, some courts are exploring other cases, including criminal, civil, and family matters; housing disputes; and environmental code violations (Berman & Fox, 2005).

Since the opening of New York City's Midtown Community Court in 1993, many courts have built upon their model (Lang, 2011). Most community courts typically rely on the following principles: enhanced information, community engagement, collaboration, individualized justice, accountability, and outcomes (Lang, 2011). The first principle, enhanced information, focuses solely on the information received and communicated through staff. The second principle, community engagement, incorporates the community to identify, prioritize, and solve local problems. The third principle, collaboration, brings together justice system actors, potential stakeholders, and social service agencies. The fourth principle, individualized justice, entails tailored community-based services, including job training, drug treatment, safety planning, and mental health counseling. The fifth principle, accountability, keeps the burden of criminal behavior on the person. The final principle is outcomes, which includes an active and ongoing analysis of the data to evaluate the effectiveness of their operation (Wolf, 2007).

The standard procedural steps of the community court include initial police action, report to the bail commissioner, report to the state's attorney, court appearance, report to social services, community service, and case dismissal (Johnstone, 2001). As an alternative to traditional case processing in low-level, non-violent crimes, community courts stress community service and social services involvement rather than focusing on punishment (Grommon et al., 2016). Participants are often required to conduct some form of community reparation and attend programs for mental health, addiction, education, and career planning (Clear & Karp, 1998).

The implementation of community courts varies from state to state (Lang, 2011). The average planning period is around two years due to the extent of any necessary construction and success in securing funds and support from the community and government institutions (Lang, 2011). Community courts typically reach out to community residents, social service providers, neighborhood institutions, justice partners, and local merchants to establish community participation and determine local concerns (Lang, 2011). Community participation is promoted through neighborhood meetings, stakeholder interviews, community advisory groups, and focus groups. By responding to a community's unique needs through engagement, community courts connect citizens with law enforcement.

Scope of adoption/culture

Since the creation of the Midtown Community Court, community courts have been introduced throughout the United States and internationally. As of 2007, there were 52 community courts in operation across the globe (Karafin, 2008). The North Liverpool Community Justice Center in the United Kingdom was the earliest international community court implemented in 2004. This court model follows the Midtown general model. The goal of the North Liverpool Community Justice Centre was to reduce fear of crime and promote public confidence, increase satisfaction within the system, increase compliance with community sentences, and reduce low-level offending and antisocial behavior (McKenna, 2007). However, the court closed in 2013 due to funding cuts and a failure to provide sufficient data (Gavin & Sabbagh, 2019).

The first community court to open in Australia was in 2007, created by the Victorian Labor Government and a Community Liaison Committee targeting the underlying causes of offending (Murray & May, 2018). This model is also very similar to US models, with the addition of a "Neighborhood Justice Officer," who assists people with hearings and facilitates problem-solving meetings (Murray & May, 2018). Also in 2007, Ireland opened its first community court at the suggestion of the Irish National Crime Council. Highlighted characteristics of this court include a dedicated judge, pre-trial assessment, a guilty plea, a problem-solving focus, a team-based approach and on-site provision of critical services, rigorous monitoring of court-order compliance, community restitution, and involvement of the local community—all characteristics found in the US model (National Crime Council, 2007).

In Canada, the first community court to open was in 2008 in Vancouver, British Columbia, as a response to chronic re-offending in the community (Slinger & Roesch, 2010). The overall design of this court was primarily influenced by Red Hook, focusing on timeliness, integration, and connection to the community (Slinger & Roesch, 2010). This particular community court is very similar to the structure of community courts in the United States; sanctions for community courts vary and are generally at the judge's discretion (Slinger & Roesch, 2010).

Finally, the most recent community court to be implemented was in 2017 in Israel. This community court was implemented as an experimental program and followed the model of the US community court with modifications (Gal & Dancig-Rosenberg, 2017). The similarities to the US model include collaboration between criminal justice and social service actors, individualized participant evaluation, and treatment plans (Gal & Dancig-Rosenberg, 2017). The differences to the US model include its operation within larger magistrate courts; reliance on existing social services available for every citizen; an intense, long-term intervention that addresses health, welfare, employment, support networks, and law-following; and the hearing of more severe crimes (Gal & Dancig-Rosenberg, 2017). Community courts have been introduced both across the United States and internationally to enhance communities and reduce low-level crime rates.

Science

Community courts are based on the sciences of theory-based therapeutic and restorative justice, problem-solving, and community justice principles (Gal & Dancig-Rosenberg, 2017). The theory behind community courts stems from community policing principles (Berman & Fox, 2005; Manning,

1984). For example, according to the broken windows theory, visible conditions of disorder in a neighborhood indicate that the community is in disarray and does not enforce social norms; therefore, more crimes are being committed (Kelling & Wilson, 1982). Building from this idea, community courts typically focus on quality-of-life crimes to improve the neighborhood and community outlooks on the justice system (Lee et al., 2013).

As discussed with drug courts, therapeutic jurisprudence requires legal actors to be aware of how law affects others, specifically regarding the potential for rehabilitation. Restorative justice also targets the potential for rehabilitation by requiring restitution. The focus of restorative justice includes using the criminal justice system to help the court participant and the victim (Svirdoff et al., 2002). The problem-solving principles aim to respond to the particular problems and needs of participants, understanding and targeting the root causes of offending behavior (Karafin, 2008). Finally, the community justice principles include promoting partnerships between neighborhoods, agencies, social services, and treatment providers. These partnerships encourage the development of community justice to promote a collaborative relationship between all parties and decrease rates of crimes (Gal & Dancig-Rosenberg, 2017). In conclusion, community courts aim to reduce neighborhood crime rates by responding to a community's unique needs through the sciences of therapeutic and restorative justice.

Domestic violence courts

History

The next court of discussion is the domestic violence court, created in light of a growing conversation surrounding the domestic violence and women's rights. It is difficult to pinpoint the exact first iteration of a domestic violence court due to the strain surrounding domestic violence in earlier years. However, domestic violence became a more expansive conversation due to the feminist movement in the 1970s (Tsai, 2000; see also Cissner & Thomforde Hauser, 2021). Most domestic violence courts were founded in the 1990s after the US Congress passed the Violence Against Women Act in 1994. As of 2013, there are 200 domestic violence courts in the United States (US Department of Justice, 2013). It is estimated that over 300 judicial systems have specialized processes for domestic violence cases; however, there is a wide variety in how each system defines itself as a domestic violence court

(Keilitz et al., 2000). In response to frustration among domestic violence victim advocates and the feminist movement of the 1970s, domestic violence courts were created to improve accountability, efficiency, and consistency.

Operations

The operations of domestic violence courts vary by jurisdiction. Four different types of domestic violence courts operate within the United States. These models include the criminal model, the civil model, the integrated model, and the "Justice Courts" model. The criminal model views domestic violence charges as criminal charges. The civil model views domestic violence charges as civil charges. The integrated model combines civil and criminal court aspects to address domestic violence completely. The "Justice Courts" model views domestic violence as a misdemeanor and does not offer the same protections as an integrated court (Ross, 2011).

Regarding implementation requirements in domestic violence courts, there does not appear to be a consistent requirement (Labriola et al., 2009). Instead, each court is tailored to its community and its existing judicial system (Karan et al., 1999). Some common factors across domestic violence courts in the United States, however, include batterer programs, substance/alcohol abuse treatment, and mental health treatment (Labriola et al., 2009).

All treatment programs delivered in domestic violence courts aim to address the cause of domestic violence instead of just punishing the action itself (Labriola et al., 2009). Although the operations of domestic violence courts vary, all of them aim for individualized treatment.

Scope of adoption/culture

Domestic violence courts exist both in the United States and globally. Adoptions of domestic violence courts have occurred in Canada, the United Kingdom, and across Europe. Like the US model, there is little consistency across domestic violence courts. Although there is no overarching model for domestic violence courts in Canada, each court has its operating model (e.g., Toronto, Winnipeg, Calgary). These courts provide services and advocacy for the victim and offer rehabilitation services and programs for court participants (Van de Veen, 2004). For example, the domestic violence court in Calgary resulted from extensive community consultation and discussion, and was modeled after courts in Toronto, Winnipeg, and San Diego (Van de Veen, 2004). The main features of domestic violence courts in Canada include integrating the criminal justice system with the community treatment agencies and coordinating treatment and resources (Van de Veen, 2004). There have been reforms to the Canadian Criminal Code to include domestic violence context as an aggravating factor for sentencing. However, domestic violence is still not the subject of a specific criminal offense.(Koshan, 2018). Estimates suggest there are over 50 domestic violence courts in Canada (Koshan, 2018).

In the United Kingdom, domestic violence courts focus on two philosophies: a victim-focused philosophy and a criminal justice-focused philosophy. The victim-focused philosophy highlights the importance of specialist case workers for victims of domestic violence, speedy referral of victims, victim's access to both services and information about case progress, opportunities for the victims to be heard in court, and the courthouse as a safe space (Bowen et al., 2013). The criminal justice-focused philosophy highlights the prompt scheduling of domestic violence cases into a dedicated court sitting, specially trained court players, being "ready on the day," and sentencing (Bowen et al., 2013). Like Canada, the court process centers around providing services for the victim and prosecuting court participants (Bowen et al., 2013). Estimates suggest that, as of December 2013, there were 138 officially accredited domestic violence courts in England and Wales (Bowen et al., 2013).

In the European Union, the treatment model, as well as the philosophy for domestic violence courts, is different for each country. The European Commission passed wide-sweeping resolutions to combat domestic violence across Europe (Mujuzi, 2016). In addition, in 2015, the European Court of Human Rights obliged European countries to address domestic violence. Some examples consist of Croatia including education, cooperation with NGOs, and financing; Romania providing "financing to prevent domestic violence"; Moldova enforcing compulsory medical treatment for those with a history of violence; and Germany examining "custody for preventative purposes," and cooperation with the Church (Mujuzi, 2016). Domestic violence courts in the European Union primarily focus on protecting victims of domestic violence, as it is viewed as a human rights violation by the European Court of Human Rights (Mujuzi, 2016). Domestic violence courts exist throughout Europe, Canada, and the United Kingdom. These courts are aimed at victim advocacy, participant accountability, and treatment.

Science

Like many PSCs, domestic violence courts use the science of therapeutic jurisprudence. Most domestic violence courts address that domestic violence might result from other underlying causes. This is evidenced by domestic violence courts' connections with other specialty courts and programs to combat the actual cause of domestic violence (e.g., Labriola et al., 2009). For example, if drug or substance abuse is of concern, a participant will also undergo treatment for those issues (Labriola et al., 2009). Domestic violence courts also use batterer programs, which share some uniform standards (e.g., Austin & Dankwort, 1999). However, the effectiveness of such programs is still relatively unclear because of how much programs vary (Labriola et al., 2009) and because of methodological issues in evaluations (Feder & Wilson, 2005).

Due to the nature of the involvement in domestic violence courts, there is a wide breadth of research examining medicine and domestic violence. Medical professionals are often the first to respond to domestic violence, and medical records are used as evidence in court hearings (Isaac & Enos, 2000). Patients who get screened for domestic violence, however, seem to vary. Medical professionals working in low-income communities and medical professionals who perform universal domestic violence screening procedures in their offices independently predicted more victim identification (Bloom & Tavrow, 2018).

Further, training on domestic violence identification and screening did not make a difference in victim identification. As such, medical records that support evidence for domestic violence seem to rely on, at least in part, a medical professional's implicit bias that low-income patients are most likely to be victims of domestic violence (Bloom & Tavrow, 2018). According to the American Medical Association's diagnostic and treatment guidelines on domestic violence, for medical records to be admissible in court the physician or attending medical professional who wrote the record should be prepared to testify that (1) the records were made during the regular course of business "at the time of the examination or interview, (2) the records were made by routinely followed procedures, and (3) the records have been properly stored, and their access has been limited to professional staff" (AMA, 1992). Therefore, the best approach for integrating medicine into domestic violence courts is that domestic violence screening is made universal in each medical office for records to be held admissible in court.

A fair amount of technology is used within domestic violence courts, especially from the criminal justice perspective. For example, since 1996, the legal system's use of GPS tracking technology has gradually increased nationwide (Erez et al., 2012). Further evaluation studies suggest more courts are using GPS tracking instead of the traditional methods of radio frequency (i.e., ankle bracelet) or non-technology-based supervision (Grommon et al., 2017). These studies, which incorporate technology on both sides, are essential when developing a domestic violence court because technology is becoming more critical in people's lives and more enmeshed with people's relationships.

Overall, domestic violence courts use the science of therapeutic justice to target domestic violence in light of the view that underlying criminogenic factors could contribute to domestic violence. By targeting those factors, these courts aim to treat court participants and reduce their likelihood of re-offending.

Human trafficking courts

History

Another type of PSC in operation is the human trafficking court. Historically, victims of human trafficking were most often charged with prostitution and prosecuted accordingly. It was not until relatively recently (2000) that human trafficking was recognized as a reason for prostitution, and the focus turned from prosecuting the victims to prosecuting the traffickers and the buyers of commercial sex (see, generally, Douds et al., 2021). Before 2000, traffickers most often walked away without consequence. In New York, preceding the establishment of Human Trafficking Intervention Courts (HTIC), prostitution cases proceeded like any other misdemeanors (Gruber et al., 2016). In a community court in Manhattan, however, social workers offered service programs to defendants (Gruber et al., 2016).

In 2003, Washington became the first state in the United States to pass anti-human trafficking legislation, followed by Texas that same year. The legislation passed in Texas called for justice and restitution for the victims, decriminalization to ensure victims are not prosecuted or convicted of prostitution, and the provision of services for the victims of human trafficking, which included the creation of a specialty court to handle such issues. Other states soon followed, with New York creating its first human trafficking court in 2013 and Michigan in 2014. It is estimated that there are currently 32 human trafficking courts in operation across seven states. In 2019, there were 606 criminal human trafficking cases in the US court system, with 1,058 active criminal defendants (Ross, 2019). After the recognition that human trafficking was a reason for prostitution, human trafficking courts were introduced to prosecute the traffickers and consumers of commercial sex.

Operations

The operations of human trafficking courts are not formally defined. While HTICs were first created in 2013, they have no foundational documents outlining their parameters (Gruber et al., 2016). With the relative newness of human trafficking courts in the realm of specialty courts, the Center for Court Innovation released a report in June 2015 outlining a "planning toolkit" that was designed to help courts and communities assess their approach to human trafficking (in particular sex trafficking) and to develop and enhance a court-based approach to human trafficking (Center for Court Innovation, 2015).

To help facilitate the creation of human trafficking courts, the Office for Victims of Crime recommends the following six characteristics (Kulig & Butler, 2019):

1. Specify responsibility for the identification and assessment of potential victims.
2. Use trauma-informed courtroom protocols.
3. Establish referrals to community-based services.
4. Monitor judicial compliance to ensure regular updates.
5. Collaborate with local task forces and service providers.
6. Evaluate the court and create performance indicators to monitor and assess the goal achievement of the court.

Human trafficking courts designed to handle specific criminal offenses can be used to ensure that women and children charged with prostitution, many of whom are trafficking victims, get the services they need rather than incarceration (Desai, 2013). The structure of human trafficking courts differs significantly by state because some states have clear legislation guiding the formation of the courts (e.g., Washington and Texas). In contrast, other states have no foundational documents guiding how the courts should be run (e.g., New York).

Broadly, human trafficking courts are intended to use treatment-oriented protocols to address the offenses committed by the participant and the trauma associated with being trafficked. This holds the three goals of identifying and diverting a potential trafficking victim from the traditional justice system, delivering trauma-informed responses, and addressing the underlying root causes of vulnerability to prevent future victimization (Kulig & Butler, 2019).

Human trafficking courts often exclude violent offenders and labor trafficking (Kendis, 2019). Victims of human trafficking (specific treatment in the courts does vary by age), human traffickers, and buyers of commercial sex are also served (Kulig & Butler, 2019). Even though there are no documented operations for human trafficking courts, a vast majority are aimed at ensuring victims receive the resources they need while diverting them from the system.

Scope of adoption/culture

Outside of the United States, similar operations of human trafficking courts exist in Canada, the United Kingdom, and throughout Europe. Canada implemented its first domestic human trafficking legislation in 2005 under the Criminal Code of Canada (Canada, 2012; Roots, 2013). The legislation passed, however, has received criticism for being too vague, thus making it difficult to distinguish human trafficking from other criminal acts in Canada (Roots, 2013). Later, Roots and De Shalit (2015) concluded that the anti-trafficking position stemmed from a policy-led perspective rather than an evidence-based initiative. However, Canada, like many other international bodies, began implementing the use of best practices, the 4-Pillars (i.e., the 4-Ps) (Canada, 2012):

1. Prevention of human trafficking,
2. Protection of victims,
3. Prosecution of offenders, and
4. Partnership with others both domestically and internationally.

With a focus on serving the victims of human trafficking identified by the Royal Canadian Mounted Police (Canada, 2012), the Canadian government allocated funds through The Victims Fund to projects that improve services to victims of human trafficking (Canada, 2012).

In 2015, the United Kingdom passed the Modern Slavery Act to restructure the criminal offenses linked to trafficking, implement more formidable sentencing powers, and create a new post of Modern Slavery Commissioner (now titled the Independent Anti-Slavery Commissioner). The United Kingdom further adopted the definition of human trafficking from the UN "Palermo Protocol" and has implemented two interpretations of trafficking—one for adults and one for children (Gravett, 2015). The United Kingdom's approach to combating human trafficking is distinct from the approach in the United States and the rest of Europe because they nationally created the UK Trafficking Centre. This victim-focused organization focuses on identifying, recovering, supporting, and repatriating human trafficking victims (Gravett, 2015). In addition, the United Kingdom has national partnerships to combat human trafficking, local law enforcement, and other smaller sectors of the criminal justice system (Gravett, 2015).

Europe's human trafficking courts look different than what has already been discussed because there is no specialty court. Instead, there is a European initiative to combat human trafficking, and these cases are heard in a more traditional criminal court. The 2005 Council of Europe Convention adopted the Action Against Trafficking in Human Beings and the 2011 European Union Anti-Trafficking Directive; both use a comprehensive approach to combating human trafficking following the "three Ps": prevention, protection and prosecution (Milano, 2017).

These "three Ps" are intended to prioritize human rights, allowing for a structure of a human rights-based approach to human trafficking (Milano, 2017). This approach is endorsed by both the Council of Europe and the European Court of Human Rights (ECtHR). The ECtHR hears cases in which a plaintiff believed their state did not hold up or failed to comply with Council's 2005 adoption of the Action Against Human Trafficking (e.g., *L.E. v. Greece*). The ECtHR must consider the case of human trafficking, which is not guaranteed (Milano, 2017). Overall, international efforts to target human trafficking have occurred internationally, with courts established in Canada and task initiatives and progression policies in the United Kingdom and the European Union.

Science

Human trafficking courts use the science of therapeutic jurisprudence to reduce recidivism and rehabilitate participants to be independent and self-sufficient (Desai, 2013). In addition, therapeutic jurisprudence is used to provide the children and youth directly affected by sex trafficking with appropriate services and treatment and to provide them with an appropriate response from the criminal justice system (Liles et al., 2016).

Human trafficking courts raise additional concerns not often found in other PSCs. First, most human trafficking court participants decide to take part in these programs as a way to avoid a jail sentence, which can be triggering to those coming from the commercial sex trade (Kendis, 2019). Second, the use of coercion in human trafficking courts has the potential to cause anti-therapeutic effects (Kendis, 2019).

When considering human trafficking courts from a medicinal perspective, medical professionals are often the first line of defense in identifying human trafficking victims, along with teachers, social workers, coaches, and public employees (Atkins et al., 2016). Medical professionals in seven US states, as of 2016, are mandatory reporters (California, Colorado, Florida, Illinois, Maryland, Massachusetts, and North Carolina). This means that these medical professionals must report the following details (Atkins et al., 2016):

1. Names and addresses of the child and the child's parents or caretakers;
2. Child's age;
3. Nature and extent of abuse, including any evidence of previous abuse;
4. Names and addresses of the school that the child attends or last attended;
5. Names of the persons responsible for the abuse or neglect;
6. Family composition, including names, ages, sexes, and races of other children; and
7. Actions taken by the reporting source, including taking photographs and x-rays, placing the child in temporary custody, or notifying the medical examiner/coroner.

There also exists a need for medical interventions for victims of human trafficking, as physical health issues are common but are often not systematically documented (Palmer, 2010; Williamson et al., 2009). Through the science of therapeutic justice, human trafficking courts use mandatory medical reports to aid victims of human trafficking.

Gambling courts

History

Another PSC in operation is the gambling court. Gambling courts are relatively new, both nationally and internationally. The first gambling court opened, in 2001, in Amherst, New York, and was modeled after successful drug and mental health PSCs. Since then, three more gambling courts/programs have been established worldwide.

In 2001, Amherst Town Court opened a Therapeutic Gambling Treatment Court in New York. The court was initially created to help participants with gambling addictions (Town of Amherst, 2018). Taking cues from drug and MHCs, the Therapeutic Gambling Treatment Court attempts to solve gamblers' problems (Hinshaw, 2005). In addition, participants are linked to gambling treatment agencies to address psychosocial issues and improve their quality of life (Town of Amherst, 2018).

While not many gambling courts exist, a few gambling courts and gambling court programs are currently in operation. Nationally, the Amherst Gambling Treatment Court was the first to be implemented and was shortly followed by the Gambling Treatment Referral Program in Louisiana in 2005 and the Voluntary Gambling Treatment Program in Nevada in 2009. Internationally, one gambling court exists in Australia, the South Australian Court Gambling Intervention Program (SACGIP). The SACGIP is modeled after the Amherst Gambling Treatment Court and was implemented in 2015.

Operations

Gambling courts focus on solving gambling addictions that might lead to illegal activities (Guenaga, 2011). Senior Justice Mark Farrell started the first gambling court to address the underserved population of gambling addicts (Hinshaw, 2005). Since 1980, the American Psychiatric Association has classified gambling disorders within the *Diagnostic and Statistical Manual of Mental Disorders* (DSM). The fifth edition of this manual—the DSM-5—defines gambling disorder as "persistent and recurrent problematic gambling behavior leading to clinically significant impairment or distress" (APA, 2022). Although the medical profession has recognized gambling as an illness for over four decades, the criminal justice system has not (Hinshaw, 2005).

Using previous drug and MHCs as inspiration, Judge Ferrell shaped the first gambling court around the concepts of therapeutic justice. Participants in the gambling court must comply with the program rules, including pleading guilty and waiving all rights to plea-bargain upon acceptance into the program (Hinshaw, 2005).

The implementation of gambling courts and programs varies from state to state, but each program has been modeled after the Amherst gambling court. Following New York's lead, Louisiana declared a statewide expansion of its Gambling Treatment Referral Program in 2005 (Guenaga, 2011). The purpose of Louisiana's program is to divert first- and second-time non-violent offenders into treatment (Guenaga, 2011). The overarching goal of the Gambling Treatment Referral Program is to help decrease the crowded dockets while matching participants to adequate treatment services (Guenaga, 2011). Like the Amherst court, many offenses are eligible for program participation as long as the offense links to a gambling problem. Ineligibility for Louisiana's Gambling Treatment and Referral Program includes individuals who have caused death or serious bodily injury, have prior convictions for a violent crime, or have used force (Guenaga, 2011).

In 2009, Nevada's legislature passed Assembly Bill 102, which authorized the creation of a voluntary treatment program for problem gamblers. As with the New York and Louisiana programs, the inclusion criteria for Nevada's voluntary gambling treatment program are broad. However, the exclusionary criteria are more defined. An individual is not eligible for the program if they have committed a felony or gross misdemeanor against someone else, a crime against a child, a sexual offense, or an act that constitutes domestic violence (Guenaga, 2011). In conjunction with medical professionals, the court works to evaluate whether or not a person would benefit from the treatment program. If the participant moves forward with enrolling in the program, they must participate in counseling and support sessions, educational sessions about the impact of gambling, and any necessary substance abuse treatment (Guenaga, 2011). All three court/gambling programs share the goal of targeting the underlying gambling disorder.

Scope of adoption/culture

Since the creation of the Amherst Gambling Treatment Court, three gambling courts and gambling programs have been introduced in the United States and around the world. Australia, as previously mentioned, houses a gambling court, the SACGIP, which was implemented in 2015 and modeled after the Amherst Gambling Treatment Court.

As the SACGIP was modeled after the Amherst Gambling Treatment Court, the scope of adaptation is not much different. Potential participants are selected based on an established set of screening criteria. This criterion includes: (1) having been charged with a criminal offense, (2) pleading guilty to the charges, (3) having committed an offense related to problem gambling, and (4) being willing to participate in a gambling treatment program (Adolphe et al., 2019).The SACGIP program includes one weekly, one-hour-long, one-on-one session with a trained psychologist. Depending on the treatment program for that participant, some form of mandatory treatment will take place. For example, the SACGIP relies on cognitive behavioral therapy and cue exposure therapy (Adolphe et al., 2019). The program lasts six months and requires two-month check-ins with the magistrate to review progress (Adolphe et al., 2019).

No other gambling courts exist outside the United States yet, but discussions of the implementation of gambling courts have occurred in Canada (Smith & Simpson, 2014).

Science

Gambling courts are based on science theory-based therapeutic justice, incorporating psychological therapeutic techniques (Guenaga, 2011). As discussed with previous PSCs, therapeutic jurisprudence requires legal actors to be aware of how their actions affect others, specifically regarding the potential for rehabilitation. This is no different for gambling courts, as the inclusion of therapeutic justice rests with the primary goal of ensuring that treatment is a part of sentencing and that all involved parties cooperate in that participation (Hinshaw, 2005).

Gambling courts also rely on specific psychological therapeutic techniques to consider problem gambling behaviors. These techniques include cognitive behavior therapy and cue exposure therapy (Guenaga, 2011). Acknowledging that problem gambling is a psychiatric disorder, these courts allow medically screened participants who qualify to enter supervised care and receive formal treatment (Simpson, 2014).

Cue exposure therapy, which is heavily used in Australia's gambling court, is a clinical intervention focusing on extinction learning (Riley et al., 2018). Such interventions can reduce cravings and relapse in substance-related and behavioral addictions (Riley et al., 2018). Cue exposure therapy procedures comprise a relaxation period followed by in-vivo exposure with response prevention in a gambling environment (Riley et al., 2018). By incorporating techniques such as therapeutic jurisprudence and cognitive-behavioral therapy, gambling courts can address a more extensive scope of participants who experience gambling problems.

Prostitution courts

History

The next PSC is the prostitution court. Prostitution courts are comparatively new within the United States but have proliferated. First implemented in 1990, but not widely adopted until the 2000s, prostitution courts saw an increase of 125% in new court implementation from 2009 to 2014 (Marlowe et al., 2016). Nationally, there are currently more than 20 prostitution courts in operation, with an additional eight court-based prostitution programs (Blakey, 2017; Huddleston & Marlowe, 2011; Mueller, 2012; Roe-Sepowitz et al., 2011). The rapid increase in prostitution courts can be attributed, in part, to Texas legislation, which requires counties with 200,000 or more residents to create a prostitution prevention program (Douglas & Guidry, 2013).

The first prostitution court was implemented in New York in 1990 (Cohen, 2016). Prostitution as a social issue is distinctive because many other PSCs incorporate elements of addressing prostitution-related actions within their overarching goals. For example, many community courts have a prostitution offense "arm." Human trafficking courts and sex trafficking courts also address prostitution. While many community courts address prostitution, among other issues, implementation of specific prostitution courts and prevention programs that explicitly focus on prostitution offense-related issues has occurred (Sanchez & Miller, 2009).

There is no evidence of prostitution courts existing outside the United States. Many countries outside of the United States have never considered prostitution a crime or have decriminalized prostitution statutes.

Operations

Most PSCs are modeled after the 10 Key Components of drug courts, and prostitution courts are no exception (Marlowe et al., 2016). Empirical research has shown that adopting the 10 Key Components contributes to more positive outcomes for PSCs (Blakey et al., 2017). Many times, prostitution programs are housed in other PSCs as an extension of services. One example is the Prostitution Protocol Program housed in the Hartford Community Court. Commonly, prostitution courts provide services and resources to help leave the profession (Sanchez & Miller, 2009; Wolf, 2011), deter people from seeking prostitutes' services (Johnstone, 2001), and work toward preventing recidivism (Updegrove & Muftic, 2019).

Another prostitution program housed in a PSC court is the Services to Access Resources and Safety (STARS) program, created in 2009 by the Midtown Community Court. The STARS program addresses the physical, sexual, and emotional violence that is associated with the prostitution experience (Schweig et al., 2012). The STARS program is an alternative to incarceration; court-based case managers screen participants to connect them to services provided by on-site partners (Schweig et al., 2012). Many prostitution court programs have adopted the STARS structure, such as the Bronx Community Solutions and the Queens County Prostitution Diversion Court (Schweig et al., 2012).

There are different types of sole prostitution courts currently in operation. Some are court-monitored diversion or pre-sentencing courts, while others are community-based outpatient programs (Leon & Shdaimah, 2012; Roe-Sepowitz et al., 2011; Schweig et al., 2012; Shdaimah & Wiechelt, 2012; Wahab, 2005, 2006; Wiechelt & Shdaimah, 2011). The handling of charges is also done on a court-by-court basis (Blakey et al., 2017). Regardless of the type of prostitution court or prostitution program, the overarching goal is to address the underlying causes surrounding prostitution.

Scope of adoption/culture

To our knowledge, no prostitution courts have been adopted outside of the United States.

Science

Like many other PSCs, prostitution courts are based on the sciences of theory-based therapeutic justice and restorative justice and they incorporate psychological educational techniques (Schweig et al., 2012). As discussed with other PSCs, therapeutic jurisprudence requires legal actors to be aware of how their actions affect others, specifically regarding the potential for rehabilitation. Restorative justice also targets the potential for rehabilitation by requiring individual and community restitution. This uses the criminal justice system to help the court participant and the victim (Schweig et al., 2012; Svirdoff et al., 2002). The problem-solving principles aim to respond to the particular needs of participants by understanding and targeting the root causes of behavior surrounding prostitution (Karafin, 2008; Schweig et al., 2012).

With the inclusion of psychological education techniques, many prostitution courts and programs apply evidence-based interventions to help participants end the revolving door of victimization and recidivism (Schweig et al., 2012). This includes adopting a trauma-informed approach, such as engaging with social services and building trust with every client (Schweig et al., 2012). Through the science of therapeutic justice, restorative justice, and psychological techniques, prostitution courts attempt to aid those who are involved with issues of prostitution.

Veterans' treatment courts

History

Veterans' treatment courts (VTCs) are another PSC in operation. Many veterans, especially those with combat experience, are at a higher risk of developing severe or persistent psychological health problems (Friedman, 2006; see also Michaels & Douds, 2021). This can include mental health issues, combat-related trauma, and substance abuse, increasing a person's likelihood of coming into contact with the criminal justice system (Britton et al., 2012; Holcomb et al., 2007; Jacobson et al., 2008). More than 70,000 inmates are veterans, representing 9% of the United States' inmate population (Greenberg & Rosenheck, 2008; McCaffrey, 2013).

VTCs were created to target the criminogenic risk factors and unique needs of veterans who come into contact with the criminal justice system (Douds et al., 2017). These courts apply problem-solving approaches to address veterans' specific needs while under correctional supervision (Russell, 2009). The first VTC was created in 2004 in Alaska (Berenson, 2010; Ruggeri, 2009); the first sustained VTC was established in Buffalo, New York, in 2008 (Russel, 2009). As of 2017, there were 461 VTCs throughout the United States across 41 states (US Department of Veterans Affairs, 2017). The recognized need for a specialized court for veterans has led to the creation of VTCs throughout the country.

Operations

VTCs focus their operations on responding to the unique needs of veterans by providing services such as treatment for substance abuse or mental health issues (Belasco, 2014). Veterans convicted of a crime can avoid incarceration, receive a reduced sentence, or have their charges dropped upon completing the program (Clark et al., 2010). While the operations of these courts vary by jurisdiction, there are five standard components:

1. Identifying eligible participants,
2. Establishing eligibility requirements,
3. Using a VTC team and consistent team meetings,
4. Individualizing program tracks for each participant, and
5. Tracking court participant data.

Most courts adapt these components and take various approaches to meet the unique needs of veterans in their jurisdictions (Douds et al., 2017).

VTCs are operated by a court team consisting of a judge, an assistant district attorney, a public defender, probation personnel, treatment personnel, and an administrator (Douds et al., 2017). Many VTCs also have a Veterans Justice Outreach Coordinator (VJO) who is representative of the veterans' association. VJOs intervene at critical junctures in the criminal justice system to reduce the criminalization of mental health and substance abuse issues and reduce rates of offending among veterans overall (Blue-Howells et al., 2013). They also are a critical avenue for the court team to assess VTC eligibility, treatment needs, and available benefits: VJOs can review the discharge status, criminal record, deployment history, and service history of veterans (U.S. Department of Veterans Affairs, 2015). Many VTCs also use a mentoring program that is not typically a feature of other PSCs. Mentors might act as social support figures or advisors to help the participant navigate the VTC program (Cavanaugh, 2011; Russell, 2009).

Participants for VTCs typically enter the program after entering a plea deal (Zweig et al., 2011); however, people can also enter the program via referral (Douds et al., 2017). After identifying potential participants, the court team arranges a clinical assessment of the court participant, including their criminal history, family history, and amenability to treatment. There are eight considerations that VTCs look for when determining eligibility (Douds et al., 2017):

1. Military discharge status,
2. Combat experience,
3. Treatment needs and the available treatment options,
4. The relationship between the offense and military service,
5. The type of offense,
6. Criminal history,
7. Victim input (if applicable), and
8. Plea requirements.

These considerations are present among many VTCs; however, eligibility requirements vary by jurisdiction. Therefore, each court must adequately determine program inclusivity and tailor programs to the specific needs of their population (Douds et al., 2017). For example, some courts might only accept veterans with military-related mental health conditions; combat veterans; or Operation Enduring Freedom (OEF), Operation Iraqi Freedom (OIF), and Operation New Dawn (OND) veterans (Douds et al., 2017). Further, some VTCs only accept misdemeanor charges, others accept only felonies, while courts accept both (Douds et al., 2017).

Most VTC participants are White, unmarried, male, and in their 40s. Most participants have also had at least a high school education and a monthly income above $1000 (Tsai et al., 2018). In addition, about one-third of participants have a criminal history, one-half report substance abuse, and over one-third show symptoms of posttraumatic stress disorder (Tsai et al., 2018). In sum, the operations of VTCs vary by jurisdiction. However, similarities exist in standard components, court teams, eligibility, and participant demographics.

Scope of adoption/culture

Although VTCs provide necessary treatment for veterans' criminogenic needs, they have not been introduced internationally. There has been support for the introduction of VTCs in the United Kingdom, highlighting the specialized needs of veterans and the obligation that courts have to help divert veterans from prison and into rehabilitation (Solicitor & Barrister, 2011). However, there are currently no specialized courts within the United Kingdom that address participants with a specific background; only specialized courts that cater to offenses. Because there is no established precedent for courts that focus on a participant's background, it is difficult for penal reform organizations to argue for their implementation (Solicitor & Barrister,

2011). Some critics of VTCs also argue that veterans should not be treated differently within the system and that it would be unjust to give them special treatment (Solicitor & Barrister, 2011).

Similarly, Australian courts have faced difficulties in determining how to deal with veterans appropriately, with some courts being too lenient on ex-soldiers and others failing to consider veterans' social and mental health issues (Nedim, 2015). The belief that veterans are a distinct social group with complex issues and the inconsistency in sentencing among veterans has led to arguments and discussions that VTCs are a necessary addition to the Australian court system (Nedim, 2015). Supporters of this idea argue that acknowledging the issues that veterans face can play a part in reducing rates of re-offending. Overall, these arguments are part of a broader conversation aimed at generating support for more treatment-oriented courts within the Australian court system that focuses on tackling the causes of crime rather than one focused on imprisonment (Nedim, 2015). Despite this discussion, VTCs have not been formally introduced in Australia. Although the need for specialized veteran's courts has been recognized globally, these courts have not been implemented outside of the United States.

Science

VTCs use the same therapeutic justice model that many other PSCs follow and are typically a hybrid of drug courts, DWI courts, and MHCs (Russell, 2009). A veteran's offending behavior might result from underlying causes such as mental health issues, substance abuse, or combat-related trauma, directly or indirectly, caused by military involvement. VTCs promote specialized services and programs to target the root of criminogenic behavior (Douds et al., 2017). Participants might receive mental health treatment, substance abuse treatment, residential treatment, or other services to ensure their distinctive needs are met (Smee et al., 2013). Courts might also use individual or group therapy to promote therapeutic benefits within the program further (Belenko, 2015).

VTCs also use a collaborative justice approach, in which multiple agencies communicate and work toward the participant's rehabilitation. Participants additionally undergo drug and alcohol testing to hold them accountable (Douds et al., 2017). In conclusion, VTCs recognize a participant's background as a veteran, consider how it has affected their lives and behavior, and apply individualized treatment and collaborative justice to work toward aiding veterans within the criminal justice system.

Aboriginal courts

History

Next for consideration is the Aboriginal court, which originated in Australia. "Aboriginal" court is a loose term; other names include "Nunga courts," "Murri courts," "Koorie courts," "Gladue courts," or "Indigenous Peoples Court" (Marchetti & Daly, 2004; Steps to Justice, 2019). Aboriginal courts are only the formal introduction of Indigenous participation in sentencing procedures in Australia; informally, it has occurred in multiple remote communities for quite some time, with proper formalization beginning in the 1990s (Marchetti & Daly, 2004).

Aboriginal courts have emerged for a variety of reasons. Indigenous Peoples are overrepresented in the criminal justice system in Australia and are 15 times more likely to be in prison than non-Indigenous persons (ABS, 2003; Briggs & Auty, 2003). The Royal Commission into Aboriginal Deaths in Custody (RCIADIC) recommends that Aboriginal courts increase Indigenous Peoples' participation in the justice system and reduce the number of Indigenous incarcerations. There has also been a recognized need for partnerships between state governments and Aboriginal organizations to promote a better justice system for Indigenous Peoples (Birggs & Auty, 2003; Whonnock, 2008).

The first Aboriginal court was implemented in Port Adelaide, South Australia, in 1999. A few years before, in 1996, Magistrate Criss Vass began working with local ndigenous groups, the Aboriginal Legal Rights Movement, and the Department of Aboriginal Affairs to address Indigenous Peoples' deep distrust toward the criminal justice system (Birggs & Auty, 2003). These discussions created an Aboriginal Court Day; a day in which the court tried specifically Aboriginal cases (Birggs & Auty, 2003). This then evolved into what became known as the Nunga Court. From there, more Aboriginal courts emerged throughout Australia. Although Aboriginal courts exist for several reasons, they were created in light of the overrepresentation of Aboriginal populations in the criminal justice system and the goal of connecting Aboriginal communities with law enforcement in a positive manner.

Operations

As with many other types of PSCs, the operations of Aboriginal courts vary depending on the jurisdiction. Typically, they uniquely highlight local magistrates and Indigenous Peoples (Marchetti & Daly, 2004). The aims of Aboriginal courts include making court processes culturally appropriate, improving trust between Indigenous communities and judicial officers, and permitting informal and open exchange of information (Marchetti & Daly, 2004).

Aboriginal courts deal with all criminal offenses; however, in most jurisdictions, they only handle bail hearings and sentencing hearings and avoid handling trials and preliminary hearings (Steps to Justice, 2019). Typical benchmarks of Aboriginal courts include that the participant must be Indigenous (or South Sea Islander), they must plead guilty, the offenses can only be heard by the court if the crime occurred in the geographical area that court covers, the magistrate retains ultimate power in sentencing, and the court is assisted by advice/representations of Aboriginal elders (Marchetti & Daly, 2004).

Aboriginal courts also attempt to incorporate Indigenous culture and understandings of justice into the court process; for example, a court might start with a locally recognized ceremony or have an elder start with a song (Steps to Justice, 2019). However, overall, there is a degree of informality that is not often common in traditional courts; there is considerably more time taken for each matter, court participants are offered a "support person" to sit by them at trial, and even people in the public gallery could be asked to speak (Marchetti & Daly, 2004).

There are currently six Aboriginal courts operating in Australia: New South Wales Circle Sentencing Court, Queensland, Victoria, Western Australia Circle Court, Northern Territory, and South Australian Nunga Court. Each court functions independently, focusing on its community and jurisdiction. The New South Wales Circle Sentencing Court was designed for people with severe and repeat offenses, aimed at achieving full community involvement in sentencing processes (Aboriginal Justice Advisory Committee, 2000). The Queensland court uses community norms and mechanisms of Indigenous social control to respond to crime and provide pre-sentence advice to judicial officers (Marchetti & Daly, 2004). The Victoria court takes custody of Indigenous court participants, arranges legal advice for participants, communicates with the participants' families, and provides information about the participants' backgrounds to judicial officers at sentencing (ATSIC, 1997). The Western Australia Circle Court follows a traditional courtroom model of a prosecutor and defense counsel presenting cases while two elders and the magistrate converse separately about sentencing options (Marchetti & Daly, 2004). The Northern Territory court considers "payback" (Indigenous punishment) as a mitigating factor in sentencing, and judicial officers are expected to get advice from the community (ATSIC, 1997). The South Australian Nunga Court is the most informal Aboriginal court in that there is no process of vetting participants before the entrance to the court (Marchetti & Daly, 2004). While each Aboriginal court highlights unique aspects, all courts incorporate Aboriginal culture into justice and foster trust between the Aboriginal community and law enforcement.

Scope of adoption/culture

Versions of Aboriginal courts exist in Canada and Columbia. In Canada, these courts are commonly called "Gladue Courts." The word "Gladue" comes from a Supreme Court of Canada case, *R v. Gladue*. The first court in Canada was the Tsuu T'ina First Nation Court, established in 2000 in Alberta. It oversees criminal, youth, and bylaw offenses committed on the Tsuu T'ina reserve. Other notable Aboriginal courts include the Cree-speaking Circuit Court in Saskatchewan, the Gladue Court in Ontario (the first urban court), and the First Nation Court in British Columbia (Whonnock, 2008).

While the operations of these courts are very similar to operations in Australia, one notable difference is that all courts in Canada must follow Gladue principles, even if it is not a designated Gladue court. These principles include consideration of a participant's Indigenous background and the impact and history of discrimination against Indigenous Peoples by Canada and the criminal justice system (Steps to Justice, 2019). When a jail sentence is given, the court must apply the principles to the length of the sentence (Steps to Justice, 2019). Some Gladue courts also offer Indigenous diversion as an alternative to going to trial and pleading guilty, typically a procedure reserved for minor criminal charges (e.g., theft or failure to follow bail conditions). Many provinces and territories across Canada also use an Indigenous Court Worker Program, which provides caseworker support throughout the court process (Department of Justice Canada, 2008).

Typically, people processed through the Gladue courts identify as Indigenous, Métis, First Nations, or Inuit (Steps to Justice, 2019). Depending on how the court is structured, non-Indigenous people might be tried within an Indigenous court; some argue that this is necessary because the location of a crime should determine where judgment takes place, while others argue that a specialized Indigenous court is not appropriate for non-Indigenous people (Department of Justice Canada, 2013).

Although there is no formal court system to process Indigenous Peoples, Columbia was the first country in the Americas to recognize Indigenous jurisdictions. In 1991, using a model described as "plurinational constitutionalism," they amended their constitution in 1991 to recognize that decisions in Indigenous jurisdictions were valid (Muñoz Chamorro, 2021). In sum, efforts to incorporate Indigenous cultures into court practices have been integrated in Australia, Canada, and Columbia, although each country varies in their approach.

Science

The science behind Aboriginal courts relies heavily on cultural considerations for the Indigenous community. Culture includes the values, behavior, and social structures unique to specific groups worldwide (Boehnlein et al., 2005). All aspects of society include culture, and it is used to help determine acceptable behavior patterns within society. Therefore, culture is essential in interacting with social systems, such as the law and criminal justice process (Boehnlein et al., 2005). Aboriginal courts use cultural science by considering factors within a court participant's life and seeking a complete understanding of their behavior. By using cultural considerations of Indigenous Peoples within the sentencing process, Aboriginal courts promote a positive relationship between the government and the Indigenous community while also considering how culture affects a person's behavior.

Child support courts

History

The next PSC, the child support court, was created in light of changing family dynamics and the need for consistent family mediation. The Industrial Revolution created a more complex and developed society in the United States, and family structures throughout the country changed. As a result, the rate of divorce and the rate of children born outside of marriage increased, contributing to the problem of inadequate financial support for single-family households (Carlson, 2009). In response, the issue of child support for dependent children was given to local courts in the form of child abandonment proceedings and child support awards from divorces (Chase-Lansdale & Brooks-Gunn, 1995). Research suggested that fathers benefited financially from divorces, while mothers and children often fell into poverty (Pao, 2015). To ensure that single mothers and their children were supported, the US child support collection system was established in 1975 (Cassetty, 1978).

This system's initial goal was to replicate the "nuclear family" structure present before divorce; the father was the breadwinner (through paying child support), and the mother was the homemaker (through taking custody of the child). However, this system began to fail as the 1980s and 1990s saw more changes in the US's social, economic, and demographic landscape (Pao, 2015). The typical "nuclear" family was no longer the norm. Courts were imposing child support obligations that failed to consider modern family dynamics. Often, these child support obligations did not balance the child's needs and the father's needs to support themselves, leading to over $113 billion worth of child support payments going unpaid (Lee, 2012). This promoted the argument that a problem-solving approach was needed to encourage and reward co-parenting and produce better results for children overall (Lee, 2012).

In the early 1980s, many community-based organizations introduced fathering programs to present the benefits of father involvement to the community rather than solely focusing on punishment as the response (National Center for Fathering, n.d.). Court actors recognized the benefits of these programs and began focusing on these issues when addressing child support enforcement (Lee, 2012). Parents who fail to pay child support (non-compliant parents, or NCPs) cycled through non-payment, incarceration, release, and repeat (Lee, 2012). As an alternative to incarceration, the first court centered on child support enforcement was introduced in 1998 in Jackson County, Missouri (Lee, 2012). As family dynamics changed, the justice system found a need to change its approach toward child support enforcement.

Operations

The actual operation of child support courts differs among jurisdictions. However, there are many shared goals, the most common being addressing NCPs who need to meet child support guidelines (Lee, 2012). Other shared goals include the cycle of non-payments and other issues that contribute to non-payments (Simpson, 2012). Child support courts provide adequate funding and emotional support for the child and the custodial parent (CP). They also decrease the financial cost of incarcerating NCPs when support is unpaid (Lee, 2012).

Child support courts follow many problem-solving principles in drug courts, such as judicial interaction with case participants, behavior monitoring, and sanctions and incentives (Simpson, 2012). To address the underlying issues that contribute to non-payment, NCPs are screened, assessed, and placed into an appropriate program by a court official. These programs can be dedicated to substance abuse, mental health concerns, literacy/vocational skills, employment opportunities, visitation planning, or other issues.

Programs are typically one year long, and participation is voluntary. Before admittance, parents are required to consent to participation and agree to two requirements (Simpson, 2012):

1. The non-compliant parent will maintain full-time employment, not re-offend, and pay for all child support obligations through wage withholding; and
2. Both parents will support the development of a visitation schedule for all minor children.

While the operations of child support courts vary by jurisdiction, there are similarities in their primary goals and program requirements.

Scope of adoption/culture

Child support courts have yet to be adopted outside of the United States, but many countries have guiding legal mandates regarding child support (Martin, 2017). Citizens of countries within the European Union can take claims to court and make payment orders enforceable in any EU country, and NCPs are also not allowed to leave their country to avoid paying (Martin, 2017).

Canada uniquely uses a Child Support Initiative focused on strengthening federal assistance for enforcement procedures and guidelines. The initiative also provides financial help to provinces and territories and monitors the effect of guidelines post-implementation (Canadian Department of Justice, n.d.). China determines child support based on parental income and standard of living, encouraging mutual agreements for custody and considering statutory factors (Zhao & Zhang, 2019). Globally, the Office of Child Support Enforcement is an agency based in the United States devoted to child support. Over 40 countries use this office, which assists families seeking support when family members live in different countries (Office of

Child Support Enforcement, 2020). Although child support courts have only been formally introduced in the United States, there have been efforts to aid in child support enforcement in other countries.

Science

Child support courts apply the science of problem-solving principles and therapeutic justice, similar to many of the other PSCs discussed (Lee, 2012; Farole et al., 2005). The combination of therapeutic programs and court-sanctioned enforcement shows this. Child support courts aim to target the specialized needs and issues each participant faces and connect them to social services to support them financially and emotionally (Lee, 2012).

Most PSCs implement a collaborative team approach to decision-making; a judge serves as a team leader and directly interacts with program participants (Lee, 2012). Because most child support courts also use therapeutic programs to target these issues, they also follow the ideals of therapeutic justice. All court processes are conducted to enforce the law and encourage health and positive growth in their participants (Rottman & Casey, 1999). By combining therapeutic programs targeting the specialized needs of each case, child support courts follow the science of therapeutic justice in their efforts of child support enforcement.

Family dependency treatment courts

History

Another type of PSC, the family dependency treatment court (FDTC), was created as an intervention to rising rates of child maltreatment (see Honardoost & Ahlin, 2021). Since the 1980s, there has been a dramatic increase in child abuse and neglect cases. Each year, more than 1 million cases of child abuse and neglect are filed and verified (U.S. Department of Health and Human Services, 2001). The cause of this escalation is substance abuse and other factors, such as poverty, domestic violence, and loss of family support systems (U.S. Department of Health and Human Services, 2001). The increase in cases poses problems for the criminal justice system. These issues include overwhelming caseloads and the inability to attain treatment for families that is timely (Center for Substance Abuse Treatment, 2004). As a result, parents were likely to continue their cycle of addiction while their children went to foster care (Center for Substance Abuse Treatment, 2004).

To treat both the cycle of substance abuse and child maltreatment, actors in the criminal justice system, child protective services, and substance abuse treatment systems looked to the adult drug court model to create their intervention (Center for Substance Abuse Treatment, 2004).

The first FDTC opened in 1995 in Reno, Nevada. The FDTC was explicitly dedicated to cases of child abuse and neglect that involve substance abuse by the child's parents/caregivers (Center for Substance Abuse Treatment, 2004). This court focused on eight guiding principles (Huddleston et al., 2008):

1. Permeance in the safety and welfare of neglected children and the needs of parents.
2. Early intervention involves parents in appropriate, comprehensive services with increased supervision from judicial agencies.
3. A holistic approach to improving family function.
4. Individualized case planning based on a case-by-case comprehensive assessment.
5. It ensured legal rights, advocacy, and confidentiality for all families.
6. Regular staffing and judicial court reviews.
7. A system of graduated sanctions and incentives.
8. A commitment to measuring program outcomes.

Following the principles set forth by the first FDTC, 38 states had at least one FDTC in operation by the mid-2000s (Huddleston et al., 2008). As of 2012, there were 343 FDTCs in operation in the United States (NDCRC, 2012). Aimed at treating cases of child abuse and neglect that involve substance abuse, FDTCs have been created and implemented countrywide.

Operations

FDTCs operate with the primary goal of protecting children from abuse and neglect by addressing the issues of both the parents and the children. As FDTCs are treatment courts dedicated explicitly to cases of child abuse and neglect that involve substance abuse by the child's parents/caregivers, the court's operation is more complicated than some of the other PSCs (Center for Substance Abuse Treatment, 2004). A collaborative effort is required from the court, treatment providers, and child welfare advocates to conduct a comprehensive assessment of the child and parent's needs. In FDTCs, the entire family participates. Even though decisions for treatment plans are created with the child's best interest in mind, the court parallels this focus on the interests of the parents as well (Center for Substance Abuse Treatment, 2004). By encouraging parents to address the issues in their lives, such as substance abuse, sobriety, and recovery, FDTCs promote safe and nurturing home environments in the long run. However, family reunification depends on the parent's demonstrated ability to care for their child's safety and well-being (Center for Substance Abuse Treatment, 2004). Essential components of FDTCs include regular hearings, judicial monitoring, timely treatment and detox referrals, frequent drug testing, sanctions and incentives, and wrap-around services (Edward & Ray, 2005).

There are three different models for FDTC—the integrated model, the dual-track model, and the parallel model (Boles et al., 2007). The integrated model consists of a single-family court judge who oversees parental compliance with substance abuse treatment and all dependency-related petitions for each case. The dual-track model consists of an FDTC judge who only monitors substance abuse treatment compliance for participants who initially failed to partake in court-ordered services. At the same time, dependency-related case proceedings are handled in a separate court. Lastly, the parallel model consists of dependency-related case proceedings conducted in court while a specialized court officer oversees parental compliance with treatment and recovery (Boles et al., 2007). While FDTCs are based on the drug court model, the difference between the two courts lies in the types of treatment services and the eligibility criteria (Moore et al., 2020). In conclusion, the three models of FDTC operate in conjunction with collaborative efforts to protect children from further abuse.

Scope of adoption/culture

The same focus on FDTCs is not present in other countries as compared to the United States. Although PSCs have seemingly been adopted globally, it seems that FDTCs have not been adopted outside the United States. However, drug treatment courts themselves have been adopted on a global scale, with many world governments and justice systems recognizing that drug dependence is a disease, so incarceration alone cannot alleviate the problems of substance abuse (Franco, 2010). Although the United States has shown a recognized need for a specialized court dedicated to child maltreatment and substance abuse, this need has not been formally recognized internationally.

Science

Like other PSCs, FDTCs are rooted in therapeutic jurisprudence and problem-solving principles. When implementing the ideas of therapeutic jurisprudence in building the FDTC, the team should include judges, treatment providers, child welfare specialists, attorneys, and other key service providers to act as therapeutic agents for the parents and children they are serving (Winnick, 2003). The philosophy of therapeutic jurisprudence, when applied to FDTCs, also encourages practices drawn from psychology and social work (Wiener et al., 2010).

The problem-solving principles of FDTC are grounded in addressing the root causes of crime (Karafin, 2008) while focusing on eliminating substance use and encouraging positive parenting practices. FDTC pulls from the drug court model, especially when implementing effective intervention into the problem-solving principles. Like drug courts, FDTCs also incorporate the eight main principles of effective intervention (Andrews & Bonta, 2006; Gendreau et al., 1996). As substance abuse is one of the main focuses of the FDTC, adapting the drug court treatment model proves beneficial (Marlowe & Carey, 2012). In sum, FDTCs use therapeutic justice and problem-solving principles, as well as effective interventions, to target the underlying needs of court participants and reduce child neglect and substance abuse.

Reentry courts

History

Reentry courts are another type of PSC in operation, created in response to the growing re-offending rates throughout the criminal justice system (see Hassoun Ayoub & Rempel, 2021). Almost all people (95%) who are convicted of a crime and incarcerated will, at some point, return to the community (Jonson & Cullen, 2015). Whether these people recidivate, however, depends on the services offered when incarcerated and immediately after their release (Jonson & Cullen, 2015). An estimated 4.5 million people are on probation or parole in the United States (one in 55 adults) (Kaeble, 2018). In 2018 alone, 600,000 people were released from federal and state prisons (Jonson & Cullen, 2015).

Although community supervision works for some, more than one-third of prison population growth can be attributed to rearrest following a violation of parole (McNeeley, 2018). In 2016, an estimated one-half of people on probation/parole still needed to complete the terms of their supervised release (Kaeble, 2018). There is also a "supervision effect" taking place; the more a person comes into contact with their probation officer, the more likely the officer will find something deviant (Hamilton, 2010; Rodriguez & Webb, 2007). Intensive monitoring can also have unintended consequences, especially for participants with a low risk of recidivating (Lowencamp & Latessa, 2005). Because community supervision does not work for everyone, it is necessary to consider programming that promotes the most successful reentry possible and ensures that a person no longer engages in antisocial behavior (Rizzo, 2020).

Current state and federal reentry courts and community supervision can be traced to the Sentencing Reform Act (SRA), which eliminated federal parole and determinate sentencing (U.S. Sentencing Commission, 2010). As a result, offenders in the federal justice system could no longer finish their sentences on parole, and the US Congress created the concept of supervised release (Driscoll, 2018). Supervised release is unique to the federal system; a person remains under the court's jurisdiction after release, focusing on "facilitating reintegration" (Driscoll, 2018).

The concept of reentry courts was proposed in 2000 as part of the Reentry Courts Initiative (RCI), including nine sites around the country in California, Colorado, Delaware (2 sites), Florida, Iowa, Kentucky (2 sites), New York, Ohio, and West Virginia (Lindquist et al., 2004; Vance, 2011). As of 2018, 43 state and 46 federal reentry courts were active within the United States (Driscoll, 2018). As a whole, reentry courts were created to reduce the rate of re-offending.

Operations

In their operations, reentry courts improve the use of oversight, incentives, sanctions, and positive resources to support reintegration and reduce re-offending rates (Bureau of Justice Assistance, 2010). Reentry courts were created to address the critical needs of returning prisoners, particularly immediately after release, with an overall goal of seamlessly transitioning prisoners back into the community through accountability and social services (Bureau of Justice Assistance, 2010). Research suggests that the most practical interventions encourage reduced recidivism and successful reentry, target people at a particular risk level, address specific needs, and deliver services to maximize responsibility (Andrews & Bonta, 1998; Smith et al., 2009).

While drug courts and other PSC models have been standardized, reentry courts still need to be. Programs tend to be distinctive and shaped by available resources, including the local population of returning offenders and the level of collaboration between courts, probation officers, and federal offices (Wolf, 2011). However, new reentry courts still turn to established programs in their early stages of development (Driscoll, 2018; Meierhoefer, 2011). The Six Key Principles of reentry courts include (Lindquist et al., 2018):

1. Assessment and planning,
2. Active oversight,
3. Management of support services,
4. Accountability to the community,
5. Graduated and parsimonious sanctions, and
6. Rewards for success.

Along with the Six Key Principles, successful reentry programs should also focus on the "accompanying narrative" that incarcerated people can become productive members of society with the assistance of reentry programs and other social services (Cullen et al., 2016; Maruna & Lebel, 2003). The population served through reentry courts differs in each jurisdiction. Several courts in the United States work primarily with high-risk court participants, some work with primarily low-risk, and some accept all potential participants (Wolf, 2011). While operations among reentry programs might vary, the vast majority share six fundamental principles and the overall goal of reducing recidivism by targeting the needs of returning participants to the justice system.

Scope of adoption/culture

Many other countries use similar models to reentry courts in the United States; however, a few specific courts are dedicated to reentry globally. The United Kingdom follows the US reentry court model components to assist in reentry, such as collaboration, social welfare organizations, and treatment programs (Ministry of Justice, 2015). In England and Wales, the judiciary has minimal interaction with participants' post-sentence supervision; however, there is a parole board for high-risk participants with sentences of 15 years or more (Criminal Justice Alliance, 2015). Although there has been some trialing with post-incarceration intervention, it has not been widespread. However, there is a push for reentry-like programs due to the success of reentry programs elsewhere (Criminal Justice Alliance, 2015).

One program, the Circles of Support and Accountability Program, is a community-based initiative to help convicted sex offenders by reintegrating them into the community through building trust, friendship, and accountability between court participants and trained volunteers (Wilson et al., 2013). This program has been implemented worldwide, including in Australia, Brazil, Canada, the Netherlands, South Korea, the United Kingdom, and the United States. The overall goal is to focus on collaboration between multiple agencies and to approach management and reintegration of court participants on a case-by-case basis to promote community safety, decrease re-offending risk, and encourage pro-social behavior. Although rare, sex offender courts exist in the United States, Canada, and South Africa (Kilmer & Emmert, 2021). All arose out of the country's social and political recognition of the problem of sex offenses and have goals of monitoring, controlling, and sanctioning sex offenders in order to protect communities.

France has a twist on a reentry court called "juges de l'application des peines" (Herzog-Evans, 2016). Judges in this model have a variety of responsibilities, ranging from releasing prisoners from custodial sentences to determining placement in the community through semi-freedom or electronic monitoring (Herzog-Evans, 2016). Judges also supervise and manage all community sentences and release measures, work closely with participants, and use community services to help participants with the post-incarceration period (Herzog-Evans, 2015). Although this is not necessarily an exact reentry court, the main principles model reentry court techniques (Herzog-Evans, 2015). Although there are no formal reentry courts outside the United States, efforts to curb re-offending rates have occurred internationally in France and the United Kingdom.

Science

Reentry courts use the sciences of therapeutic jurisprudence, problem-solving principles, and procedural justice, similar to many other PSCs. The focus of therapeutic justice in reentry courts allows the law to be a therapeutic agent if restructured to better align with therapeutic principles and can positively impact psychological well-being (Wexler & Winick, 2008). The judge is crucial to court function and is a supporter of court participants (Popovic, 2002). They emphasize accountability and have a more active, engaged, and less formal relationship with participants compared to the traditional court setting (Popovic, 2002).

Problem-solving principles and procedural justice address the specialized needs of specific populations of court participants (DeMatteo et al., 2019) (see Chapter 3 in this volume for more). The emphasis on procedural justice provides a perception that courts act in just and legitimate ways; if people believe they are treated with respect and dignity, they are more likely to view the system positively (Warren, 2000). Overall, principles of therapeutic justice, supportive interactions between participants and judges, immediate intervention, and clear rules/goals lead to heightened procedural justice and legitimacy, which in turn encourages compliance and reduced recidivism (Kaiser & Holtfreter, 2016; Rizzo, 2020).

Animal courts

History

The next PSC to be discussed is the animal court, the first of which opened in Pima, Arizona, in 2012. This court was created with the County Attorney's office, Justice Court staff, Pima Animal Care Center Officers, Arizona Game and Fish Department, Pima County Sheriff's Department, and defense attorneys (Animals and Society Institute, 2020). Animal courts serve defendants accused of misdemeanor offenses or repeat offenders involving animal abuse, as well as defendants with animals deemed "dangerous" (e.g., incidents of dogs biting) (Animals and Society Institute, 2020). Overall, there are few courts specific to animal welfare (Patronek, 1999). Although few animal courts are in operation, they were created to combat animal abuse.

Operations

Animal courts typically follow the same general components and goals as other PSCs, but they have unique operations depending on the jurisdiction. As of 2016, three animal courts are in operation in the United States: Prima County, Arizona; Bernalillo County, New Mexico; and Boutetourt County, Virginia. Although the exact numbers of operations vary, the Animal Welfare Court in Bernalillo County reviewed approximately 40,000 animal control complaints in 2014 (Animals & Society Institute, n.d.). Due to the limited nature of animal courts, there is no standardization in the operation of these courts. However, the few courts that do exist seem to have three components in common: punishment, education, counseling/behavior management (Animals and Society Institute, 2020).

Punishments often include a fine, relinquishing of the animal, and probation. Education includes lessons on how to care for an animal properly. Finally, counseling/behavior management addresses the likely causes of animal mistreatment (e.g., substance abuse, mental health problems, anger issues) (Animals and Society Institute, 2020).

Beyond these three components, each animal court has specialized operation processes. For example, the Animal Welfare court in Pima, Arizona, has implemented fines, probation, and jail time while also offering intervention and treatment programs (Animals and Society Institute, 2020). The Pre-Adjudication Animal Welfare Court in New Mexico offers the option of diversion in therapy (New Mexico Courts, n.d.) While each court shows unique qualities in its operation, there are also similarities in its overall goals.

Scope of adoption/culture

There is no evidence of animal courts outside of the United States.

Science

In the most minimal sense, animal courts rely on components from psychology to assist in their operations (e.g., anger management therapy and counseling sessions) (Animals and Society Institute, 2020). These components focus on the counseling/behavior management component of animal courts.

Gun courts

History

Another PSC, the gun court, has been introduced due to the rise in violent firearms-related crimes. There are a wide variety of gun violence interventions in the United States, including legislative action (adopting new laws regarding carry permits), changes in policing (such as targeting guns through direct enforcement), and judicial measures (revising sentencing guidelines) (Nobles, 2008). However, gun violence interventions have varied; some programs are believed to be promising, while others seem to have no effect whatsoever (Sherman, 2001).

After determining that violent firearm crimes were rising, Providence and Bristol country in Rhode Island created a "gun court calendar." Although this was not a separate court, it placed firearms crimes on a different schedule to be handled by assigned personnel (Noble, 2008). Seeing the potential success of handling firearms cases separately, Birmingham, Alabama, created the first gun court in 1995 as a branch of the city's Family Court (Noble, 2008). This gun court, like the majority of PSCs, took inspiration from the drug court movement of the 1990s and the calendar schedule in Rhode Island (Wellford et al., 2004). Multiple agencies, including the Alabama Department of Youth Services, local nonprofits, the Department of Probation, and the County Sheriff's Office, worked together to create the gun court.

Gun courts exist in the juvenile justice system as well. The use of gun courts, particularly for juveniles, is related to the high rates of gun violence among adolescents (Office of Juvenile Justice and Delinquency Prevention, 1999). In 2006, 3,184 children/teens died from gun-related incidents in the United States, which included 2,225 homicides (Children's Defense Fund, 2009). The firearm homicide rate for adolescents in the United States is 15 to 16 times higher than that of 25 other industrialized countries combined (Office of Juvenile Justice and Delinquency Prevention, 1999). Typically, juvenile gun courts focus on providing intervention for youths while also holding them accountable (Noble, 2008). Along with efforts in gun control reform and changes in policing, gun courts were established to target and reduce violent crimes involving firearms.

Operations

The actual operation of gun courts varies by jurisdiction, but they share similar components and goals. Gun courts generally target particular offenses for processing in a community-based court (Wellford et al., 2004). Overall, they attempt to move gun-related offenses through the system efficiently and, in a majority of cases, implement harsher punishments (Noble, 2008). Key components of gun court include (Sheppard & Kelly, 2002):

1. Early intervention (in most cases, before court proceedings);
2. Short-term, intensive programming;
3. Intensive educational emphasis on gun education and the harms of unlawful gun use; and
4. Inclusion of court and law enforcement personnel, as well as community members.

While gun courts operate differently across jurisdictions, standard features include small caseloads, frequent hearings, immediate sanctions, family involvement, and treatment services (Wellford et al., 2004). The Birmingham gun court typically targets first-time juvenile delinquents (Nobles, 2008). The New York City gun court, created in 2003, handles felony gun possession cases (Nobles, 2008). The Philadelphia gun court, implemented in 2005, hears cases in which the most serious offense is a Violation of the Uniform Firearms Act (Nobles, 2008). Whereas Birmingham and New York City courts focus on deterrence and sanctions, the Philadelphia court focuses on rehabilitation and education (Nobles, 2008). Each gun court operates in its own way, but commonalities exist in many areas.

Scope of adoption/culture

As not many nations experience the number of firearm-related incidents as the United States, there are few gun courts or gun control measures in other countries (Nobles, 2008). However, gun courts were initially conceived in Jamaica in 1974 with the passing of the Gun Court Act (Calathes, 1990). This act authorized a specialized court to process cases involving the illegal possession/use of firearms and ammunition. This was in response to increased gun violence, stemming from political unrest and poor economic conditions (Calathes, 1990). Another country that attempted to implement gun courts was Australia. Australia initiated and implemented a gun court but abandoned it in 2004. An evaluation found that the rates of firearm violence were too low to justify expenses (Samuels, 2004). Overall, gun courts are limited to within the United States and Jamaica, as gun-related incidents are much lower in other countries.

Science

Gun courts implement the science of judicial authority and the philosophy of deterrence to target the root problems of crime and ultimately change the behavior of court participants (Huddleson et al., 2008; Nobles, 2008). Deterrence is using negative consequences to deter criminal behavior at an individual level and as an aggregate unit of analysis (Gibbs, 1975; Jervis, 1979; Zimring & Hawkins, 1973). At the individual level, deterrence acts as a conduit to avoid crime after being caught and punished. At the aggregate level, deterrence acts as a conduit for decreased rates of crime corresponding with changes in legislation, policy, and enforcement (Zimring & Hawkins, 1973). Gun courts are positioned as "get tough" measures aimed at illegal firearms and gun violence, promoting deterrence through harsher sentencing and by punishing court participants considered the most "at-risk" for gun-related crime (Nobles, 2008).

Homelessness courts

History

The next PSC to discuss is the homelessness court. First implemented in 1989 in San Diego, California, homelessness courts have grown slowly (see Troeger & Douds, 2021) Today, there are about 10 homelessness courts throughout the United States. The goal of homelessness courts is to aid with issues related to mental health, employment, life skills, substance abuse, and legal issues (Lopez, 2018). The first court implemented in San Diego in 1989 was the Homeless Court Program (HCP). It was held at local shelters for homeless veterans to resolve outstanding misdemeanor criminal cases (ABA, 2006). The HCP worked with local social services providers to find solutions for homelessness. This includes but is not limited to economic catastrophe, the inability to thrive because of child support owed, employment that does not pay enough to rent an apartment, or severe mental health issues (ABA, 2006).

Due to the success the HCP experienced in its first year of operation, expansion took place quickly. In 1990, the HCP was expanded to include women's and cold weather shelters in 1994, and by 1995, the HCP serviced the general homeless population at large (ABA, 2006). Since 1995, nine more states nationally and one country internationally have implemented homelessness courts in their criminal justice systems.

Operations

Ten states have developed courts to help justice-involved people experiencing homelessness: Arizona, California, Colorado, Michigan, Missouri, New Mexico, South Carolina, Texas, Utah, and Washington. Homelessness courts aim to help the participants navigate complicated legal matters while providing resources to attain self-sufficiency (Lopez, 2018).

As this population is mainly vagrant, participants do not always enter court through the traditional tracks. Participants can be introduced to homelessness courts in two ways: they sign themselves up for court, or they are referred through the system (Troeger & Douds, 2021). From there, eligibility is examined. While the various courts around the country have their eligibility criteria, three standards are present at every court. First, the person is actively experiencing homelessness; second, their offense must be nonviolent; and third, they are willing to work toward the end goal of self-sufficiency (Troeger & Douds, 2021).

The typical homelessness court operates with the traditional pure dismissal model, meaning participants are offered an action plan agreed upon by a judge and related service provider, which the participant must accept to move forward (Troeger & Douds, 2021). If the participant chooses to accept, their related fines and incarceration times are waived. Once the program is completed, evidence of progress is given by the service provider to dismiss the charges and release the participant from the program (Troeger & Douds, 2021).

Most homelessness courts meet outside traditional court buildings, often in shelters or public spaces like libraries. Court days usually include hygiene offerings, food, group therapy, access to attorneys and social service providers, and court sessions (Troeger & Douds, 2021). While each court operates separately, there is a consistent overlap between these processes.

Scope of adoption/culture

One other country has adopted processes similar to those of the homelessness courts located in the United States. Canada has developed homelessness-related diversion programs for both pre-arrest and pre-trial for their MHC participants (Public Safety Canada, 2004). Only participants proceeding through the mental health PSC are eligible for these types of programming. However, criminal justice actors within Canada have provided suggestions for ways to expand services for homelessness, including more targeted diversion programming (Public Safety Canada, 2004).

Other than the diversion programs currently available in Canada, there is no clear evidence of homelessness PSC existing in other international countries.

Science

Like many other PSCs, homelessness courts are based on the sciences of theory-based therapeutic justice and rehabilitation and encompass a community-based approach (ABA, 2006). As discussed with other PSCs, therapeutic jurisprudence requires legal actors to be aware of how their actions affect others. The problem-solving principles aim to respond to the particular problems and needs of participants, to understand and target the root causes of homelessness, and to provide tools and resources to become self-sustaining permanently (ABA, 2006).

Including the community-based approach makes it crucial to understand the importance of service providers in this particular PSC. Homeless service providers serve as a critical link between the court system and people experiencing homelessness (ABA, 2006). The providers offer solutions that participants might not encounter if they were proceeding through the regular criminal justice system process (ABA, 2006). Service providers take on many roles in homelessness courts, including advocating for participants. The providers often ensure the participant is ready to resolve their case and reintegrate into society successfully (ABA, 2006).

US tribal courts

History

Tribal courts are another PSC within the United States. The history of tribal courts in the United States can be traced back to the 1880s and the creation of the "Courts of Indian Offenses:" the US government's response to the perceived lack of law enforcement and justice in Indian Country (Jones, 2000; see also Aseline & João Lobo Antunes, 2021). These courts aimed to handle less severe criminal actions and disputes among tribal members. In addition, many of these courts aimed to integrate Indigenous Peoples into non-Indigenous society and did not reflect Indigenous values and customs, trying to alter those values into culturally dominant ones that society viewed as necessary (Jones, 2000).

The Indian Reorganization Act of 1934 allowed Indian tribes to set their own justice codes and operate their own court systems to enforce tribal laws enacted by Indian tribes. In response, tribes developed their own governing methods, integrating a traditional court model and elements of tribal law and peacemaking (Jones, 2000). Today, there are approximately 400 tribal courts throughout the United States (Bureau of Indian Affairs, n.d.). The power to establish courts in their own jurisdictions is inherently recognized within the US Constitution, court decisions, treaties, and federal statutes, which consider Indian Tribes sovereign nations (Florey, 2013).

However, some tribes choose not to enact their codes and operate by the Code of Indian Offense in the Code of Federal Regulation (CFR). Some tribes cannot afford to create or operate their court systems and use CFR courts operated by the Bureau of Indian Affairs (Jones, 2000). These courts are similar to tribal courts, with the exception that they are funded and administered by the Bureau of Indian Affairs, as well as being restricted from hearing internal tribal disputes (Jones, 2000). The United States has five regional CFR courts: Albuquerque, the Southern Plains, the Western Region, the Eastern Oklahoma Region, and the Southwest Region (Bureau of Indian Affairs, n.d.) Overall, tribal courts were introduced to recognize the unique status of Indian tribes within the United States and have been established throughout the country.

Operations

Many tribal courts operate with procedures similar to state and federal courts (Jones, 2000). However, one key difference is that those juries in tribal courts consist of only six members, all of whom are tribal members. Many tribal court judges are trained attorneys; however, tribal courts might also have respected tribal members serve as judges due to their knowledge of a tribe's customs and traditions. Tribal judges are typically appointed by the tribe's governing body or are elected to their positions. In larger tribal courts, there are often both law-trained and non-attorney judges (Jones, 2000).

Many tribal courts use both law-trained attorneys and "lay advocates," who are tribal members who are knowledgeable of tribal law and represent court participants (Jones, 2000). Some courts might require lay advocates to take a bar exam before being allowed to practice. However, most court systems only require an admission fee and adequate study of the Tribal code. Tribal courts are not required to appoint or pay for an attorney for a person who cannot afford legal counsel, but most tribal courts have a public defender system (Jones, 2000).

Another significant difference in tribal courts is their limit on court authority in some instances and persons, which is set out through certain acts of congress and decisions by the United States Supreme Court (Jones, 2000). The US Supreme Court has stated that Indian tribes lack the authority to regulate non-Indian criminal conduct and can only prosecute any Indian person who commits a crime within the reservation. For example, a non-Indian who commits a crime on an Indian reservation cannot be prosecuted through a tribal court and instead will be processed through state or federal courts, depending on case circumstances (Jones, 2000).

Tribal courts are also limited in the types of sentences that can be imposed on court participants. Currently, federal law prohibits tribal courts from imposing a jail sentence exceeding one year for any crime. As a result, many tribal courts only oversee civil and low-level criminal cases and avoid prosecuting severe crimes, which are delegated to the federal court system (Jones, 2000). Many tribal courts also hear child abuse and domestic violence cases, with mandatory arrest and hold provisions to protect victims after a crime is reported (Jones, 2000).

Many tribal courts implement one of three approaches in their overall operations (Tribal-State Judicial Consortium, n.d.). Some courts operate traditionally, following their laws, customs, and traditions, and the tribes' governing council or tribal leaders decide cases. Other courts take a contemporary approach and have a tribal court judge preside over cases and apply the tribe's written laws, codes, and treaties. Finally, some courts use traditional and contemporary approaches, in which tribal leaders settle some cases while others are settled by a tribal court judge (Tribal-State Judicial Consortium, n.d.).

In a few states, Indian tribes (as identified through the law) do not operate court systems or will operate systems that hear minimal cases. These states are Public Law 280 states and can prosecute all persons, Indian and non-Indian, who commit crimes on Indian reservations. However, some of these states still have tribal courts that hear certain types of disputes, such as violations of hunting/fishing codes or cases involving the Indian Child Welfare Act (Jones, 2000). While the exact operations of tribal courts vary state by state, they follow similar proceedings to traditional courts, including tribal members and cultural considerations.

Scope of adoption/culture

While tribal courts are unique to US jurisdictions, some countries have implemented court systems of their own to account for Indigenous tribes that are located within their regions. Most notable are the Aboriginal court systems in Australia and Canada, which were created to increase the participation of Indigenous Peoples in the justice system and improve partnerships between state governments and Aboriginal organizations (Birggs & Auty, 2003; Whonnock, 2008). Similar to US tribal courts, Indigenous courts typically only process people of Indigenous heritage. However, Indigenous courts are less formal than US tribal courts and often only handle bail hearings and sentence hearings rather than trial and preliminary hearings (Steps to Justice, 2019). The need to recognize and collaborate with Indigenous groups in specialized court settings has been recognized internationally in the United States, Canada, and Australia.

Science

The focus of tribal courts is cultural considerations for the Indigenous community. The aim is to recognize tribal nations and their unique jurisdictions while operating under a PSC model. Tribal courts use cultural considerations of Indigenous Peoples within the sentencing process to promote a positive relationship between the government and the Indigenous community. In conjunction with the inclusion of cultural science, tribal courts can better account for factors within a participant's life while also considering how culture affects behavior.

Elder protection courts

History

The last PSC to discuss is the elder protection court, which was created to aid in elder abuse cases. About one in 10 Americans over the age of 60 have experienced elder abuse in some capacity (Acierno et al., 2010). Elder abuse is defined as "any knowing, intended, or careless act that causes harm or serious risk of harm to an older person either physically, mentally, emotionally, or financially" (National Center on Elder Abuse, 2017).

The most common form of elder abuse is neglect (National Center on Elder Abuse, 2017). Crimes against elderly victims are similar to domestic violence in that they frequently go unreported: the New York City Department for the Aging reports that for every elder abuse case reported to programs/agencies, 23.5 cases went unreported (2011). Many victims might be unable to report their own elder abuse due to limitations, isolation, emotional/financial dependency on their abuser, or an overall desire to protect the abuser (Banks et al., 2014).

Many cases that fall under elder abuse can be heard in multiple jurisdictions, such as those specializing in crime, probation, guardianship, or civil matters. Elder abuse not only creates legal and healthcare costs but it also reduces older people's participation in community life (Dong & Simon, 2013). Without accessible social services, the elderly population becomes more at risk through aging (National Center on Elder Abuse, 2017). By 2030, the number of adults aged 65 and older will represent nearly 20% of the US population, likely creating different and greater demands on the legal system concerning elder abuse (Banks et al., 2014).

As a result of the high rates of elder abuse, an increasing elder population, and a system that did not accurately assist our elderly population, the first elder protection court in the nation was established in Alameda County, California, in 2002 by Judge Julie Conger (Banks et al., 2014). Using a specialized judge and calendar dedicated to processing elder abuse cases, the elder protection court became the docket for all felony elder cases in the county (Banks et al., 2014).

Although the importance of elder protection courts has been noted, few jurisdictions have developed specialized programs explicitly targeting elder abuse. While the Alameda County court no longer operates, an adaptation of the court was created in Ventura County, California, in 2009 (Banks et al., 2014).

Operations

Elder protection courts operate with a focus on the victim of the crime rather than the perpetrator. Their sole purposes are making the court more accessible to victims of elder abuse, providing individualized attention to the needs of victims, and providing a single venue where cases can be resolved efficiently and compassionately (Banks et al., 2014). According to Judge Conger, the key to a successful elder protection court is the assignment of a case manager, who offers comprehensive resolution by reviewing the court's database and determining if pending cases have the same victim (Banks et al., 2014). Case managers also review all domestic violence and civil harassment claims for evidence of elder abuse (Banks et al., 2014). Further, Judge Conger highlights the importance of collaboration and investment from multiple actors, including presiding judges, workgroups, task forces, elder access groups, justice partners, case managers, court coordinators, and other trained court personnel (Banks et al., 2014).

There are many challenges that elder protection courts face, not only in their creation but also in their successful continuation (Banks et al., 2014). Funding issues include training on aging issues for all levels of court personnel and eliminating physical barriers for the elderly inside and outside the court space (e.g., accessible ramps, transportation, and assistive listening devices) (Banks et al., 2014). Finally, securing confidence in victims of elder abuse is a difficulty all courts face: as a group, the elderly are reluctant to turn to the court system and might not be aware of the services available to them (Banks et al., 2014). While elder protection courts represent a vital step toward reducing the victimization of the elderly, legislative expansion of mandatory reporting requirements and more substantial penalties for not reporting abuse is still needed (Banks et al., 2014). To support victims of elder abuse and make the courts more accessible, elder protection courts work to aid victims in all aspects of the court process.

Scope of adoption/culture

Elder protection courts have not been introduced outside of the United States. Overall, the prevalence of elder abuse reported across the globe is around 5%, with the most common type being psychological abuse, followed by financial, physical, and sexual abuse (Salsi et al., 2015). Despite elder abuse rates raising concern throughout the world, no jurisdictions outside of the United States have a court system dedicated to prosecuting elder abuse cases.

However, one country, Italy, has recognized the importance of combating elder abuse (Salsi et al., 2015). Specific articles in their penal code target crimes against those who mistreat family, cohabitants, or other people under their care. Crimes in which a person abuses the "needs, passions, or inexperience" of a member of a disadvantaged population are also mentioned in the penal code (Salsi et al., 2015). Although many researchers have recognized the need for more elder abuse legislation, little progress has been made. While elder protection courts only exist formally within the United States, the need to protect elders from abuse is recognized globally.

Science

Elder protection courts focus heavily on the science of problem-solving approaches. They are dedicated to responding to elder abuse and the legal needs of seniors in a problem-solving and holistic manner (Banks et al., 2014). Courts focus primarily on the victim rather than the perpetrator. Court actors pay attention to any potential underlying problems by assessing participants to see if specialized treatment programs are needed (Banks et al., 2014). These treatment programs are typically substance abuse or mental health treatment (Banks et al., 2014). Because elder protection courts target a participant's needs, they apply a problem-solving approach. Using problem-solving principles, the root causes of offending behavior are targeted through treatment programs and other programs for participants (Karafin, 2008).

Similarities and differences among problem-solving courts

PSCs were created to help participants in an individualized and specialized way, aiming to reduce recidivism. Since the implementation of the first PSC, the model of PSCs has been adapted to address various issues that plague people in contact with the criminal justice system. As a result, many commonalities span across the different PSCs. These similarities might be reflected in the court's practices, policies, science, or theory. However, the variance between PSCs also exists. This section examines those similarities and differences.

One of the most common similarities in these courts is how they function. Most PSCs fall under two categories: diversionary programs or alternative sentencing programs. PSCs that act as diversionary programs address the needs of a person who has committed a crime but has yet to receive a sentence. Rather than proceed through the traditional court process, the person might be eligible to proceed through a PSC. In looking at PSCs as alternative sentencing programs, the involvement in PSCs follows a conviction.

Another shared similarity in PSCs stems from the theoretical foundations of different courts. PSCs' most recurring justice principles include therapeutic jurisprudence, procedural justice, and restorative justice. Therapeutic jurisprudence, which focuses on implementing the law through a therapeutic approach (Wexler, 2000), can help guide PSCs. The essence of therapeutic jurisprudence centers on the therapeutic and anti-therapeutic consequences of the law. This requires legal actors to be aware of how their actions affect others, specifically regarding the potential for participant rehabilitation. This does not exclude retributive responses, if necessary, but shifts the onus to the criminal justice practitioners and their role in court processes (Miller et al., 2020) (see Chapter 3 in this volume for more on the justice of PSCs).

Procedural justice focuses on treating people through the legal system (Thibaut & Walker, 1975). Procedural justice emphasizes that court participants should have a voice throughout their case, be treated with dignity and respect as they proceed through the legal process, and be treated equally (Hinds & Murphy, 2007). In addition, many PSCs use procedural justice to promote higher compliance regarding social services (Winick, 2003). Examples of procedural justice used in PSCs include the judge speaking directly to the participant, using the participant's name, allowing space for the participant to ask questions, and seeking input from the participant (e.g., Gatowski et al., 2013; Gover et al., 2007).

Restorative justice is an approach to justice that focuses on restoration, healing, and accountability (Poulson, 2003). Restorative justice encourages participants to take ownership of their actions, encouraging the victims to be active in the legal proceedings (Poulson, 2003). These principles are often found in the PSCs that incorporate a community component into their model (Miller et al., 2020). The incorporation allows the community to have an input in the legal process while permitting the participant to give back to their community.

Although PSCs have many similarities, there are many differences present as well. The most common differences in PSCs include the target population as well as the delivery of the court model. Target populations differ among PSCs due to the nature of the court. For example, drug courts target people who commit crimes involving drugs; community courts target people who commit quality-of-life crimes; VTCs target veterans who commit crimes. In addition, PSCs are created with eligibility criteria to serve a specified population. Eligibility criteria allow PSCs to deliver intentional and customized services (Huddleston & Marlowe, 2011). Unlike the traditional court system, which does not differentiate based on offense, the different target populations of PSCs allow for an individualized experience.

Another difference, not only between different PSCs but between courts in the United States and other countries, is the delivery of the court model. As discussed in this chapter, PSCs have spread far beyond the United States. In adapting PSCs in other countries, many delivery modifications have occurred. Most notably, the US and foreign courts differ in legal actors' roles; for example, English judges play a much smaller role than US judges because they have other actors to rely on (Nolan, 2009). Another difference is how judges interact with court participants; for instance, judges in the United States tend to be more emotionally invested in the process, whereas judges in Scotland, England, and Ireland are more business-like (Nolan, 2009). Finally, there is a clear difference in the philosophies and beliefs that underlie PSCs when comparing the United States to other countries. For example, courts in Canada function under the notion that domestic violence is a learned behavior to be addressed by education, whereas courts in the United States treat it as an illness to be addressed through treatment (Nolan, 2009). These differences in delivery models can be traced back to the individual court, target population, and the methods behind the original implementation.

Conclusion

As the court system has evolved from an exclusively traditional adversarial process to a system that includes specialty courts, PSCs are no longer just a US phenomenon nor the only focus on substance abuse. PSCs in the United States and across the globe have been formed to address mental health, prostitution, gambling, domestic violence, animal issues, gun violations, and various other social issues related to crime. Some PSCs are designed to address multiple problems, while others focus on the group of participants rather than the offense committed. Each PSC, whether implemented nationally or internationally, has its unique history, societal differences, and science of each type of PSC.

SECTION 2
THE SCIENCE OF PROBLEM-SOLVING COURTS

3
The Justice Principles of Problem-Solving Courts

Logan A. Yelderman, Mia A. Holbrook, Jennifer L. Lanterman, Alicia DeVault, and Monica K. Miller

Applications of Justice in Problem-Solving Courts

Criminal "justice" refers to the practice by which people are treated appropriately and fairly given their criminal actions. Although words like "appropriate" and "fair" then beg a definition, the idea of justice involves deservingness and fairness. This chapter will discuss the various justice principles found within the context of criminal justice associated with problem-solving courts (PSCs), including adversarial processes, therapeutic jurisprudence (TJ), procedural justice (PJ), restorative justice (RJ), legitimacy, and community sentiment. Some PSCs specifically rely on one or two specific justice principles, while others might rely on more or none. Some PSCs even use different terms but still apply many of the same justice techniques as other courts.

Justice and fairness are often assessed by examining the processes (e.g., judicial treatment) that involve defendants in criminal cases and assessing the outcomes (e.g., case dispositions). Justice might involve moral questions, such as which crime should be considered more severe? The answer then helps the courts and legal system determine which crime should receive harsher punishments. Justice might also involve the protection of vulnerable populations, such as those with intellectual disabilities, mental health issues, physiological impairments, and children. With many of these populations, intent and instructional comprehension might be viewed differently than in non-vulnerable populations. Justice prioritizes all parties involved rather than one party. The involvement of all parties in this conceptualization is critical because it allows the word "justice" to be applied universally. Although

Society, Science, and Problem-Solving Courts. Monica K. Miller, Mia A. Holbrook, Logan A. Yelderman, and Kylie Kulak, Oxford University Press. © Oxford University Press 2025. DOI: 10.1093/oso/9780190059804.003.0003

the term "justice" needs and requires no modifier, several emerging areas of research involving differing foci apply descriptive terms to situate justice within a respective area of interest or context. Terms such as "procedural justice" and "restorative justice" refer to the universal justice applied to the procedures used when handling offenders and the restoration of the bonds between the offender and victims or community.

Fairness in the criminal justice system, on the other hand, refers to the equal treatment of offenders and the assurance of constitutional and legal protections (e.g., due process). It is fairness that tasks the criminal justice process to be void of bias, discrimination, and prejudice or any form of impartiality. These features of fairness help achieve the goal of treating all people equally under the law. It is only the law that differentiates cases, punishments, and procedures, not irrelevant or uncontrollable characteristics, such as race, sex, and religion.

Common depictions of Lady Justice, a symbolic representation of law and order, include her holding scales, and sometimes a sword as well, and (usually) being blindfolded. The scales and sword represent justice and the blindfold represents fairness. The current chapter discusses how justice and fairness manifest in the use and application of PSCs in the criminal justice system. First, structural fairness, in the form of the adversarial process, is discussed followed by various justice principles and how these operate in the context of PSCs.

Adversarial Process

Many countries, including the United States, Canada, and Australia, use the adversarial process to settle public, legal disagreements (Miller et al., 2020; Newmark et al., 2004; Visher et al., 2008, 2007). The adversarial system is characterized as a classification of procedures that relies on a neutral fact finder to resolve disputes (Landsman, 1984; Sward, 1989). Formal proceedings in an adversarial system consist of contending parties presenting evidence and information on their behalf in a dispute-resolving mechanism (Landsman, 1984). While the various court structures within the United States apply the adversarial process differently, the criminal court system employs the adversary method in its most basic form. In practice, the opposing parties of the prosecution and defense present evidence to a judge and/or jury. The judge and/or jury act as the neutral fact finder in an effort to reach a resolution. Each side represented in a legal case (prosecution/plaintiff and defense) has the autonomy and discretion to pursue and present evidence of their respective case within the context of legal standards. In this process, the ultimate legal decision is made by the judge and/or jury. The influence of the adversarial process can be seen throughout the criminal justice and courts system, and in many countries, the adversarial system creates the foundation by which fairness and justice can be applied.

The adversarial process in the criminal justice system in general

In general, the US criminal justice system relies on an adversarial system for criminal court proceedings. The adversarial model supposes that justice is best served through the development and demonstration of one case from different perspectives (Marcus, 1992). Thus, this adversarial system is composed of two opposing sides (who each present a case) and one neutral party, who listens to each case and evaluates. The two opposing sides are comprised of the prosecution and the defense, who are often put at odds with one another. The purpose of the two opposing parties is that this will lead to the truth being discovered. Judges play the neutral role in this model, serving a detached and passive part in the adversarial process. Part of the judges' function is to ensure the procedures of due process, determining how the law should be applied, and fact-finding when necessary (Marcus, 1992).

The procedures for the use of the adversarial process in the US criminal justice system are standardized. Each adversarial trial follows a similar format: the prosecution and the defense will each have time to present their case, starting with opening statements, calling witnesses, conducting cross-examinations, and providing closing statements. The judge presiding over the case will oversee each side's presentation, guaranteeing that due process is being upheld and all parties are adhering to the rules of procedure. If the trial involves a jury, the jury becomes an extension of the neutral party. The judge will provide the jury with a review of the legal questions at hand, the procedures the jury should follow, and how to evaluate the presentations of the case to reach a decision.

The adversarial model places the onus on the opposing parties to present the paramount case to convince the neutral party to rule in their favor. Although a desirable outcome might be mutual agreement, each party sets out with the purpose of presenting a stronger argument of the evidence (Marcus, 1992). Because of this approach, the rulings and outcomes that stem from the traditional adversarial process in the United States tend to be more punitive overall (Miller et al., 2020).

The adversarial process and problem-solving courts

One of the key foundational principles of the PSC model is the belief in non-adversarial engagement and team collaboration. In PSCs, the adversarial process shifts to a collaborative process and fundamentally changes the role of attorneys from competitor to problem-solver (Rogers, 2006). This puts team-based decision-making at the center of the model, with the focus solely on the participant, rather than the competition. For the PSC process to be most effective, criminal justice practitioners, treatment professionals, and support services must work together in a cooperative and organized fashion (van Wormer, 2010). For this collaborative model to be established, various professionals must come together, including the judge, prosecutor, and defense attorney, and commit to the process of creating policies and procedures that will support the goals of the PSC (Berman & Feinblatt, 2005).

Various PSCs have modified the approach to the courtroom, including, at times, interweaving components of the adversarial process. Some of the more common sanctions from the adversarial process were adopted in the development of many PSCs' programming (Berman & Feinblatt, 2001). One example of this can be seen reflected in many drug courts, where the prosecuting and defense attorneys work together to create both a reward system and a sanction system for participants moving through the drug court (van Wormer, 2010). This is similar to an adversarial system, where the attorneys will agree upon sanctions for the defendant but with a focus and emphasis on collaboration.

Not only does the role of attorneys change, but the role of judges will often change as well in a PSC setting. The adoption of the adversarial process for PSCs often focuses less on the idea of judges being neutral fact finders and more on judges engaging in a more hands-on fashion. This might include forming a relationship with the participants, organizing meetings, following-up on progress, and maintaining connections with service providers (Berman & Feinblatt, 2001).

While preserving traditional criminal court processes can be beneficial in certain circumstances, the unique and individualist approach of PSCs makes it imperative to understand how the remnants of the traditional process might relate to achieving specific program outcomes (Miller et al., 2020). As previously discussed, the adversarial process entails a more punitive approach. However, the adoption of certain adversarial traits in a non-adversarial PSC setting allows the actors of the court to better address the needs of the participant.

Although there are similarities and overlap between the traditional court adversarial process and the non-adversarial engagement and team collaboration process of PSCs, these courts inherently lean toward less adversarial methods. One of the cornerstones of the PSC model is the collaborative team. The development of such a team allows for coordination, supervision, and support as the participant proceeds through the court. This process promotes the idea that everyone involved in the PSC shares a common goal (Wolf, 2005). This common goal might include working toward effective treatment, successful re-entry, or positive life events, among others. This translates to the judge, attorneys, social services, and stakeholders recognizing and upholding their distinctive roles in the PSC process (Wolf, 2005).

The adversarial process is beneficial in societies that value human rights, the presumptions of innocence, and protection from corruption or government coercion (i.e., a free society; Freedman, 1998). However, PSCs opt to achieve the same goals but without the adversarial system. To help achieve this, PSCs employ a number of other processes and practices that help enhance justice and fairness despite a lack of a formal adversarial system.

Therapeutic Jurisprudence

The practice of the law can have anticipated and unanticipated effects. Applying the law can have positive and negative outcomes. These outcomes and effects can impact victims, witnesses, defendants, families, etc. TJ is concerned with how the law affects and influences all of the people involved in the process, with a specific focus on those who are most directly impacted by its application and their well-being (Wexler, 1992; Winick, 2003). TJ is specifically concerned with outcomes of a process; it is very much a results-driven endeavor. According to Wexler (1992), the law can produce therapeutic outcomes and anti-therapeutic outcomes. Therapeutic outcomes would be those related to the enhancement of a person's well-being or situation, and anti-therapeutic outcomes would be those that diminish the well-being or situation of a person (Wexler, 1992; Winick, 2003). The view of TJ is premised on the notion that the law and its application can have therapeutic effects on the people to whom it is applied. TJ presupposes a societal value placed on the individual person, inherent human dignity, and compassion for others (Yamada, 2021). This is a very similar (if not the same) foundation as the one on which the adversarial process is based.

Originating in mental health law, TJ is often used as a multi- or interdisciplinary framework used to better understand what affects laws and related processes have and how changes can be made to improve those effects (Hora et al., 1999). Because TJ involves the examination of cause and effect analyses, behavioral science is heavily engaged and statistical analysis is strongly integrated, or at least they should be (Hora et al., 1999). Scholarship on TJ has increased over the last several decades and will likely continue to do so as more disciplines become involved and research tools improve. Nevertheless, given the extent to which TJ is optimally applied, there is great confidence that the courts and legal system will become fairer (see Perlin, 2024).

Therapeutic jurisprudence in the criminal justice system in general

TJ principles can be found in most areas of the criminal justice system. Examples of TJ in the traditional criminal justice system are best explained in terms of therapeutic and anti-therapeutic consequences because the therapeutic effects of the law and its application of course preceded the development of a framework used for labeling, categorizing, and studying just as thoughts and behavior preceded the development of social science theories.

Consideration of therapeutic consequences can be found in much of the mental health and disability law. One good example of a TJ practice that has therapeutic effects is the reading of Miranda rights to suspects taken into police custody. These Miranda rights provide suspects with information that might be beneficial to their criminal status and their well-being if it helps them provide a defense, achieve bond, or avoid self-incrimination. Various forms of defenses, such as *mens rea* defenses, insanity defenses, or other mental health defenses, provide defendants with defenses that incorporate their mental health, need for treatment, and overall well-being. These could be considered therapeutic.

Another example of a law with therapeutic consequences is the law allowing the use of closed-circuit television (CCTV) in court for child witnesses. In this case, the purpose of using CCTV is to enhance the well-being of the child without sacrificing impartiality toward the defendant. CCTV use in Canada has been supported by judges and prosecuting attorneys because it reduces the trauma and anxiety that children experience when asked to testify against their accuser in the courtroom, which can sometimes be a family member (Bala et al., 2000). Specific therapeutic effects might be reductions in pre-trial anxiety and increased accuracy of child witness statements (Goodman et al., 1998). Additionally, anti-therapeutic effects would have to be minimized, which in this case could be any biasing effect toward the defendant; however, Goodman et al. (1998) found no biasing effect related to defendant guilt.

The death penalty, on the other hand, is often considered anti-therapeutic because of the trauma imposed on the victim's family by witnessing the execution (Adcock, 2009). Witnesses experience traumatic images and sometimes guilt-induced states of disturbance. Another anti-therapeutic consequence is that of solitary confinement. Solitary confinement is intended to separate an inmate from the rest of the population, for a number of statutorily defined reasons, either to serve as punishment or protection. However, solitary confinement has produced detrimental effects on the mental health and well-being of prisoners (Haney, 2018). There is even evidence that it has produced changes in brain activity after a short period of time (Grassian, 2006). These are considered anti-therapeutic consequences under TJ. The anti-therapeutic consequences of solitary confinement, like the development and onset of new diagnosed mental illness, have also been raised in countries outside of the United States, such as in Denmark where pre-trial solitary confinement has been a target of criticism (Smith, 2006).

Therapeutic goals could be applied to a number of other criminal justice processes, such as post release therapeutic communities for drug abusers, services for people with intellectual and developmental disabilities, and in child abuse or custody cases (Hora, 2002; Marinos & Whittingham, 2019; Marlowe, 2002). One prominent program intimately tied to the discussion and scholarship of TJ is the PSC.

Therapeutic jurisprudence in problem-solving courts

When PSCs first began, they lacked any clear theoretical foundation (Winick, 2003). Yet, with the popularity of drug courts and the excitement around mental health courts (MHCs), these PSCs began to grow at a very fast rate that outpaced any development of theory or empirical foundation for them (Castellano, 2011; Hughes & Peak, 2012). Because of the early markers of success in drug courts and the popularity of other PSCs, like MHCs and community courts, there was a need for theory and empirical understanding in the scholarship of these courts. TJ seemed to fit this role quite conveniently because it uses science to evaluate therapeutic legal impacts (DeMatteo et al., 2019). Not only were PSCs outcome-oriented, as was TJ, but many of the PSCs operated under the goal of providing therapy to participants in need of therapy rather than detention/imprisonment. So, they seemed therapeutic in essence. And, for the most part, they are, particularly MHCs (e.g., Miller et al., 2020; Redlich et al., 2006). In fact, PSCs are often described in the literature as being based on, guided by, or oriented toward TJ (Bakht, 2005; Kaiser & Rhodes, 2019; King, 2011; Porter et al., 2010; Rottman & Casey, 1999).

PSCs are non-traditional courts that address social and psychological problems associated with crimes. Therefore, the nature of their problems favors therapy as a treatment or solution. However, PSCs are also different from the traditional criminal justice system in that they are diversion programs, which involve collaborative teams, led by a judge. The judge plays a significant role and is highly influential in the type of experience the participants have the outcomes (Hora & Stalcup, 2008). Judges develop plans for participants after getting input from numerous team members, often including mental health and treatment professionals in drug, mental health, and community courts; therefore, the extent to which PSCs produce therapeutic consequences rests largely on the judge's shoulders (Duffy, 2011; Simmons, 1999).

Many PSCs use practices that align with TJ, such as motivational shocking in MHCs and open-ended questioning, as in some domestic violence courts (Castellano, 2017; Mirchandani, 2008). In Wiener et al.'s (2010) TJ model of PSCs, courts produce therapeutic consequences through two paths: one through increased perceptions of fairness and legitimacy of the law, and the other through motivation and empowerment of the individual. One question remains, which is whether or not courts that integrate TJ more have better outcomes. Although research is limited, it appears that PSCs which more strongly integrate TJ into their practices have better outcomes (Shaffer, 2011).

All of this is not to say that PSCs have perfected the application of TJ (see Wolff, 2002 for discussion of how to improve therapeutic consequences in MHCs). Often, TJ runs counter to traditional criminal justice goals (Johnston, 2012). Many of the "cons" discussed in Chapter 11 might undermine TJ. Moreover, TJ might be best achieved with a more holistic approach taken by community courts, for example, but the sub-specializations of drug, prostitution, and MHCs might minimize the influence and benefits of the TJ in these courts (Dorf & Fagan, 2003). Veterans' treatment courts (VTCs) focus on the victim, and are different from most other PSCs, so it is possible that TJ applies to those courts differently, even though they still seek therapeutic consequences (King, 2011). To the extent to which recovery and rehabilitation are viewed as autonomous and discretionary outcomes, TJ might flourish, but if they are viewed as forced and coerced, therapeutic outcomes might begin to disappear (see Burns & Peyrot, 2003).

Orienting PSCs through TJ might not work everywhere. For example, in China, TJ might be difficult to apply because the courts are less focused on the individual than in the United States (Li & Liu, 2019). Also, the therapeutic consequences in some courts might be masked by other contextual factors; for instance, in an Australian mental health diversion court, the therapeutic consequences were better explained by pre-program risk and mental well-being (Lim & Day, 2016).

As TJ is applied to and tested within PSCs, it is possible that what is learned from this research can be applied outside of PSCs (Schneider, 2010). Hopefully, court models can be improved, and widely shared recommended practices can have a meaningful impact on improving the well-being of offenders and reducing crime overall.

Procedural Justice

Procedural justice (PJ) is the notion that the way in which a dispute or legal case is handled is important in shaping a person's perception of how they were treated (Tyler & Lind, 2002). PJ focuses on perceptions of fairness and legitimacy. *Fairness* refers to the fair process of the law applied to those under its imposition, and *legitimacy* refers to the extent to which authority is ascribed to a decision-maker (e.g., judges or police) by those under the decision-maker's influence (e.g., citizens). Tyler (2003) describes PJ as the extent to which people accept and comply with laws because they believe that those who uphold the laws are effective at their job and do their job in a fair manner. Moreover, this fairness is based on trust (e.g., reliance and proven accountability) and legitimacy (e.g., acceptable values, ethics, and behaviors).

PJ involves several practical functions in daily life. It provides an understanding of how feedback plays a role in power dynamics between the authority and the governed. It also helps life to be more predictable and less uncertain, and it helps instill and uphold (or often reflect) a collective morality (Vermunt & Steensma, 2016). In essence, PJ involves both perceptions of fairness and legitimacy and includes the goals of increasing social cohesion, obedience of the law, and the well-being of the population.

Procedural fairness in the criminal justice system in general

As mentioned earlier in this chapter, the use of the adversarial process involves a goal of procedural fairness. Indeed, the adversarial system is considered the fairest system when compared to many other criminal justice and legal systems (Thibaut et al., 1974). This is likely due to the fair processes and procedures employed in the adversarial system, such as due process, the belief in the idea of one being innocent-until-proven-guilty, the right to criminal defense representation, etc.

PJ is often considered when people interact with the legal and criminal justice system. A primary focus in the PJ literature is police and the courts (Tyler, 2003). The police are an obvious target of fairness perceptions because they are probably the first point of contact with the legal and criminal justice system with any particular procedure associated with it (i.e., albeit the first interaction would be the awareness of the law or signs posted describing/explaining the law, but interactions with these require no procedure beyond sensational attention and cognitive awareness). The police enforce the law and implement the law at its initial stage, which is whether a law officer observed or had reason to believe that a person violated the law. In this instance, the person is either ticketed, arrested, or verbally warned regarding their violative behavior. When coming in contact with police, people might be faced, for the first time, with the question of whether or not they think the law is fair. It is quite possible that people are not confronted with the thought of whether or not a law is fair until they are faced with a conflict between what they want to do and what the law allows them to do. Nevertheless, their assessment of police fairness either coincides with fairness judgments of the law itself or operates independent of their judgments of the law. Thus, their perception of police fairness is some combination of the view of the police and the law.

Once the person is finished with law enforcement, contact with the legal system is initiated, typically through contact with the courts. This would include discussions with attorneys and meetings with judges. In both contact with law enforcement and contact with the courts, people tend to judge the fairness of how they were treated and processed. In the courts, people assess the fairness of the judge, the attorneys (e.g., settlements and plea deals), and the punishment (e.g., sentencing guidelines or judge's discretion). Again, people are likely judging, for the first time, the fairness of legal punishments at the same time they are judging the fairness of how the judge treats them. Procedural fairness involves the simultaneous judgment of the laws and statutes (and the processes set forth by them) and the actors involved in the processes (see Tyler, 1987).

Procedural fairness prioritizes process over outcome, often striking a balance between outcome importance and the risks and drawbacks of getting there (Solum, 2004; Tyler, 1987). Fairness might naturally be scrutinized more when the stakes are higher, such as with hefty damages or significant jail time. However, fairness is generally a societal good, consisting of judgments pertaining to the genuine pursuit of ethicality, morality, and honesty, and the avoidance of exploiting fairness for a purely manipulative societal or political tool (Tankebe, 2009; Tyler, 1987, 1988).

Procedural fairness in problem-solving courts

PSCs are ripe for PJ application (see DeMatteo et al., 2019). Specifically, providing participants with autonomy and opportunity to earn some level of reduced punitiveness increases perceptions of fairness. With PJ elements in PSCs, participants would likely become more compliant with the demands and requirements of the programs (Weiner et al., 2010). Such elements might include the judge giving the participant a voice during their meetings (Farole Jr., et al., 2005).

Procedural fairness is one of the hallmark features of MHCs, where much of the TJ work originated, and is often considered a guiding framework (Fisler, 2015; Perlin, 2018). These elements are also found in Israeli community courts (Gal & Dancig-Rosenberg, 2020). Although judges are often considered to be playing the primary role in fair procedures, attorneys are also capable of engaging in procedurally just processes that contribute to participants' perceptions of fairness in MHCs and community courts (Perlin, 2018; Calabrese, 2002). As a culmination of procedurally fair practices, whether from judges, attorneys, or court structure, participants in PSCs, particularly MHCs, tend to view the court fair and just, more so than traditional court (Ray & Dollar, 2014; Wales et al., 2010).

Evidence supports the effectiveness of implementing PJ elements in PSCs as well. Dollar et al. (2018) found judicial PJ was related to favorable court outcomes, specifically court completion. In addition, procedural fairness was related to higher reunification rates, quicker case closures, and increased participation in a family drug court (Fessinger et al., 2020). Thus, PJ seems to facilitate, or have the potential to facilitate, positive outcomes in PSCs.

PJ might not apply equally across all participant demographic groups. Rottman claims that the effect of PJ is robust across majority and minority groups, but Atkin-Plunk et al. (2019) suggest that perceptions of PJ are lower among Black PSC participants. These two claims are not necessarily in contrast; even though groups might differ in initial perceptions, the effect of PJ could still be the same. However, not much research has examined moderating effects of PJ on PSC participants' outcomes.

An additional concern in PJ is the identification of several aspects that might undermine the benefits of PJ and fairness. One is the extent to which the court operates with a more coercive and supervision focus, removing the voice of the participant and any feelings of autonomy, such as in prostitution courts (Kendis, 2019). Another aspect is the extent to which team members do not share the same views or goals of the court and instead align with a more anti-therapeutic orientation, undermining the cohesive PJ framework (Franke & Shdaimah, 2022). It appears that PJ must be adopted through the court structure and by the court team members to maximize its effect, and any defecting team members or practices could undermine its benefits.

Legitimacy in the criminal justice system in general

Perceived legitimacy is sometimes considered a component of PJ or a result of PJ. Often legitimacy results from PJ; specifically from fair and just processes that are considered effective (McIvor, 2009; Tyler & Jackson, 2013). Sometimes, legitimacy is related to other external factors. However, as with fairness, legitimacy is more closely aligned with perceptions of the processes courts or authorities use more so than the outcomes (Tyler & Sevier, 2013). Although this idea seems to imply that legitimacy is fully in the hands of the perceiver, it is probably more accurate to say that legitimacy is negotiated through interactions between the perceiver and the perceived (Bottoms & Tankebe, 2012). Nevertheless, the hope is that legitimacy leads to compliance or satisfaction with legal services and outcomes, given ethical considerations, and a meta-analysis supported this in that legitimacy beliefs were related to intentions to comply with the law (Walters & Bolger, 2019). However, perceptions of legitimacy can be eroded from the use of dehumanizing practices, such as videoconferencing in Australia (Rowden, 2018), targeting identity groups (Ford, 2012), and institutionalizing bias against Indigenous Peoples, like in Canada (EagleWoman, 2019).

Legitimacy often occurs at the interaction level, and individual interactions with authorities can produce perceptions of legitimacy of the broader authority body. Moreover, perceptions of the broader authority body can impact perceptions of individual interactions, such as with police interactions during traffic stops. For example, in corrections, an inmate's interaction (or family's interaction) with a correctional officer might carry some level of evaluative weight regarding legitimacy, but these perceptions are also likely shaped by perceptions of general legitimacy in the corrections system more broadly. Moreover, perceptions of legitimacy of one particular organization could impact adjacent organizations, showing a transference effect (e.g., Caldeira & Gibson, 1995; Wang et al., 2023). Thus, PSCs could obtain their legitimacy, at least in part, from the perceptions of the broader criminal justice system.

The extent to which authorities and the public share goals and values could facilitate perceptions of the authority's legitimacy (Grosfeld et al., 2022). However, when authorities are viewed as legitimate, as it has been established, they can gain a level of approval despite misalignment with public sentiment (Nunn, 2017). Thus, for example, when authorities go against the grain of society, the extent to which this is accepted depends on if that authority is viewed as legitimate or not. Legitimacy is not necessarily determined once and then remains solidified from that point on; it is shaped and reevaluated throughout repeated interactions. When there is an inflection point, or when a new or revised alternative is introduced, legitimacy perceptions are re-evaluated because what was used to initially evaluate legitimacy has changed (Rabinovich-Einy, 2015). PSCs were introduced as new alternatives to the traditional justice system, so they garnered a new evaluation of legitimacy, during which the policies, processes, and outcomes were assessed to make such judgments.

Legitimacy in problem-solving courts

Perceptions of PSCs' legitimacy are most likely a summation of legitimacy beliefs about the law, courts, juvenile justice system, judges, attorneys, and treatment (Klein, 2016). Because PSCs are judicially led, the legitimacy of the judges provides a significant impact on the court's legitimacy, which is evidenced by the influence of the judge in court satisfaction and the tendency for biases toward judges to impact perceptions of legitimacy (Audette & Weaver, 2015; Heck & Roussell, 2007; Kennedy, 2012). Also, in PSCs, more so than other courts and legal authorities, legitimacy is heavily influenced by outcomes (i.e., effectiveness; Casey, 2004). This reliance on effectiveness might be semantically obvious because the name "problem-solving court" creates an expectation of a solution so if there is no solution, then these are not legitimate programs as they violate the promise implied in their name.

Some PSCs gain legitimacy by the narrowed focus alone. For example, drug courts might be considered legitimate because of the specificity in their goals—to address drug abuse. VTCs gain legitimacy because they target a specific population with specific needs and stoke a sense of national responsibility and gratitude for those who risked their lives for the country (Baldwin & Brooke, 2019; Gallagher & Ashford, 2021; Kieckhaefer & Luna, 2020). In this way, the legitimacy lies in the intentions of the court, not only the processes or the outcomes, which appears to be unique to PSCs and potentially just VTCs.

Overall, perceived legitimacy of PSCs seems to be uniquely situated in an embedded view of legitimacy of the criminal justice system, intentions of the specific court, and perceptions of the legal professionals who make up the team. However, Dalke (2020) poses an interesting question when discussing community courts in a review of Zozula's (2019) text, *Courting the Community Court: Legitimacy and Punishment in a Community Court*, which is if these courts are considered legitimate, then why are they not gaining in popularity? Perhaps the influence of legitimacy on the longevity of PSCs is weak, if not complicated.

Restorative Justice

Restorative justice (RJ) is a collaborative approach to dealing with criminal offending whereby stakeholders in a particular criminal offense (e.g., offender, victim, and community) collectively discuss and make decisions about the present and future implications of the crime and outcome for the offender (Daly, 2017; Marshall, 1999). RJ is often considered more of an approach than a theory or specific process because it includes a number of diverse theories, processes, structures, and policies that adhere to a similar central theme of engaging in practices that restore the relationships and bonds between people and communities through moral socialization (Braithwaite, 1999; Johnstone & Van Ness, 2007). Some assumptions of RJ are that all parties involved know the process, understand the implications, and agree to participate (Cohen, 2016). Although there is no singular consensus definition, Chris Marshall provides a definition that is quite comprehensive and inclusive of the elements in most definitions:

> Restorative justice involves a voluntary, relational process whereby those with a personal stake in an offence or conflict or injustice come together, in a safe and respectful environment, with the help of skilled facilitators, to speak truthfully about what happened and its impact on their lives, to clarify accountability for the harms that have occurred and to resolve together how best to promote repair and bring about positive changes for all. (2020, pp. 103–104)

RJ can often extend beyond the criminal justice system into homes, schools, or local organizations, such as churches (Marshall, 2020). For example, RJ practices in schools are associated with a reduction in violent incidents, school suspensions, and absenteeism and tardiness (Fronius et al., 2016).

Restorative justice in the criminal justice system in general

RJ most likely gained popularity in the face of declining confidence in the traditional criminal justice system (Marshall, 2020). RJ was viewed as a new alternative, although many acknowledge its historical roots. While sometimes associated with the TJ movement, RJ involves using a more inclusive process of responsibility and accountability, which puts more of a focus on reparation and reintegration than punishment or rehabilitation (Gal, 2020; Marshall, 1999, 2020; Nolan, Jr., 2003). RJ emphasizes human dignity, reduces power inequality, and increases offender reintegration. Goals of RJ are to restore and satisfy victims, offenders, and communities, enhance freedom and justice, and reduce and deter crime (Braithwaite, 2002). RJ practices have been used internationally historically and might even reflect a more traditional form of justice systems observed in Indigenous societies around the world (Braithwaite, 1999; Lanterman, 2020). It has received global praise and has been used in a number of international settings, such as the courts, prisons, law enforcement, and schools (Van Ness, 2005). Some scholars even support RJ as an ideal, such that the criminal justice system *should* be providing the opportunity for victims and offenders to come together (e.g., Latimer et al., 2005). Much of this excitement stems from its success. According to a report in the United Kingdom, RJ practices were related to reductions in feelings of revenge among victims and recidivism among offenders.

Research indicates that participation in RJ practices can produce a range of positive outcomes for victims, including reduced emotional symptoms, reduced fear of future victimization, victim empowerment, restored autonomy and self-respect, and reduced posttraumatic stress (Angel et al., 2014; Miller, 2011; Sherman et al., 2015a; Sherman & Strang, 2007; Tamarit & Luque, 2016). The primary offender-related outcome of interest is recidivism reduction. Research has also indicated that participation in well-facilitated RJ can result in the reduced likelihood of recidivism (Hayes & Daly, 2003; Latimer et al., 2005; Maxwell & Morris, 2001; McGarrell, 2001; Nugent et al., 2001; Rodriguez, 2007; Sherman et al., 2000, 2015a, 2015b). In a recent meta-analysis of RJ programs, these programs seemed to slightly reduce recidivism for general crimes but not violent crimes (Fulham et al., 2023). Such successes have led to the implementation of RJ in a number of criminal justice settings, including PSCs.

Restorative justice in problem-solving courts

PSCs have often been linked to RJ, whether suggesting that PSCs are founded in RJ or whether PSCs use a RJ model (Berman & Feinblatt, 2001; Butts, 2001; Nolan Jr., 2003). Several of these courts might be particularly well-positioned to incorporate RJ approaches because of the way they are set up, such as the community courts and domestic violence courts. Some critics of the current drug court model emphasize a move toward a more RJ framework and programmatic structure than the current structure (O'Hear, 2009). While there is not much evidence of the effectiveness of specific RJ PSC programs compared to non-restorative programs, PSCs seem to be a worthy avenue for implementing conferences between victims and offenders under formal facilitation to improve the outcomes for the offender and the community (a shared goal of both PSCs and RJ; Menkel-Meadow, 2007).

RJ does have some limitations (Daly, 2007). RJ does not have a universally agreed upon definition, and it is often described and defined differently in the literature. It also has a heavy emphasis and focus on the punishment side of a case rather than the investigation side. Moreover, RJ might enhance attitudes of fairness but find it difficult to achieve restorative change and secure genuine and sincere apologies from offenders. Some offenses might be too harmful and cause too much suffering for RJ to even be an option. Finally, the popularity of RJ might significantly outperform the effects of it. While effective, RJ might have only moderate influence over outcomes for victims and offenders (Daly, 2007). Moreover, RJ approaches used in PSCs might solve problems unrelated to the criminogenic needs of the offender, which might prevent a meaningful effect on recidivism (Schaefer & Beriman, 2019). Nevertheless, research related to RJ effectiveness in PSCs is severely lacking and would benefit from empirical attention.

Community Sentiment

Social scientists from many backgrounds have noted the importance of gaining community support for legal (and non-legal) endeavors. Some PSCs were formed specifically to address community sentiment, but all programs should pay close attention to sentiment. The sentiment of various communities (e.g., the general population, judges, lawmakers) is important because it affects perceived legitimacy of the legal system (Miller et al., 2015). Additionally, PSCs are often integrated into communities, and so their initial success is dependent upon community support. Many courts are short-lived because community sentiment or resources are low.

The success of courts likely reflects the public support for courts and the buy-in from stakeholders (e.g., businesses, treatment centers, shelters, schools, and food services). This public sentiment might be considered under the idea of PJ or legal authority. However, what seems to be clear is that the public holds influential attitudes about the legal and criminal justice system and how they operate. The public's ideas about the effectiveness of criminal justice will likely shape their support for alternative programs. Moreover, the community holds a direct stake in these programs, which is community safety and the dangers posed by the participants in these programs.

To exemplify community sentiment that might be detrimental to programs like PSCs, this is a resident's comment regarding a hypothetical prisoner reentry program:

> How much more of our resources are going to be used to help people with issues that did not come from our county. Yes, we ARE our Brothers Keepers, but we have people right here . . . commiting crimes and going to prison who will be right back here, why aren't our resources being devoted to their re entry into society . . . this is too much . . . one thing after another, the sex trafficking victims facility that saw a disturbance from their in the first weeks it was opened, the state school which our school district already helps, and now this . . . and these are the ones that I can think of from memory . . . I say enough is enough. . . . but no one wants to put a stop to MORE criminal activity possible for the citizens . . . we are going to end up being a blight to our surrounding neighbors because of the facilities and helping that is going on here. To say nothing of our property values going down.

Community sentiment in the criminal justice system in general

Between the 1960s and 1980s, the public supported a harsher and more punitive court system and general punitive attitudes were related to greater support for the courts (Flanagan et al., 1985). Although support for harsher courts might have declined in the subsequent decades, those who support state or local courts tend to be more educated, from lower crime areas, and have a good working knowledge and understanding of the court system (Benesh, 2006). In an Australian study, the public thought the courts were too lenient in their sentencing, but they also supported alternatives to traditional sentencing, which suggests that the desire for harsher sentences and the support for alternatives can co-occur (Mackenzie et al., 2012). Perhaps, this is because the public wants harsher sentences for violent and sex offenders, but they want alternatives for low-level offenders. PSCs provide avenues for lower-level offenders and some violent offenders (i.e., domestic violence courts).

Community sentiment in problem-solving courts

The public generally supports PSCs (Casey & Rottman, 2005). Moreover, there is little to no variation in these views from country to country (Murphy et al., 2024). Support for PSCs is linked to support for rehabilitation, TJ, and explanations of crime that lend themselves to treatment, proactive policies, and responses to crime, such as those considered procedurally just (Miller, 2020; Murphy et al., 2024; Schaefer & Beriman, 2019). For example, MHCs are often supported because crime is viewed as a symptom of mental illness and because treating mental illness and reducing the revolving door of the criminal justice system for offenders with mental illness is a common goal of judges, researchers, and the public (e.g., Goodale et al., 2013; Simonsson et al., 2020). Moreover, community courts in Canada are often supported to the extent to which they contribute to overall national public health goals (Garcia et al., 2019). This is probably the best summary of how and why the public would support PSCs, which is because they are solving problems that promote societal health. Drug courts help promote physical health. Domestic violence courts improve family and relational health. MHCs promote mental health. Community courts promote local and community well-being. Prostitution courts promote community well-being, sexual health, and physical health. VTCs promote physical and mental health. PSCs, in general, promote societal values placed on the health and well-being of the people in that society, and as long as the courts are viewed as working toward those goals and those goals remain valuable to society, public support for PSCs should remain strong. Although the courts' effectiveness might impact overall support to some degree, their support is likely driven by virtue of their purpose.

Conclusion

PSCs provide an important junction at which ideal justice principles meet criminal justice systems. The most widely used justice principles in PSCs are TJ and PJ, and the least used was community sentiment (Miller et al., 2020). Although all PSCs incorporate some elements of TJ, PJ, or RJ, it is still unclear as to how this affects overall societal level crime rates. However, initial analysis indicates that the adversarial process and community sentiment have strong impacts on outcomes whereas social support has the weakest impact (Miller et al., 2020). Nevertheless, these principles are guiding frameworks for PSCs. RJ seems to be particularly strong in Australia through restorative conferences. PJ is important in countries with high crime rates and heavy policing, such as the United States. Moreover, the use of PSCs to correct for unjust treatment of Indigenous populations through the implementation of policies that align with the justice principles discussed in this chapter are critical to building communities in countries like Canada and Australia. Some places, such as China, might benefit from applying some of these justice principles, like RJ, but find it difficult to apply others, like TJ, due to the political and structural dynamics of the country. However, it is clear that advocates for PSCs view them as the frontier for enacting more just treatment of offenders and restoring communities.

4
The Psychology of Problem-Solving Courts

Psychological Foundations in Problem-Solving Courts

The law can be a driving force for a person's behavior (Miller et al., 2020; Wexler, 2000). Laws have historically led to positive societal trends, and some have led to negative societal trends, resulting in abolition or reversals from the highest courts. A seemingly perpetual question is how the law should be applied to motivate positive and constructive civil behavior. Problem-solving Courts (PSCs) attempt to address this inquiry.

Offenders who enter into programs in PSCs are typically identified by crimes associated with quality of life, status, person/society relationships, or mental health. For example, prostitution courts and substance use courts (e.g., drug courts and DWI/DUI courts) address quality of life. Veterans' treatment courts (VTCs) address special at-risk statuses, and community courts address issues of person/society relationships (although they admittedly also include quality of life issues). Mental health courts (MHCs) address mental health issues. Inherent in any PSC is the application of numerous psychological principles. While this could be said of all courts, PSCs extend their reach and specifically categorize court types by offender/offense types, highlighting the unique underlying psychological implications. The goal of PSCs is to provide a unique court structure and processes that will help address these specific societal problems.

Built into the name PSCs, these courts are created to solve social issues rather than rely on traditional forms of punishment. If PSCs aim to address societal problems, then it is a logical assumption to suggest that the courts would vary across societies, which inevitably would vary in social problems. However, there are core underlying psychological processes that might explain the successes and potential failures of PSCs and how and why they work. These also might provide insight into why they were established and

Society, Science, and Problem-Solving Courts. Monica K. Miller, Mia A. Holbrook, Logan A. Yelderman, and Kylie Kulak, Oxford University Press. © Oxford University Press 2025. DOI: 10.1093/oso/9780190059804.003.0004

how their current structure evolved. This chapter will discuss the psychological concepts associated with PSCs; specifically, the rational actor model (RAM), the psychological legal decision-making model, anticipated emotion, operant conditioning, social support, social norms, authority, and the moralizing nature of the courts. Most courts do not explicitly rely on psychological theories, but these are built-in and provide a workable framework to better comprehend the processes and outcomes of PSCs. The application of psychological principles and theories could provide insights into offender behavior, along with court success, which is the focus of this chapter.

Rational Actor Model of Legal Decision-Making

The RAM is based on rational choice theory and expected utility theory. According to the RAM, participants in any given situation are provided options from which to make a decision. This decision is made by considering the costs and benefits, or risks and rewards, associated with pursuing one option and leaving the other option(s) behind and by comparing these outcomes to the decisional goals. Both preference and probability of outcome success factor into the objective and subjective assessments of risk and reward (Friedman & Savage, 1948; Goldthorpe, 1998; Kahneman & Tversky, 1979; Monroe &Maher, 1995; Scott, 2000). In general, people tend to pursue and maximize rewards and benefits and minimize risks and costs; however, the valuation of what is rewarding and what is costly is a subjective judgment that is specific to each person and situation. Purely logical and objective assessments of costs and benefits related to the outcome alone are insufficient to explain human behavior, which is why other models of human behavior, such as the cognitivist model (Boudon, 1996) and RAM, better describe decision-making.

In the legal system, RAM proposes that people make decisions within the legal or criminal justice system based on a cost–benefit analysis (Korobkin & Ulen, 2000; Wiener et al., 2010). In PSCs, participants weigh the costs and benefits of participating in the program versus their punishment if they do not to participate in the program (e.g., detention, supervision requirements, or fines). According to RAM, judges can encourage particular participant behaviors by identifying costs and benefits and by describing them in such a way that the rational, or logical, decision would be to participate in a PSC program. PSCs (which ideally have minimal costs with potentially significant benefits) would position the participant to reap the benefits and avoid the costs of punishment or negative behavioral consequences (Wiener et al., 2010).

One notable limitation to this approach is that PSCs often punish offenders who engage in program violations with a very costly punishment that the participants rationally choose the program to avoid. In some cases, the program might be more restrictive than the original punishment would have been if the PSC requires more time and effort than traditional probation (see also Chapter 11). It is possible that the costs and benefits are both immediate and long-term and that the rational analysis of costs made at the beginning of the program to avoid the impending jail time or detention is not as great as the long-term costs associated with committing to a lengthy program with a high degree of supervision. Once participants are in the program, each decision comes with a new set of costs and benefits, so rational choice becomes a frequent basis for engaging in various behaviors. If participants truly made rational choices, then the program staff would need to discern their subjective preferences and develop a plan that includes the appropriate rational calculus for each participant. Ideally, this would lead to an extremely high graduation and completion rate and lower recidivism. However, this is not the case across all PSCs (Berman & Feinblatt, 2001; Kaiser & Rhodes, 2019; Weiner et al., 2010).

In addition to evolving cost–benefit analyses throughout the program, another limitation of the RAM is that not all criminals weigh costs and benefits in the same way. Perhaps, some participants believe that the cost of a short prison sentence is less than the cost of giving up their livelihood (selling drugs) or way of life (using drugs). People do not always make rational choices and can sometimes act against their best interests. Thus, the application of this theory, while well-intentioned, is not a perfect predictor of court participation or program completion. Judges, attorneys, and program staff should discuss the costs and benefits of participating in the court with the offenders to get an idea of how they view the different outcomes rather than assuming that the offenders have thought through all possible benefits and costs. Also, there are many barriers to logic-based rationality, such as neurological damage, emotional instability, or impulsivity associated with prolonged drug use or trauma and compromised self-control.

One final point to make on the RAM is the way in which sequential rational decisions are treated within PSCs. For example, in many PSCs, if several rational choices are made (e.g., curfew compliance, negative drug screens, or timeliness for court appointments), then participants might be given verbal praise, a curfew extension, or a prize of some sort. However, if a single violation occurs, presumably from a non-rational choice, then punishments (e.g., detention, program expulsion, or fines worth much more than program prizes) might be incurred. This suggests a strong negative response to a single non-rational choice and a weak or non-existent response to a series of rational choices. Strong negative responses, in contrast with weak positive responses, could skew and reshape how participants view costs and benefits without the court judge and staff's awareness, leading to misjudgments of behavioral expectations by the program and court teams. To better understand the possible rational choices for each person, there must be levels of social, economic, and cultural considerations in determining how costs and benefits apply to participants. Assuming that "all people would rationally make this specific choice" neglects the subjective nature of cost–benefit analyses at the individual level and could cause PSC programs to fail.

The takeaway from the RAM is not that it never applies but rather that it might be limited in its ability to explain and predict PSCs participants' behaviors. Other theories might better explain participant behavior, replacing the RAM. It is also possible that the RAM can be integrated with another model to more comprehensively address participant decision-making.

The Psychological Model of Legal Decision-Making

Because of some of the limitations of the RAM, some researchers have proposed a different, more social-psychological model to explain why offenders behave in certain ways (Wiener et al., 2010; also see Wiener & Georges, 2013). This model, described as the psychological model of legal decision-making, incorporates justice principles (e.g., therapeutic jurisprudence [TJ] and procedural justice [PJ]; see Chapter 3) while also acknowledging the psychological factors that might influence offender behavior. This model also was developed primarily for the legal context. More specifically, the model references motivational and emotional states as potentially driving forces behind offender behavior, which can be interpreted through PSC contexts.

Motivational approaches using the psychological model of legal decision-making

Underlying many of the PSCs lies motivational features: achieving sobriety, avoiding jail, leaving prostitution, rehabilitating mental illness, reestablishing community relationships, etc. The courts' understanding of these motivations can help structure programs and situate offenders to align motivations with programmatic progress. Two motivational theories that apply to PSCs are the theory of reasoned action and the theory of planned behavior. Both theories describe the extent to which a person aspires to a particular behavior, and the enactment of that behavior is dependent upon their attitudes toward the behavior, subjective norms associated with the behavior, and steps outlined to achieve the behavior (Sheeran & Orbell, 1999). In this case, offenders would be most successful when they view their current behaviors negatively and their new behavior positively. Success is most likely to occur when they believe the new behavior is good and socially acceptable, and there are concrete steps outlined to help adopt the new behavior.

One direct application of the theory of planned behavior and the theory of reasoned action is the use of behavioral contracts. Behavioral contracts provide students with target behaviors and associated behaviors with positive outcomes, and provide clear consequences for lack of behavior engagement (see Bowman-Perrott et al., 2015; Downing, 2002; Edgemon et al., 2021). The use of a prevention motivational state (i.e., the desire to seek safety and security by avoiding an undesirable end state, such as prison) is likely to lead to increased success in PSCs (Wiener et al., 2010; Wiener & Georges, 2013). This is primarily because the offender is motivated to behave in a way to avoid jail. Here, jail or detention acts as the primary agent of deterrence.

Based on regulatory focus theory, people might adopt a prevention motivation, a motivation to avoid failures or unsuccessful actions, when protecting the integrity of their duties, responsibilities, and obligations (Crowe & Higgins, 1997; Higgins, 1998). The prevention aspect, here, is the desire to avoid making a mistake and violating one's role. In a PSC, a person adopts the role of a court participant by agreeing to sidestep detention or other punitive alternatives and instead adopt the responsibilities associated with the PSC. Therefore, to succeed in the court, a person would likely take a prevention-focused approach and avoid failure in every context (Wiener et al., 2010; Wiener & Georges, 2013). Yet, as Higgins (1998) points out, understanding motivation from a promotion and prevention focus moves beyond the hedonic principle. These motivations to achieve aspiration or prevent failures undoubtedly come with an expected emotional experience to occur, given one of the two outcomes. Literature on anticipated emotions sheds light on how future emotions might influence behaviors.

Anticipated emotion in the psychological model of legal decision-making

The model also involves emotion, particularly anticipated emotion, in determining offender behavior (Wiener et al., 2010; Wiener & Georges, 2013). Anticipated emotions are those that people think will occur, given their behavior and the expected outcome. Negative anticipated emotions typically discourage behavior, and positive anticipated emotions typically encourage behavior (Kotabe et al., 2019). Anticipated emotion is premised on accurate outcome expectations, the influence of prior emotions, and a general avoidance of negative emotions (Ellsworth & Scherer, 2003). Additionally, people tend to engage in positive behaviors if they expect positive consequences (Richard et al., 1996). For example, if an offender has a negative experience in a drug court and subsequently feels anger, frustration, or annoyance, they are likely to anticipate feeling this way in future proceedings and avoid the behavior that produced the feeling (e.g., dropping out of the drug court or not engaging in services). If, however, the offender has a positive experience in a drug court, and subsequently feels a sense of achievement, relief, or satisfaction, they are likely to anticipate feeling this way in future proceedings. Anticipated emotions motivate behavior by giving people a basis for how they would feel if found in a similar situation again (Baumeister et al., 2007; Wiener et al., 2010).

Setting goals is an important component of PSCs, and achieving goals can induce happiness and a sense of accomplishment (Higgins et al., 1997), which would increase the likelihood of future behavioral engagement because it produced a positive emotion. By anticipating these positive emotions, offenders might behave in ways that encourage them to go to future court hearings (e.g., continuing in the court and using services) and could potentially increase the chance of successful completion and less recidivism.

Essentially, the psychological model of legal decision-making is a countermodel to the RAM—it does not assume that people behave in rational ways, but instead assumes that certain personal and social psychological factors can influence behavior (Wiener et al., 2010; see also Wiener & Georges, 2013). Understanding the use of motivation and emotion can help PSCs become more effective. By encouraging participants to have prevention motivation strategies and by making sure that participants have experiences that are as positive as possible, judges can help shape future behavior so that participants are likely to succeed in PSCs.

Motivation and emotion in the legal system

Motivation and emotion theories can be applied to the legal system, and many clear examples exist. For instance, if an offender experiences negative emotion while in court, they might anticipate the same negative emotion in future court hearings (see Wiener et al., 2010). This would then directly impact the offender's mindset when in court, such as fearing the court. However, too much emphasis on past experiences might suggest a deterministic view, neglecting the possibility of other intervening or affective events.

Focalism is a term used to describe how people tend to focus too much on a particular aspect of an event when making related judgments, such as using past events to define future events while discounting other events (Wilson et al., 2000). Similar to anticipated emotion, offenders could overestimate negative or positive emotion by not considering other aspects in their lives that are happening at the same time (Wilson et al., 2000). This could be new employment, negative drug screens, positive relationships, or birthdays.

To prevent being outcome-focused, it is also critical to examine offenders' experiences and perceptions of the process that leads to those outcomes. The process might drive affective reactions to criminal justice experiences. For example, it is important for a defendant to feel that their voice and perspective are heard when stating their case (McIvor, 2009). Moreover, when there is mutual respect and the offender develops a positive relationship with the court officials, progress made by the offender might be more sustainable (McIvor, 2009). Offenders' perceptions of fairness can increase positive emotional experiences and can also lead to increased compliance and perceptions of legitimacy (Tyler, 2004, 2006; see also Chapter 3 of this text). Therefore, positive perceptions of the process and positive emotions have a reciprocal relationship, which are facilitated by police, courts, and program staff, and can lead to positive outcomes.

Anticipated emotion in problem-solving courts

PSC judges and staff are tasked with cultivating environments that support, motivate, and encourage offenders' participation to achieve positive changes and outcomes for the offender (Weiner et al., 2010). In addition, judges are able to use or encourage various techniques, such as motivational interviewing and active listening, to elicit mutual respect among people in the courtroom (Elek, 2019). This is accomplished by fostering a system that seems legitimate and fair to the offender, which should translate to positive emotions (Wiener et al., 2010). Moreover, judges and court staff should be able to read and anticipate participants' emotions, assisting in the court's ability to tailor hearings or programs to elicit positive outcomes conducive to offender improvement and productivity (Elek, 2019). However, this might be difficult because offenders have difficulty anticipating their own emotions given court hearings and program outcomes (Gilbert & Wilson, 2000). Although emotional support is important (Miller & Johnson, 2009), not all cultures embrace free and open discussion of outcomes, emotions, or feelings (Nolan, 2009), which might prevent judges and court staff from identifying and predicting offenders' emotional responses. Nevertheless, anticipated emotions for oneself and others can play an important role in developing and implementing programs in PSCs.

Operant Conditioning

Similar to parents who implement rules and schedules to train and discipline children, courts create programs, schedules, and rules for participants. However, instead of promoting general positive behaviors, these training schedules target very specific behaviors. Many services involve holistic approaches, but the programs associated with PSCs are pre-determined and defined by the behaviors that the courts set out to remedy. This type of programming is based on operant conditioning principles in which behavior is shaped through rewards and punishments.

According to operant conditioning, behavior is likely to be repeated if followed by a reward, and stopped if followed by punishment (Bozza, 2011; Miller et al., 2020). For example, people might buy more scratch-off lottery tickets if they win, repeating a rewarded behavior. Also, people might drive slower if they have received a ticket before, hoping to avoid the punishment of another ticket. Thus, rewards and punishments could be used to manipulate or regulate behavior (Bozza, 2007). Regular application of operant conditioning principles can lead to habits or long-term behavioral trends, using consequences to control the course of desired behaviors (Staddon & Cerutti, 2003). However, to be the most effective in eliciting behaviors, rewards and punishments must be enacted within a reasonable timeframe so the target behavior and reward or punishment are associated (Staddon & Cerutti, 2003). In a social setting, rewards and punishments lay the groundwork for establishing group norms (Burgess & Akers, 1966).

Operant conditioning in the legal system

Operant conditioning in the legal system most notably takes the form of sanctions and punishments for breaking the law. This includes tickets, fines, arrests, imprisonment, or supervision. In some cases, the legal system includes rewards, such as the opportunity to take defensive driving to remove a ticket if a person has not received traffic violations in the recent past or early prison release (parole) for good behavior. Crimes outline behaviors that will be punished. People then weigh the benefits against the punishment. If the punishment is worse, the behavior is less likely. This idea underlies both the assumption of rational thinking and the goal of deterrence (Jervis, 1989). However, if the reward is greater or if the behavior is more strongly reinforced then it is likely to be repeated (e.g., Burgess & Akers, 1966). Reinforcements can come from the behavior's immediate tangible rewards or peers' reinforcement (Lanza-Kaduce et al., 1984; Triplett & Payne, 2004). If the behavior is not motivated by reinforcement, then the punishment might be ineffective (e.g., Bouhours & Daly, 2007).

The extent to which people obey laws also depends on the legitimacy they attribute to the law and those enforcing the law and the likelihood of getting caught (Tyler, 2006). For example, people might obey traffic laws to the extent they think they might get caught and the extent they consider traffic laws to be important and police officers to fairly and justly apply traffic laws.

Operant conditioning in problem-solving courts

The ultimate goal for PSCs is to modify behavior to reduce the likelihood of recidivism. A way PSCs use operant conditioning is by providing incentives and sanctions to reinforce or diminish certain behaviors (Miller et al., 2020). Enforcing positive reinforcement is the most productive way to alter behavior (Choi, 2012; Marlowe & Kirby, 1999). This is especially important in family drug courts in which successful participants earn sobriety and are able to reunify with their families, but unsuccessful participants do not get these rewards and might experience family separation, re-arrests, and imprisonment (Choi, 2012). In juvenile drug treatment courts, the use of strengths-based incentives can be critical to motivating youth and potentially enhancing youth outcomes (Schiller et al., 2019).

Some issues can arise when using operant conditioning in PSCs. Timing is important when reinforcing or diminishing a behavior. The time interval between the behavior and the incentive or sanction should be short to allow the person to associate it with their behavior (Miller et al., 2020). Sanctions should also be consistent between people who express the same negative behaviors and also ensure that sanctions are swift and firm (Miller et al., 2020). These principles are often used in drug courts (Bullard & Thrasher, 2016).

Variation in the use of operant conditioning

The United States has a punitive criminal justice system with harsh punishments for breaking the laws (Tyler, 2006). These strong sanctions are used to encourage compliance with the law. However, excessive punitiveness and the overreliance on punishment might undermine perceptions of legitimacy regarding the laws and law enforcement. As a result, there are efforts to move away from punitiveness and toward a more rehabilitative approach through TJ (Tyler, 2006; see Chapter 3 for more on these justice principles). In this framework, which would align more with rewards-based incentives, the courts would provide a rehabilitative role in offenders' lives rather than a strict punitive role. Although other countries might have less punitive criminal justice systems, American citizens might not necessarily hold more punitive attitudes at the individual level (Kugler et al., 2013). PSCs might be part of the response to less punitive means to deal with crime in the United States and across the globe.

Social Norms

The next psychology theory discussed in this chapter is that of social norms, a concept that works hand-in-hand with operant conditioning. Social norms are the "rules" of society, set forth by behavioral expectations implied by group behaviors and internalized by people (Schultz & Tabanico, 2009). For instance, in one society it is counter-normative to pick your nose in public. There are sanctions if you violate norms (e.g., people will make fun of you, tell you that you are gross, or not hang around you). On the other hand, there are rewards for following the norms of the community. For instance, in communities that value athletic success, a star athlete will be featured in the newspaper and might receive awards and scholarships. People generally obey the norms of their social groups to avoid punishment and receive acceptance or rewards.

According to the focus theory of normative conduct, there are two types of norms, which are descriptive norms and injunctive norms (Cialdini et al., 1990; Cialdini et al., 1991). Descriptive norms provide information as to how a person should expect to behave in a situation. This is an information-based understanding of what to do and when. Injunctive norms are norms established by observing behaviors and noting which are rewarded and which are punished or processing information about behaviors that have been rewarded or punished. These norms operate on an operant conditioning foundation. Descriptive norms provide information about what *is* done, and injunctive norms provide information about what *should* be done (see Schultz & Tabanico, 2009). However, normative behavior does not often require much repetition because one great reward or severe punishment could start or stop a behavior after only occurring once.

Norms are typically learned through socialization (Bicchieri et al., 2018), and socialization occurs throughout one's lifespan. Although each setting has its own norms, there are general norms held by society that people are taught as they grow up. These norms are internalized and manifest in motivations, attitudes, and behavioral habits. The assumption is that normative attitudes provide a behavioral prescription, and the goal is to elicit conformity. Normative attitudes enable translatability across contexts; however, it is unclear how and when normative attitudes directly relate to normative behaviors (Bicchieri & Funcke, 2018; Bicchieri & McNally, 2018). It is possible that normative attitudes and behaviors in some situations might not align. This might be best characterized by the saying, "do as I say, not as I do."

Even though norms are primarily used to communicate which behaviors are unacceptable, they can provide foundations for behavioral guidelines within social networks that are reinforced quickly, often from trusted sources, and with little consequence or cost (Bicchieri & Funcke, 2018; Bicchieri & McNally, 2018; Schultz & Tabanico, 2009). Norms can be enshrined as law to capture people's consensus as to which behaviors should be regulated with legal punishment (e.g., Wingrove et al., 2011). However, norms require societal organization or consensus for both development (unless developed by few and enforced upon many) and maintenance (otherwise, rebellion or apathy might settle in; Rose & Clear, 1998). Additionally, laws require enforcement. Symbolic laws that aim to establish a norm but remove the threat of punishment might cease to exist after a period of time without any consequences for violations. Norms are patterns of behaviors within a society upheld by attitudes that value those behaviors. These require some cohesiveness in society and often the endorsement by the majority. When norms are formalized into laws, they require legal enforcement and legal punishment.

Social norms in the legal system

Norms establish a foundation for which behaviors should be rewarded and which should be punished. This includes rewards, such as military medals of valor and bravery, and punishments, such as execution. The application of social norms extends to nearly every area of human life, in criminal and civil courts, and in private and public behavior. Social norms and laws have an intimate relationship. On the one hand, social norms can be formalized into law. For example, as marijuana use became more prevalent and its negative perception declined, states across the United States began adopting laws legalizing marijuana consumption and possession. On the other hand, laws can establish norms and impact social perception (Salazar et al., 2003). For example, smoking in the United States declined dramatically after the passing of the Federal Cigarette Labeling and Advertising Act of 1965 and the Public Health Cigarette Smoking Act of 1969, which required a health warning label on cigarette packages, regulations on cigarette advertising, and regular updated health information reports about the dangers of cigarettes

(Center for Disease Control [CDC], 2021). Laws can mold and shape societal behavior, creating a structure of approved actions and interactions, and the effectiveness of these laws and social structures to control behavior depends on the geographic and demographic characteristics of the region in which they are applied (Funk, 2005; see also Schultz & Tabanico, 2009).

The relationship between laws and norms can be reciprocal (see Chapter 7). For example, the social norms of women's liberation and changing family dynamics likely led to the passing of no-fault divorce laws in many states across the United States in the 1960s. Shortly after these laws were passed, divorce rates rose expeditiously, which likely strengthened the growing downward trend of negative public perceptions surrounding divorce. This is quite implicative of the dynamics shared between socially negotiated behavior and the development and enforcement of law and punishment. However, one critical understanding of laws and norms is that they are based on the premise that people can learn and correct behavior as a result of potential or actualized punishment and consequences (Burgess & Akers, 1966). For example, if a person sees a neighborhood watch sign, then the only way that norms and laws could work is if that sign elicits a thought or feeling that the person has an increased chance of being punished or losing social relationships if caught committing a crime (see Schultz & Tabanico, 2009).

Laws and norms can work in tandem. The laws, or formalized norms, establish a legal punishment, but the informal norms establish a social punishment. For example, committing a crime incurs a punishment. That punishment often includes a status, such as a sex offender or convicted felon. These statuses then impact life opportunities, such as employment or relationships. The reason that criminal statuses impact life opportunities is because of established norms that sexually victimizing others is bad and breaking the law is bad. This perceived "badness" then manifests in interactions with others, such as neighbors, employers, and family members, through fear, avoidance, or confrontation (see Wenzel, 2004). As a result, the offender might experience negative emotions. This is, in fact, how norms work. Norms, when violated, result in consequences and internalized guilt and shame (Funk, 2005; Weibull & Villa, 2005). Importantly, these negative emotions are purposefully elicited to motivate better behavior more consistent with the laws and norms and reparative behavior to re-establish relationships and social standing (Rodriguez, 2007). This is precisely why norms rely on learning and why the impact of norms relies on the application of consequences. Without consequences or with insufficient consequences, social norms can begin to weaken or change, and criminal and deviant behavior might rise and spread throughout the population, potentially establishing a new norm of misconduct (Weibull & Villa, 2005).

Social norms in problem-solving courts

PSCs still use punishment to correct behavior, whether it is the revocation of privileges or expulsion from the program. However, PSCs also operate to change the norms surrounding the offender's behaviors and how they view interactions with others. In the restorative justice (RJ) framework, offenders work through a series of processes, such as negotiations, mediations, or reparations to repair and re-establish relationships or connections with the victims or the community (Rodriguez, 2007; Zehr, 1995). This promotes norms of responsibility, accountability, forgiveness, and repentance. Through the process of RJ, communities can reiterate their norms to the offender and hold the offender accountable while also allowing the offender time to develop and internalize those local norms (Rodriguez, 2007). Through RJ practices, communities can have agency in the rehabilitation and restoration of the offender, which emphasizes the importance of community membership and reifies the community norms (King, 2008).

Social norms apply to PSC offenders in several ways. Offenders might associate with groups that value crime. Thus, the goal is to change the perceptions of the norms. The judge is tasked with communicating that broader society does not value law-breaking by rewarding law abiding behavior and punishing law-breaking behavior. RJ provides an avenue by which judges and courts can accomplish this (see Chapter 3).

In family courts, programs help families define and reinstitute family roles and the norms surrounding those roles. In community courts, the offender's role in the community is redefined, and the norms of the community are clarified and imposed upon the offender. In drug courts, abstinence norms are introduced to replace norms of drug use. In MHCs, mental health is destigmatized. In each of these courts, norms are reshaped, and through this, the offender's behavior is expected to change; at least, that is the goal.

Countries might vary in the specific norms they set, but social norms are used in most places. For example, the United States and the United Kingdom both enforce the social norm of less drug use in drug courts, but the United

States focuses more on abstinence and the United Kingdom focuses more on reduction (Nolan, 2009). Additionally, the Liverpool Community Court uses RJ practices to help reinforce social norms (Nolan, 2009). There are a variety of ways that PSCs rely on the power of social norms. By doing so, they encourage compliance with judicial orders and society's norms more generally. As this section noted, the role of society and social connections is essential.

Social Support

When trying to change behavior or when people go through loss, they often look for help from others. The help, or aid, from others, is called social support, and it can come from family, friends, and strangers in the community (Cullen, 1994). Social support is typically broken down into emotional support, instrumental support, informational support, and appraisal support (Heaney & Israel, 2008; House, 1981). Emotional support is affectional support communicating love, care, and compassion for the person in need. Instrumental support is the direct help by the provision of finances, services, or other tangible resources. Informational support is the provision of information or the transfer of knowledge that is directly applicable in helping a person find a resolution to a problem. For example, this might be providing someone with the phone number of someone who can help or talking someone through the steps of how to do something. Appraisal support is typically words and behaviors that help reaffirm a person, reiterate their value and worth, and enhance their self-concept (Colvin et al., 2002; House, 1981).

Social support is related to healthier self-esteem, better overall well-being, less depression, less stress, less alcohol use, better coping, lower mortality and morbidity risk, and better community-level problem-solving (Cobb, 1976; Colvin et al., 2002; Heaney & Israel, 2008; House et al., 1988; Miller et al., 2020). Familial social support can reduce distress and problematic behavior and can be aided by policies that increase a family's ability to provide support (Colvin et al., 2002). In some cases, people might need help building social support networks. Institutions and organizations can provide support structures through mentoring programs, therapeutic or support groups, and programs that facilitate or provide institutionally derived support (Heaney & Israel, 2008). However, if the support provided by these institutions and organizations is inconsistent and fickle, then this can undermine the benefits of social support and potentially have negative effects (e.g., Colvin et al., 2002).

Social support in the legal system

Social support is integrated in the legal system in many different ways. In some cases, it is used as a rehabilitative mechanism; in other cases, it is used as a crime prevention mechanism (Colvin et al., 2002; Cullen, 1994). Strong family support can be a buffer against juvenile delinquency (Loeber & Stouthamer-Loeber, 1986), and several justice-related programs offer mentoring. Moreover, social support can assist crime victims as well (Mitchell & Hodson, 1986; Yap & Devilly, 2004). The effectiveness of social support programs is an ongoing investigation, and a reasonable conclusion is that any program's effectiveness will depend on the context and fidelity to the program. However, the goal of social support programs is admirable in its intention and attractiveness (Cullen et al., 1999).

Social support can be tied to perverse incentives, and the people providing it might have nefarious motivations. This creates a problem of illegitimate social support, which can contribute to the development of poor behavioral habits and criminal motivations (Colvin et al., 2002; Hagan & McCarthy, 1997). In these instances, what might appear to be beneficial social support at first, ends up being an avenue back into (or further into) a criminal lifestyle.

Although it seems clear that social support might help offenders who have already been convicted, incarceration and various other punishments sever ties with family, friends, religious institutions, and employment (Cochran, 2014; Miller et al., 2020). Thus, the source of social support is the very thing the offender loses. This creates isolation from potential aid. Such social support mechanisms are not replaced or reproduced within jails and prisons, and the potential for illegitimate social support increases significantly in these situations (see Cullen, 1994).

Offenders who are able to maintain social support connections fare better than those who are unable to maintain such connections (Cochran, 2014; Miller et al., 2020). Understanding the importance of social support in reducing the likelihood for an offender to recidivate, many PSCs have integrated services that allow offenders to keep close ties with their family and their community (e.g., family engagement services; Henggeler et al., 2012; Miller et al., 2020).

Social support in problem-solving courts

PSCs have flexibility in how they deliver services. This positions PSCs to offer various social support services and potentially integrate social support programs into the PSC. Among juvenile offenders, social support programs (e.g., family intervention programs) can improve family dynamics and reduce recidivism (Darnell & Schuler, 2015). Juvenile drug courts often implement mentoring programs, and courts find that these can have a meaningful impact, but several barriers exist, which can prevent program fidelity or mentorship accessibility (Yelderman, 2017).

In community courts, part of the rehabilitation process is strengthening the offender's ties with the community and between the community and law enforcement (Gal & Dancig- Rosenburg, 2017). This creates a mutual social support system and an integrated network of people and entities that provide resources to and for each other. Drug courts also increase resources for offenders, such as therapy and transportation, and help balance the need for treatment for the offender and the need for public safety or the community (Koetzle et al., 2015). In MHCs, participants might view the court as an entity of social support in addition to the people in their support groups who show interest in their progress and share the same mental health burdens or situations (Canada & Gunn, 2013).

Social support mechanisms, such as those found in PSCs, should be strengthened and maintained not to create a false pretense of social support but enhance the offender's ability to be rehabilitated through maximizing social integration and social aid while reducing the reliance on illegitimate social support and potential criminality (Braithwaite, 1989; Colvin, 2000; Colvin et al., 2002). To help ensure the sustainability and maintenance of these types of programs, some courts use policies that increase consistency and reduce errors in miscommunication. One such program is the "one family, one judge" policy that keeps a family with the same judge rather than handing off the family between judges (Spinak, 2008). This policy reduces the likelihood that some element of need or aid is lost in translation. Policies like these increase accountability and consistency and could help establish social support networks with longevity.

Variation in the use of social support

Social support is found in various iterations of courts cross-culturally. Social support is integrated into Canadian domestic violence courts through familial support and in French juvenile courts, which also emphasize familial support (Blatier, 1998; Nolan, 2009). In the United States, there is a specific court dedicated to social support through mentoring, which is a mentoring court. This court provides probationers with a mentor to help reduce recidivism by providing a specific support person (Taylor, 2020). In each of these, social support is either an aspect of courts or encouraged through court programs. Except in mentoring courts, social support might not be the primary court component, but it is often integrated in some way throughout PSCs.

Authority

Since Stanley Milgram's (1974) study on obedience, research has applied the principles of obedience and authority across numerous contexts. One notable theory related to obedience is that of PJ, in which authority produces compliance at higher rates to the extent the authority is seen as legitimate (Tyler & Lind, 2002). The goals of a trusted and legitimate authority might be viewed as beneficial and in the best interest of those who comply. Through socialization, these goals are integrated and adopted as societal goals at the individual level, increasing compliance, creating informal social accountability in compliance, and eventually creating individualized extensions of the original goals contributing to societal cohesion and order (Tyler & Jackson, 2014). Beyond the authority of law, judges, law enforcement, and other official personnel throughout the legal system can be viewed as figures of authority and can elicit compliance, reducing legal trouble through various means. For youth, parents are figures of authority and can help youth reduce negative health behaviors (Mouttapa et al., 2003).

Other forms of authority can emerge through relationships with trusted and respected people, such as teachers, coaches, or religious leaders. These authority figures can be taught to younger people through socialization and reinforcement (e.g., norms; Burger, 2009; Milgram, 1974). Moreover, some positions or careers carry an element of authority with them because they include some sort of specialized training, such as medical doctors, psychologists, economists, and lawyers. Even politicians can carry a level of authority because they are elected and viewed as a representative authority by consensus with decision-making power. In each of these cases, authority figures are designated a role of requesting or encouraging compliance, conformity, and obedience. This often occurs through societal structures, such as laws, rules, delegations, policies, programs, or any societal structure that produces an authority hierarchy and places some level of power or decision-making ability with a person or group. The legal system is set up in the same way, instilling power and authority to different people and groups in a hierarchical manner.

Not all people respond to authority and power similarly (Damen et al., 2014). Religious beliefs shape how people view religious, legal, and scientific authorities (Cacciatore et al., 2018; Skitka et al., 2009). Additionally, individual differences, such as the need for closure, uncertainty reduction, heuristic processing, and ambiguity avoidance, might increase a person's reliance on authority figures (Grzyb et al., 2018; Kruglanski et al., 1993; Petty & Cacioppo, 1996).

Authority in the legal system

While the authority in the legal system seems obvious, its effectiveness might depend on people's views of the court's authority. Compliance with authority likely depends on people's perceptions of justice, fairness, and legitimacy of the court, which would include the perception that the court acts in an ethical manner and treats people in the court with some level of respect and humanity (Tyler, 1990; Tyler, 2006; Tyler & Jackson, 2014; see Chapter 3 of this text for a full discussion). A person's obedience to legal authority might also depend on the extent to which there will be punishment if a law is broken. For example, fear of being punished was negatively related to music piracy and illegal downloading behavior (Wingrove et al., 2011).

In some cases, especially in PSCs, the participants or offenders have the chance to provide input in their participation. This gives the participant a degree of agency and volition. To the extent that this is granted to them and taken seriously, the person's view of legitimacy and trust in the authority can increase along with positive outcomes for the participant (Tyler, 1990; McIvor, 2009). Judges are primary figures in courts, especially PSCs. This gives them an authority that can be quite effective in its influence. For example, the involvement of judicial review decreased non-compliance among batterer program participants (Gondolf, 2000). Because judges assume different roles in PSCs, they have a significant and influential authority.

Authority in problem-solving courts

In general, judges are expected to be neutral in their interpretation and application of the law; however, in PSCs, judges' roles are more flexible and allow for a more advocative and supervisory position, which can enhance participant trust and compliance (Burton, 2006; King, 2010). This type of role can be especially beneficial in treatment (Casey, 2004). In drug courts, judges are able to take familial and cultural factors into consideration and provide supervision and interventions to increase positive behavior among participants (Choi, 2012; King, 2010). In MHCs, judges' active involvement and participation in the participant's case and with the participant enhanced participant outcomes (Kopelovich et al., 2013).

Judges not only act as authority figures for the participants but are also authority figures on PSC teams, often acting as the leader of the court team (see Wiener et al., 2010). The teams collectively can use their positions and authority in the context to coordinate a wide range of community resources and leverage them in favor of the participants (McIvor, 2009). Numerous organizations provide resources for judges in PSCs, including the National Council of Juvenile and Family Court Judges. They provide workshops, conferences, and training for judges and teams working in PSCs and other juvenile and family courts.

In the United States, judges take a less traditional role and engage with the youth in the courtroom and also with the community and stakeholders (Nolan, 2012). This allows the judge to act as an authority but also express genuine investment in the participant's progress. In some places, such as England, the system might not be structured to allow for such flexibility in the judge's or magistrate's role, and the magistrates might prefer to act strictly as a judge and not as a counselor; in addition, some international courts dismiss or dislike the less formal role of the judges in US PSCs (Nolan, 2012). However, the US courts have also provided a model that has been adopted throughout many international PSCs.

In Scotland, drug courts maximize positive relationships between participants and authorities by enhancing communication and involvement of the Drug Court Sheriffs in the participant's case and progress (McIvor, 2009). Participants even commented on the difference between the authority of the drug courts and the authority of the traditional courts. Judges in Canada and Australia also take on a more flexible authority role through an increase in agency in making program decisions for the participant (Nolan, 2009).

Moral Psychology

Moral psychology involves the understanding of how people think and behave in moral or ethical contexts, which inevitably becomes a study of how people perceive, interpret, and act on decisions or attitudes of right and wrong (Doris et al., 2020). Moral judgments are often made at the behest of moral intuitions and moral reasoning. Moral intuitions are more instinctual moral judgments, whereas moral reasoning is a structured and patterned way by which a person formulates a moral justification for a decision, which underlies a particular moral argument. (Doris et al., 2020; Haidt, 2007). Moral reasoning can override or correct moral intuitions, and people can shape each other's moral intuitions and reasoning, and this stems from a genuine interest in people's own and others' morality, particularly in the social context (Haidt, 2001).

As people age throughout childhood and into adulthood, their views and understanding of morality change (Kohlberg & Hersh, 1977). Initially, morality and judgments of right and wrong are tied directly to physical or verbal reprimand for their actions. Then these judgments of right and wrong begin to align with family values and the values of other social groups, independent of their immediate effect on the person. Finally, these moral judgments begin to contain value independent of any source of authority or group designation, but attitudes and behaviors (and rules) are judged based on the inherent value of the act or attitude itself independent of the group affiliation (Kohlberg & Hersh, 1977). In childhood, the physical consequences and immediate family/peer values strongly shape moral judgments, which can lead to higher susceptibility in children to define or redefine moral judgments, especially when taught by authority figures (Raaijmakers et al., 2005). It is possible that youth engaged in delinquency use different moral judgment strategies than those engaged in non-delinquent behaviors (Kohlberg, 1974). Additionally, understanding moral reasoning among youth might help inform court programming for youth, and this is likely true for adults as well. Encouraging the use of moral reasoning that incorporates an understanding of value and judgments of right and wrong and attributing right and wrong to the behavior itself rather than mimicking the moral judgments of family and friends might help reduce illegal and illicit behavior (Raaijmakers et al., 2005; Rest, 1994).

One way of aiding moral judgments is to work with program participants to set goals that align with progress, program goals, and personal goals. Allowing the person to have agency in their own goals might increase intrinsic commitment to the program. Additionally, by using a joint effort to establish these goals, the program team can be sure that clear moral reasoning behind each goal is explained and reiterate the connection between the program goals and good or right behavior. Therefore, establishing goals and plans to complete goals can enhance behavior change and the successful achievements of those goals (see Frink & Ferris, 1998).

With each program-related behavior, participants either progress toward or away from their goals. Participants are often given feedback on their behavior to help reaffirm the program's goals and the moral reasoning behind the goals. This serves as a system of accountability, which provides reinforcement through rewards and punishment to encourage or discourage behavior (Frink & Ferris, 1998). When paired with moral reasoning, accountability can be used to help guide people to engage in goal-directed behavior (Pitesa & Thau, 2013).

Moral psychology in the legal system

The legal system, particularly the criminal justice system, implies morality by formally defining right and wrong behavior for its citizens. Negative behavior is punished through fines, required programs, detention, or supervision. Although appropriate behavior is not necessarily rewarded by the legal system, in the absence of negative behavior, it is reinforced through norms and informal social structures. Laws and punishments serve to instill morality and punish behaviors or actions that are detrimental to society. The goals of society might include social harmony, liberty, the ability to live without suffering, etc. If a behavior imposes upon these societal goals, then it might be punished, which reinforces that those behaviors are wrong. However, as discussed in the norms section of this chapter, what is right and wrong and what is punished might differ across subcultures or in immediate and local environments in which wrong behavior might be rewarded to a degree. This chapter will not discuss the morality of law or point out every place in the legal system that formalizes what is right and wrong; however, it is important to understand how and where moral psychology surfaces, most obviously, in PSCs.

Moral psychology in problem-solving courts

PSCs approach negative behaviors from the perspective that they have some underlying causal factors (Hora & Stalcup, 2007). In many courts, this includes that the problem behavior might be a result of inappropriate views of right and wrong or positive attitudes toward a particular negative behavior. For example, it is possible that batterers in domestic violence court think it is acceptable to physically abuse a partner or spouse if that person is "out of line" or disrespectful. This might be viewed as right or acceptable because they witnessed this growing up, were taught this way, or acted this way and decided that because they are doing it and the abused is not calling the authorities or running away, it is probably fine. In drug courts, drug users might have positive perceptions of drug use because it helps them cope with something or because they were taught that there is nothing wrong with it. This is especially complicated for youth whose parents drink alcohol and might even let them drink alcohol in their presence, which is sometimes the case in juvenile drug courts. PSCs often include the family to help create a program that incorporates the most immediate influences and better understand the youth's environment. The youth might believe that drinking alcohol is acceptable but forget that when their parents are not around, it is illegal (as several states allow minors to consume alcohol under parental supervision). Moreover, more states are legalizing marijuana, so drug courts treating offenders with marijuana charges might be frustrated by mixed messages from society. PSCs, especially the judges, assess and address issues at the intersection of the participant, the participant's family, and the community (Berman, 2000).

To counter favorable views of criminal behavior, PSCs establish moral dictates through supervision and program structure. In essence, PSCs play a moralizing role by reshaping participants' views regarding what is moral (see Steinberg, 2018). Paired with the previous discussion on social norms,

PSCs encourage participants to adopt new attitudes and beliefs about right and wrong behavior and encourage the adoption of new social norms. In PSCs, this can be done through goal setting and accountability. Moreover, judges play a critical role in establishing morality through PSCs. Judges have wider discretion in PSCs than in traditional courts, and because of this, they are able to address a wider range of behavior than just the criminal behavior related to the offense. Judges also demonstrate and model moral behavior through empathy, compassion, respect, and understanding (Hueston, 2021; Winick, 2003).

Goal-setting is found in most PSCs, as each court has program goals for each participant. More specifically, many courts will use behavior contracts in which the participant and the court team come together and develop unique goals for that participant. These behavioral contracts are then used as an accountability measure to compare performance throughout the tenure in the program. The use of behavioral contracts might increase program adherence and reduce violations (Winick, 2003). Although mostly used in the educational setting (Bowman-Perrott et al., 2015), behavioral contracts have been adapted to many PSCs (e.g., Deschenes et al., 1995).

Accountability often accompanies programs with high rates of supervision, and PSCs involve multiple aspects of supervision. Perhaps, one of the most well-known areas of accountability is the regular meeting between the participant and the judge or court authority. In these instances, participants will often give a quick update on their progress and answer any questions or challenges. This serves as regular feedback to keep the participants accountable for their actions from week to week. Additionally, many PSCs, especially drug courts, have regular drug testing, keeping participants accountable for their drug use. Community courts involve a host of community partners, which makes the network of accountability denser and increases the geographical coverage of the program's accountability network.

Accountability and morality might manifest differently in various problem-solving settings. Borrowing from US PSC influence, the Croydon domestic violence court, in England, used a regular review process for participants' rehabilitation compliance in hopes of increasing accountability and reducing negative behaviors (Nolan, 2009). In a Calgary, Alberta, domestic violence court, judges use more varied discretion regarding when they want to interact with the program participants. It can be a few weeks or a few months. It is not as frequently prescribed as in the United States and more frequently than every three months, like in some UK courts. Thus, the regular accountability structure is tailored to the participant rather than being a concrete standard across all PSCs and for all participants (Nolan, 2009).

Conclusions

PSCs incorporate a wide variety of social science phenomena with a particular reliance on and incorporation of many psychological principles. This chapter reviewed many of them and pointed out various ways in which a basic understanding of psychology can help inform and understand effective (or ineffective) practices in PSCs. Also, as noted, these principles have some universality to them, although there are variations in where and how they are applied.

One of the critical implications of the incorporation of psychology into PSCs is that as psychological research progresses, the potential for PSCs to be effective improves. However, this assumes a foundation of ethical and valid research conducted by psychologists, research organizations, and universities. Practitioners use the information from researchers to design and implement interventions. The interventions can only be successful to the point they are guided by sound and valid research. Unreliable and invalid research will lead to ineffective interventions, wasted money (often taxpayer dollars), and, most importantly, underserved program participants. Just as sick people do not want ineffective medical care, offenders do not want ineffective rehabilitation programming. This places a large burden on the researchers, but it is the very reason that much of this psychological research is conducted in the first place.

Another critical component in the psychology and PSC relationship is the openness to and use of psychology research in PSCs. This is apparent in the trend toward using evidence-based practices. To gain insights from psychological research and understand the psychology of some of the problem behaviors among the participants in PSCs, judges and program coordinators must be willing to look at the psychology research on the related topics, or at least consult treatment professionals and psychologists when developing programs and plans. A major strength of the PSC is the team approach, which enhances the court's ability to include professionals from various backgrounds and gain insights from multiple fields. The critical juncture is the integration of these insights into program development and delivery.

The use of psychology in PSCs, of course, has variations internationally because much of the ability to use lessons learned in psychological research depends on the national, societal, and cultural structure within which the courts operate. However, PSCs seem to have a natural inclination toward including psychology research as a basis for programming and how to best help participants, and the future of PSCs will likely depend, in part, on the future of social scientific research and our collective ability to better understand human behavior.

5

Scientific Methodology Used in Evaluations of Problem-Solving Courts

Differences in Evaluating Problem-Solving Courts

This chapter discusses the scientific evaluations of problem-solving courts (PSCs), comparing how scientific evaluations might differ by society. The evaluation of PSCs often considers various justice principles and psychology concepts such as therapeutic jurisprudence (TJ), procedural justice (PJ), community sentiment, and social support (see Chapters 3 and 4). The *application* of justice and psychology theories can also vary in PSC evaluations. Courts might emphasize different theories in their design and operation, and researchers might use specific theoretical frameworks to guide their evaluations. Scientific evaluations of PSCs can differ depending on the country in which they are conducted. Different legal systems, cultural norms, scientific backgrounds, and resources might influence the evaluation criteria, methods, and outcomes (see DeMatteo et al., 2019 for discussion of methodological challenges).

Building off of the work by Miller, Block, and DeVault (2020), this chapter will examine and compare PSC evaluations nationally and globally. Many evaluations of PSCs use recidivism as a dependent variable to assess the effectiveness of these courts. However, how recidivism is defined and operationalized can vary among evaluations, potentially affecting the results and comparability of studies. The type of PSC being evaluated can also significantly impact the evaluation process. For example, community courts prioritize community outcomes, while mental health courts (MHCs) focus on cognitive health-related outcomes. These variations in outcome measures can influence the evaluation's design and findings. This same sentiment applies to the methods used in PSC evaluations. Factors such as sample size, participant selection, research design, and data collection methods can differ among evaluations, leading to variations in rigor.

Society, Science, and Problem-Solving Courts. Monica K. Miller, Mia A. Holbrook, Logan A. Yelderman, and Kylie Kulak, Oxford University Press. © Oxford University Press 2025. DOI: 10.1093/oso/9780190059804.003.0005

Although PSC evaluation is common in the literature, there has yet to be a global comparison. Evaluations of PSCs in different countries might employ distinct methodologies and approaches due to differences in legal systems, cultural considerations, and available resources. Comparing evaluations from various countries can offer a deeper understanding of the global effectiveness of PSCs and how science and culture factor into the process. Understanding these variations is crucial for obtaining a comprehensive understanding of the impact and effectiveness of PSCs across different settings and jurisdictions.

Problem-solving courts and evaluations

It is imperative to scrutinize the effectiveness of PSCs to assess whether they are achieving their intended objectives, to identify any unforeseen consequences, and to make informed decisions regarding whether PSCs should be sustained, extended, or scaled back. PSCs were initially established to tackle the root causes of criminal behavior, aiming to diminish repeat offenses and offer rehabilitation and associated services to offenders.

There are multiple approaches to assess the effectiveness of PSCs. The Maryland Scientific Methods Scale (Farrington et al., 2002) categorizes research designs in ascending order of rigor:

1. A pre- and post-court assessment of a treatment group or a cross-sectional comparison of a treatment group and a non-treatment group *without* using control variables.
2. A pre- and post-court assessment of a treatment group or a cross-sectional comparison of a treatment group and a non-treatment group *with* the incorporation of control variables.
3. The use of a non-treatment comparison group with thorough control of differences between the comparison group and treatment group through methods like regression or matching, although significant differences might still exist.
4. A quasi-experimental design assumes treatment is the sole distinguishing factor between the non-treatment comparison group and the treatment group.
5. A randomized controlled trial representing the highest level of research rigor.

Moreover, PSCs exhibit variability in their chosen outcome measures. The most prevalent metric is whether the defendant has recidivated by committing additional offenses. As a result, the predominant focus of evaluations on PSCs centers on assessing recidivism rates or determining whether they have effectively aided court participants in addressing and mitigating the underlying issues that led to their involvement in criminal behavior. The duration of this measurement period can range from months to years. Furthermore, the definition of recidivism might encompass minor infractions or exclusively include serious crimes or offenses akin to the initial violation. Sometimes, PSCs consider alternative outcome measures, such as mental health or community-related outcomes.

The justice foundations of each court will vary based on the court's intent. As outlined in Chapter 3, there are many justice principles upon which PSCs rely, such as the adversarial process, TJ, and PJ, among others. The evaluations of each court will also differ, as a result, based on the variety of justice principles and psychological theories used. The analysis conducted for this chapter will examine how such justice and psychological principles are incorporated into PSCs, both nationally and globally.

This chapter discusses each type of PSC and the scientific process for evaluating these courts. This chapter will also compare PSC evaluations by society in the United States and globally.

Methods in Current Study

For this chapter, we conducted a comprehensive examination of PSC evaluations. For each type of PSC, previously published evaluations were collected and coded for relevant information. Each evaluation underwent a comprehensive coding process encompassing multiple aspects, including methodology, dependent variables, operationalization, use of justice principles, application of psychology principles, and consideration of global variations.

Selection of evaluations and coding

Each evaluation was coded for six different categories: methodology, dependent variables, operationalization of dependent variables, justice principles employed, psychology principles used, and differences globally. When coding for methodology, variation in methods, rigor, sample size, and selection of participants were examined. The number of dependent variables and their various operationalizations were noted when coding for dependent variables. This allowed for comparing how PSCs operationalized effectiveness within similar courts, across different courts, and globally. When coding for justice and psychology principles, each evaluation was examined for the principles included, highlighting the common themes for different types of PSCs. When coding for global consideration, comparisons were drawn for disparities and deviations between evaluations in other countries.

Specific criteria were employed to identify usable evaluations. The evaluation needed to focus explicitly on a PSC. Studies not exclusively focused on PSCs were not included in the analysis. This encompassed any evaluations of a stand-alone program, such as a substance abuse treatment program held outside the reach of a drug court. As discussed previously, many PSCs span multiple jurisdictions or collaborate to provide multiple services (e.g., a community court addressing prostitution, vandalism, and minor drug possessions). In these cases, the evaluations were included with the overarching PSC type.

Previous evaluations were required to provide a sufficient description of the PSC to determine whether it incorporated the components of interest, such as operationalized variables and justice principles. The search for these evaluations was conducted separately for each type of PSC, using keywords in numerous scholarly and government databases. Every PSC was searched, and eligible evaluations were reviewed to ensure an exhaustive approach.

Classification of methodology

Each evaluation was categorized according to its design and methodology. Adopting the Maryland Scientific Methods Scale (Farrington et al., 2002), the following definitions were used:

1. A pre- and post-assessment of the treatment group or cross-sectional comparison of the treatment group and non-treatment group *without* control variables.
2. A pre- and post-assessment of the treatment group or cross-sectional comparison of the treatment group and non-treatment group *with* control variables.

3. A non-treatment comparison group was used, and adequate control of differences across the comparison group and treatment group through regression or matching, but essential differences might remain.
4. Quasi-experimental design that allows for the assumption that treatment is the only difference between the non-treatment comparison group and treatment group.
5. Randomized controlled trial.

Designs outside these definitions were also categorized, although they were less common. These included designs such as surveys and meta-analyses. The rigor of methodology was also assessed, based on the definition of a three or higher on the Scientific Methods Scale.

Categorizing variables

In our analysis, the categorization of dependent variables was dependent on the evaluation. The most common dependent variable was recidivism. Recidivism is one of the most critical outcomes for criminal justice and court systems. Each evaluation adopted its definition of recidivism; they differed on the follow-up timeframe and whether they considered technical violations and specific re-offenses.

Other standard dependent variables included court effectiveness, drug use or sobriety, mental health outcomes, community engagement, and case processing. No variable elimination or reduction occurred, but each type of PSC was evaluated based on the identified variables.

Identifying justice and psychological principles

We implemented a coding process for justice and psychological principles to assess the existence of specific components within each PSC. These components included problem-solving, adversarial process, TJ, PJ, legitimacy/operant conditioning, restorative justice (RJ), community sentiment, effective intervention, and operant conditioning (see Chapter 3 for more on justice principles).

For a PSC to be classified under the problem-solving component, it needed to include the fundamental philosophy of PSCs. These courts are designed to go beyond traditional punitive approaches and address the root causes of criminal behavior by focusing on individualized interventions and treatment. Examples include an individualized approach, collaboration, balancing justice and therapeutic methodologies, and problem-solving adjudication.

For a PSC to be classified under the adversarial process component, it must incorporate at least one element of the traditional adversarial criminal court process (Harrell et al., 2007; Newmark et al., 2004). Common features included intensive supervision by probation/parole departments and requirements to abstain from alcohol and drug use with regular testing.

For a PSC to be classified under the TJ component, it must have incorporated either offender treatment related to the specific type of PSC or increased offender access to social services. Examples included substance abuse treatment, intervention programming, and assistance in obtaining housing or employment.

For a PSC to be classified under the PJ component, it needed to incorporate participant contact with the judge as a central tenet of the court. Examples included judicial follow-ups with participants or having the judge explain the PSC process to participants.

For a PSC to be classified under the legitimacy/operant conditioning component, it must incorporate rewards and sanctions to change an offender's behavior. This is linked to legitimacy in the sense of following authority orders in relation to rewards and sanctions (see Chapter 3 for more). Common sanctions included jail time in response to positive drug tests or increased court appearances due to lack of involvement. Common rewards included reduction in required court appearances or fewer drug tests.

For a PSC to be classified under the RJ component, it must incorporate victim advocacy, offender accountability, or community service elements. Common examples included the presence of victim advocates during court proceedings or a requirement of involvement in the local community for the participant.

For a PSC to be classified under the community sentiment component, it needed to incorporate input from the community in court proceedings. Examples included seeking community input regarding the problems that needed addressing and seeking community input on addressing issues troubling society.

For a PSC to be classified under the effective intervention component, it needed to incorporate addressing the root causes of the related behavior and promote positive change for future behavior. Examples included using research and evidence-based approaches and access and matching to treatment and support services.

Classification of evaluation differences globally

A significant contribution of this analysis is examining the differences between PSC evaluations globally. Some assessed components included differences in justice principles, distinctions in evaluation measures, alterations in variable categorization and operationalization, and definitions of effective programming.

Results by Court Type

Drug courts

Drug courts are the most evaluated specialty courts to date. As drug courts were the first PSCs to be established, many evaluations are available in the literature.

Evaluation methods

The variation in methods employed to assess the effectiveness of drug courts is diverse, reflecting the complexity of evaluating such programs. In a broad sense, the most common approach is an experimental design incorporating a control group. However, quasi-experimental designs are also prevalent, matching participants and non-participants based on similar drug charges. Some studies use meta-analyses and survey research methods as well.

Experimental designs, as highlighted by Koetzle et al. (2015), often compare a drug court participant group with a non-treatment group. The non-treatment group consists of drug offenders on probation who were eligible for drug court but chose not to participate. Quasi-experimental designs, exemplified by Krebs et al. (2007), involve comparing drug court participants with a matched comparison group in traditional court settings.

Meta-analyses studies, such as those conducted by Brown (2010) and Shaffer (2011), offer a comprehensive overview by reviewing outcomes research from quasi-experimental and randomized control studies. Brown (2010) explores the effectiveness literature for drug courts, while Shaffer (2011) identifies characteristics influencing drug court effectiveness.

Additional methodological approaches include randomized control designs, as examined by Brown (2010), in which drug offenders are randomly assigned to treatment or non-treatment groups, and survey research, as demonstrated by Nored and Carlan (2008), measuring perceptions of drug court judges to examine critical factors contributing to program success.

Systematic reviews, as conducted by the US General Accountability Office (2005) and Wilson et al. (2006), offer a synthesis of multiple evaluations, providing a comprehensive understanding of drug court effectiveness for both juvenile and adult offenders.

Belenko (2001) emphasizes that evaluations typically encompass various aspects, including the number of admissions, program retention, client characteristics, program or treatment service information, in-program drug test results, cost analysis, and post-program recidivism with a comparison group. Additionally, some evaluations incorporate qualitative interviews with staff, clients, and/or participants, enhancing the depth of understanding regarding drug court dynamics and outcomes.

The variation in sample sizes across studies evaluating drug courts is notable. It is uncommon to encounter studies with sample sizes below 100 participants; most typically fall within the 100 to 500 participants' range. Smaller drug court analyses often exhibit smaller sample sizes, with Belenko (2001) noting one of the lowest at (n = 27).

In contrast, more extensive studies with sample sizes exceeding 500 are not uncommon, especially in research that analyzes multiple drug courts or conducts meta-analyses of multiple evaluations, as Belenko (2001) highlighted. The distribution of sample sizes between the test and control groups is generally even. For instance, in the study by Krebs et al. (2007), there were 475 participants in total, with 274 in the drug court group and 201 in the traditional court group.

In the context of meta-analyses, Brown (2010) used 44 reports for their analysis, with 29 explicitly evaluating drug treatment court outcomes. Drawing on a diverse set of studies, this collective approach allows for a more comprehensive understanding of the impact of drug courts across varying sample sizes and settings.

The variation in the rigor of drug court evaluations is crucial to understanding these studies' methodological strengths and weaknesses. Mitchell et al. (2012) classified drug court evaluations into four categories based on the Maryland Scientific Methods Scale, distinguishing between weak quasi-experiments, standard experiments, rigorous experiments, and random experiments or studies with unclear information. Of 154 evaluations, 25 were rated as "weak" in methodological rigor, 75 as "standard," and 36 as "rigorous." The remaining evaluations fell into the categories of random experiments or had insufficient information.

Rigorous experiments typically employed subject-level matching on key variables or propensity score matching, enhancing the internal validity of the findings. On the other hand, standard experiments used a historical comparison group or a group of offenders eligible for but not referred to the drug court program. Weaker experiments often compared drug court participants to people who were eligible for participation but either refused or were rejected. These weaker experiments are considered less robust in terms of internal validity due to potential differences in factors, such as pre-treatment motivation, perceived seriousness of drug problems, and self-efficacy among participants.

Most evaluations fell within the "standard" or "rigorous" categories in terms of methodological rigor, according to the Maryland Scientific Methods Scale. However, Saum and Hiller (2009) note that the most rigorous design, a truly experimental approach, is rare due to ethical considerations (e.g., denying treatment to a control group), limited resources for evaluation, and challenges associated with the operational and organizational culture of justice system agencies. Consequently, less rigorous quasi-experimental methods are typically employed in drug court evaluations. This reflects a pragmatic approach to balancing ethical considerations, resource constraints, and the practicalities of justice system operations.

The selection of participants in evaluations of drug courts exhibits substantial variability, with a range of methodologies employed across different studies. Notably, various common selection processes have been identified, drawing from studies such as those conducted by Belenko (1998) and Mitchell et al. (2012). For participants in drug courts, methods include:

- The random assignment of offenders to a probation track,
- The random selection of offenders who committed felony drug offenses and were identified as potential candidates for drug court, and
- The random selection of juveniles arrested for misdemeanor drug possession.

Control group participants are selected through methods such as "historical control," involving a comparison with offenders who would have been eligible for drug court at the time of their offense and charging, eligible defendants who opted not to enter a drug court program, and defendants with felony drug charges who were ineligible for drug court. Belenko (2001) noted that evaluations often used convenience samples rather than random samples of clients and staff. In the context of meta-analyses, Brown (2010) employed a comprehensive approach, using multiple academic fields, sources, and databases to obtain titles and abstracts, subsequently reviewing and assembling appropriate literature for the meta-analysis.

Dependent variables

Dependent variables in the evaluation of drug courts are multifaceted, commonly focusing on recidivism rates post-release, as is observed in many PSCs. The operationalization of recidivism varies across studies. Belenko (2001) considered recidivism based on both drug use and criminal activity, while Koetzle et al. (2015) defined recidivism as measured by "new charges," and Krebs et al. (2007) assessed recidivism through arrests after completing the court program. Notably, different studies employed distinct time frames and criteria for defining recidivism, such as rearrests within one year after drug court admission, recidivism during program participation (including both drug usage and criminal charges), rearrests two years after program release, reconvictions 12 months after program completion, reconviction 15 to 24 months after the initial arrest, and rearrest data six months post-admission.

Another common dependent variable is drug use, both within the program and after program completion, with "drug use" typically encompassing the use of any drug, especially those associated with the offender's original charge. Some studies delve into drug courts' cost-effectiveness and social benefits, comparing the costs of supervising participants in drug courts to those in correctional facilities. Analyses might also consider the salaries of drug court personnel compared to correctional institution personnel, and social benefits might be outlined by employment rates or employment-related activities post-program graduation.

Jensen and Mosher (2006) measured both in-program and post-program outcomes, providing a comprehensive understanding of the longitudinal effects of drug court interventions. Belenko (2001) included additional dependent variables, such as retention and graduation rates, drug use within the program, recidivism during the program (as discussed earlier), and general recidivism. These varied dependent variables contribute to a comprehensive evaluation of drug court effectiveness, capturing criminal justice outcomes and the broader impact on drug use, cost-effectiveness, and social well-being.

Justice and psychology principles

A wide range of justice and psychology principles can be found in drug court evaluations, including TJ, problem-solving principles, effective intervention, adversarial components, PJ, psychological/medical advancements to assist in the healing process of addiction, community sentiment, and operant conditioning. The most common justice and psychology principles in drug court evaluations were TJ, effective intervention, and PJ. Many studies touch on psychological/medical advancements in healing addiction, as to why conducting the study was necessary.

Global examination

Global evaluations of drug courts employ diverse methodologies and examine various dependent variables, offering insights into the effectiveness of these interventions in different jurisdictions. In Australia, Makkai and Veraar (2003) conducted a retrospective analysis of drug court participant offense records post-completion, comparing outcomes to offenders who refused drug court and followed the traditional route, as well as ex-prisoners known to have been under the influence at the time of the offense. In Scotland, McIvor (2004) opted for a qualitative approach, conducting interviews with offenders, sheriffs (judges), and other court personnel. In New Zealand, Payne (2005) used qualitative interviews with past drug court participants and compared the group in the drug court to those referred to the program but declined participation. In Canada, Somers and colleagues (2012) adopted a retrospective longitudinal cohort design, including all drug court participants and using propensity score matching for the comparison group selection.

The dependent variables assessed in these global studies vary. In Australia, Makkai and Veraar (2003) focused on re-offending, the time to the first offense, and the offending frequency. In New Zealand, Payne (2005) examined recidivism, specifically the time taken to re-offend, re-offending frequency, and program completion. In Canada, Somers and colleagues (2012) defined recidivism as court appearances for offenses, not necessarily all arrests or crimes.

Sample sizes in these global evaluations differ across studies. In Australia, Makkai and Veraar (2003) analyzed 259 drug court participants, 97 refusals, and 107 in the "prisoner comparison group." In New Zealand, Payne (2005) included 120 offenders who started the program, with subgroups for program completion and recidivism analysis. In Canada, Somers and colleagues (2012) worked with a sample size of 360, with 180 participants in each group.

The guiding principles in these global evaluations vary as well. In Scotland, McIvor (2004) emphasized PJ and TJ. Similarly, Somers and colleagues (2012) also adopted TJ principles in Canada. Collectively, these global studies contribute to a nuanced understanding of the effectiveness of drug courts, considering cultural and jurisdictional differences in their evaluations.

There are many overlaps between US and global drug court evaluations. These include the choice of dependent variables, primarily focusing on recidivism, the methodology employed, sample size considerations, and TJ principles. Differences can be attributed to the cultural context surrounding drugs, legal definitions, and treatment approaches.

DWI/DUI courts

Evaluations consistently affirm the efficacy of driving while impaired/driving under the influence (DWI/DUI) courts, which draw upon the drug court model. Twenty-eight evaluations have been conducted up until now on DWI/DUI court, with the majority of them finding a positive impact of the PSC.

Evaluation methods

Various methodological approaches have been employed in evaluating DWI/DUI courts. Random assignment studies, as highlighted by Breckenridge et al. (2000), Jones (2005), MacDonald et al. (2007), and involve the random allocation of eligible offenders to either DWI/DUI court or alternative dispositions. However, such studies acknowledge the ethical concern of withholding treatment. Quasi-experimental studies, as discussed by Cavanaugh and Franklin (2012), compare DWI/DUI court outcomes to those who did not enter DWI/DUI court, often using matched comparisons. Examples include Mackin et al. (2009), who used a matched comparison from probation, and Meredith (2007), who employed historically matched comparisons.

Longitudinal and experimental designs, exemplified by Carey et al. (2008), involve collecting data on DWI/DUI court participants for at least one year following program completion, with a comparison group of offenders. This comprehensive approach includes site visits to observe structure, procedures, and routines featured in the study. Additionally, meta-analyses, such as those conducted by Marlowe et al. (2009) and Mitchell et al. (2012), aggregate findings from multiple studies for a broader understanding of DWI/DUI court effectiveness.

The rigor in evaluating DWI/DUI courts, as discussed by Saum and Hiller (2009), closely mirrors that of drug courts. Although the ideal preference leans toward a proper experimental design, the practical reality often involves using quasi-experimental models. These models are rigorous if the control group is appropriately matched and if an "intent-to-treat" design is implemented. However, the rigor diminishes if "refusals" or "rejecters" are included in the control groups. Marlowe et al. (2009) further elaborate that most DWI/DUI evaluations are classified as "standard" in terms of rigor, with only a few studies meeting the criteria for a rigorous design, while some are perceived as weaker. Aligning with the evaluation scale applied by the Maryland Scientific Methods Scale, most DWI/DUI court studies fall within the "standard" category, with "rigorous" and "weak" studies being roughly comparable in number.

Variations in sample size within evaluations are quite diverse. The sample sizes generally range from 100 to 500 participants, with studies demonstrating fluctuations in participant numbers. For instance, Fell et al. (2011) encompassed 363 graduated offenders, 259 terminated offenders, 270 people in a retrospective comparison group, and 450 in a contemporary comparison group. Breckenridge et al. (2000) in Texas examined 133 DWI/DUI offenders in the experimental group compared to 954 members in the control group. Other studies, such as Saum & Hiller (2009), Jones (2005), Lapham et al. (2006), MacDonald et al. (2007), and Meredith (2007) presented varying sample sizes.

Variability in selecting participants for DWI/DUI court evaluations is crucial, as emphasized in the *Introductory Handbook for DWI Court Program Evaluations*. The handbook underscores the significance of assessing all participants associated with a DWI court, irrespective of program completion. It stresses the importance of forming a control group with participants unlikely to be influenced by factors affecting outcomes. Notably, the outcomes of participants who refused to enter were denied access, dropped out, or terminated from the DWI/DUI court and should not be compared to DWI/DUI court outcomes. Many studies include all participants entering the program, while some focus solely on program graduates. Notable examples like Casey et al. (2008), Hiller & Saum (2009), Jones (2005), Mackin et al. (2009), and Meredith (2007) exhibit this inclusive approach. Propensity score matching, a prevalent method in the last decade, involves matching based on various factors such as prior DWIs/DUIs, felony records, demographic characteristics, and risk and needs assessment scores compiled by probation officers. Comparison groups typically consist of offenders from one or two years prior to program implementation, meeting eligibility criteria but not participating, or people on probation with DWI/DUI court-eligible criminal histories. Random assignment studies often employ a comparison group randomly selected to a probation group from those eligible for drug court.

Dependent variables

The two main dependent variables found in DWI/DUI court evaluations were recidivism and sobriety. Recidivism was typically operationalized as new DWI/DUI arrests or moving traffic violations. However, many studies also included any criminal charge or arrest post-program completion. Some measurements of recidivism specified a rearrest after completion of the program, starting collection at six months up through six years post-completion (Carey et al., 2015; Cavanaugh & Franklin, 2012; Mackin et al., 2009; Marlowe et al., 2009). Others included self-reported DWI/DUI or alcohol abuse (Marlowe et al., 2009).

Justice and psychology principles

As DWI/DUI PSCs are rooted in a similar framework to drug courts, there is an overlap in which justice and psychology principles are employed. The most common principles include TJ, problem-solving principles, adversarial process, effective intervention, operant conditioning, and PJ.

Global examination

There is no clear evidence that DWI/DUI courts have been implemented outside of the United States, which results in no evaluations to examine. However, as discussed in Chapter 2, many driver-rehabilitation programs have been implemented throughout Europe.

Mental health courts

Overall, evaluations of MHCs show positive effects on recidivism. Roughly 17 evaluations have been conducted globally and nationally in the adult and juvenile systems.

Evaluation methods

Variation in methodologies employed to evaluate MHCs is evident across studies. Quasi-experimental designs, as used by Behnken et al. (2017), followed a one-group pre-test and post-test design. Using a between-subject comparison, Christy et al. (2005) compared MHC defendants with a matched sample from a county without an MHC. Hiday & Ray (2010) and Lowder et al. (2016) performed between-subject comparisons and examined individual characteristics and process factors, by comparing MHC participants and a Treatment-As-Usual (TAU) group. Nonequivalent comparison group/matched sample designs, exemplified by Boothroyd et al. (2005), matched MHC defendants with those in a traditional court based on demographic and clinical characteristics. In some instances, such as Cosden et al. (2005), randomized trials were used to randomly assign participants to MHC or TAU. Post-test-only comparison designs, such as in Dirks-Linhorst & Linhorst (2012), involved secondary data analysis, exploring rearrest rates one year after discharge. Longitudinal studies, like Steadman et al. (2011), and retrospective observational approaches, like McNiel & Binder (2007), compared criminal charges for MHC entrants and other adults with mental disorders in jail. Qualitative and quantitative interviews and data are incorporated in studies like Wales et al. (2010) and Trupin et al. (2001), showcasing the diverse methodological landscape of MHC evaluations.

When juxtaposed with DWI/DUI and drug courts, the assessments of MHCs exhibit a lesser degree of rigor. Most MHCs evaluations align with the "standard" category of the Maryland Scientific Methods Scale, with only a few meeting the criteria for "rigorous" standards. Additionally, many of these evaluations are categorized as weak regarding methodological rigor.

Variation in sample sizes within MHC evaluations shows a tendency for slightly smaller numbers than DWI/DUI and drug courts, although some studies still feature sample sizes exceeding 500. For instance, Behnken et al. (2017) reported a sample size of n = 63, Boothroyd et al. (2005) involved 97 participants in MHC and 77 in the control group, while Christy et al. (2005)

worked with 116 in MHC and 101 in the control group. Cosden et al. (2005) conducted their study with 235 participants, 137 in MHC and 98 in the control group. Dirks-Linhorst (2012) reported a sample size of 351 in MHC, including 137 terminated and 89 non-participants. Lowder et al. (2016) worked with 98 participants in total, consisting of 58 in MHC (30 graduates and 28 non-completers) and 40 in the TAU control group. McNiel & Binder (2007) had a sample size of 170 in MHC and 8,068 in criminal court. Wales et al. (2010) engaged 1669 people in regular court, 527 in MHCs, and conducted 80 interviews. Trupin et al. (2001) conducted 128 interviews and analyzed data for 404 new referrals to MHC.

The selection of participants is consistent across evaluations. Experimental groups typically encompass all participants enrolled in a MHC, often including participants from a voluntary pool within the court. Control groups vary, with the most common being a TAU group, a pool of people eligible for MHC who opted not to participate or those who exited the program prematurely. In Behnken et al.'s (2017) study, all juveniles who completed court-ordered probation and graduated from the court were included. Boothroyd et al. (2005) offered voluntary participation to defendants from both mental health and traditional courts. Cosden et al. (2005) included all eligible offenders booked into the county jail, using premature terminations and refusals as the "treatment-as-is" control group. Dirks-Linhorst (2012) considered all cases admitted that completed the program, were terminated, or chose not to participate but were eligible. Lowder et al. (2016) included all participants exiting MHC in its first three years, comparing them to a group of offenders adjudicated in the same timeframe who did not participate but received TAU. McNiel & Binder (2007) encompassed all people with a diagnosed mental disorder, whether in MHC or criminal court. Wales et al. (2010) interviewed participants during their MHC treatment or within six months of release, with additional data collected from a subsample in the court's waiting area.

Dependent variables

Many dependent variables are employed to gauge the effectiveness of these specialized programs. Similar to DWI/DUI and drug courts, pre- and post-specialty court recidivism is a commonly used dependent variable in MHC evaluations. Behnken et al. (2017) defined recidivism as an arrest, while Dirks-Linhorst (2012) considered it an arrest for a new crime within one year after discharge from the program. Lowder et al. (2016) also examined post-program charges, convictions, and jail days within one year from program release or case disposition. McNiel & Binder (2007) focused on rearrest for any offense, particularly violent crimes, and Trupin et al. (2001) assess any "booking" or jail time. Christy et al. (2005) offered a comprehensive definition of recidivism, including time spent in jail, rearrests, and self-reported violent/aggressive behavior within one year of post-study enrollment, distinguishing between aggressive and violent acts based on specific criteria.

Clinical status and mental health assessment were other prevalent dependent variables in MHC evaluations. Boothroyd et al. (2005) used the Psychiatric Ratings Scale, a 7-point scale based on self-report and behavioral observations during clinical interviews, while Cosden et al. (2005) conducted assessments at six-month intervals for 24 months, covering the Global Assessment of Functioning, Lehman Quality of Life Scale, Behavior and Symptom Identification Scale, and the Addiction Severity Index.

Additionally, post-program service use is examined. Boothroyd et al. (2005) investigated whether participants received treatment within eight months after their initial court appearance, relying on self-reported services during face-to-face interviews. Lastly, participants' perceptions of PJ are considered, Wales et al. (2010) explored what participants liked best and least about the program and used a civil commitment survey to discuss their views on their treatment experience. These diverse dependent variables collectively contribute to an understanding of the outcomes and impact of MHCs on participants.

Justice and psychology principles

The most common justice and psychology principles for MHCs include TJ, PJ, adversarial process, and operant conditioning.

Global examination

MHCs have been implemented in Australia and Canada, albeit less extensively than in the United States, leading to a scarcity of evaluations in these regions. In instances in which evaluations exist, they often mirror the models employed in the United States, emphasizing TJ. In Canada, Dunford and Haag (2020) identified a need for more literature on the evaluations and day-to-day practices of MHCs, prompting them to devise their questionnaire for investigation. Similarly, Watts and Weinrath (2017) acknowledged the limited research on evaluations and undertook a pre-test–post-test design with a sample size of 35 to compare rates of criminal justice involvement. Davis

(2014) conducted a retrospective assessment of secondary data, comparing 127 participants who completed the program with those who did not. Lim and Day (2014) employed a retrospective analysis in Canada, identifying MHC participants and their initial offenses and assessing the re-offending rates of program completers versus those who entered but did not complete the program (n = 219). Davidson et al. (2016) used qualitative interviews and a written survey distributed to willing program participants in Australia. Skrzypiec et al. (2004) conducted a pre- and post-program comparison, examining the number of charges and offenses (n = 157). These diverse evaluation approaches contribute to the understanding of MHC effectiveness globally.

Community courts

Although the establishment and execution of community courts have made significant progress, evaluations of their efficacy yield varied outcomes.

Evaluation methods

Variation in the evaluation methods of community courts is evident, showcasing diverse approaches to assess their effectiveness. In quasi-experimental studies, Eckberg (2001) employed two comparison groups, one from the same time period and one from the previous year, matched on demographic characteristics and case similarities. Grommon et al. (2017) adopted a retrospective design, comparing community court participants with those referred but declined, using a propensity score adjustment. Lee et al. (2013) employed a similar approach, comparing data on adult criminal and juvenile delinquency cases using propensity score adjustment. Katz (2009) evaluated defendants arrested pre-program implementation and post-implementation, while Nugent-Borakove (2009) used a pre-test–post-test design with a control group. Hakuta, Soroushian, and Kralistein (2008) measured outcomes between misdemeanor defendants arraigned in community courts and criminal courts.

Qualitative surveys were also conducted, adding a nuanced perspective. Eckberg (2001) surveyed community members, offering a cross-sectional comparison of community court participants and non-participants. Lee et al. (2013) conducted group and individual interviews with various stakeholders, including court staff, attorneys, police commanders, community leaders, and partners, employing propensity score adjustment to enhance the qualitative insights. Additionally, some studies employed pre-test–post-test designs with control groups, and a few included non-treatment groups with controls (Ross et al., 2009; Sviridoff et al., 2002).

The assessment of community courts reveals a common acknowledgment among studies that, although an ideal evaluation would involve an experimental design, practical constraints related to operations and budget limitations within community courts preclude such approaches. According to the Maryland Scientific Methods Scale, most evaluations exhibited either low or moderate levels of rigor, with only one study demonstrating a high level of rigor in assessing community courts. This variation in rigor across evaluations highlights the pragmatic hurdles in conducting stringent assessments of community court effectiveness.

The variation in sample sizes across evaluations of community courts is notable, reflecting the diverse scopes and contexts of these studies. In Eckberg's (2001) survey-based study, 405 community members and 133 offenders were included, providing a comprehensive perspective on community perceptions. Grommon et al. (2017) engaged a substantial sample with 388 participants in community courts and 186 in the control group, allowing for a comparative analysis of participant outcomes. Katz's (2009) evaluation encompassed an extensive sample of 22,753 participants, with 15,138 assessed in the pre-implementation phase and 15,039 in the post-implementation phase, ensuring a robust examination of temporal changes. Lee et al.'s (2013) study involved 3,247 cases, with 1,576 in community courts and 1,671 in criminal courts, contributing to a nuanced understanding of case dispositions. Nugent-Borakove's (2009) evaluation included 439 participants, with 209 in the community court group and 230 in the control group, offering insights into program impacts. Lastly, Hakuta, Soroshian, and Kralistein's (2008) comprehensive study involved 27,472 participants, with 4,169 in the treatment group and 23,303 in the control group, providing a large-scale assessment of the court's overall impact.

The selection of participants in evaluations of community courts varies by study. In Eckberg (2001), the comparison group comprised cases with similar offenses managed during the same time period and those from the previous year, contributing to a robust analysis of temporal trends. Grommon et al. (2017) had the treatment group encompassing participants through the community court, while the control group comprised people who were processed through a traditional court but were offered community court participation.

Lee et al. (2013) focused on all cases processed within the community court during a specific time period for the treatment group, while the control group included all defendants arraigned on misdemeanor criminal charges in criminal or family court during the same timeframe. Nugent-Borakove (2009) employed a temporal dimension, assessing defendants who entered community court within a specified timeframe and collecting data from 18 months before and after the community court intervention. The control group for this study was drawn from defendants who were offered community court participation but did not engage, ensuring a meaningful comparison.

Dependent variables

The dependent variables used in community court evaluations exhibit a broad spectrum. Like other PSCs, recidivism was the main dependent variable in most community court evaluations. Grommon et al. (2017) focused on recidivism, defining it as an arrest for a new offense following the qualifying arrest and referral to the community court over 36 months. Lee et al. (2013) considered recidivism as any felony or misdemeanor arrest within their evaluation. Nugent-Borakove (2009) extended the definition of recidivism to encompass any new offense or re-offense before and after community court intervention.

Case processing efficiency was another common variable. Hakuta, Soroushian, and Kralistein (2008) compared the average number of days between initial arrest and case resolution. The restoration was also examined through community members' perceptions of crime rates, feelings of safety, satisfaction with the criminal justice system's handling of livability crime, and satisfaction with community service projects (Eckberg, 2001).

Furthermore, Eckberg (2001) explored information-related variables such as community knowledge about the court process, comfort levels with court proceedings, and satisfaction with the accessibility of social services. Proximity, measured as community satisfaction with the current community location, was also considered in Eckberg's (2001) evaluation.

Finally, sentencing outcomes were scrutinized in studies by Katz (2009) and Hakuta, Soroushian, and Kralistein (2008), encompassing alternative sanctions, jail sentences, and penalties. This diverse array of dependent variables underscores the multifaceted nature of community court evaluations, capturing both criminal justice metrics and community-centric perspectives.

Justice and psychology principles

Community courts show a much lower level of intensity when adapting and implementing justice and psychology principles compared to other PSCs. Common justice and psychology principles include TJ, PJ, RJ, adversarial process, community sentiment, and operant conditioning.

Global examination

Although limited in number, global evaluations of community courts often adopt site-specific assessments grounded in experimental designs, as noted by Slinger and Roesch (2010). In contrast, Ross et al. (2009) employed a non-treatment comparison group of 300 participants, emphasizing the integration of TJ, RJ, and PJ. This global perspective contributes to the broader understanding of community courts, emphasizing varied methodologies across geographical contexts.

Domestic violence courts

There is a limited number of evaluations on domestic violence courts, and overall findings are varied. Approximately 10 evaluations have been conducted globally on these courts. Their distinct creation processes pose a challenge in comparing evaluations.

Evaluation methods

Between the 10 evaluations that have been conducted on domestic violence courts five sets of methods have been used. The most common being quasi-experimental with a comparison group (Gover et al., 2007; Harrell et al., 2007) as well as mixed methods that included survey components (Keilitz, 2000; Labriola et al., 2009), and site visits (Labriola et al., 2009). Like many other PSC evaluations, some domestic violence court evaluations used secondary data analysis provided by the court (Newmark et al., 2004). Data collected from these domestic violence court evaluations would be considered not to meet the standard of the Maryland Scientific Methods Scale and qualify as low in rigor.

The sample size for these evaluations is widely varied, depending on the study. The largest sample included 1,368 cases (Harrell et al., 2007), while the smallest sample included 136 cases (Newmark et al., 2004). Many domestic violence court evaluations hovered in the middle, some with around 400 cases (Gover et al., 2003).

The selection of participants also varied depending on the methodology and chosen sample size. Some evaluations incorporated random sampling and matching (Gover et al., 2003), while others used availability samples (Harrell et al., 2007).

Dependent variables

Like many other PSCs, recidivism is the main dependent variable examined in domestic violence court evaluations. Gover et al. (2003) examined rearrests for domestic violence, simple assaults, or aggravated assaults, measuring incidents 18 months after the initial domestic violence arrest. Harrell et al. (2007) employed self-reports to capture new threats, intimidation, or violence, as well as any arrests during the year after disposition, with specific attention to the nature and frequency of domestic violence arrests and probation revocations. Newmark et al. (2004) considered probation violations and arrests as indicators of recidivism.

Other important dependent variables included the frequency of monthly domestic violence arrests, specifically in simple and aggravated assault cases (Grover et al., 2003). Victim and offender experiences with service and justice agencies form another critical dimension (Harrell et al., 2007). Offender accountability is gauged through the severity and certainty of consequences (Harrell et al., 2007), victim wellbeing as assessed through interviews (Harrell et al., 2007), and case outcomes and case processing (Newmark et al., 2004).

Justice and psychology principles

The justice and psychology principles used to evaluate domestic violence courts included PJ, RJ, adversarial processes, TJ, and operant conditioning.

Global examination

Two domestic violence evaluations have been conducted globally, both occurring in Canada—one evaluation used retrospective case analysis for a sample of 474 (Dawson & Dinovitzer, 2001). The dependent variables for this evaluation were the likelihood of prosecution and victim cooperation. The justice principle focused on restorative justice components for this study (Dawson & Dinovitzer, 2001).

The second evaluation conducted a pre-test–post-test evaluation examining domestic violence crime rates before and after the implementation of the domestic violence court (Tutty & Koshan, 2013). This study has been the largest domestic violence court evaluation conducted to date, with a sample of 6,407 (Tutty & Koshan, 2013). This evaluation's justice and psychology principles included TJ and RJ.

Comparatively, overlap exists between the US domestic violence court evaluations and the Canadian domestic violence court evaluations. There are similarities in methodological approach, dependent variables, and justice and psychology principles.

Human trafficking courts

With the first human trafficking court opening in 2013, there is not yet a breadth of information available to evaluate.

Evaluation methods

The primary evaluation for human trafficking courts examined one court throughout a five-year period, collecting quantitative data from an exhaustive case file review (Bath et al., 2020). Data was collected for 364 total cases and considered low in rigor. In addition to demographic information, this evaluation gathered data on involvement within the justice system and involvement with treatment agencies for all participants.

Dependent variables

Three dependent variables were used for this study, including identification of mental health and substance use, service linkage to mental health and substance use treatment, and stability indicators—the identification of mental health operationalized through mental health diagnoses and psychiatric evolutions. The identification of substance abuse was operationalized through self-report measures. The service linkage variable was operationalized as the number of victims in the human trafficking court connected with mental health services and substance use treatment. Stability indicators were categorized as child welfare contact, running away from home, and involvement in the justice system (Bath et al., 2020).

Justice and psychology principles

The justice and psychology principles evaluated for human trafficking courts included TJ, problem-solving principles, and RJ.

Global examination

To the best of our knowledge, no human trafficking courts outside of the United States have been evaluated yet.

Gambling courts

As of 2023, there have not been any systematic evaluations conducted on gambling courts. However, there have been examinations of the program effectiveness of the Nevada gambling program and the Australian gambling court.

Nevada's gambling program is currently in the developmental stages and manages a comparatively small caseload. Suggestions for improvement include screening protocols for gambling programs and attorney training for gambling-specific risks (Laux, 2019).

Global examination

The Australia Gambling Court was initiated in 2015 and underwent a review in 2019 to assess its effectiveness. Given the court's relatively recent establishment, there is limited available data for comprehensive evaluation. Nevertheless, the pilot phase of the gambling court received positive recognition from the South Australian Office for Problem Gambling, suggesting initial success (Adolphe et al., 2019). Although these courts are still in their early stages, the emerging findings indicate a positive trend.

Prostitution courts

Prostitution courts are a recent development in the United States, which has led to a lack of evaluations. Often, the components of prostitution courts are integrated into other PSCs as an extension of services. Consequently, while there might be limited dedicated evaluations of prostitution courts, segments of the program have probably been assessed within the context of broader PSC evaluations. Three evaluations have been completed evaluating prostitution courts.

Evaluation methods

Prostitution court evaluations employ various methods to assess their effectiveness. Two descriptive analyses focused on arrest and recidivism data concerning participants in these courts (Mueller, 2012; Sviridoff et al.,

2000). Additionally, one evaluation consisted of exploratory research, which involved comparing three groups in terms of recidivism (Miner-Romanoff, 2015). All people were eligible for the court, but only 64 participated. The remaining people underwent community supervision or received no intervention (Miner-Romanoff, 2015).

Notably, sample sizes vary across studies, with one comprising 131 participants, another involving 448, and a third comprising 344. Two of the studies specifically examine the recidivism rates of court participants within a designated time frame. At the same time, the third extends its analysis to encompass all eligible people for the program. These diverse approaches contribute to an understanding of the impact and outcomes associated with prostitution courts.

Dependent variables

In evaluating prostitution courts, various dependent variables are employed to assess the program's impact on participants. Recidivism is a key measure, defined as any new arrest occurring either during or after program participation. Program completion is another dependent variable, with completion status categorized based on whether participants successfully finished the program, were terminated, or were still actively engaged. Housing status is also considered, acting as an indicator of stable housing. Lastly, substance use is a significant variable measured in terms of the number of days participants remain sober. These dependent variables collectively provide a comprehensive framework for evaluating the effectiveness of prostitution courts, capturing elements related to legal outcomes, program engagement, housing stability, and substance use patterns among participants.

Justice and psychology principles

The justice and psychology principles evaluated for prosecution courts included TJ and key components of problem-solving.

Global examination

No prostitution courts have been adopted outside of the United States.

Veterans' treatment courts

A few evaluations have been done on veterans' treatment courts (VTCs) since their creation.

Evaluation methods

The most common method used in VTC evaluations was a pre–post comparison with no control group (Knudsen & Wingenfeld, 2016; Slattery et al., 2013; Smith, 2012; Tsai et al., 2018). Although most evaluations favored that approach, one evaluation was compared with a non-treatment control group (Hartley & Baldwin, 2019).

Most evaluations contained a sample smaller than 200 participants, although one evaluation had a sample of 7,931 veterans (Tsai et al., 2018). In terms of the sample selection, every evaluation examined all eligible participants. When a control group was included, it encompassed veterans eligible for PSC programming but chose not to participate (Hartley & Baldwin, 2016). Most of these studies would be considered low to moderate in rigor.

Dependent variables

The two most common dependent variables used were recidivism and treatment effectiveness. Recidivism was operationalized differently for each evaluation, ranging from any new arrest after participation begins (Hartley & Baldwin, 2016) to any new arrest during program participation or within one year after completion (Knudsen & Wingenfeld, 2014; Slattery et al., 2013; Smith, 2013), to any new incarceration while in program (Tsai et al., 2018).

Treatment effectiveness was operationalized similarly for all evaluations, capturing improved quality of life, psychiatric symptoms, and recovery. Some evaluations measured treatment effectiveness in intervals, such as before the program, six months post-program completion, and twelve months post-program completion (Knudsen & Wingenfeld, 2014; Slattery et al., 2013). Others measured only post-program completion, examining the status of housing, employment, and VA benefits to support treatment effectiveness (Tsai et al., 2018).

Justice and psychology principles

The justice and psychology principles evaluated for VTCs included the adversarial processes, TJ, PJ, problem-solving, and social support.

Global examination

VTCs have not been introduced globally so no comparisons can be made on evaluations.

Aboriginal courts

Recognizing the challenges and nuances associated with evaluating Aboriginal courts is essential, especially given their limited presence and the cultural aspects involved. Aboriginal courts are not widespread, and their implementation can vary significantly among Indigenous communities and regions.

Evaluation methods

Evaluating Aboriginal courts often involves assessing their impact from a cultural standpoint. These courts are designed to incorporate Indigenous cultural values, traditions, and practices into the justice system. The most prominent evaluation published on Aboriginal courts used a qualitative analysis methodology (Gant & Gabosky, 2000). The analysis comprised interviews with members of justice groups and community members. This included corrective staff, policing staff, community organizations, and associated staff. Police and community records were also examined as supplemental analysis.

Other, more detailed information about the evaluation methodology, such as sampling selection and follow-up, was not provided. According to the Maryland Scientific Methods Scale, this evaluation ranked a 2 in terms of rigor.

Dependent variables

The dependent variables of this study were diversion from the criminal justice system, sanctioning of anti-social behavior, resolving family disputes, and reducing levels of personal space and property crime (Gant & Gabosky, 2000). The variable of diversion from the criminal justice system was operationalized as a decline of rates in the number of juvenile charges after implementation of the court. The sanction of the anti-social behavior variable was operationalized as a decline in juvenile activity. The variable of resolving family disputes was operationalized as a decline in family disputes after court participation. Reducing personal space and property crime levels was operationalized as the perceived level of these types of crimes and measured through respondents' opinions of the court itself (Gant & Gabosky, 2000).

Justice and psychology principles

The justice and psychology principles evaluated for Aboriginal courts included TJ, community sentiment, and cultural consideration.

Global examination

Although Aboriginal courts exist in Canada, there are no evaluations of court success.

Child support courts

Similar to other smaller PSCs, there are few evaluations of child support court success.

Evaluation methods

One main evaluation has been conducted on child support courts; it employed a non-treatment comparison group methodology (Simpson, 2012). The study comprised one group of randomly selected participants participating in the child support court compared to one group of people eligible for child support court but electing not to participate.

The sample size was 63 participants, 31 in the treatment group and 32 in the comparison group. This evaluation is moderate in rigor.

Dependent variables

Two dependent variables were examined: collection of child support payments and jail time (Simpson, 2012). Child support payment collection was operationalized as the amount an individual owes before and after program admittance. Supplemental data was examined in the number of payments made in the six months before program participation and in the six months post-program participation (Simpson, 2012). Jail time was operationalized as the time spent in jail 12 months before and 12 months post-program participation.

Justice and psychology principles

The justice and psychology principles evaluated for child support courts included TJ, problem-solving principles, and operational conditioning.

Global examination

Child support courts themselves have not been introduced globally. However, Canada and many EU countries use operational conditioning components in their legal codes regarding child support, so there are some similarities.

Family dependency treatment courts

Since its establishment in 1995, numerous family dependency treatment court (FDTC) evaluations have consistently revealed positive outcomes.

Methods

A quasi-experimental methodology was the sole selection of evaluation methodology for FDTC. All current evaluations used a quasi-experimental approach, which consisted of two treatment groups and a TAU group (Ashford, 2004); outcomes for FDTC treatment compared to outcomes from non-FDTC treatment (Boles et al., 2007); nonequivalent control group design (Green et al., 2007); and non-randomized comparison group design matched on propensity score (Worcel et al., 2008).

The sample size varied from large to small based on the study, but no studies were in between. The largest sample sizes were 1,718 (Boles et al., 2007) and 1,220 (Worcel et al., 2008), with the smaller sample sizes being 120 (Ashford, 2004) and 100 (Green et al., 2009).

The selection of participants varied from study to study. Ashford (2004) collected data on all people referred to the court for experimental groups, using historical data collection and matching techniques for control groups. Boles et al. (2007) established a comparison group comprising families who entered the dependency system six months before the program's implementation. The treatment group, in contrast, consisted of families entering the dependency system and being mandated to receive program treatment. Worcel et al. (2008) also established a comparison group, which included eligible participants subjected to traditional case processing and a second comparison group from two matched comparison counties. The treatment group consists of all cases within the FDTC (Worcel et al., 2008). Green et al. (2009) focused on the primary parent, typically the mother, and all children within the study.

Dependent variables

The evaluation of FTDCs involves the consideration of various dependent variables that provide insights into their effectiveness in addressing the complex issues associated with families in the child welfare system. The most common dependent variables included recidivism, treatment status, treatment engagement, and child welfare outcomes.

Similar to other courts, recidivism is the most prevalent dependent variable measured. Some studies, such as Boles et al. (2007), examined recidivism and reentry. Recidivism was measured as the percentage of children returning to out-of-home care following a new allegation after the closure of their previous case. Reentry, on the other hand, refers to the percentage of children initially reunified with their families during the program but later returned to out-of-home care before the case was closed.

Another significant dependent variable is substance abuse/treatment status, drawing parallels with drug courts and DWI/DUI courts, as outlined by Ashford (2004). In this context, any substance use is categorized as "recidivism." Additionally, Boles et al. (2007) considered treatment completion as a marker of success, a perspective reiterated by Green et al. (2009), in which the successful completion of treatment is regarded as an important outcome.

Treatment engagement is assessed based on the metrics provided by Ashford (2004), which examines the number of family members entering treatment, those in residential treatment, and those completing treatment.

Child welfare outcomes are multifaceted, considering various dimensions. Boles et al. (2007) evaluated outcomes such as a child's return to parent(s) and permanency decisions regarding custody. Green et al. (2009) focused on the date a child is placed back into permanent placement and the reunification of at least one child with their original parent(s). Worcel et al. (2008) explore aspects such as out-of-home placement, the likelihood of spending time in such placement, the duration spent in out-of-home placement, the time taken for permanent placement, and the reunification with the original parent(s).

Justice and psychology principles

As FDTCs are comparable in structure and implementation to drug courts, both courts focus on similar underlying justice and psychology principles. The principles in FDTC evaluations included TJ, problem-solving principles, effective intervention, adversarial components, PJ, psychological/medical advancements to assist in the healing process of addiction, community sentiment, and operant conditioning.

Global examination

Although drug treatment courts have been implemented on a global scale, the need to treat family dependency has not been recognized globally.

Reentry courts

Reentry courts are one of the more recent PSCs, resulting in few effectiveness evaluations thus far.

Evaluation methods

Four major evaluations have been conducted on reentry courts. Three evaluations employed a quasi-experimental method (Hamilton, 2010; Rizzo, 2020; Taylor, 2017), while one used a randomized control trial supplemented with interviews (Ayoub & Pooler, 2015).

Each quasi-experimental study included a matched sample, either comparing the treatment group of reentry court participants to a matched sample of people in supervised release (Taylor, 2017), comparing the treatment group of reentry court participants to a matched sample of people under probation supervision (Rizzo, 2020) or comparing the treatment group of reentry court participants to a matched sample of traditionally supervised parolees (Hamilton, 2010). These evaluations would be considered moderately high in terms of rigor.

Sample sizes for the completed reentry court evaluations were congruent, ranging from 400 to 530, with one study housing a sample of roughly 950 participants. The population selection was also consistent, with all reentry court participants making up the treatment groups and matched comparisons from probation and parole making up the comparison groups.

Dependent variables

Recidivism was a dependent variable for all four evaluations of reentry court. Post-program employment status and educational attainment were supplemental dependent variables in some evaluations (Ayoub & Pooler, 2015; Rizzo, 2020; Taylor, 2017).

Operationalization of recidivism included a new arrest or supervision revocation within 18 months (Taylor, 2017), rearrest, reconviction, or parole revocation (Ayoub & Pooler, 2015), a new arrest within an 18–36-month period (Rizzo, 2020), and any rearrests, reconviction, or parole reconviction measured at one, two-, and three-years post-release (Hamilton, 2010).

Employment status and educational attainment were operationalized as any employment or educational attainment occurring within 18 months to three years post-release (Ayoub & Pooler, 2015; Rizzo, 2020; Taylor, 2017).

Justice and psychology principles
The justice and psychology principles evaluated for elder protection courts included TJ, PJ, and key components of problem-solving.

Global examination
Principles of reentry courts exist throughout EU countries and Canada, but a PSC system has not been devoted to reentry outside the United States.

Animal courts

There are no evaluations available for animal courts.

Gun courts

Limited attention has been devoted to evaluating gun courts' effectiveness and operational aspects, as noted by Nobles (2008). The bulk of insights regarding US-based gun courts stem from an evaluation conducted on the Juvenile Gun Court in Birmingham, Alabama, as documented by Wellford et al. (2004) and the Office of Juvenile Justice and Delinquency Prevention (2002).

Evaluation methods
The evaluation of gun courts employed a mixed-methods approach encompassing qualitative and quantitative analyses. Qualitative insights were gathered through interviews with the court's judges. These interviews aimed to capture nuanced perspectives on the program's functioning and effectiveness. The quantitative analysis involved an examination of overall crime trends, focusing specifically on juvenile gun charges and overall violent crime rates before and after the program's implementation. The quasi-experimental component of the evaluation assessed case processing records and recidivism rates for court participants and a control group. Although interviews were conducted voluntarily, the treatment group comprised all court participants within a specific timeframe, historically matched to pre-implementation cases.

However, the rigor of the evaluation was noted to be low to standard for all aspects. A limitation of this evaluation lies in the small sample size, with only three interviews conducted, and challenges in obtaining information on the quasi-experimental component, resulting in limited data availability.

Dependent variables

Various dependent variables are employed to comprehensively gauge the program's impact in evaluating gun courts. One significant aspect involves assessing participant perceptions of the program. Participants are asked to share their opinions, providing insights into whether they perceive any benefits, a deterrent effect, or overall changes in crime rates resulting from their involvement in the program. These subjective insights contribute valuable qualitative data to complement more quantitative measures. Recidivism is a key quantitative metric, defined within the evaluation as any new arrest or conviction among participants, providing a clear measure of the program's effectiveness in preventing repeat offenses. Additionally, the evaluation delves into societal impacts by examining overall crime trends. Specifically, analyzing juvenile gun charges and general crime rates both before and after the implementation of the gun court program, offering a comprehensive understanding of the program's effectiveness in influencing both individual behaviors and broader patterns of criminal activity.

Justice and psychology principles

The justice and psychology principles evaluated for gun courts included PJ and key components of problem-solving.

Global examination

Gun courts have not yet been implemented globally.

Homelessness courts

There are only two evaluations currently published examining the effectiveness of homelessness courts.

Evaluation methods

The evaluation of the homelessness court involves using both qualitative and quantitative methodologies to assess its impact on participants and its effectiveness in addressing issues related to homelessness. Two distinct approaches involving qualitative data analysis and experimental designs were used for homelessness court evaluations.

Although both evaluations (Buenaventura, 2018; Pennell & Kerry, 2001) used experimental design components and qualitative components, the outcomes measured differed. One study used experimental design to compare recidivism and arrest data between two groups: offenders who actively participated in the court and those who failed to appear. The treatment group comprised participants who attended court and participated within a specified timeframe. In contrast, the control group was composed of participants who failed to attend court, with a matching process applied to a group found in the service registry.

Another experimental design focused on housing outcomes, comparing all participants who partook in the court against those listed in the service registry during the same time period. The treatment group consisted of participants actively participating in the court and tracked for housing outcomes. The control group, in one instance, was composed of people matched from the service registry, while in the other, it included people who signed up for the court but did not attend. This design facilitates a thorough exploration of the court's effectiveness in improving housing stability for participants.

Both experimental designs boast substantial sample sizes in the 300s, enhancing the statistical robustness of the findings. Including a control group in each design, selected based on service registry information or non-attendance at court, strengthens the study's internal validity.

Dependent variables

Like most PSCs, recidivism was the main dependent variable measured in both studies. Both evaluations operationalized recidivism as rearrest (Buenaventura, 2018; Pennell & Kerry, 2001). Due to the nature of the court, a secondary variable that was also examined is housing outcomes. Housing outcomes were defined as the number of participants placed in transitional or permanent housing post-program involvement or law enforcement contact. Buenaventura (2018) considered the usage of housing services in addition to housing outcomes, framing the variables as the number of days using housing services before and post-enrollment in court.

Justice and psychology principles

The justice and psychology principles evaluated for homelessness courts included TJ, community sentiment, and key components of problem-solving.

Global examination

Although there is one diversionary program in Canada, there are no evaluations of court success.

US tribal courts

Two evaluations have been conducted on US tribal courts to date.

Methods

The evaluation of US tribal courts primarily used qualitative survey analysis in two separate studies. One study compared cases in nearby areas that did not participate in tribal courts, offering valuable insights into the court's unique impact. Interviews were a key component, involving stakeholders, community members, court actors, and court participants. In another approach, a non-treatment comparison group was established, collecting data, including recidivism information, and comparing it to similar cases in nearby counties. A descriptive analysis was undertaken in one study, gaining access to tribal court records and conducting a detailed examination of participant and case characteristics.

Despite the richness of insights garnered, sample sizes in these evaluations were small, ranging from 29 to just under 200 (Fortson & Carbaugh, 2014; Gross, 1999; Nesheim, 2010). Interviews were voluntary, ensuring participant willingness. For treatment groups, participants were drawn from all court participants within a specific timeframe. If a control group was involved, it was derived from similar case data in a neighboring county within the timeframe.

Dependent variables

In evaluating US tribal courts, several dependent variables were used to assess the court's impact and effectiveness comprehensively. Participant perceptions of fairness and "hozho," a Navajo term embodying balance, harmony, and beauty, serve as qualitative measures. Participants were asked to express whether they believe the court promotes these cultural ideals. Recidivism was a key quantitative variable, defined as any new arrest or criminal charge occurring within five years of post-court involvement. To capture diverse perspectives, stakeholder and participant perceptions were considered. Participants were asked about factors they perceive as effective in the court, areas that could be improved, and whether the court is the most suitable avenue to address the identified issues. Additionally, opinions on tribal youth crime, its changes over time, and perceived root causes provided valuable insights into the broader societal impact of the tribal court. This approach, combining cultural considerations, quantitative recidivism data, and stakeholder perspectives, offers a holistic evaluation of the tribal court's functioning and its role in addressing justice issues within the community.

Justice and psychology principles

The justice and psychology principles evaluated for US tribal courts included RJ and community sentiment.

Global examination

There are no evaluations to compare, as tribal courts are unique to US jurisdictions.

Elder protection courts

Chapter 2 notes that elder protection courts are not widespread, so this analysis has few evaluations to consider.

Evaluation methods

The most notable evaluation of elder protection courts used a mixed methods approach (Banks et al., 2014). This comprised qualitative interviews with court stakeholders and key informants and a document review of court case files to provide quantitative data. Sixty-eight case files were reviewed for quantitative data, which were all the cases from that court available for review. Each case file included relevant information and demographic characteristics of the victim and perpetrator.

Dependent variables

The dependent variables used in this evaluation included access to justice, victim safety and prevention of elder abuse, prosecution of elder abuse, case processing efficiency, assistance provided to victims, and case outcomes (Banks et al., 2014). Access to justice was operationalized as the number of elders who received easy access to criminal justice aid. Victim safety and prevention of elder abuse was operationalized as an effort taken to determine if abusive situations have desisted and/or if the perpetrator of abuse has been held accountable. Prosecution of elder abuse was operationalized as the number of elder abuse cases prosecuted in the county. Case processing efficiency was operationalized as the efficiency of processing elder protection court cases compared to traditional case processing. The final dependent variable, the assistance provided to victims and case outcomes, was operationalized as support provided to elders in criminal justice matters, such as help with filing a protection order, using testimony as evidence, restitution, issue of civil or criminal protective order (Banks et al., 2014).

Justice and psychology principles

The justice and psychology principles evaluated for elder protection courts included TJ and key components of problem-solving.

Global examination

Elder protection courts have not been implemented globally, so there are no evaluations to consider.

Discussion

Comparing PSC evaluations between the United States and other countries reveals commonalities and differences in the approaches, outcomes, and challenges these specialized judicial interventions face. US and global PSCs emphasize rehabilitation, reducing recidivism, and addressing the underlying issues contributing to criminal behavior. The goal is to break the cycle of recidivism through tailored interventions. PSCs in both settings often involve collaboration among stakeholders, including judges, prosecutors, defense attorneys, social services, and treatment providers. The multidisciplinary approach aims to provide comprehensive support to participants. US and global PSCs prioritize individualized approaches, recognizing that effective interventions must be tailored to each participant's unique needs and circumstances.

Some differences between US and global court evaluations included legal and cultural differences, such as adopting certain courts or including certain behaviors considered problematic. The types of offenses addressed by PSCs can vary. In the United States, these courts often focus on issues like drug addiction or mental health. In contrast, globally, PSCs might address a broader range of social issues, depending on local priorities. The policy and legal context surrounding PSCs and how they are evaluated can also differ significantly. Variations in legal systems, sentencing practices, and government priorities shape the landscape in which PSCs operate. Evaluation metrics and research focus might vary based on PSCs' regional goals and priorities. Cultural and legal nuances might lead to variations in measured outcomes and evaluation methodologies.

When deciding whom to include in the analysis of PSCs, compelling evidence suggests that it is crucial to assess outcomes for all participants, regardless of whether they completed the program. This approach aligns with an "intent-to-treat" analysis, which examines outcomes for all participants for whom the program is intended to provide treatment (as explained in the *Introductory Handbook for DWI Court Program*).

Regarding research rigor, some evaluations lacked sufficient methodological rigor to draw robust conclusions, primarily due to inadequate control groups (Wood et al., 2018). Numerous studies involved people who declined participation or were ineligible for the program. However, these people are likely to differ systematically from the experimental group on various factors, such as motivation, self-efficacy, and their perception of the seriousness of the problem (Mitchell et al., 2012).

Conclusion

The examination and evaluation of PSCs is critical for several reasons. It helps assess whether the PSCs accomplish their intended goals, identifies unintended consequences, and informs decisions about maintaining, expanding, or contracting these specialized courts. Determining whether specialty courts are more effective than traditional courts is paramount due to the potentially high costs associated with implementing PSCs and the possible disadvantages related to their specialized nature. Evaluations serve to gather empirical evidence to answer this fundamental question. Furthermore, evaluations offer insights into whether a program needs to adapt its structure or methods to enhance effectiveness and optimize resource use. Suppose the evaluations indicate that a court successfully achieves its objectives. In that case, it provides a compelling case for maintaining and expanding the reach of that court to serve more people and communities effectively. Chapter 6 will highlight the effectiveness component of PSC evaluations, comparing what makes programs more or less effective.

6

Effectiveness of Problem-Solving Courts

Mia A. Holbrook and Mary Dhondt

What Do Problem-Solving Court Evaluations Tell Us?

Chapter 5 discussed the methodology used in evaluations of problem-solving courts (PSCs). This chapter will expand on this by addressing whether evaluations have revealed if the PSCs are effective. Considering the 18 types of courts first discussed in Chapter 2, this chapter assesses whether the scientific evaluations suggest that the courts are successful. This chapter will examine evaluations of the most common 18 types of PSCs: drug courts, DWI/DUI courts, mental health courts (MHCs), community courts, domestic violence courts, human trafficking courts, gambling courts, prostitution courts, veterans' treatment courts (VTCs), Aboriginal courts, child support courts, family dependency treatment courts, reentry courts, animal courts, gun courts, homelessness courts, US tribal courts, and elder protection courts. Each court section will include a thorough assessment of completed evaluations, considering the methods and findings of each evaluation.

A significant component of the science behind PSCs is the evaluations used to determine their effectiveness. Evaluations of PSCs typically involve measuring outcomes related to participant behavior, such as substance abuse, mental health, employment, housing stability, and criminal justice involvement. Depending on the research question and available resources, evaluations can use various methods, such as randomized controlled trials, quasi-experimental designs, and process evaluations (see Chapter 5). The results of evaluations assist in making evidence-based decisions regarding the implementation and expansion of PSCs. This chapter will highlight the similarities and differences in evaluating PSCs and discuss why some courts might be more successful.

Society, Science, and Problem-Solving Courts. Monica K. Miller, Mia A. Holbrook, Logan A. Yelderman, and Kylie Kulak, Oxford University Press. © Oxford University Press 2025. DOI: 10.1093/oso/9780190059804.003.0006

Drug court evaluations

Due to their popularity and scope, drug courts are among the most heavily researched and evaluated PSCs. The community-based, problem-solving nature of drug courts and therapeutic justice has prompted widespread support and political popularity throughout the United States. Overall, adult drug court participants show lower recidivism rates than non-participants, supporting the conclusion that drug courts reduce recidivism (Mitchell et al., 2012). Reported drug use and criminal activity are "relatively reduced" during program participation, but long-term effects are less clear, with an average of 47% of drug court participants reaching program completion (Belenko, 2001). Overall, drug court participants are less likely to re-offend than those who proceed through a traditional court setting, especially participants who complete the program (Wilson et al., 2006).

Program completion is essential because it provides positive outcomes in long-term behavioral changes (Lowenkamp et al., 2005). For example, when evaluating drug court participants against non-drug court participants, 20% of graduating participants recidivated compared to 51% of the comparative population that received traditional treatment (Wolfe et al., 2002). Additionally, most drug courts provide long-term treatment to participants with histories of drug use, contact with the criminal justice system, and previous treatment failures (Jensen & Mosher, 2006). Most scientific evaluations support the idea that drug courts assist in reducing recidivism.

DWI/DUI court evaluations

Evaluations generally support the effectiveness of DWI/DUI courts. DWI/DUI courts are based on the proven drug court model, effectively reducing recidivism and addiction (Wallace, 2011). The outcomes of DWI/DUI courts are not statistically different from traditional courts (Bouffard & Richardson, 2007; Franklin, 2010). In identifying 28 evaluations of DWI/DUI courts, a large majority (85%) supported their effectiveness (Mitchell et al., 2012).

DWI/DUI court participants are less likely to recidivate than those who do not participate in treatment (Carey et al., 2008). Participants also show fewer reconvictions than members of control groups in multiple evaluations (Breckenridge et al., 2000; Carey et al., 2015; Hiller et al., 2010). DWI/DUI recidivism and general recidivism are reduced by an average of more than 12%, with some courts reducing recidivism rates by 50–60% (Mitchell et al., 2012). The percentage of court participants who test positive for drugs and alcohol also significantly decreases over time (Carey et al., 2015).

Reductions in recidivism and drug use greatly benefit public health, safety, and economics. For example, DWI/DUI courts produced an average net cost savings of $1,505 per participant and $5,436 savings per graduate, primarily due to lowered recidivism rates (Mackin et al., 2009). In addition, even though DWI/DUI courts provide more intensive and expensive treatment services than traditional courts, they cost less to administer due to a shorter period of supervision (Wallace, 2011). Most scientific evaluations of DWI/DUI courts suggest they effectively reduce recidivism and save money.

Mental health court evaluations

Overall, evaluations of mental health courts (MHCs) show positive effects on recidivism and promote treating mental health issues. For example, people in MHCs tend to have lower rates of new charges while under court supervision (Almquist & Dodd, 2009). In addition, participants in MHCs show reduced recidivism, are less likely to be arrested on new charges, and have fewer bookings into jail than people who show mental health issues that go through a traditional court setting (Cosden et al., 2005; McNiel & Binder, 2007; Moore & Hiday, 2006; Trupin et al., 2001).

MHCs link people with treatment services more effectively than traditional court systems (Almquist & Dodd, 2009). MHCs increase participants' access to treatment services; court participants who complete the program are more likely to continue treatment after completion (Boothroyd et al., 2005). Participants report improved independent functioning, less distress, decreased substance use, and improved life satisfaction compared to those who went through a traditional court (Cosden et al., 2005). Participants in MHCs also report having a more favorable view of the justice system and believe they received fair treatment (Cosden et al., 2005).

MHCs have the potential to lead to long-term cost savings through success in lower recidivism rates and the associated costs of charging, incarcerating, and hospitalizing inmates who have mental illnesses (Almquist & Dodd, 2009). In addition, it is worth noting that MHCs do not substantially increase costs, at least in the short term (Ridgel et al., 2007). In sum, the evaluations of MHCs promote that they are effective in reducing recidivism, promoting mental health treatment, and reducing the costs of incarceration.

Community court evaluations

Although community courts have had strides in their creation and implementation, evaluations of their effectiveness provide mixed results (Grommon et al., 2017). Community courts relate to reductions in arrests and motor vehicle theft, residential and commercial burglaries, and illegal vending in prostitution (Ross et al., 2009; Sviridoff et al., 2002). Felony and misdemeanor arrests in neighborhoods adjacent to a community court area have had similar reductions (Lee et al., 2013). Evaluation results regarding individual outcomes are mixed as well. For example, Red Hook Community Court showed slight recidivism reductions two years post-arrest. However, recidivism outcomes after one year were not statistically significant (Lee et al., 2013). Seattle Community Court showed no differences in recidivism after 18 months of admission (Nugent-Borakove, 2009).

The evidence suggests that the Midtown Community Court has largely succeeded in its mission; local crime was reduced by as much as 56% in the case of prostitution, and thousands of hours of community service work is being performed in the Midtown neighborhood each year (Sviridoff et al., 2000). Like Midtown, Red Hook Community Court also proved successful by reducing incarceration, improving compliance with community service mandates, and garnering high opinions from residents (Berman et al., 2003).

A lack of a specific target population or underlying criminogenic factors could be to blame for mixed results (Mitchell et al., 2012; Sarteschi et al., 2011). The underlying issues are quality-of-life offenses that affect the community rather than a specific issue concerning the participants, which could, in turn, dilute the anticipated effect of the model (Ammann, 2000). However, community courts have improved in many areas over the years, including the timeline of case processing (Lee et al., 2013), increased community service completion rates (Sviridoff et al., 2000; Weidner & Davis, 2000), reduced use of the time served and jail sentences (Hakuta et al., 2008; Lee et al., 2013), and substantial cost savings for local government offices (Lee et al., 2013; Nugent-Borakove, 2009). Although the Midtown and Red Hook community courts have shown positive effects in reducing local crime and incarceration, evaluations of other courts have shown mixed results.

Domestic violence court evaluations

Evaluations of domestic violence courts are scarce and show mixed results overall. Roughly 10 evaluations have been completed on domestic violence courts across the world. Unlike other PSCs, these courts are created differently, which makes evaluations challenging to compare. Some courts show no significant differences in the re-arrest rates between domestic violence court participants and non-court participants but have reports of a high level of safety and well-being among victims (Harrell et al., 2007). Other courts show that domestic violence court participants are less likely to be re-arrested for domestic violence than those who go through traditional courts (Harrell et al., 2007).

Evaluations of international domestic violence courts also vary. For example, domestic violence courts in Canada show increased victim cooperation in using domestic violence courts (Dawson & Dinovitzer, 2001; Tutty & Koshan, 2013). Domestic violence courts in the United Kingdom show reduced recidivism rates for domestic court participants in Cardiff and Wolverhampton courts. In contrast, the West London court showed decreased case processing time. Although there are few evaluations of domestic violence courts, reviews of their effectiveness are mixed; however, some evaluations show positive outcomes in recidivism, victim compliance, and overall victim advocacy.

Human trafficking court evaluations

Overall, evaluations of human trafficking courts show positive results. Involvement in human trafficking courts for US youth impacted by commercial sexual exploitation suggests an increase in the identification of mental health struggles, substance use needs, and linkages and referrals to mental health and substance use treatment services (Bath et al., 2020). Further, it is suggested that there was an increased stabilization, indicated by decreased substantiated child welfare allegations, fewer running away episodes, and fewer placements and criminal involvement (Bath et al., 2020).

Human trafficking courts have been criticized for treating commercial sex involvement as a behavioral problem or addiction and placing primary emphasis on treating underlying trauma and substance use problems (Kendis,

2019). Human trafficking courts currently fail to address structural barriers to well-being, which often underlie commercial sex involvement (Kendis, 2019). Such obstacles might include housing, gender identity discrimination, immigration concerns, and economic insecurity. Kendis (2019) finds that the effectiveness of these courts is directly tied to the available resources in the surrounding area and funding to ensure participants have access to the resources they need, including culturally competent services to participants, which has proven to be challenging for some programs. Although evaluations of human trafficking courts show increased care for mental health and substance use issues and stabilization, there is still room for improvement in addressing victims' well-being.

Gambling court evaluations

As of 2023, no systematic evaluations have been conducted on gambling courts. However, the Nevada gambling program and the Australian gambling court have been examined regarding program effectiveness. As these courts are relatively new and small, both assessments are considered effective in serving the intended population (Adolphe et al., 2019; Laux, 2019).

Nevada's gambling program is still building and maintains a relatively small caseload (Laux, 2019). However, suggestions for improvement include increasing attorney awareness of gambling addiction diversion and implementing a gambling problem screening protocol for all defendants (Laux, 2019).

First launched in 2015, the Australia Gambling Court was reviewed in 2019 to ensure service effectiveness. As the gambling court is still relatively new, there is not much data to evaluate as of yet. However, the pilot of the gambling court was regarded as a success by the South Australian Office for Problem Gambling (Adolphe et al., 2019). Although these courts are still reasonably new, findings are skewing positive.

Prostitution court evaluations

Prosecution courts are relatively new within the United States, which lends to a lack of completed evaluations. Many times, prostitution courts are housed in other PSCs as an extension of services, so it is likely that though there are not many evaluations of prostitution courts, the program itself has been evaluated before.

The Chicago Coalition for the Homeless highlighted the work of a handful of PSCs or programs across the United States that addressed prostitution (Mueller, 2012). Recommendations that followed focused on improving the court process, eligibility, and identification of victims, services, and safety for participants (Mueller, 2012). Other PSCs that have prostitution programs existing within them that have been previously evaluated include the Services to Access Resources and Safety (STARS) program housed within the Midtown Community Court (Schweig et al., 2012). When focusing on prostitution-related cases, the STARS program evaluation has shown effectiveness; local crime relating to prostitution was reduced by as much as 56% (Sviridoff et al., 2000). Overall, the program also proved successful by reducing incarceration, improving compliance with community service mandates, and garnering high opinions from residents (Berman et al., 2000).

Similarly positive results were also found in an evaluation of the Changing Actions to Change Habits (CATCH) specialized docket in Franklin County, Columbus, Ohio. Participants who completed the program experienced reduced drug additions, strengthened relationships, and reduced recidivism rates (Miner-Romanoff, 2015).

Veterans' treatment court evaluations

There needs to be a more comprehensive analysis of VTC outcomes and their effect on outcomes such as recidivism, housing, employment, and health, which are mixed (Tsai et al., 2018). A large amount of research supports that VTCs are successful in lowering recidivism rates (Hartley & Baldwin, 2019), providing better housing and employment outcomes (Tsai et al., 2018), and improving mental health (Knudsen & Wingenfeld, 2016). Veterans who participate in and complete VTC programs show consistently lower rates of recidivism than people who are processed in a traditional court. (Hartley & Baldwin, 2016). Participants often had better employment and housing outcomes than veterans who had not participated in the program (Tsai et al., 2018). VTCs can also improve mental health, overall functioning, and social connectedness (Knudsen & Wingenfeld, 2016).

VTC participants had positive outcomes in recidivism, housing, employment, and veterans administration (VA) benefits (Tsai et al., 2018).

Approximately 14% of program participants re-offended during their time, which is lower than the 23–46% average one-year recidivism rate in the traditional court system (Tsai et al., 2018). Court participants have also shown increased rates in housing and VA benefits (Tsai et al., 2018).

Participants with past incarcerations, unaddressed substance abuse problems, property offenses, or probation/parole violations were at higher risk for new incarcerations (Tsai et al., 2018). Typically, there is no change in employment from program admission to exit. These results show a potential need for more rigorous treatment in VTCs and more in-depth targeting of homelessness and substantial employment issues among veterans (Tsai et al., 2018). However, most VTCs positively affect recidivism, housing, and employment.

Aboriginal court evaluations

Evaluations and opinions toward Aboriginal courts vary. Although the movement toward including Indigenous populations is viewed positively by many, there is criticism over the overall development. Notably, the most significant criticism is that Aboriginal courts represent a continual practice of colonizing Indigenous traditions. For example, the practice of Aboriginal courts is viewed similarly to taking "Native Police" officers from a different geographical area to police Indigenous communities during the colonial period (Cunneen, 2001). However, the difference between the two is that in modern times, court members are members of the communities and share kinship and identity with the population ultimately being tried in the court (Marchetti & Daly, 2004).

Another area of concern is that of a "hybridized system" (VDOJ, 2002). Aboriginal courts can only process and represent the Indigenous systems of laws, so there is a natural conflict in managing differing loyalties (VDOJ, 2002). The role of "elders" has been strongly endorsed by Indigenous actors within the justice system. However, the difficulties of finding appropriate people who fit within this category can prove to be one major roadblock (VDOJ, 2002).

The development and improvement of Aboriginal courts in Queensland, Australia, showed effective outcomes in combating high levels of personal and property crime and providing re-empowerment to Aboriginal communities (Gant & Grabosky, 2000). Implementing these courts has opened the flow of conversation between state governments and Indigenous communities (Gant & Grabosky, 2000). However, although Aboriginal courts have shown positive outcomes in reducing crime rates and incorporating Indigenous culture into justice proceedings, many argue that separating Aboriginal communities from traditional justice has adverse effects.

Child support court evaluations

There are few empirical evaluations of child support courts. However, some assumptions can be made about their success, primarily concerning participants who complete the program (Simpson, 2012). For custodial parents (CPs), successful participation results in consistent child support payments. For non-compliant parents (NCPs), an opportunity to be involved in their child's life and escape the cycle of imprisonment is presented as an alternative to incarceration. Most importantly, children receive financial and emotional support from two parties (Simpson, 2012). In an analysis of child support courts in the US state of Georgia, researchers found that as NCPs progressed through the program, they showed improvements in attitude, increased connections with court programs, and increased child support payments (Simpson, 2012).

However, not all people can complete the program. This could be due to the social services not correctly meeting the population's needs, the program's rigorousness, or a family structure that is "too broken" to fix (Simpson, 2012). Multiple courts reported that untreated substance abuse was an issue for multiple participants (Lee, 2012). In sum, although not all child support court participants complete the program, it can be assumed that participants who complete child support programs see positive outcomes.

Family dependency treatment court evaluations

Since its creation in 1995, multiple family dependency treatment courts (FDTCs) have been evaluated, and these evaluations have shown positive results overall. FDTCs provide significantly better outcomes when compared to traditional family reunification services, including a more extended stay in treatment and higher rates of parental participation and family reunification (Marlowe & Carey, 2012). FDTC models also have the potential to improve short-term treatment outcomes among caregivers with substance abuse problems (Ashford, 2004; Boles et al., 2007; Green et al., 2007; Worcel et al., 2008). These courts also show greater overall engagement in treatment participation, retention of the program, satisfaction with services, improved clinical/social functioning, and more successful family reunification than traditional courts (Boles et al., 2007; Green et al., 2009). Families in FDTCs were found to be twice as likely to achieve family reunification than non-FDTC families (Lloyd, 2015; Zhang et al., 2019). However, family reunification is only one of the multiple permanent placement options for children; between 16% and 24% do not achieve permanent placement (Bruns et al., 2012). Participation in an FDTC shows a positive effect on family reunification and re-entry into care; families who participated in the court were much more likely to be reunited with one another and were less likely to re-enter care one year after program completion in comparison to families who did not participate (Chuang et al., 2012).

Due to the high volume of families impacted by substance abuse, FDTCs serve only 7–10% of families involved in the child welfare system (Young & Marlowe, 2014). It also can take families over four months to enter a program, contributing to the system becoming overburdened and families not receiving timely treatment (Brook et al., 2015; Bruns et al., 2012). However, although their impact is shortened by the sheer volume of families affected by substance abuse, FDTCs show many positive outcomes, primarily in family reunification.

Reentry court evaluations

As reentry courts appeared less than two decades ago, there is limited research on evaluations of effectiveness (Rizzo, 2020). Because reentry courts monitor participants closely, research suggests that there should be an increased report of violations due to the supervision effect (Albonetti & Hepburn, 1997). However, it is worth noting that reentry court participants might also be given more leniency. Because the judge can exercise discretion on the implications of unlawful behavior, this could counter the supervision effect (Taylor, 2017). Overall, the supervision effect differs in the measure of recidivism used (Hamilton, 2010).

Some evaluations suggest that participation in reentry reduces recidivism rates, particularly after successful completion of the court (Ayoub & Pooler,

2015; Taylor, 2017). It is suggested that reentry court participants were significantly less likely to have their supervision revoked and that those who graduated from the court were significantly less likely to be re-arrested than the comparison group from a traditional court (Taylor, 2017). Regardless of graduation status, participants predicted higher employment rates and less frequent supervision revocation (Taylor, 2017). This finding is consistent in other evaluations, with graduation from the court ultimately linked to a long-term reduction in recidivism (Rizzo, 2020). Reentry court parolees (both those who graduated and those who did not) were less likely to be arrested; parolees were less likely to be reconvicted, which was significant after one-, two-, and three-years post-participation; and those who completed the program experienced lower rates of re-arrest and revocation (Hamilton, 2010).

Significant issues identified to improve reentry courts include identifying and incorporating evidence-based practices, improving the use of sanctions and incentives, strengthening recruitment training of people who work in reentry courts, and cultivating greater community and system support (Wolf, 2011). Although there are areas for improvement, reentry courts show positive outcomes in reducing recidivism and promoting law-abiding behavior.

Animal court evaluations

There is no evidence of program evaluations that have been conducted and no mention of recidivism rates.

Gun court evaluations

Few evaluations address gun courts' effectiveness and operations direction (Nobles, 2008). Most knowledge from US-based courts comes from an evaluation of the Juvenile Gun Court in Birmingham, Alabama (Office of Juvenile Justice and Delinquency Prevention, 2002; Wellford et al., 2004). Although the court saw an increase in gun-related cases in its first year, gun-related crimes have decreased since then; 1996/1997 and 1997/1998 saw a 38.7% reduction in juvenile gun-related crimes (Wellford et al., 2004). There was also a reduction in recidivism rates, with participants in the gun court showing lower rates of re-offending than people who participated in a traditional court (Wellford et al., 2004). Although evaluations of gun courts are scarce, they generally show positive effects on gun-related crimes and recidivism rates.

Homelessness court evaluations

There are minimal evaluations published examining the effectiveness of homelessness courts. Within the body of limited research, findings show that homelessness courts are most effective with stable community partnerships (Hennick, 2017). These relationships allow more opportunities for success for participants (Hennick, 2017). Echoing results from other PSC evaluations, participants who successfully graduated from the homelessness court program experienced a significant increase in their abilities to sustain permanent housing successfully (Buenaventura, 2018). These results rang true for up to two years following the completion of the homelessness court program (Buenaventura, 2018). Although there are not many evaluations to consider, the ones completed in homelessness courts generally portray a positive outcome for graduated participants.

US tribal court evaluations

There is little research on the effects of tribal courts on delinquency among American Indians. Of the limited available research, it is hypothesized that tribal courts are more effective than traditional courts when dealing with crimes committed in American Indian communities (Fortson & Carbaugh, 2014). Court participants express more significant feelings of fairness, higher levels of settlement, and overall more satisfaction with the Navajo Family Court than participants surveyed in a traditional family court (Gross, 1999). However, the long-term recidivism rate of court participants is not statistically different from that of people processed through a state court system (Nesheim, 2010). Most tribal courts are viewed positively for recognizing tribal justice in conjunction with state and federal law.

Elder protection court evaluations

Because elder protection courts are not widespread, very few evaluations of their success exist. However, Judge Conger notes many positive outcomes stemming from the Alameda County court. These included early and efficient resolution of matters, reduction of recidivism, and greater compliance with monetary restitution/treatment programs (when applicable). The court also showed effective collaboration between agencies, improved addressing underlying issues such as substance abuse or mental illness, and provided a supportive environment to elderly victims through trained judges and court personnel that addressed their specialized needs (Banks et al., 2014).

Elder courts are positioned to create programs that educate court actors and the general population on the rights and remedies for elder abuse (Banks et al., 2014). Consolidating ancillary cases involving the same victim creates a consistent and therapeutic outcome for all parties involved. Elder protection courts also encourage the development of precedent-setting elder law cases and the recognition of the physical, sensory, and mental/cognitive changes that can be present in the elderly population (Banks et al., 2014). Overall, elder protection courts show positive outcomes in the resolution and court proceedings of elder abuse cases and provide support for elderly victims.

Similarities and Differences among Problem-Solving Court Evaluations

The evaluation of PSCs will vary depending on the type of court being evaluated and the specific goals and outcomes being assessed. This chapter examined the evaluations conducted on 18 different types of PSCs. Through this analysis, some similarities were present in most evaluations, and some differences were defined between evaluations.

Each PSC type has unique goals, strategies, and outcomes, which will dictate the necessary evaluation methods. However, because many PSCs have overlapping approaches and intended objectives, many evaluations use similar criteria. The most common similarities in PSC evaluations include measuring recidivism, assessing participants' satisfaction, gauging the impact on the local community, and examining cost–benefits concerning effectiveness. Reducing recidivism is a common component of every PSC, so every evaluation must consider recidivism when examining the court's effectiveness. Similarly, PSCs are often voluntary programs, so it is crucial to assess participants' satisfaction when evaluating these programs. Nearly every court evaluation discussed in this chapter included one or all of these concepts in their study. Although there are many similarities in evaluations, there are also many differences.

Because each type of PSC has unique goals, there are also many differences in the various PSC evaluations. These differences include the evaluation methods, the outcome measures in addition to recidivism, and the contextual factors in the evaluation analysis. The evaluations examined for this chapter covered quantitative and qualitative methods, often decided by the resources and time available. Outcomes measured were another difference within the various PSC evaluations; different courts have different goals, so the outcomes measured will often be distinctive. For example, drug court outcomes measuring effectiveness will considerably differ from child support court outcomes measuring effectiveness. Although there might be differences in the evaluation of PSCs, all evaluations aim to determine the effectiveness and success of these courts.

Comparing the evaluations of different types of PSCs can provide insights into their relative effectiveness and inform the development of best practices. However, it is essential to note that evaluating PSCs is complex and requires consideration of multiple factors, including the unique characteristics of the court, the population it serves, and the local context.

Conclusion

A significant component of the science behind PSCs is the evaluations used to determine their effectiveness. As detailed in this chapter, some courts (e.g., drug courts) have an abundance of evaluations, while others have very minimal evaluations (e.g., homelessness courts). One court, animal courts, has no record of any evaluation conducted as of yet. Evaluations are used to determine the effectiveness of PSCs in achieving their goals, such as reducing recidivism rates, improving participant well-being, and enhancing public safety. Evaluations are also used to identify improvement areas and inform policy decisions related to PSCs. For example, if evaluations show that a PSC effectively reduces recidivism rates among a specific population, policymakers might decide to expand the program to serve more people. Alternatively, if evaluations show that a PSC is ineffective, policymakers might discontinue the program or make changes to improve its effectiveness. The science behind these evaluations is crucial to expanding successful PSCs and discontinuing unsuccessful PSCs.

Various evaluation methods and measures have been used to assess the effectiveness and success of PSCs. However, there are still many courts with minimal evaluations. Overall, evaluations are a critical component of the science behind PSCs because they provide evidence-based information on the effectiveness of these programs.

SECTION 3

SOCIETY AND PROBLEM-SOLVING COURTS

7

When Law and Culture Collide

Law and Culture's Symbiotic Relationship

The previous chapter evaluated the success of problem-solving courts (PSCs) through a scientific lens, providing insight as to why certain PSCs have retained success. This current chapter begins a new section in this book, *society and law*. Here, we discuss a major feature of society—culture—and how culture can have a discordant relationship with the law. The consequences of this relationship can impact society's relationship with the law, particularly how members of society interact with the law. When culture and law are not harmonious, an interaction with the law might result in unfortunate consequences.

As law and culture are usually considered distinct concepts, we will begin by discussing the definition of culture, particularly the lack of agreement regarding a definition. As culture is unbounded and intricate, often those who share cultures and meaning systems find themselves in conflicts and confusion regarding the proper way to follow the stipulations of said culture. The lack of coherence in a definition of culture and, ostensibly, subcultures can be a product of law. Law defines the differences regarding assigned meanings (culture) and incoherence regarding that given meaning, but law can also produce and influence culture itself.

After elaborating on the relationship between culture and law, we will illustrate cultural differences apparent in cultures and subcultures that could affect the likelihood of a person interacting with the justice system and the subsequent outcomes of that interaction. We will consider tightness–looseness theory (Gelfand et al., 2006; Harrington & Gelfand, 2014); that is, the notion that certain cultures tolerate deviance less and enforce stronger social norms compared to others. We will also consider cultural differences in light of incremental versus entity views, such that people in some cultures believe that they (as individual people) are malleable and flexible, but their environments are stable compared to believing they themselves are stable, but their environments are malleable and flexible. Therefore, cultures that

Society, Science, and Problem-Solving Courts. Monica K. Miller, Mia A. Holbrook, Logan A. Yelderman, and Kylie Kulak, Oxford University Press. © Oxford University Press 2025. DOI: 10.1093/oso/9780190059804.003.0007

hold an incremental view of themselves will be more likely to reform after a crime (believing they can change themselves), whereas those from consistent cultures would believe that who they are is unchanging.

With the established theoretical background, we will identify and discuss some subcultural phenomena, such as cultures of honor, urban survival syndrome, black rage, hate crimes, and individual demographic differences that might play a role in the relationship between culture and law. We will then tie in the discussed theories and subcultural phenomena with some real-world cases in which culture and law were at odds. After providing some real case examples, we will discuss how these cultural differences and subcultural practices can have implications for the legal system. Specifically, we will discuss how these differences can make a person more likely to interact with the legal system, affect the court process, and, ultimately, affect judicial decision-making. Implications for judges are discussed at the end of this chapter.

Defining Culture and Law

The law and culture are seemingly simple concepts that, under the surface, are more complicated to define (see generally, Miller et al., 2020). Law, in its most basic form, can be generally defined as a set of formal rules and regulations enacted by judicial decisions and constitution. Culture's meaning is highly contested, but it can be generally defined as a set of shared meanings, symbols, or practices. The contested meaning arises from the fact that, although there are shared meanings, symbols, and practices, culture is simultaneously always in flux—challenging and contradicting what is normally considered a coherent, bounded culture.

Law and culture are often posited as separate realms, with law being considered irrelevant or minimal to culture, and culture considered peripherally to legal questions (Mezey, 2001). Instead, law and culture are in a symbiotic relationship with one another. Culture produces the law people follow; law produces cultures centered around those laws. In other words, law participates in the formation of culture and simultaneously is a product of a culture (Mezey, 2001). To illustrate this point, consider the court case *Roe v Wade* (1973). Not only has this case (and its later reversal) had an impact on the legality of abortions, but it has affected cultural practices in the speech, media, and meanings of abortions and reproductive health (Lempinen & Brice, 2022). Thus, culture and law are products of one another.

Theories of Culture and Law

In the field of cultural psychology, two methodological approaches are most often used for researching and theorizing about culture. One approach posits that the investigation should center around one culture, such that the investigation should focus on understanding one culture's unique factors by the definitions of that culture. The alternative approach opts for understanding a culture through its underlying differences with other cultures. Here, we are going to use the second approach, using theories to discover underlying differences amongst cultures to better understand those cultures.

Tightness–looseness

Tightness–looseness is one theoretical distinction used to understand various cultures (Harrington & Gelfand, 2014). This section discusses this theory in general, and then as applied to PSCs.

Tightness–looseness in general

Particularly, the distinction between tightness and looseness describes how punitive a society/social system will be in terms of punishment versus permissiveness. Tight societies (e.g., China, South Korea, Singapore) have stricter rules, more social order, more coordination, and less tolerance for deviant behavior than loose societies. Loose societies (e.g., the United States, Spain, Brazil) have significantly more tolerance for deviant behavior, being characterized by openness and the promotion of creativity, less order, and less coordination (Gelfand et al., 2006; Harrington & Gelfand, 2014).

Tight societies are more likely to be characterized by order; authoritarian governments; higher population densities; fewer natural resources; and more incidences of ecological, territorial, and historical threats. These societies have fewer civil liberties and more restrictions regarding media in comparison to loose societies. The threats tight societies face are posited to explain why these societies heavily sanction deviant behavior and develop strong social norms, due to their history of threats (Gelfand et al., 2006; Harrington & Gelfand, 2014). Threats include instances of conflict or ecological threats (e.g., hurricanes, tornados, droughts). These sanctions and norms aid in the survival of the citizens through coordinated social action. In contrast, loose societies have fewer ecological and historical threats and can "afford" more deviant actions.

Research from the United States suggests that states that were identified as tight (e.g., Mississippi, Alabama, Arkansas) were associated with a history of ecological threats, such as a higher incidence of natural disasters and fewer natural resources in comparison to loose states. Tight states had reportedly higher incarceration and discrimination rates, but lower social disorganization and lower rates of homelessness and alcohol and drug abuse compared to loose states. Tight states also had lower rates of trait openness, creativity, and overall happiness in contrast to loose states (Harrington & Gelfand, 2014). Tightness–looseness in the United States, in particular, could also be related to subcultures. The United States overall is deemed loose despite having some of the highest incarceration rates in the world (Widra & Herring, 2021); subcultures might explain why some states are considered loose whereas others are considered tight. For example, states that are considered tight are often states that have "cultures of honor," which will be discussed later in this chapter.

Tightness–looseness applied to problem-solving courts

Tight cultures, at first glance, seem to have a clearer relationship with law compared to loose cultures and subcultures. However, if tight states possess higher incarceration rates compared to loose states, perhaps some tolerance for deviation and room for creativity could aid certain states to lessening those rates. If culture is paradoxically coherent and in flux, loose cultures might permit the relationship between culture and law to be symbiotic, reproducing one another as they are intended. Thus, loose cultures might promote and find more efficacy with PSCs because of their endorsement of creativity and leniency toward deviancy. In contrast, tight states might be opposed to PSCs altogether because those states believe a violation of the social order is beyond rehabilitation. The former statements are hypotheses yet to be tested.

Incremental versus entity selves

Another theory from cultural research that can offer insight into the discordant relationship between culture and law is incremental versus entity selves. This section discusses this theory in general, and then as applied to PSCs.

Incremental versus entity selves in general

This perspective posits that people who hold entity perspectives believe that people hold fixed dispositions, reasonably assuming that other's behaviors can be assigned to these behaviors. In contrast, those who hold incremental perspectives believe that the attributes of a person are flexible and can adapt to a current situation, goals, needs, and emotions (Dweck et al., 1995).

Holding a more incremental perspective, East Asians are more likely to believe that they are flexible and malleable (Heine, 2010). They tend to believe situations around them constantly change and prefer to view both positive and negative aspects of situations (Ji et al., 2001). East Asians would be more likely to believe that it would take effort to reduce any deviant behaviors (Holloway, 1988) and would persist in those efforts (Heine et al., 2001). This motivation is exacerbated if they believed they were harming their group with their behaviors, as group harmony is emphasized (Markus & Kitayama, 1991; Miyamoto & Eggen, 2013). These persons are more likely to engage in cognitive reappraisal (Tamir et al., 2007) and regulate their emotions to match those around them (Matsumoto, 2007).

Those who hold incremental views endorse less extreme stereotypes (Levy et al., 1998) and make more situational, rather than dispositional, attributions compared to those who hold entity views. In contrast, those who hold entity views are more likely to engage in the fundamental attribution error. The fundamental attribution error is erroneously assigning dispositional rather than situational attributions to a person or situation (Dweck et al., 1995, Plaks et al., 2001). Although some research suggests that those who hold incremental views are more likely to engage in immoral behavior (Huang et al., 2017), most research suggests the opposite. For example, incrementalists hold more positive judgments of offender rehabilitation (Leith et al., 2014), are more likely to forgive and trust after apologies (Haselhuhn et al., 2010), and are overall less negative and punitive toward immoral targets (Gervey et al., 1999) as they believe immoral persons can be reformed (Kammarath & Peetz, 2012). In contrast, entity persons believe moral traits are fixed, thus holding more negative perceptions toward immoral targets and believing them more likely to recidivate (Tam et al., 2013).

Incremental versus entity selves applied to problem-solving courts

Societies that hold more incremental perspectives of themselves (East Asian cultures) would likely have a more harmonious relationship between law and culture and be more receptive to introduction of PSCs. Furthermore, members of those societies that interact with PSCs would likely be more successful in their efforts to rehabilitate (Holloway, 1988) and would persist in those efforts (Heine et al., 2001), especially if they believed the wrongdoers were harming their group with any immoral behaviors (Miyamoto & Eggen, 2013). In contrast, because entity perspective societies (Westernized cultures) tend to engage in the fundamental attribution error, they might attribute their deviant or immoral behaviors to situational causes for themselves but not for others (Heine, 2010; Ross, 1977). Thus, PSCs might not only be less welcomed in entity perspective societies, but those members who interact with a PSC might be less likely to persist in rehabilitative efforts. Furthermore, as mentioned, those who hold entity perspectives tend to believe that immoral persons are more likely to recidivate, likely due to their belief that traits are fixed (Tam et al., 2013). Of note, the former statements are hypotheses yet to be tested.

Subculture and Law

Cultural differences do not always have to be on a macro level, as some subcultural phenomena might develop within a larger culture that distinguishes some members from others. Here, we will discuss some subcultures that have developed out of certain socioeconomic and demographic differences that could impact the likelihood that someone will interact with the legal system. This is not to assume, however, that all subcultures are birthed from larger, coherent culture or that all subcultures are equally prevalent (Mezey, 2001); yet, the tenets of these included subcultures are, as we will discuss, discordant with what law dictates as appropriate behaviors.

Cultures of honor in general

Most common in the US South and the Mediterranean, cultures of honor were originally developed in response to weak laws and easily stolen property (e.g., farm animals). Because these areas were characterized by and relied on agricultural income, men were required to exert toughness and retaliate aggressively in response to an attempted robbery. States not reliant on such forms of income (and thus not developing an honor culture due to a lack of such theft concerns) are deemed dignity states (e.g., the US North). Honor cultures are defined by a patriarchal structure (i.e., women are expected to be submissive) and beliefs embodying dignity, honesty, and reciprocity. The masculine honor mentality has led to more excessive risk-taking, resulting in high rates of accidental deaths compared to dignity cultures; the mentality also leads to more support for aggressive responses to a national-level provocation (Barnes et al., 2012). Both the men and women in these cultures hold these views (Guerra et al., 2013).

Honor cultures experience more interpersonal, intergroup, and collective violence compared to dignity cultures (Nisbett & Cohen, 1996). Societies classified by an honor culture experience more homicides, more permissive gun control legislation, representatives who vote for more aggressive foreign policies, more lenient laws toward domestic violence, greater tolerance for corporal punishment in schools, and self-defense laws that result in milder sentences for people who use violence in defense of self or property (Nisbett & Cohen, 1996). Furthermore, higher levels of social organization (defined by residential and family stability) are associated with more violence and more violent policies in the South (Cohen, 1998). Southern White males are more likely than Northerners to endorse violence when it is used for self-protection (e.g., a man has the right to kill a person to defend his house) and to defend one's honor (e.g., the violent response to an insult is justified; Cohen & Nisbett, 1994). Employers in honor states are more cooperative and understanding toward job candidates with criminal records in honor related conflict than employers in non-honor/dignity states (Cohen & Nisbett, 1997).

Culture of honor applied to problem-solving courts

People from honor cultures as a subculture would likely have a discordant relationship with law. Furthermore, the endorsement of violence and corporal punishment are not values concordant with the values of a PSC. Regions that adopt honor culture would likely opt to not adopt PSCs as an alternative to regular criminal courts. We also hypothesize that a person who endorses honor culture might actually prefer to be sentenced to a punishment rather than a rehabilitative PSC.

Urban survival syndrome in general

Used four times so far as a defense to crimes in legal trials (cases of Daimon Osby, Torino Roosevelt Boney, Felicia Morgan, Gerald Hampton), urban survival syndrome is a defense implying that a crime that would seem abhorrent to an ordinary person might be a reasonable reaction to someone raised in a violent, indignant neighborhood (Liggins, 1999). Urban survival syndrome has sometimes been labeled as a variant of posttraumatic stress disorder (PTSD); persons using the syndrome as a defense claim they were in a different state of mind during the incident (Borders, 2015; Liggins, 1999).

In the case of Daimon Osby (*State v. Osby*), the defendant, an African American man, shot and killed Marcus and Willie Brooks in Fort Worth, Texas. Osby believed that his only option for eliminating the repeated threats and harassment from the victims was to kill them. Osby and his counsel argued that his crime was a result of Osby's routine exposure to violence from living in one of the most dangerous neighborhoods in the country. Osby's upbringing led him to believe that lethal force to defend himself was reasonable given the circumstances (Borders, 2015). In the first trial, the jury was hung, believing that in conjunction with the urban survival defense that Osby did in fact only shoot the victims in self-defense. However, at the second trial, Osby was not allowed to admit a psychologist that would testify that Osby was experiencing similar symptoms to PTSD (the urban survival syndrome). The usage of the syndrome was impactful in the first trial, but when not mentioned in the second trial, the trial led to conviction.

Urban survival syndrome applied to problem-solving courts

Once again, such a subculture is not concordant with law, ostensibly leading to a conflict within law and culture's interconnected nature. Urban survival syndrome is synonymous with the tenets of a PSC. Using a trauma-informed perspective, PSCs could consider the consequences of growing up in such a violent environment had upon the defendant when considering rehabilitative options. Areas characterized by high crime, however, are likely to be areas in which cultures of honor are present, or are a "tight" society, thus being unlikely to adopt a PSC.

Black rage

Black rage is a legal strategy that is a defense exploring the connection between environment and crime. America's history of pervasive racism toward Black persons can result in racial stress and anger and subsequently a mental disturbance due to prolonged exposure to racism. Subtle insults fester into rage due to a "healthy cultural paranoia Black people develop in response to racism" (Grier & Cobbs, 1968; as cited by Sneirson, 1995, p. 2256). The Black rage defense is a path to explaining to the jury and judge that the society itself was a contributing factor to a criminal act; the defense establishes a state-of-mind defense that influences the court to consider environmental hardship (Harris, 2020). Some people agree with the usage of the Black rage defense, whereas others use this as an excuse to be even more prejudiced by purporting that the defense is a mask of racial hatred toward White persons (Sneirson, 1999).

Black rage applied to problem-solving courts

Like urban survival syndrome, Black rage is a defense that might not be consistent with the law, but it highlights the importance of contextual factors that are often neglected by the criminal justice system. PSCs (and the criminal justice system) must consider environmental context when determining a rehabilitative option. For example, rehabilitative options that place a Black person back in the violent environment that precipitated the criminal action in the first place would be extremely insufficient.

Demographics

Beyond some larger subcultural phenomena, some subcultures are relegated to certain socioeconomic or demographics that nonetheless impact how the members of these subcultures interact with the legal system and influence the relationship between culture and law. Although there might be many other subcultures prevalent, here we discuss subcultures of the rich and subcultures of racism.

Cultures of the rich: Affluenza

The case of Ethan Couch (Howerton, 2023) exemplified a specific subculture—a culture of the rich—when Couch used the so-called affluenza defense to explain his reckless behavior. Bringing a "wealthy people are above the law" ideal to the courtroom, affluenza is a social condition which allegedly makes it difficult for someone who has had a lot of money but no accountability to understand that their behaviors are wrong (Eckenroth, 2015). Ethan Couch was 16 years old at the time when he had drunkenly crashed his father's truck, subsequently killing four and injuring nine others in Burleson, Texas. Sergio Melina, Couch's passenger, became paralyzed from the waist down as a result of the crash.

Couch's attorney claimed an affluenza defense for Couch's behavior. Affluenza was intended to portray to the judge that Couch was so rich and privileged that he had no inherent differentiation between right and wrong. His parents had very rarely punished him or made him face consequences for his wrong behavior. Thus, he did not develop a normal understanding of wrongful behavior. In the end, Couch was given only 10 years of probation. During that probation time, Couch and his mother fled to Mexico.

Cultures of racism: Hate crimes

A hate crime is crime that demonstrates evidence of prejudice based on a demographic, such as race, gender, sexual orientation, religion, or disability (Hate Crime Statistic Act, 28 U.S.C. § 534). Twenty-five-year-old Ahmaud Arbery was jogging in Satilla Shores, Georgia, when he was shot and murdered by three White men. Evidence presented at trial revealed that two of the men armed themselves before chasing Arbery. The third defendant joined the pursuit after the men who were chasing Arbery passed his residence. The three men attempted to box Arbery in, chasing him through the neighborhood for three to five minutes. Evidence shows that Arbery was completely unarmed, had his hands in plain view, and never spoke a word to the defendants. The men claimed that they believed Arbery was a burglar but had made assumptions entirely based upon his race (United States Department of Justice, 2021). Additional evidence demonstrated that all three men had an extensive history of racial prejudice toward Black people. The three men involved were sentenced to prison, with two receiving sentences of life in prison for the killing of Arbery (Office for Public Affairs, 2022).

Another recent instance of a culture of racism through the act of hate crimes occurred during the COVID-19 pandemic. Hate crimes against people of Asian descent increased exponentially during the pandemic, posited to be stemmed from a fear of foreigners, national insecurity, and general xenophobia (Vachuska, 2020). One of the catalysts for this trend was former president Donald Trump's usage of the terms "China virus" for COVID-19 in various statements posted to Twitter (now known as X) (Fallows, 2020). This event coincided with a sharp rise in hate incidents against Asian Americans, cultivating an environment for hate crimes to occur (Jeung et al., 2020). After the labels "Kung Flu" and "Chinese virus" began to be used publicly, hate crimes against Asian Americans particularly surged (Han et al., 2023).

The affluenza defense and hate crimes are prime examples of when law and culture collide in a catastrophic manner, the latter being a much more devastating occurrence. What is novel about these examples is that these subcultures have been manifested and maintained against an unchanging law. Perhaps these subcultures were born out of opposition to the law, particularly hate crimes. Members of this subculture could suppose that treating people of color equally is against their core beliefs, developing in opposition of the law. Nevertheless, these subcultures are a prime example of when culture and law are extremely disconnected.

Case Examples in Which Culture and Law Collided

Ideally, culture and law should have a symbiotic relationship. Nevertheless, there are plenty of examples in the courtroom and beyond that demonstrate what happens when culture and law happen to collide. The current section provides some case summaries of real court cases that have taken place in the past in which some sort of cultural defense has been used, varying in effectiveness.

Two Cambodian refugees sparked outrage when they were gifted with a German Shepherd, but instead of treating it like a pet, they hit the dog over the head with a blunt instrument, slit the dog's throat and began to skin it. The judge ruled that the dog was killed for food and in a non-cruel manner, which is legal under US law. Years of national outrage followed this event, leaving the general public questioning whether this was a case of culture clash or just plain animal cruelty (Haldane, 1989). This is just a singular example of a case in which law and culture had a disjointed relationship.

In the case of *Poddar v. People* (1972), the defendant, Poddar, was a student at the University of California, Berkeley. Before migrating to the United States, he was part of the affluent Harijan caste known as untouchables. Poddar killed Tanya Tarsoff because she rejected his romantic advances;

Poddar was later found guilty of second-degree murder. In Poddar's appeal, he wanted to have an anthropologist testify that it was a big shift from simple Indian culture to complex American culture and he was accustomed to arranged marriages. Poddar argued that this expert evidence should have been admitted as evidence of diminished capacity at the time of the murder.

In the case of *People v. Aphaylath* (1986) the defendant, a Laotian refugee, killed his wife due to jealousy. She was receiving phone calls from and displayed affection for an "unattached man." According to Laotian culture, what the defendant's wife and the other man did brought upon enough shame to trigger a significant loss of control in the defendant. At trial, the defendant was hindered by his inability to speak English. Furthermore, the court excluded testimony from two expert witnesses who would have testified about the stress of assimilating into American culture. Particularly, the testimony would have stated that the defendant's status of being a refugee was unconsciously influencing his actions in the foreground in conjunction with the immediate cause, which was jealousy toward his wife.

In the case of the *United States of America v. Jose Alejandro Escalante-Escovar* (2015) the defendant, Escalante-Escovar, pleaded guilty in the US District Court for the Southern District of Florida to illegal reentry of a deported alien. Escalante-Escovar had attempted to appeal these charges. However, Escalante-Escovar had a prior charge of lewd battery of a minor, which subsequently resulted in the impregnation of the minor victim. Escalante-Escovar claimed it was normal in his culture to marry someone so young. Escalante-Escovar was 27 years old and he had married someone who was 15 years old. Furthermore, he claimed that if he was deported, he could no longer support his family that resided in the United States. When rejecting Escalante-Escovar's appeal, the court reasoned that honor killings are also a cultural norm, but nonetheless would be improper to dismiss in the United States.

In the case of *Dang Vang v. Vang Xiong X. Toyed* (1991) the defendant, Xiong, was appealing after the plaintiffs asserted that Xiong had raped them during his employment at the Washington State Employment Security Office. Xiong attempted to challenge the testimony of Marshall Hurlich, an epidemiologist who testified about Hmong culture at the trial. Hurlich mentioned that Hmong women are expected to be submissive, such that they are raised to obey men and are relegated to a specific role concerning intercourse and marriage. Furthermore, Hurlich suggested that Hmong refugees are reliant on government assistance to survive, thus admiring the federal position Xiong was occupying.

In the case of *People v. Wu* (1991), defendant Helen Wu strangled her son, Sidney, to death with a window blind cord and then attempted to take her own life by slashing her wrists. The defense claimed that Wu had killed her son to take care of him in the afterlife, which was a cultural defense. In Asian culture, if a mother commits suicide and leaves her children behind, she is considered irresponsible. Thus, in the context of Asian culture, Wu's actions were considered an act of altruism. The prosecution argued something different: that Wu was exacting revenge upon Sidney's father, who was having an extramarital affair. The prosecution also argued that Wu also snapped because her son was born out of wedlock, and a paternal grandmother (the only person who was nice to Sidney) was dying from cancer. Wu was convicted of first-degree murder and her later appeal was denied.

Although normal in Afghani culture, kissing a child in their genitalia is considered sexual assault in the United States. Afghani culture permits a parent to kiss a child all over their body, including the penis, which is not considered a holy body part. In the case of *State v. Kagnar* (1996), Mohammad Kagnar, the defendant, testified that the practice was permitted until the child was three, four, or five and that, because the penis was an unclean body part, kissing it was a testament of how much he loved his child. Kagnar was found guilty on two counts of gross sexual assault. This case is reminiscent of another event in 1990 in South America in which an immigrant in Georgia was investigated for stroking her four-year-old son's genitals in an effort to put him to sleep, which was normal in her culture (LaCayo, 1993). Charges were never brought against her.

An example outside of the courtroom is that some cultures consider letting an infant "cry it out" as abusive, whereas others consider this practice commonplace. In countries or tribes under high risk or facing constant threat, an infants' survival would be treated with extreme care and alert. As such, some cultures' responses to their infant crying are immediate, a response not as common in Western cultures (Stork, 1993). This practice could also be related to the tightness–looseness theory as discussed earlier; cultures that are experiencing ecological threats have less tolerance for deviance and social disorder, so these cultures might endorse addressing an infant crying immediately as a survival tactic.

Another example is an event from 2004. Child Protective Services (CPS) became involved with a six-week-old Vietnamese infant presenting with bone fractures at a routine pediatrician check-up. CPS removed both the infant and the three-year-old sister from the home. It is commonplace to sleep on floor mats in Vietnamese culture, and the three-year-old happened to be playing with the infant on the floor mat in such a manner that caused the bone fractures. The fractures were not caused by abuse (Carlson, 2004; Reisig & Miller, 2009).

Likewise, in 2002, a Chinese immigrant mother beat her child with a broomstick for bad grades. This practice is acceptable and normal in her culture, but the mother was surprised to learn of the opposing American child abuse laws (Reisig & Miller, 2009; Zhao, 2002). This might have occurred due to the East Asian belief of incremental selves. The mother might have believed her son could persist in his efforts to become a better student, disciplining him in a manner common in her culture.

All of the former cases present real-life examples of law and culture not aligning. As discussed, law and culture can collide on the topics of marriage, parenting, and even what is considered food. The following section uses these cases to further elaborate on the consequences of law and culture not aligning and how PSCs might reconcile these instances.

Possible Consequences of Law and Culture Not Aligning

The cases above depict concrete instances of when culture and law did not align, despite the symbiotic relationship between culture and law. Beyond emotional reactivity to culture clashes, serious legal consequences can result from these collisions between law and culture. Here, we discuss one of the foremost consequences of this discordance and what PSCs can learn and apply from these consequences.

Increased interactions with the law

As illustrated by the examples above, the most obvious and unfortunate consequences of cultural clashes are increased interactions with the law. A cultural practice that is a norm could be outlawed in that person's place of residence, resulting in a surprising legal consequence. Cultures that are considered "tight" will be more punitive than loose cultures because tight cultures deal with more crime overall. Similarly, cultures that hold entity views would be less likely to believe that the culture-based deviant behavior is a fixed trait about this person, rather than caused by factors of the situation. Thus, if someone from a loose culture or incremental self enters the opposing culture, this could lead to law-related consequences and misunderstandings.

The United States, for example, has a unique criminal justice system compared to numerous nations in Europe, Asia, and Latin America. Law, in the United States is used to change society or the behaviors of others with an end goal of justice. Juries are also relatively unique to the United States, especially civil juries, as no other country allows juries to decide civil trials (Denver Trial Lawyers, 2018; Miller, 2013). Other countries might have authoritarian systems, or at the opposite extreme, laws that are not strictly enforced. For example, a Chinese couple tried to bribe a woman who their son had sexually assaulted to get him out of trouble. Charges were dropped against the couple because they were acting in accordance with cultural norms. Despite being a tight country in most domains of the law, most sexual crimes in China go unpunished and the Chinese government has habitually pressured citizens to drop lawsuits against certain groups (Miller, 2019). With such examples of law and culture colliding, how might courts, particularly PSCs, reconcile these differences.

Conclusion

PSCs have a rehabilitative, rather than punitive, focus. When focusing on rehabilitation, this rehabilitation should be both culturally informed and trauma informed. Procedural justice is one route that could be taken to promote a rehabilitative focus. When people have more amicable interactions with law enforcement, they are more likely to believe in and abide by the law (Tyler, 2003). Procedural justice can be heightened by cultural considerations in court, giving litigants a voice, respect, neutrality, and understanding (Center for Court Innovation, n.d.). PSCs' implementation and consideration of culture's role in the law could lead to a successful, rather than discordant, relationship between culture and law.

A considerable misstep would be to attempt to edit or remove culture's place in a society to be compliant with the law. For example, following the Columbine High School shooting, Congress attempted to regulate youth culture (e.g., violent media) rather than law-related legislature (e.g., introduce gun control legislature; Mezey, 2001). As the relationship between culture and law is symbiotic, one cannot exist without influencing the other. However, in cases such as subcultures of affluenza and racism, we are not suggesting that the law or PSCs consider these cultures in the same manner as other cultural differences.

Instead, PSCs should take a multiculturalism approach. Multicularism is an approach that encourages keeping numerous ethnic and cultural groups politically relevant in policy and decision-making. This approach would be especially potent in a country like the United States, which is composed of ethnically diverse communities and considers the interests of both society as a whole and the individual. Facets of economic efficiency, social justice, and cultural identity are considered. Current laws should be assessed for what principal cultural values are reflected within the law and which cultural values could be accommodated. If the implications of accommodating certain values are positive, a change consistent with the basic principles and structure of that society should be considered and proposed (Kearney, 1990).

PSCs could be the key to keeping law and culture aligned through considering the various cultures and subcultures. The current chapter discussed different cultural and subcultural ideas and practices that could collide with the law, as well as real-life court cases in which culture directly collided with the law. Consequences of this collision were highlighted, encouraging PSCs to focus upon procedural justice and multiculturalism approaches to realign culture and law. The following chapter on the Social Mind-set model, discusses how the model aids in predicting how and why some cultures accept or reject PSCs based upon a culture-influenced mindset.

8

Problem-Solving Courts and the Social Mind-set Model

Monica K. Miller, Kylie Kulak, and Amber Westbrook

The Social Mind-set Model

The last chapter provided a discussion of *how* societies around the world differ, and this chapter offers an explanation for *why*. Monica Miller and Amber Westbrook (2021) offer a general Social Mind-set (SMS) model (see Figure 8.1) that attempts to explain why societies differ in what they consider to be a crime and in what they consider to be the proper response to that crime. For instance, one country might have access to scientific research suggesting how causes of crime can be addressed that another country does not. This science is one of the six factors in the SMS model. In this chapter, the SMS model is discussed generally and then applied to the topic of problem-solving courts (PSCs).

Societies around the world can vary greatly in their responses, with one society considering a behavior to be a crime and another not. Even when societies do agree that a specific behavior is a crime, they might disagree on the response. The SMS model builds off the frameworks by Herbert Blumer (1973) and John W. Kingdon (2003), who offer complementary explanations for how social issues become law. Those authors discuss how a social issue is recognized as a problem worthy of legal action—and the resulting processes that result in legal action. Yet, those models stop short of explaining *why* the legal actions that are adopted differ from one country to the next. They do, however, acknowledge that the policy process is influenced by social factors (e.g., high-profile cases and social movements), beliefs, and ideologies. These are some of the factors that comprise what Miller and Westbrook (2021) call the SMS model.

Society, Science, and Problem-Solving Courts. Monica K. Miller, Mia A. Holbrook, Logan A. Yelderman, and Kylie Kulak, Oxford University Press. © Oxford University Press 2025. DOI: 10.1093/oso/9780190059804.003.0008

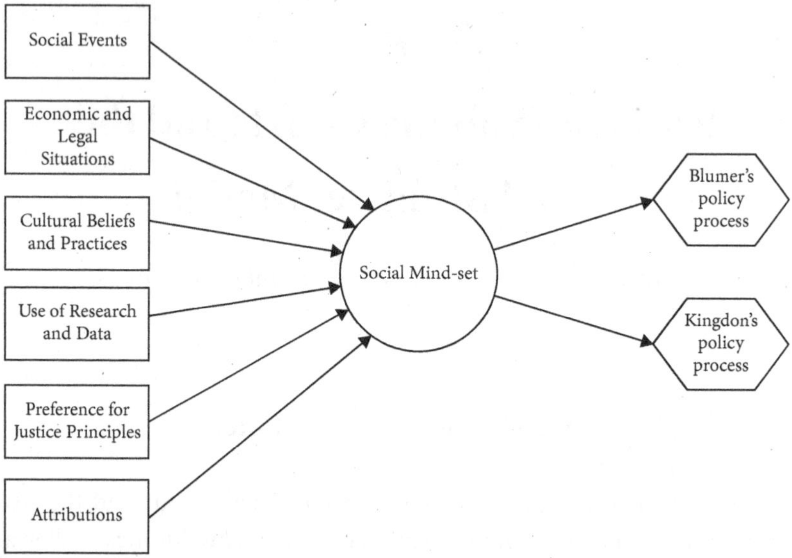

Figure 8.1 The Social Mind-set Model (initially published in Miller & Westbrook, 2021)

The SMS model proposes that social mind-sets are precursors to the policy processes described by Blumer and Kingdon. Specifically, the model suggests six social and psychological factors that influence the social mind-set of a society, which in turn shapes the policy processes described by Blumer and Kingdon. These six factors include the society's: (1) high-profile events and social movements, (2) economic and legal situations, (3) cultural beliefs and practices, (4) use of scientific research and data, (5) preference for justice principles, and (6) attributions for behavior. These social and psychological explanations add to the understanding of *why* societies differ—often dramatically—in the laws and policies they adopt. In general, a cross-society analysis can help explain how social mind-sets are formed and changed (Miller & Westbrook, 2021). This chapter examines these possible explanations in depth by offering examples from multiple countries. This chapter is the first application of the SMS model to a particular context: PSCs. The SMS model might explain why some countries have PSCs, have courts for some issues but not others, and differ in the ways their PSCs work. Each factor in the SMS model could contribute to this understanding, as discussed in the next six sections.

Factor 1: High-profile Events and Social Movements

The first factor in the SMS model is how social movements and high-profile events can influence policymakers to take action and how these actions vary by culture and country (Miller & Westbrook, 2021). A social movement is characterized by members of a community or society who collaborate to achieve a specific goal that is typically social or political. This movement can exist regardless of a high-profile event that captures the attention of the public (Miller & Westbrook, 2021). This section provides a few general examples of how high-profile events and social movements can shape a social mind-set, followed by an example of how this part of the SMS model applies to PSCs.

High-profile events and social movements shape the social mind-set

Some events are so impactful that there is a sharp and permanent shift in the social mind-set, thus influencing the laws and policies that were in place and subsequently put into action. The Civil Rights Movement in the United States put pressure on politicians and policymakers to change legislation regarding segregation and equal rights for all Americans (Lang, 2013). Past and current legal actions in the United States (e.g., gay rights, equal gender pay) have been shaped by this movement. Other societies that did not experience a social movement similar to the Civil Rights Movement are unlikely to have commonality in legislation with the United States in regard to equality.

In 2012, Canada experienced a social movement called Idle No More led by a group of Indigenous women. The Canadian government's failure to consult with Indigenous leaders when considering a bill that would have major effects on the Indigenous Peoples sparked this movement. The movement was characterized by protests, flash mobs, blockades, and Chief Theresa Spence's hunger strike (Graveline, 2012). The outcome of this movement was a 13-point declaration signed by the Canadian government ensuring Indigenous Peoples' rights to consult on bills that affected them. Although the United States has a substantial number of Indigenous groups who have experienced similar social issues to those in Canada, the United States has not experienced a similar uprising, likely because there has not been a catalyst of the same nature as there was in Canada. The catalyst, in this case, was the series of high-profile events that prompted a movement.

One proposition of the SMS model is that societies vary in what they consider to be a social issue that needs to be addressed by the legal system. The presence of a social movement is one possible reason for such societal differences. For example, domestic violence is a crime that is not recognized as a crime or social issue in all countries. The United States did not recognize domestic violence as a social issue until the women's movement in the 1960s (Coker, 2001). In comparison, in countries such as Egypt, there is no law that forbids spousal abuse (Yount & Li, 2010). Egypt might not have a law forbidding spousal abuse because a social movement prompting a response to domestic violence (and women's rights more broadly) has not occurred to the same extent as in the United States.

High-profile events could also explain why some societies have particular laws and other societies do not. Amber Hagerman's abduction and murder was a high-profile event that quickly became headline news across the United States. (Griffin & Miller, 2008). There were no large, organized social gatherings that would indicate a social movement, but the sheer attention to this case influenced the policy-making process, leading to the implementation of the AMBER Alert system (America's Missing: Broadcast Emergency Response) by the US government. Countries that have not had a similar high-profile event would be less likely to have a policy or notification system like AMBER Alert.

High-profile events and social movements could affect the social mindset of a society, particularly both its current and future legislation regarding the issue. If one country experiences a devastating high-profile event, there will likely be a subsequent action to address the issue; a country that has not experienced such an event is less likely to take action. This hypothesis could apply to PSCs, as discussed next.

High-profile events and problem-solving courts

As a response to the perceived widespread drug abuse problem and the "War on Drugs" political movement, drug courts emerged in the United States. According to James Nolan (2012), the Dade County drug court in Miami, Florida, was the first PSC in the United States. Nolan explains that this court was introduced in response to the crack epidemic that began in the 1980s. Had this crack epidemic not reached such a high level of concern amongst the general public and political leaders, there might have been fewer (or no) drug courts offered as a solution to this social issue. The United States began using these PSCs as a means to address the overcrowded jails throughout the country that were home to many repeat offenders with drug addiction issues. The drug courts were used as an alternative to present the cases and sentence the offenders to rehabilitation-focused programming like community service and drug treatment programs (Nolan, 2012). It was not long before other countries began to take notice and incorporate the use of PSCs in their communities. Some of the countries that Nolan (2012) identified as using the US model of these PSCs include England, Australia, South Africa, Norway, and Canada.

Similar to drug courts, domestic violence courts also evolved in part due to social movements. The women's movement of the 1960s was likely a contributor to the creation of domestic violence courts to address domestic abuse issues. Some jurisdictions have domestic violence courts to address the root of the problem causing the violence in the home or in interpersonal relationships of the offender. Some of the conditions placed on people who are given this rehabilitative option include therapy (both one-on-one and family), anger management courses, and even drug testing if deemed appropriate. These rehabilitative programs are an attempt at solving the root cause of the abuse. The social mind-set behind the creation of these courts is that if a person is only incarcerated as a consequence of their abuse, they will likely not learn skills that would prevent future abuse. In contrast, a court can assist the offender in addressing their problems (e.g., anger management). By providing tools and resources to target the deeper issue, the court can potentially prevent the offender from engaging in future abuse.

As discussed throughout this section, high-profile events and social movements are the first factor that could influence the social mind-set and PSCs. The existence of such PSCs will vary among societies depending on what events are experienced and the seriousness of said events in triggering any social movements.

Factor 2: Socio-political-economic Situations

The second factor in the SMS model illustrates how societies that face difficulties in socio-political-economic arenas are likely to have different social mind-sets than societies who do not face those difficulties (Miller & Westbrook, 2021). In societies in which people struggle to meet their basic needs (e.g., clean water, housing), values and priorities might be different than for people in countries without such struggles. In turn, how people in struggling countries meet their needs to survive can be controversial to people in more affluent societies. An example is prostitution: in some countries where money or food are scarce, sex work is viewed as a means to survive. Those who live in societies in which the struggle to meet basic needs is common are likely to believe that people commit crimes out of necessity. This section gives some examples of how socio-political-economic situations of countries might affect the social mind-set in general, followed by an example of how the socio-political-economic situation of a country could affect PSCs.

Socio-political-economic situations shape the social mind-set

Columbia, along with other countries that are similar in terms of economic and social struggles (e.g., drug cartels, arms conflicts, and human rights violations) are focused on economic and social issues which restrict the legal system's ability to address remaining issues (Miller, 2020). These major issues require substantial attention and resources, making it difficult to address citizens' basic needs such as food and shelter.

The African nation of Ghana has substantial corruption in its political, business, and legal systems (Rahman, 2018). Some common corrupt activities include bribery, fraud, misappropriation, and bias. Although actions have been taken to decrease corruption and increase accountability for corrupt behaviors, the effect remains relatively minimal. In turn, citizens might experience a lack of trust in their leaders. Political culture and/or events, along with corruption, influence the norms, stereotypes, and beliefs of a country's social mind-set.

Generally speaking, countries with high economic strife and underdeveloped legal systems lack the resources to provide services to address many of the crimes currently present. Additionally, in countries where terrorist groups or drug cartels are active, leadership will likely focus their efforts on these issues. Countries that do not face challenges such as corruption, terrorist groups, or drug cartels are more equipped to address nuanced criminal problems, such as driving under the influence (DUI), prostitution, or gambling-related crimes. As such, the social mind-set and resulting legal actions differ among countries.

Socio-political-economic situations and problem-solving courts

Socio-political-economic situations can lead to the creation of or inform PSCs as a means to address social issues. PSCs typically are not present in less developed or third-world countries, especially those that do not recognize drugs or drug use as an issue of addiction or illness. In countries like Mexico, there are no drug courts, mostly because there is no formal recognition of drug usage as a personal rehabilitative issue. Therefore, drug courts would not be viewed as an option to address drug-involved crimes and addiction.

As this section discussed, the socio-political-economic situation of a society is the second factor that could influence the social mind-set and adoption of PSCs in that society. PSCs will likely not be implemented in societies that experience high poverty and/or hunger. If the basic needs of the people are not met, there are likely few resources available to address other criminal or social needs.

Factor 3: Cultural Beliefs and Practices

The third factor in the SMS model addresses the cultural beliefs, practices, and traditions that are passed down generationally by the people who inhabit a given society. An example of cultural beliefs is whether the society largely practices individualism or collectivism. According to Markus Kemmelmeier and colleagues (2003), individualism is characterized by personal freedoms, choices, and rights, whereas collectivism is characterized by a focus on group goals and social norms. Individualism and collectivism each produce a different social mind-set, thus resulting in different policy responses. As individualism is characterized by having a strong focus on the self rather than the community, policy responses tend to reflect that sentiment through laws and expectations of the general public. In communities in which collectivism is embraced, the policy response then reflects what is in the best interest of the "greater good." This section presents some examples of how cultural beliefs and practices within any given country could affect the social mind-set in general, followed by an example of how these beliefs and practices could affect PSCs.

Cultural beliefs and practices shape the social mind-set

Individualistic societies have policies that are highly focused on things like freedom of speech or personal rights. These policies and viewpoints are focused more on the person and less on the interest of the larger society. Collectivist societies tend to focus more on obedience to authority, emphasizing policies that might not be beneficial for a particular person but are most beneficial to the community as a whole.

An example illustrating how cultural beliefs, practices, and social mind-sets are intertwined is whether or not children are perceived as needing protection from sex/marriage or being used as a form of property to ensure the well-being of the family. In some countries, such as Sudan, it is culturally acceptable for adult men take a "child bride," meaning the young woman is likely just coming into puberty and is not yet 18 years of age (even though the country formally outlawed child marriage in 1990; UNICEF, 2016). In Western cultures, such practices are counter-normative at minimum and punishable under the law at maximum. Whether a country is at one of these two extremes or somewhere in the middle is part of a social mind-set that affects laws regulating sexual behavior and the contracts to be entered into by juveniles.

In the United States, there is an assumption that minors cannot consent and are in need of protection; therefore, anyone engaging in sexual activity with a minor is deemed an offender (Hanson & Bussiere, 1998). Sex offender laws are sometimes used to prosecute a young adult male with a juvenile girlfriend, requiring the offender to register as a sex offender. However, some states have adopted "Romeo and Juliet" laws, meaning that an adult can have sex with a minor given that the minor is not significantly younger than the adult (typically four or fewer years younger; Volokh, 2015). In the case of *Genarlow Wilson v. State of Georgia*, Wilson successfully appealed an aggravated child molestation conviction for having oral sex (at age 17) with a 15-year-old, claiming the state failed to apply the "Romeo and Juliet" law retroactively.

Many countries do not view juvenile relationships as problematic or in need of protection. For example, in the case cited above, Wilson was 17 years old, and the minor was 15, thus the "Romeo and Juliet" law should have been applied because this type of relationship would not be considered inherently problematic. In contrast, Brazilian law generally has a different perspective on statutory rape; it is a crime only when someone 18 years of age or older has sex with someone who is under the age of 14 (because in Brazil the age of criminal responsibility is 18).[1]

Germany is an example of a country that does not have any nationwide registration or notification laws for juvenile sex offenders.[2] Therefore, there are no laws in place that label juveniles as sex offenders (Global Overview of Sex Offender Registration and Notification Systems, 2014). This differs from the United States, where there is an extreme focus on protecting minors (Armstrong et al., 2015). These varying beliefs about sexual behavior with juveniles have led to very different social mind-sets and thus different policies varying by country.

Cultural beliefs and practices and problem-solving courts

There are currently no PSCs or specialty courts that address matters of sexual conduct in the countries that recognize sex crimes. This is likely due to the fact that incarceration has been the go-to response for people that cause harm to juveniles. Therefore, as long as sexual engagement with a minor by an adult is viewed as a crime under the law that causes harm to a child there will not be specialty courts to address these crimes.

However, there are examples of specialty courts that address certain cases that are a matter of cultural significance in other countries. Some PSCs in the United States address and rehabilitate citizens that have participated in prostitution (National Institute of Justice, 2020), whereas other countries would not consider prostitution to be a problem (World Population Review, 2023). Another example of a specialty court is that some PSCs in the United States address homelessness (National Institute of Justice, 2020), whereas some countries do not consider courts responsible to handle homelessness because churches often offer shelter to people experiencing homelessness, as discussed in Chapters 9 and 10 (New York Times, 2022). In sum, some countries might consider a cultural topic to be the court's responsibility to

[1] This information came from one of the informants from the study reported in Chapters 9 and 10.

[2] This information came from one of the informants from the study reported in Chapters 9 and 10.

solve, whereas others might not see the cultural topic as a common, everyday occurrence.

Factor 4: Use of Research and Data

The fourth factor in the SMS model is how science based on valid research and data can have a meaningful impact on the social mind-set of a society in terms of policy response. For instance, there has been recent data collected on incidents of domestic violence in the United States. The data suggests the deterrent that is most effective at preventing future domestic violence is to arrest the person who was engaging in the abusive behavior (Amaral et al., 2023). This discovery impacts the social mind-set of that society in terms of the best method and/or policy to implement to address the issues of domestic violence. A country that does not have access to research on domestic violence could not even have policies in effect to address the issue, much less enact consequences. This section provides examples of how the research conducted can affect the social mind-set in general, followed by an example of how the use of data and research can inform the implementation of PSCs.

Use of research and data shape the social mind-set

In countries where there is little or no funding available to produce valid and reliable research, research can have little impact on the social mind-set of that society. Consider domestic violence: if a country is lacking the ability to conduct research on it, then there will not be informed policy changes implemented. Research and data are impactful elements to consider when attempting to understand how a country could hold a social mind-set that is dramatically different from other countries. In the United States, there has been a considerable amount of research focused on domestic violence to better understand causes and potential treatments. According to the National Center for Biotechnology Information (NCBI), "Domestic violence is a serious and challenging public health problem. Approximately 1 in 3 women and 1 in 10 men 18 years of age or older experience domestic violence" (Huecker et al., 2023). This statistic, and others like it, are readily available due to the research that has gone into understanding domestic violence.

In contrast, countries that have not recognized domestic violence as a social issue that requires attention are likely to not have research that would offer solutions. The rates and prevalence of domestic violence can be identified, but there is not much available in terms of research on the foundational causes for it. For instance, the research that has been conducted on domestic violence in Africa has been completed by researchers from other geographical locations. Therefore, the social mind-set in Africa differs from countries like the United States who have identified domestic violence as an important issue.

Use of research and data and problem-solving courts

Research is a major element in the development of PSCs. Research produces data that indicates the need for the PSCs. For instance, domestic violence courts have been created in numerous jurisdictions throughout the United States as a response to data demonstrating the prevalence of this type of violence. Additionally, research has shown that mere incarceration of domestic violence offenders does not solve the recurrence once released into the community (Babcock & Steiner, 1999). PSCs have addressed domestic violence by assigning the offenders to programs, some of which are anger management, therapy, and couples counseling—allowing for the possibility of rehabilitation.

In addition to demonstrating the *need* for courts, data also demonstrate the utility of PSCs. Chapters 5 and 6 discuss how researchers have studied courts and whether they have produced their intended outcomes. When scientific data demonstrate that courts are successful, it is more likely to influence other courts in that society and that others will adopt similar courts.

Factor 5: Preference for Justice Principles

The fifth factor in the SMS model is related to justice. There are multiple types of justice principles, and those a given society chooses to implement will impact their legal approach to crime and justice. In this section, the justice principles to be discussed are procedural justice (PJ), restorative justice (RJ), and legitimacy (see Chapter 3 of this volume for more discussion of various justice factors related to PSCs). Each justice type has a unique goal and varying outcomes when applied to law breaking behaviors. This section discusses a few examples of how a country's preference for a type of justice principle can greatly influence the social mind-set in general, followed by examples and discussion of how this directly impacts the use of and tools used with PSCs.

Preference for justice principles shape the social mind-set

Tyler and other researchers have studied why people follow the law (Lind et al., 1997; Tyler et al., 2015; Vermunt & Steensma, 2016). One explanation is that PJ gives a person the opportunity to state their opinion, or a voice. This opportunity can be interpreted by that person as an indicator that they are an important member of society, and thus deserve to be heard (Vermunt, 2013). This encouragement to speak one's opinion can lead the person to be more accepting of the consequences of their actions, and thus hold themself responsible for their actions (Tyler & Lind, 1992). PJ research has indicated, in general, that people will obey the law when they feel they have been treated fairly, even if the legal outcome is not what they had hoped for (e.g., they are convicted).

Another option is RJ; research suggests that RJ techniques can be helpful by acknowledging the harm victims have suffered (Cameron & Thorsborne, 2001; Umbreit, 1998). Additionally, RJ can reduce recidivism by generating increased legitimacy (belief the law enforcement are valid authorities) through perceived PJ.

Lastly, Tyler (2006) defines legitimacy as a justice principle as follows: "The belief that authorities, institutions, and social arrangements are appropriate, proper, and just." Tyler and other researchers have studied how this concept of legitimacy informs community policing (Tyler, 2006; Tyler et al., 2015; Friedmann, 1992). Community policing reflects the following premise of legitimacy based on the research by Friedmann: "A policy and a strategy aimed at achieving more effective and efficient crime control, reduced fear of crime, improved quality of life, improved police services and police legitimacy, through a proactive reliance on community resources that seeks to change crime-causing conditions" (1992, p. 1) This research indicates that people follow the law when the leaders (i.e., police officers) are perceived to be legitimate authorities.

Justice principles are not necessarily equally applied across all countries. This is due to the cultural differences and the institutional and structural differences. For example, the United States is quite retributive in nature. Historically, the United States was born out of a revolution, and the ownership of firearms is a critical feature of societal liberties. Thus, the violent nature of crimes might be a result of a high gun population, which then requires a harsh retributive justice system. The United States is, however, adopting many therapeutic jurisprudence (TJ) practices and PJ elements; for example, the United States pioneered and popularized drug courts (see Chapter 3).

Australia and New Zealand, on the other hand, have been world leaders in RJ practices, integrating RJ conferences into their courts system (Daly & Hayes, 2001). Canada, likewise, has introduced and sustained RJ practices in their courts as well (see Tomporowski et al., 2011). Some countries, such as China, have political and governmental structures in place that make it difficult to successfully employ some justice principles that are more individualizing; however communal practices, such as RJ seem promising (Li & Liu, 2019). Although countries tend to differ in the degree to which various justice principles are applied or can be adopted, these principles have now been cemented as global phenomena.

Preference for justice principles and problem-solving courts

The foundational beliefs of PJ principles can be exemplified by the case of a person who is convicted of their first DUI and is sentenced to DUI classes and drug court. The judge allows them to express their concern that they need help with alcohol addiction. As long as the person perceives the consequence as fair, they are likely to abide by the sentence and complete the requirement. In contrast, if a person in the above-described situation feels as if the consequence is unfair, they would be more likely to not complete the program(s).

The United States also has implemented other legal processes that take the PJ mindset into account. Programs in the United States help women remove themselves from prostitution by providing them with life skills classes, counseling, and prostitution diversion court (Schweig et al., 2012). The United States has these types of programs and procedures in place because the research has informed the justice system of such principles. Countries that are lacking research on PJ are unlikely to have the previously discussed policies and programs.

When observing the implementation of RJ, a primary goal is to correct the harm done by the offender to both the victim(s) and the community. Victim–offender reconciliation is an example of how RJ is used, allowing the offender to apologize and repay the victim for any losses that they incurred as a result of the crime (Sullivan & Tifft, 2001). Other countries that do not have access to research are unlikely to have legal policies that reflect these principles of RJ.

As a result of the research conducted on people following the law when leaders and those who enforce the law are perceived as legitimate, the United States has implemented procedures that reflect legitimacy, such as community policing. Institutional selection is another mechanism built upon Tyler's definition of legitimacy. Institutional selection refers to matching a person's ideologies with their institution's objectives (Tyler, 2006). For example, Pratto et al. (1997) stated that when people are choosing employment, they often will choose careers that reflect their personal objectives and beliefs. Research has found that this method of choice leads to higher levels of satisfaction and willingness to obey laws (Pratto et al., 1997; Tyler, 2006). Therefore, legitimacy influences multiple areas of peoples' lives, as well as the social mind-set of communities and countries.

Factor 6: Attributions for Behavior

The sixth and final factor in the SMS model describes how a country could attribute crime to the criminal's situation or experiences (e.g., poverty, mental illness, drug addiction) or place the blame on the criminal's personal choice. These attributions shape the social mind-sets and resulting responses from the community and policies currently in effect. Multiple explanations for different crimes can be considered what psychologists refer to as internal (i.e., person) attributions or external (i.e., situational) attributions (Carroll & Payne, 1977). Internal attributions for the cause of crime are reflected in the notion of "super predators," which is the idea that perpetrators are inherently bad and therefore need to be incapacitated because they cannot be rehabilitated. This internal attribution to crime results in punitive responses to criminal behaviors. This section discusses how the attributions for behavior directly can influence the social mind-set in general, with examples illustrating the SMS model and how it relates to PSCs.

Attributions for behavior shape the social mind-set

Internal attributions lead to a social mind-set that offenders need to be punished for being characteristically bad people, which leads to harsher legal actions. In contrast, if the cause of crime is attributed to external situations, then that country is more likely to be less punitive and more rehabilitative toward the offender (e.g., to provide help for substance abuse or mental health issues). Similarly, if a society attributes juvenile crime to parenting, peer pressure, or underdeveloped brains (external), then that country would likely be more focused on rehabilitating juvenile delinquents. In contrast, a society that attributes the crimes committed by juveniles to personal attributes (internal) would likely be more punitive (i.e., treating juveniles as adults in court proceedings).

During early European times, juveniles were not held responsible for their criminal behavior; instead, the juveniles' parents were held responsible (Goodey, 1994). Parents were expected to teach their children right from wrong and the social mind-set of this time reflected a belief that juveniles' behavior and choices were both elements that could be corrected by parenting (Goodey, 2004). Thus, the only punishment that juveniles were subjected to was from their parents without the justice system's interference.

In another example, one solution to the crime problem that was implemented in the United States was the Three Strikes Law, which dictates that a person must be sentenced to life in prison on their "third strike," given they had committed two prior offenses that were considered violent or serious in nature. The Three Strikes Law was a result of internal attribution as the cause of crime. The Three Strikes legislation is punitive and symbolic in nature (Austin et al., 1999) and punitive laws are often driven by attributions of stability regarding attributions of the person (i.e., once a criminal always a criminal; Maruna & King, 2003). The attributions for crime likely affect PSCs, as discussed next.

Attribution for behavior and problem-solving courts

The first juvenile court in the United States was opened in 1899, with a focus on rehabilitation of juvenile offenders (Steinberg & Scott, 2003). The United States now has juvenile justice courts in every state. Judges in these courts mostly support the concept that juveniles have less developed reasoning and decision-making skills than adults, and therefore they should be processed through the court system in a different manner than adults (Steinberg & Scott, 2003). In general, legal actors in the United States attribute blame to the parents of juveniles via parental responsibility laws (Brank et al., 2005). However, these laws do not absolve juveniles of all responsibility for their crimes. The social mind-set in the United States on juvenile justice is more punitive than it used to be, and it is now common for juvenile offenders to be waived (i.e., transferred) to adult court for prosecution (Kratcoski & Edelbacher, 2009). Nevertheless, the US Supreme Court has found that sentencing a juvenile to the death penalty is unconstitutional because their brains are not fully developed (Steinberg & Scott, 2003).

According to US research, juveniles do not have fully developed brains and therefore are biologically less capable of processing situations in the same manner as adults (Steinberg & Scott, 2003). This creates difficulty for juveniles to evaluate situations such that they make the best decision(s) (Steinberg & Scott, 2003). Therefore, the social mind-set prior to the 1990s in the United States was that juveniles cannot be held accountable for their criminal behavior in the same manner that adults (Kratcoski & Edelbacher, 2009). The general social mind-set was that juveniles need to be offered rehabilitation and not punitive sanctions when they are adjudicated for a nonviolent crime.

In contrast, Austria enacted the Juvenile Justice Act in 1988 which, "defined juvenile offenders as persons between the ages of 14 and 19 who had committed an offense and provided that youths who committed offenses before the age of 14 cannot be held criminally responsible" (Kratcoski & Edelbacher, 2009, p. 209). Only three jurisdictions in Austria had juvenile justice courts that were separate from the adult courts, but they have since been abolished, and all juveniles older than 14 years old are processed in the same courts as adults (Kratcoski & Edelbacher, 2009). In contrast, Austria is non-punitive regarding juveniles under the age of 14; juveniles in this age group are not held criminally responsible. In Austria, there is a belief that if a child is committing crimes at such a young age, it can be attributed to the parents or to a lack of parenting (external attributions; Kratcoski & Edelbacher, 2009).

Age is also subject to causal attributions, differing between both countries and time periods within a single country. According to Steinberg and Scott (2003), in the last 30 years, the only countries that have executed juveniles as punishment for their crimes are Congo, Iran, Yemen, Saudi Arabia, Pakistan,

Nigeria, and the United States.[3] The attribution that a country makes regarding causes of juvenile crime affects whether the response is punitive or rehabilitative, which then influences the legal actions that dictate the outcomes for juveniles in the justice system.

Attributions, along with the other five factors of the SMS model, help explain how a society develops a particular social mind-set about an issue such as PSCs. This mind-set then affects how and whether a policy process begins, which could affect whether a PSC is adopted in that society, as discussed next.

The Social Mind-set Model and the Policy Process

The previous section described the left side of the SMS model: the six factors that influence the social mind-set of a particular society (see Figure 1). Each section then applied these factors to PSCs. This section describes the right side of the SMS model: how the social mind-set of the society influences the policy process and how these policy processes can be applied to PSCs. The SMS model incorporates two policy process models, one posited by Blumer (1971) and another posited by Kingdon (2003).

Blumer's model of social problems

The SMS model suggests that social mind-sets can affect the policy process, including the process suggested by Blumer's (1971) model. Blumer created a five-stage model to explain how social problems prompt legal action: (1) a social problem emerges, (2) the social problem is selected and identified by the community or lawmakers within a country as one in need of addressing, (3) the social problem is legitimized, (4) the social problem becomes respected by the people of that community, and (5) the given culture or country mobilizes itself to address the social problem (Knauff, 2007).

Blumer (1971) explains how an event, crime, or given circumstance can become a social issue. Drug courts will be used here as an example of each of Blumer's (1971) stages. In some jurisdictions in the United States, drug courts are used as an alternative to incarceration for criminals who struggle with addiction. Although the courts rely on sanctions (including

[3] The US abolished the death penalty for juveniles in *Ropers v Simons* (2005).

incarceration), they incorporate many therapeutic elements (e.g., treatment programs, education programs). The ultimate goal of most drug courts is to reduce recidivism by helping the criminal become drug-free. (For a comprehensive review of the history, effects, and cultural elements of drug courts see Kaplan et al., 2018; Nolan, 2009; Nolan, 2017.)

Blumer's (1971) first stage is the emergence of a problem. Legal actors—especially judges—realized that many drug users reoffended shortly after being released from prison, creating a revolving door problem (Tiger, 2011). Blumer's (1971) second stage is selection of the problem as one deserving of being addressed. The Miami courts selected substance abuse as a problem that deserved their attention, with other courts and counties following suit.

In Blumer's (1971) third stage, the problem was legitimized as courts and researchers took action to solve the problem. Research examined the correlation between substance abuse and criminal activity to offer some explanations and identify which crimes were drug-related; such research was used as the bases for drug courts (Tiger, 2011). In Blumer's (1971) fourth stage, the relationship between substance abuse and criminal activity was recognized and respected as a social issue that needed to be addressed (Tiger, 2011). Blumer's (1971) fifth and final stage is mobilization. Americans, criminal justice system actors, and scholarly researchers began to work to build a new program to address the issue of substance abuse and crime. As a result, drug courts were implemented in the United States (Tiger, 2011).

The United States followed the stages as described by Blumer (1971) to recognize and address the social issue that emerged related to drug use and crime, which might not happen elsewhere or for other issues. Other countries might not even begin this five-stage process or get stalled in one of the stages. For instance, a social issue might emerge but fail to be recognized as a problem that needs to be addressed, or the problem might be recognized, but the government might not mobilize to address it. This could be because of the social mind-set in those societies; if the social mind-set is not favorable, then the process Blumer (1971) suggests cannot occur. For instance, there are no special drug courts in other countries, such as Mexico, to address the issue in a rehabilitative manner (Robertson et al., 2014). Applying Blumer's (1971) principles, countries such as Mexico arguably have not recognized the relationship between drug use and crime as a social issue that needs to be addressed. The government could also be unable to mobilize help for criminals to become drug-free. Whatever the reason, Mexico has not yet recognized a need for drug courts.

In sum, this brief analysis suggests that the SMS model might explain how a social mind-set regarding PSCs might affect the policy process as described by Blumer (1971). Although more research is needed, these few anecdotes suggest the SMS model—and Blumer's model—does help explain why some countries differ in their approach to addressing social issues through their court systems.

Kingdon's framework applied to social mind-set and problem-solving courts

Just as the social mindset might lead to the processes Blumer (1971) explained, it might also lead to the processes explained by Kingdon (2003). This section suggests such, and then uses PSCs as an example. Kingdon (2003) developed a framework to explain how policies are formed, written, and implemented. This concept, known as the multiple streams framework, is comprised of three different elements: problems, policies, and politics. When the three elements (streams) come together, policies and laws are likely to gain the attention—and action—of politicians and policymakers (Kingdon, 2003).

The first stream is an identified problem. According to Kingdon (2003), policymakers learn about existing conditions through avenues such as data and statistical indicators. This information could motivate them to take action if it leads them to conclude that the condition is a problem (Kubiak et al., 2005). We propose that the social mind-set plays a critical role in identifying a problem. Previous data suggests that courts were experiencing increased drug cases, leading Miami courts to adopt drug courts (Goldkamp & Weiland, 1993). High-profile events can also attract the attention of policymakers, even if the data does not indicate a problem. For instance, the opioid crisis made headline news and prompted judiciaries to address the problem through PSCs (Supreme Court of Ohio, 2017).

The second stream is policy. Policy solution ideas go through multiple stages, including discussion, reports, and conferences. Kingdon (2003) posits that generating a proposed solution is not difficult in itself; the difficulty lies in finding a solution that is feasible and compatible with the values (what Miller and Westbrook [2021] would call the social mind-set) of the policymakers (Kingdon, 1984; Kubiak et al., 2005). We predict that the social mind-set affects these possible solutions. For example, some people might hold values that drug issues are a personal issue, applying internal attributions to a drug user (e.g., they made that choice of their own free will; Schomerus et al., 2011). Thus, a PSC addressing said issues would have difficulty employing rehabilitative measures for offenders; according to their values, the offender has a personal flaw that led to their offense.

The third and last stream in Kingdon's theory is politics. There are three components: national mood, pressure group campaigns, and the ideology of policymakers. All components are influenced by social mind-set. First, the national mood refers to the dominant public opinion of any given country). Second, pressure groups have the ability to influence the politicians and policymakers. Third, the ideology of policymakers is important for any shift to occur. In fact, some research suggests that partisan politics plays a significant role in the amount of state-level regulation of drug court policies (Moss, 2019).

According to Kingdon's (2003) theory, when two or all present streams convene in a certain context or time, a policy window—or a period that permits initiatives for change—opens (Khayesi, 2011; Kingdon, 1984). For example, a change in political stream and problem stream can open a window allowing for policy entrepreneurs to find viable policies and adopt one (see also Craig et al., 2010) or an incremental change in an existing policy (Saint-Germain &Calamia, 1996). A possible cause of these changes in society's social mind-set is one overarching explanation. Kingdon (2003) relies heavily on concepts that are a part of the social mind-set, including public opinion, ideologies, and beliefs. Thus, Kingdon (2003) provides a foundation for the SMS model. The SMS model offers factors that contribute to the social mind-set—the ideologies and public mood to which Kingdon (2003) refers. Kingdon's (2003) idea of pressure groups is one of those factors that shapes the social mind-set, as will be discussed below. Kingdon (2003) writes about how these things affect process and timing of policy change—SMS model discusses these things as the reason why a certain direction is taken in these three streams).

In sum, the SMS model presents a potential explanation as to how a social mind-set, when applied to PSCs, could affect the policy processes originally described by Blumer (1971). The provided anecdotes suggest that the SMS model and Blumer's model have explanatory value in the discrepancy of approaches to social issues by various countries through their court systems.

Conclusion

The SMS model offers an explanation as to why there is a variance between countries in regard to which social issues and problems are addressed—and how they are addressed. For instance, PSCs will only be established in the countries that perceive issues like substance abuse and domestic violence as social issues that are in need of intervention rather than mere incapacitation or negligence. Blumer (1971) and Kingdon (2003) each provide frameworks by which we can understand what must occur for policy change to take place and for social issues to be noticed by the society as a whole or by the people in society that have the power to influence change, specifically on a legal and political level.

The use of examples among various countries allows for a multi-dimensional perspective of how issues are viewed, classified as requiring action, and how policy is enacted to address said issues. The SMS model offers an explanation as to why some issues, like child abduction and drug crimes, are addressed in some countries and not others (Miller & Westbrook, 2021). Holistically, the SMS model is a multifaceted answer to the question "why do some countries have PSCs and others do not?" The six factors suggested by the SMS model are likely all (to varying degrees) suggest explanations for why countries differ.

The SMS model (including theories by Kingdon [2003] and Blumer [1971]) is a succinct, plausible explanation as to why some countries have PSCs, yet others do not. It is our hope that this model can be tested statistically, using both PSCs and other social issues as topics. Such tests would determine whether the SMS model is useful as an explanatory tool.

Conclusion

SECTION 4

THE DEVELOPMENT (OR NOT) OF PROBLEM-SOLVING COURTS

9

Why Some Countries Have Problem-Solving Courts

Waleed A. Jami, Kylie Kulak, and Monica K. Miller

A Typology of Adoption

Problem-solving courts (PSCs) have become a staple of the American judicial system within the last 30 years (Boldt, 2017) and are also steadily becoming an element of the judicial system in other parts of the world, such as China (Li & Liu, 2019) and England (Bowen & Whitehead, 2016). However, not all societies have PSCs. Some societies might use PSCs to address specific concerns (e.g., prostitution) or these courts might emerge as a response to community sentiments (e.g., the desire to help homeless people). In comparison, in other nations, PSCs are not even considered. As such, the adoption of a PSC involves more than a reconfiguration of the legal system, but also a shift in the society's culture and values (Nolan, 2001; see also Chapter 8 of this volume). The growing prevalence of PSCs in the United States and other parts of the world can be explained by several factors that might vary across societies; these include practical concerns, changes in legal or social structures, prevalence of social issues, and even medical or technological advances (Miller, 2020). This chapter will examine reasons why numerous societies *do* adopt PSCs by describing the typology found by Miller (2020) and further investigating whether new qualitative data replicates that typology and the factors within. Chapter 10 of this volume examines the reasons why societies do *not* adopt PSCs.

Miller (2020) identified several factors that explain some of the underlying motivations behind the implementation and development of PSCs. Namely, PSCs might be established because of (1) necessity or practicality; (2) changes in social structure, such as changes in which institutions address social and personal issues; (3) advances in science (including social science) and medicine which include differences in attributions; (4) a catalyst that

Society, Science, and Problem-Solving Courts. Monica K. Miller, Mia A. Holbrook, Logan A. Yelderman, and Kylie Kulak, Oxford University Press. © Oxford University Press 2025. DOI: 10.1093/oso/9780190059804.003.0009

suddenly brings attention and change to society's sentiment toward a social issue; and (5) changes in society's sentiment toward a social issue without a catalyst. With new interview data, four out of five of the factors in the typology were replicated. All factors were replicated to various degrees, but the factor that focused on advances in science and medicine was not replicated in the new sample.

Methodology

The data presented in Chapter 9 and Chapter 10 expand and summarize the Miller (2020) typology and apply new interview data to this typology. The data came from legal professionals, scholars, and other informants who were located in various countries. All interviews were either written or oral and were semi-structured with the goals of detecting (1) how various societies used their court systems to address social issues, and (2) the reasons behind each country's adoption to that approach. All informants were experts (through education and/or experience) in sociology and/or law in their home countries. Additionally, data was collected from other sources, including books, websites, observations, and resources from the International Institute for the Sociology of Law library. Thus, the typology is based on a literature review and on informant interviews, observations, and document reviews (see Miller, 2020). The initial set of interviews included people from Spain, France, Italy, Ecuador, the United States, Canada, India, the Netherlands, Finland, Columbia, Argentina, Ghana, Scotland, and Germany. New data stemmed from some of the countries already mentioned and additional countries, including Nigeria, Moldova, Colombia, Indonesia, and Israel.

Just like the original Miller (2020) article, no direct comparisons were made, simply because, even with a semi-structured interview, informants did not have the answer to every question. Further, other constraints like language barriers and time limits made sophisticated country comparisons difficult.

Results

Analyses of the data, combined with the data from Miller (2020), indicate that there are five factors in the typology of reasons countries do have PSCs.

These factors are discussed below, with focus on both the original data from Miller (2020) and the data that is new to this chapter.

Necessity and practicality

The first factor that Miller (2020) found is that of "necessity or practicality" (see also Berman & Feinblatt, 2001; Nolan, 2009). Technical issues like prison overcrowding and high judicial caseloads could force judges and other legal professionals to reevaluate their strategy in tackling some types of cases. To illustrate, PSCs within the American context originate from a drug court in Miami-Dade County, Florida, in 1989 (Berman & Feinblatt, 2001), perhaps as a consequence of the "War on Drugs" philosophy of the government at the time (Terry, 1999). This increase in focus on drug-related crime led to a high rate of prosecutions, overcrowded prisons, and overbooked judicial dockets (Goldkamp, 1999; Terry, 1999). Furthermore, judges realized that repeat offenses were common because defendants did not have either the capability or desire to quit using drugs. Judges then focused on helping defendants to break their drug habit to reduce the chances of repeat offenses (Terry, 1999). Early on, these courts were promising; drug courts led to fewer re-arrests relative to traditional courts (Terry, 1999).

In contrast, in some parts of Europe, PSCs are not as widely available, perhaps in part because there was no "War on Drugs" to cause a rapid increase in court cases. The interviewee from Scotland indicated that judges in the United States want PSCs to address repeat offenses and the "draconian nature of available sentences." Overall, it seems there is not a pressing problem in Europe that has galvanized legal professionals to develop a PSC (Miller, 2020).

Gaining the public's trust could also be an underlying motivation (Nolan, 2009) which can be considered another practical reason, as it might improve the perceived legitimacy of the courts (Miller, 2020). There are instances in which judges are concerned that the communities they serve do not perceive the courts as legitimate authorities. When there is a prevailing social issue, a new type of PSC could emerge to tackle this issue enroute to gaining the community's trust in the courts (Nolan, 2009). Furthermore, gaining the community's trust is a stepping stone toward procedural justice (PJ)—the perceived fairness of the judicial processes (e.g., Tyler, 1989). Perceptions of PJ are vital because these perceptions can affect people's inclination to abide by the law (e.g., the judge's orders) and their perceptions that the courts are legitimate authorities (e.g., McIvor, 2009). According to an interviewee from Brazil, special courts are generally less formal and more friendly, which makes the community perceive them more favorability (e.g., as more just).

Miller (2020) also found that another "practical/necessary" reason for the emergence of PSCs pertains to finance and economics. Monetary purposes can influence the establishment of some courts, such as the drug courts in the United States. This is not always the case; the interviewee from Spain, for instance, indicated that financial concerns do not impact the way in which Spanish courts respond to social issues. Rather, courts in Spain tend to respond to social issues as necessitated by their constitution.

This factor was initially found in the Miller (2020) analysis. We replicated the factor in our data from informants from Brazil, Indonesia, Columbia, and China in more recent interviews. First, the interviewee from Brazil noted that Brazilian judges tend to have a huge caseload and the Special Courts Act of 1995 was adopted to shorten or reduce judicial procedures. Although there is no direct evaluation, special courts are believed to be viewed more positively and justly by the community. In this sense, improving relations between community members and the legal system can improve the perceived legitimacy of the courts.

Second, within the Indonesian context, PSCs emerged on the basis of necessity and practicality. For example, some PSCs in Indonesia, like the courts that tackle corruption, can require technical expertise like non-career (ad hoc) judges. The interviewee from Indonesia indicated that there are several special courts, such as special human rights courts, that specifically tackle past gross human right violations as well as courts that address corruption. The former was ultimately rejected, but the latter was compelling enough to be established because the quantity of cases increased—necessitating a special court to tackle a high caseload. More specifically, the development of this special court emerged because of two central drivers: first, the establishment of corruption criminal courts in all district capitals were based on the decision of the Constitutional Court in 2008; and second, multi-line investigators and prosecutors were in the corruption cases, such as the police, prosecutors, and corruption eradication commissions.

The juvenile courts typically examine cases in which the child defendant is between the ages of 12 to 18 with a focus on diversion. Specifically, there are several special mechanisms that are implemented, such as rehabilitation mechanisms, for drugs users or mandatory mediations in civil cases. The aim of these mechanisms is to balance the position of the parties and reduce the number of cases in court. Important to note is that the diversion mechanism is excluded for cases where the criminal threat is above seven years or constitutes recidivism. Another important factor to consider is that the typology (Miller, 2020) and the character of special courts formed in Indonesia refers to the specific cases and not social issues. For instance, although there is a special court in the form of a juvenile court, the primary consideration is not to answer social problems related to children (e.g., violence, exploitation, etc.), but to answer the judicial practice that children as perpetrators of crime must be conducted differently from that of adult offenders. In this sense, treating child defendants differently from adult defendants can be viewed as a form of practicality.

One of the interviewees from Colombia also indicated that some courts might emerge out of necessity. Arguably, there was a practical necessity to create a new jurisdiction called the Especial Jurisdiction for Peace (JEP). The JEP attempts to solve cases regarding crimes committed by former combatants of the Revolutionary Armed Forces of Colombia—People's Army (FARC-EP). The underlying motivation for this court stemmed from the notion that normal criminal procedures might make use of the police and other public servants who might be biased in the process. Another pragmatic reason is the reality that the Columbian government must address, in one way or the another, the considerable number of ex-belligerents that are re-entering society; they require education, job opportunities, and accompaniment to be rehabilitated. This opportunity to receive help from the government might have contributed to PJ, as the JEP resolved the conflict between members of society.

An interviewee from China noted that PSCs or special courts do exist in the Chinese judiciary system; this includes military courts, maritime courts, railway transportation courts, and forest courts, among others. These courts did not emerge based on a social issue, but rather from a sense of practicality. For example, the establishment of special courts, like the miliary court, was developed because of the military's embedded political interests. The latter three courts were developed to simplify the legal procedure on related disputes. Overall, special courts in China could be established from a sense of practicality above all else.

Although Nigeria does have special courts (e.g., domestic violence courts, family courts), there is a plan in progress for a particular special court, according to the interviewee from Nigeria, to address cases that entail corruption, kidnapping, and money laundering, as well as legal issues like drug sale, cybercrime, and other economic and financial crimes. The interviewee also mentioned that the success of PSCs in Nigeria will depend on whether these special courts could provide speedier trials and save costs; thus, PSCs and their future implementation seem contingent on whether or not they are practical. Indeed, the interviewee also noted that many of the crime-related issues could be in part due to poor governance. In this sense, PSCs could help improve governance quality—another practical purpose.

Changes in social or legal structure

A second important reason for the rise of PSCs stems from changes in a given social or legal structure; that is, changes in the legal and social structure might spur the need for PSCs. For instance, Miller (2020) found that one specific reason for this factor is the availability of formal legal education (e.g., law school), as well as the increase in courts which allows the development of PSCs. In the United States, professional conferences and additional education trainings can help judges in PSCs (Brank & Haby, 2013). In contrast, other societies may not have the availability of additional training, which can affect judges' support of problem solving courts (Brank & Haby, 2013).

Beyond changes in legal training norms and opportunities, changes in the law itself can also influence the establishment of PSCs (Miller, 2020). Due to the growing intricacy of laws, some courts have become specialized. General jurisdiction judges might lack the knowledge necessary to tackle the various types of cases, which fuels the need to establish specialty courts for some cases, such as bankruptcy or maritime issues. In this sense, some of these specialty courts were PSCs with judges who had additional training or experience for specific case types.

Social change can also be an impetus for the development of PSCs (Miller, 2020). For example, the legal system now handles cases that used to be addressed by churches (Berman & Feinblatt, 2001). Other private issues, such as family issues (e.g., domestic violence) or health issues (e.g., drug addiction) were not originally taken as cases by the legal system. For instance, the interviewee from Ecuador indicated that prostitution is viewed as a health problem and is thus not addressed by the courts (Miller, 2020). Moreover, the interviewee from Argentina indicated that there are family courts to provide specialized treatment.

This factor identified by Miller (2020) was replicated with new data from Brazil, Israel–Palestine, and Indonesia. Brazil illustrates an example of social change influencing the rise of PSCs, according to the interviewee. In 1988, Brazil transitioned to democracy after years under military dictatorship. The new regime was tasked with combating social inequality and poverty. This focus on youth crimes was based on the Statute for Children and Adolescents Act of 1990. Cases that involved youth crimes generally functioned similar to standard criminal trials, but if the juvenile defendant was found guilty, the sentencing of the youth would be different than that of a typical adult. In these cases, judges usually order youth to participate in a "socio-educative" program tailored to the youth defendant, which might include a combination of counseling, community service, and time in an institution, although the latter is typically a last resort according to the legislation. These institutions do offer schools and programs, as well as social workers and psychologists, to help youth defendants. Thus, social and political changes have affected which issues gain attention and, therefore, which deserve a PSC.

In Israel, there are special courts that are specific to religious groups like Jews, Muslims, Christians, and Druze, according to the interviewee from Israel. Further, there are seven rabbinical courts for the Jewish community in Israel, alongside four Muslim courts that operate across Israel. Religious courts deal with issues like marriage or custody, but there is also a wealth of other courts, like the supreme courts, to deal with general issues. Changes to the legal system can be a function of different religious groups in a given society.

The Indonesian context also provides an example of special courts potentially emerging because of social structure or change within the global context. Namely, the emergence of international organizations can influence the development of special courts. The establishment of a commercial court (the first special court after the 1998 reform) with the International Monetary Funds (IMF) as a sponsor is an example of the development of a court within the global context. The motivation behind this special court was to acquire funding and to show, on the international stage, that Indonesia was improving in terms of safety. Further, it was a way to seek assistance because of the Asia financial crisis in 1997, according to the interviewee. As of 2021, compliance is still occurring through programs, such as the small claim court mechanism in civil courts to raise the Ease of Doing Business ranking in Indonesia according to the interviewee from Indonesia; this compliance might help with acquiring future funding.

Although reasons behind the establishment of special courts in Indonesia were multifaceted, as indicated by the interviewee from Indonesia, some influence for special courts might have emerged because of social issues. For example, the establishment of a Labor Court in 2003 aimed to resolve inequalities in labor dispute resolutions. Previously, labor disputes were carried out in a bipartite manner between workers and companies, which resulted in the inequality of resources. Even with government involvement, in many cases, workers had no power against corporations, and because of this, a special court was formed to settle the disputes as parties deemed independent, impartial, and fair.

Advances in science and medicine

Advances in science and medicine have also contributed toward the development of PSCs (Miller, 2020). Medical advances have been a factor for the implementation of PSCs (Berman & Feinblatt, 2001). In the US context, addiction is now identified as a medical issue with many treatments having been developed (see Robinson & Adinoff, 2016, for a historical review). The development of mental health treatments, facilities, and diagnostic tools has made PSCs a possibility (Berman, 2000).

Miller (2020) also found that the development of technology is influential (Berman, 2000; Berman & Feinblatt, 2001). Technologies like house arrest bracelets, drug testing, and communication systems (e.g., online databases, email between judge and treatment facilities) are critical to monitoring offenders' compliance and progress. A more specific example of technology's role in courts can be identified in veterans' treatment courts (VTCs). Advancement in social science research indicates that, when veterans return to the United States, they typically have some trouble adjusting to civilian life (Elbogen et al., 2012), encouraging some jurisdictions to establish VTCs (Hawkins, 2009–2010). Veterans could struggle with mental health problems, such as posttraumatic stress disorder, substance use, and other issues that pertain to finances, family, and housing; these issues can lead veterans to be stuck in the legal system (see also Chapter 5 for more on VTCs).

VTCs typically work with the Veterans Association to help veterans in need (Huddleston & Marlowe, 2011). For example, the VTC in Buffalo, New York, pairs offenders with veteran mentors who are trained to help in rehabilitation process for offenders. This particular example illustrates the use of science and technology. For instance, a network of services requires modern communication technologies like email or the internet, and mental health and substance abuse professionals need advancements in science in order to effectively diagnose and treat these illnesses. The mentoring program for veterans might have been influenced by the findings on mentoring programs across social science research. House arrest monitoring bracelets, for instance, can track the wrongdoer and reduce or eliminate the need for incarceration, which reduces recidivism. All these advances in medicine, science, and technology combine to make VTCs possible (Miller, 2020). The United States has largely embraced the advances in medicine, science, and technology that encourage the development of PSCs. Yet, countries that have little access to technology or science would be less likely to have courts that depend on it—without certain technologies, such approaches would not be feasible.

Social science research has also elucidated some of the dynamics as to why PSCs exist, according to Miller (2020). In recent years, social scientists have uncovered the links between crime, drug addiction, and mental illness—especially with regard to attributions (Claro et al., 2015). Essentially, there are two types of attributions: external and internal (Kelley & Michela, 1980). External attributions entail the interpretation of a person's behaviors based on circumstances whereas internal attributions describe the interpretation of a person's behavior based on some internal quality like personality traits and habits. Thus, some people might view crime as a personal choice—that the act of a crime reflects the offender's character—whereas other people could perceive a criminal offense as a reflection of the offender's circumstances (e.g., poverty, mental illness, addiction).

The type of attribution that occurs can differ from person to person, and from one society to the next. For example, the theoretical foundation of drug courts in the United States was that addiction contributes to crime; hence, crime is a reflection of a situation (i.e., addiction). This viewpoint, more generally, can be seen in Argentina (Miller, 2020). The interviewee from Argentina mentioned that communities have a general belief that people do not typically commit a crime unless those people were facing problems like drug problems or mental health issues. This inference might explain why Argentinians generally prefer institutions that aid offenders, rather than favoring prisons (Miller, 2020). In contrast, the interviewee from India indicated there is little recognition of this viewpoint, and the interviewee from Columbia noted that the general population is more focused on retribution and punishment (despite the legal code's focus on rehabilitation). Therefore, some societies focus on situational attributions (e.g., Argentina or the United States) whereas other countries (e.g., Columbia) emphasize personal attributions (see generally Miller et al., 2015). These attributions could shape policy responses to crime as PSCs emerge from the recognition that social issues (e.g., addiction) contribute to lawbreaking (Miller, 2020).

Another interesting dynamic to attributions is that certain groups within society have contrasting attributions (Cochran et al., 2012). For instance, research in political psychology posits that republicans and conservatives generally adopt more personal attributions compared to democrats and liberals; their explanations as to why crime occurs is a matter of personal responsibility and culpability (Cochran et al., 2012). Potentially, states and countries that are politically and socially conservative could be unsupportive of the establishment of PSCs, according to the interviewee from Brazil. At the same time, in the United States, both democrats and republicans generally support drug courts (e.g., Maron, 2009), which might suggest that political beliefs, despite the type of attributions they might be associated with, are not consistent predictors of the kinds of courts that exist and develop. Interestingly, the interviewee from France noted that conservatives believe that courts can tackle social issues, but conservatives also desire more punishment along with rehabilitation (Miller, 2020).

This factor was not replicated with newer data. This particular typology might be more of a feature of the US context simply because of this country's leading role in academic research up until the last few years (e.g., Zhu & Liu, 2020). As other societies continue on their own advances in science and medicine, they might find more utility in PSCs and new techniques and ideas that would make PSCs more feasible.

Changes in society's sentiment toward problems with a catalyst

Miller (2020) found that a catalyst can bring attention to a social issue which can then spur the development of PSCs. Social issues must be brought to light and be viewed as a problem before they can be addressed (Blumer, 1971; Kingdon, 2003; see also Chapter 8 of this volume); without this recognition, social issues might not inspire the development of PSCs. An interviewee from Miller (2020) indicated that, in Ecuador, although gambling is illegal, it is not perceived as a problem; thus, there was no development of special courts to address gambling. In the United States, however, gambling is considered an addiction and there are a number of gambling PSCs.

Even if a country identifies that certain social issues could be addressed by special courts, it might not address other social issues in the same manner. To illustrate, the interviewee from India noted a human rights movement in the 1990s that increased awareness of social issues related to domestic violence and disabilities (Miller, 2020). Although the courts now generally assist with these social issues, they do not typically address other issues, like homelessness, drug addiction, prostitution, or gambling. In this sense, Indian society does not yet recognize them as social issues in need of the courts' attention whereas issues pertaining to domestic violence and disabilities are recognized, in part because of the movements that served as a catalyst.

Miller (2020) also argued that PSCs can be a response to social events including (1) high profile events that cause a panic, like crimes involving an offender with mental illness (Redlich, 2013); (2) a social movement like the "War on Drugs" (Nolan, 2001); or (3) a general movement, like the feminism movement that spurred the establishment of domestic violence courts in the United States (Shaver, 2013; Wolff, 2013). Regardless of the catalyst, the issue must be viewed as a concern by legal authorities, along with the perception that this problem can be tackled by a special court.

This factor was somewhat confirmed with new data from two interviewees from Colombia. These interviews indicated that a special procedure in Colombia was set up to address a specific social issue, like armed conflict, with the JEP. The JEP was created with a special court to realize criminal investigations and to establish transitional justice. This judicial process provides support for victims' reparation and comprehensive assistance. Also, the judge could help the offender receive different treatment or punishment rather than prison. However, there is general lack of use of special courts in Columbia, and the one exception is the JEP, according to one of the interviewees. The JEP has the function of administrating transitional justice and learning the truth about the crimes committed within the frame of the armed conflict (in any case, such crimes should have been committed before December 1, 2016). The goal of the JEP was to contribute to the victims' rights to justice, and contribute to their reparation, with the purpose of building a stable and lasting peace.

Arguably, the JEP was created by a catalyst because the signing of the peace agreements included victims participating in the draft of said agreements as a negotiating party. Because of this particularity, the importance of the role of the victim, usually neglected by other types of courts, increased considerably and produced the necessity of a different legal approach to the justice administration system that is now dealing with the post-conflict reality of the country.

Changes in society's sentiment toward problems without a catalyst

Another factor identified by Miller (2020) indicates that PSCs can emerge without a specific catalyst; instead, some special courts could gradually emerge because of a slow evolution of legal reforms and an incremental shift in community sentiment (see, generally, Blumer, 1971). It is possible lawmakers and other legal experts themselves might believe that some change should be done, especially in more democratic societies (see, generally, Miller et al., 2015).

In Miller (2020), an interviewee from Ecuador indicated that driving a vehicle while under the influence is viewed as a serious crime in both Ecuador and in the United States, but there is a stark contrast between the two countries. Whereas there is no help for defendants in Ecuador, there are drug courts and to a lesser extent, DWI/DUI courts in the United States. Perhaps if the concern continues, Ecuador will eventually follow suit. That is, although there are no PSCs currently, both government officials and the community are starting to realize that driving under the influence is an emerging social problem that the legal system should address. Within the Ecuadorian context, there are no social movements or an event to serve as a catalyst that could increase the demand for special courts; their constitution would allow for such a court, but gradually, special courts could emerge as a solution to a longstanding problem. Perhaps a gradual shift in attitudes and views on certain issues could spur the need for some kind of special court without needing any high-profile events or movements.

An interviewee noted that, starting in 2012, Argentina recognized battered wife syndrome as a legal defense available to a woman who harms her abusive husband (Miller, 2020). At about the same time, the country also began to include marital rape in the legal definitions of rape. Although these events had likely been occurring for many years, leaders began to recognize these abuses as serious social issues in need of legal action; that is, leaders might eventually realize the necessity of a PSC for domestic violence-related issues (Miller, 2020).

This factor was somewhat replicated in the newer data collected for this chapter, especially within the Chinese context, as some social issues are tackled by certain problem-solving tribunals which function similarly to PSCs. The interviewee from China mentioned that these problem-solving tribunals rise in response to the court's power among certain social issues. The juvenile tribunal has a focus on rehabilitation and the reduction of recidivism, ultimately addressing the social and psychological issues that youth might face. It seems that some social issues are left to the court's discretion in the use of problem-solving tribunals rather than there being a catalyst to spur changes in the legal system. It is important to note that, although these tribunals function like PSCs, they are unique in that they are independent of the courts. The interviewee from China noted that "many specialty tribunals in China are somehow functioning as foreign PSCs."

The interviewee from China also noted that there is a growing interest in actual PSCs due to limitations in tribunal courts, especially in terms of environmental protection. The tribunal courts are limited because they do not have the same legal powers in other courts in China. Relatedly, the lack of legal power, including the lack of professional judges and legal resources, hinders the perceived legitimacy of these tribunals, leading to distrust from community members. Changes in community sentiment, as well as a recognition of the ineffectiveness of environmental problem-solving tribunals, might gradually lead to the development of a PSC to address environmental concerns.

Conclusion and Future Directions

In sum, PSCs are emerging in the global context even though their origins are from a specific context in the United States—the "War on Drugs" (Terry, 1999). Miller (2020) identified five factors that could explain the establishment of PSCs. Namely, PSCs can be a response to practical concerns or out of necessity, changes in social structure, advances in science/medicine, and as a response to a catalyst or gradual attitude change by leaders and communities. The goal of this chapter was to examine whether these factors were replicated with new interviewees.

PSCs are, in part, established out of necessity or in practical terms (Miller, 2020). Very broadly, the development of these courts can help with technical issues like high recidivism and garnering community trust in the legal system. This factor might be the most robust, as it was noted by interviewees from Brazil, Indonesia, Columbia, and China. Perhaps the first and foremost drivers of PSCs are borne out of necessity and practicality. In some sense, this factor is a necessary condition for any other factor to emerge. That is, motivations for the development of PSCs tend to have a practical element to them, among other reasons. For instance, a PSC that was developed as a response to a catalyst can be viewed as necessary and pragmatic. By neglecting the impact of a catalyst, the community's perceptions of PJ could wane. In this case, responding to a catalyst with the development of a PSC can be viewed as practical.

Another factor is that of changes in social structure, which can bring about the establishment of a PSC. The kind of social change that typically calls for PSCs include changes in where and how issues get addressed, the increase in the complexity of the law, and available training for legal professionals (Miller, 2020). This typology showed some evidence of robustness, as it is found in Brazil, Israel–Palestine, and Indonesia. And each of these countries had been influenced by social changes for various reasons. Brazil's implementation of PSCs was a part of their transition to democracy, and enroute to this transition, to develop some perceived PJ in the community. Israel–Palestine's focus involved the use of religious courts to help address issues unique to each religion. Finally, the Indonesian context provides an example that has to do with globalization, as some of their development of problem courts were motivated to acquire legitimacy in the eyes of the international community.

Advances in science and medicine have also increased the feasibility of PSCs (Miller, 2020). These advances can lead to technologies that make the rehabilitative process smoother, as well as elucidating the dynamics for why some communities might be interested in PSCs, whereas others might not even consider them. This factor was not replicated in the new data, and it could have to do with other societies not having the same research focus as the United States, which only in recent years has lost its place as the leader in academic research (e.g., Zhu & Liu, 2020). Perhaps, as academic research continues to improve in other societies, the ability and interest to develop PSCs might increase.

A catalyst or major event that draws attention to a social issue can be the spark to the development of PSCs (Miller, 2020). Specific movements like the "War on Drugs," and more general social movements, like the feminist movement, can be the drivers of the establishment of PSCs. This factor was partially confirmed by interviewees from Columbia who indicated that the JEP is a special court focused on rehabilitating those who were involved with armed conflict; the catalyst of armed conflict necessitates special courts to emphasize the victims' right to justice and contribution toward reparation.

A catalyst is not always necessary, as PSCs can be considered by a society without high-profile events. For example, gradual changes in attitudes by members of society or the incremental realization of some social issue could be antecedents toward the development of PSCs. This factor was partially confirmed by the interviewee in China. The interviewee indicated that China does have tribunal courts, but because of their limited ability in addressing issues, there is some interest in developing PSCs. In this sense, the change in community sentiment might spur the development of special courts without necessarily having a high-profile event.

Some of these examples might touch on "emic," or context-specific, differences in PSCs that are unique from culture to culture. The emic approach can explain the unique contexts that give rise to PSCs in different parts of the world (see Triandis & Marin, 1983). For instance, the "War on Drugs" context can be considered a unique American context. Future studies can examine "etic," or general, cross-cultural frameworks for determining why some societies have adopted PSCs. For example, there is an etic cross-cultural framework called "tightness–looseness" (Gelfand et al., 2006). Tighter societies have stronger norms and are less tolerant of deviance, whereas looser societies have weaker social norms and are more tolerant of people engaging in unusual and non-normative behaviors. PSCs could be perceived as a form of deviance from a society's tradition, especially in tighter cultures, which would prevent some progress toward adjustments of the current system. In contrast, PSCs could be viewed as a unique or even unusual approach in tackling social issues which might intrigue these looser societies, increasing the chances of implementation.

In short, PSCs can emerge for a number of reasons, and can be beneficial in a given society (Miller, 2020). The countries discussed in this chapter provide examples of the utility of PSCs, as well as a set of typologies that can explain the interest or development of PSCs. Although not all countries have PSCs, major nations like China and Nigeria are starting to consider the possibility of implementing PSCs. As societies develop and change, PSCs could emerge to address unique issues or streamline aspects of the judicial process.

10

Why Some Countries Do Not Have Problem-Solving Courts

A Typology of Rejection

Problem-solving courts (PSCs) are courts dedicated to addressing specific problems, such as drug usage, homelessness, domestic violence, and a multitude of other social issues (Nolan, 2009). Sometimes called specialty courts, these courts deviate from the traditional one-size-fits-all approach by shifting focus to rehabilitation efforts and lowering recidivism rates (Miller, 2020). This approach involves attempting to remedy the issue at its source by integrating defendant-centered therapeutic jurisprudence (Babb, 2013; Gatowski et al., 2013) or empowering the defendant (Petrila, 2013). Despite such benefits, some countries might not possess the abilities, resources, or desire to implement such courts in their respective countries. For example, a country might not have the financial ability or adequate rehabilitation centers or might outright dismiss the idea of a PSC because their courts are not intended to be rehabilitative. Miller (2020) qualitatively analyzed how PSCs functioned outside of the United States, gathering interviews from informants in other countries. From those interviews, Miller (2020) was able to develop hypotheses as to why some countries have and others do not have PSCs. The purpose of this chapter, as well as the preceding chapter, is to revisit Miller's (2020) typology and apply new interview data to the typology to determine whether this new data supports the original typology.

Using the typology postulated by Miller (2020), Chapter 9 summarized and further elaborated as to why some countries *have* implemented PSCs. However, according to Miller (2020), various reasons exist as to why some countries have *not* adopted specialized courts. This chapter adapts the typology devised by Miller (2020) as to why certain countries do not have PSCs, including (1) a lack of case demand or resources; (2) fear of negative outcomes; (3) beliefs that maintaining equality prohibits specialized courts for only some offenders; (4) the legal requirement for all courts to provide

Society, Science, and Problem-Solving Courts. Monica K. Miller, Mia A. Holbrook, Logan A. Yelderman, and Kylie Kulak, Oxford University Press. © Oxford University Press 2025. DOI: 10.1093/oso/9780190059804.003.0010

rehabilitation; (5) beliefs that it is not the court's role to help offenders; and (6) current, broader social issues that require more of the country's attention. This chapter adds an additional factor to Miller's (2020) typology known as (7) community demands. Community demands center around the idea of community sentiment, or collective ideals, attitudes, opinions, and values held by the local community (Miller & Chamberlain, 2015). For instance, the local community might explicitly express that they do not want a PSC because they might not agree with how a PSC defines justice. The current chapter presents new data from informants across the globe and delves into sociocultural explanations regarding why certain societies have not implemented PSCs.

Methodology

Please refer to Chapter 9 for an detailed overview of how the data was collected for both of these respective chapters. The new data presented here are purely qualitative in nature and were used to support, reject, or add to the typology presented by Miller (2020).

Results

Although the data from Miller (2020) indicated that there are six factors in the typology of reasons countries do not have PSCs, the analysis of the new data included in this chapter suggests there are seven factors. These factors are discussed below, with focus on both the original data from Miller (2020) and the data that is new to this chapter.

A lack of resources

The first factor in Miller's (2020) typology for why certain countries do not have PSCs is a lack of resources. Particularly, some countries might not have the financial resources required to develop and maintain PSCs because often they are not funded by the government (see Miller & Johnson, 2009). Despite the promise that PSCs reduce costs by reducing recidivism (Marlowe et al.,

2016) or using alternative sanctions (Casey & Rottman, 2005), the preliminary costs to develop these courts are high (Nolan, 2001). For example, the United States decommissioned some PSCs because of the 2008 recession (Miller, 2020; Petrila, 2013). The new data supports this finding; an interviewee from Turkey stated that, due to an economic recession, there would not be the financial resources to develop PSCs. Similarly, an interviewee from Italy indicated that the required changes in the legal system's infrastructure would be too costly and tumultuous. Other interviewees from India, Egypt, and Brazil have also referred to the lack of funds required to develop PSCs. One particular interviewee from Israel remarked that a lack of financial resources could be a reason why neither Israel nor Palestine (Israeli courts have some jurisdiction over Palestinians) have implemented PSCs; however, this fact is contestable due to Israel's economic wealth and well-established court system.

According to Miller (2020), lack of resources to address social issues can also manifest in the form of personnel, clientele, and treatment resources. A common theme found in Miller (2020), and amongst many countries in the new data seems to be high caseloads and training personnel. In the United States, one of the major reasons PSCs are sustained is due to the caseload they can absorb from traditional courts (Casey & Rottman, 2005). One interviewee from Columbia indicated that judicial workers are constantly on strike due to such high caseloads. Another interviewee from Moldova stated that no specific trial dates are set due to high caseloads, so the timeline for all cases are often delayed. Interviewees from Indonesia and Russia have both indicated that the training required to have judges specialized in social issues is not economically feasible. An interviewee from China reported how, due to large caseloads, it would not be possible to stretch resources to further accommodate the establishment of PSCs. This interviewee reported that, because China's legal system is relatively immature, it could not handle the nuances regarding PSCs. Our interviewee from Italy offered similar reasoning, offering that Italy's infrastructure is not prepared to initiate the changes. In Nigeria, an interviewee stated a similar reasoning: that the judiciary is under-staffed, under-equipped, and not generally motivated to push for judicial reforms like PSCs. Less support was found for lack of clientele and treatment resources, as only one interviewee from Turkey cited these factors as reasons for not adopting PSCs. In sum, the first factor of Miller's (2020) typology is still strongly supported.

A fear of negative outcomes

The next factor in Miller's (2020) typology is the fear of negative outcomes as a consequence of establishing PSCs. For example, it is possible that the public might view the social issues handled by PSCs as being trivialized because they were not handled by a regular court. Essentially, treating a certain social issue, like domestic violence in India (Miller, 2020), exclusively through a PSC might result in negative perceptions from the community. The new interview data partially supports this factor. In Italy, rather than fears of how treatment of the *social issue* will be publicly received, concerns fall upon how the *offender* might be perceived. Specifically, concerns arise in how the offender could be possibly stigmatized by the community, that "stereotyped profiles" might be generated about the offenders who participate in PSCs. In a different perspective, some Colombian citizens are facing homelessness, starvation, and unemployment, and therefore would be very frustrated that attention is directed at helping offenders instead of them. Thus, rather than perceiving the offender or social issue (e.g., domestic violence, addiction) negatively, it would be the fact that other issues are receiving attention. Later in this chapter, the prevalence of larger social issues will be discussed in reference to why PSCs have not been adopted. From the current data, it seems that negative stigmatization of the social issue is a factor, but with some nuance; how the offender might be stigmatized or trivializing competing social issues can also impact whether a country adopts PSCs.

Another reason falling under the factor of negative outcomes is the fear that offenders are stripped of their due process rights when entering a PSC (Miller, 2020). Particularly, some legal professionals believe that removing the adversarial process forces offenders to admit guilt (because an admission of guilt is required to move through the court; Brank & Haby, 2013). Further, offenders are often promised that charges against them will be dropped upon completion of treatment through the PSC, a practice that could be perceived as coercive (Brank & Haby, 2013; Nolan, 2009). In Miller (2020), the interviewee from Italy mentioned that, although *judges* might be more accepting of the non-adversarial process, *attorneys* view this process as obstructing their duty to act as an advocate for their client. The new data does not support this factor. In fact, interviewees from Turkey and Columbia mentioned that, even if rehabilitation efforts are made, reduced sentences are not offered to offenders. Many interviewees (e.g., Sweden, Columbia, Italy) stated that their countries are more punitive toward offenders; therefore, the respective judicial systems seem less concerned about the offenders' due process rights.

The final reasoning under this factor in the typology is that judges might experience burnout from hearing the same type of cases rather than a variety of cases (Chase & Hora, 2000). Judges can be at risk for vicarious trauma due to being exposed to second-hand negative emotions from working with those who experience it firsthand (hearing cases involving abuse, mental illness, or violence; Chamberlain & Miller, 2009). Miller (2020) found support for this idea through an interviewee from France who noted that hearing a diversity of cases would prevent burnout for judges. Judges might also experience negative effects from becoming close with offenders. Although viewing an offender succeed and recover throughout the rehabilitation process might be rewarding, viewing an offender struggle or fail through rehabilitation might be exceptionally difficult. This might be a legitimate reason, but the new data did not find support for this. The interviewees often focused more on the level of authority judges have or the fact that judges should only be viewed as a punitive force. In terms of the overall typology, however, the factor is well supported; whether a PSC is adopted can be dependent on foreseen negative outcomes.

A belief in equal treatment

One stipulation of PSCs in the United States is that only certain offenders are selected to participate in a PSC. The judge determines the offender's need for help and considers therapeutic resource availability. Other countries, however, would find this a violation of their right to equality. In Miller's (2020) typology, interviewees from France, Germany, Italy, Netherlands, and Spain all noted that PSCs do not exist as a result of unequal treatment of offenders. In support of this, an interviewee from Egypt stated that it would be unfair to not sentence all offenders to some form of imprisonment. In Egypt, they can consider the circumstances and try to reduce the sentence, but to send an offender to rehabilitation without imprisonment is unlawful. One of the interviewees from Columbia recited similar reasons, that each single offender cannot be helped as it would be a jurisdictional issue. The interviewee provides the following example, that in the case of drug addiction, rather than helping offenders, certain locations exists where it is legal to use drugs to deter drug usage in places such as parks. In other words, rather than rehabilitation efforts, Columbia provides alternate locations so certain unlawful acts are not conducted in public community centers.

Further support was found from an interviewee in Sweden who stated that rehabilitation from a PSC would not be seen as justice, but as special treatment. The interviewee went on to state that there are plenty of state funded programs that are designed to treat social issues, so the sentiment stands that someone should "get help before" committing a crime. In Brazil, the community views PSCs as unfair, such that they would actively promote crime. In other words, the interviewee posited that PSCs would almost be viewed as a reward for committing a crime because offenders would receive rehabilitation and treatment that is not accessible to law-abiding citizens.

Less support was found for the idea that all offenders should receive rehabilitation, as it seems more countries align with the sentiment that the general public should receive access to such social services. The idea that community members might be left with inadequate treatment due to the allocation of treatment to offenders is a criticism that has been held by some US citizens as well (Casey & Rottman, 2005). The idea that equal treatment might be infringed upon if some offenders receive treatment is supported, but more in the direction that it might be perceived as unfair that regular citizens do not have access to such treatments.

A requirement for rehabilitation

Some countries do not have *special* rehabilitative PSCs because *every* court serves as a PSC, for instance by providing rehabilitation. For example, US tribal courts serve the same function as PSCs. US tribal courts follow a one-size-fits-all approach but employ restorative justice (RJ) and honoring culture to every single case. Miller (2020) found that countries including Spain, France, and Italy are bound by law to provide some form of rehabilitative response for offenders. An interviewee from Argentina stated that special courts are unnecessary because according to criminal code Article 34, judges must consider social context as mitigating evidence for all offenders (Miller, 2020). The code instructs that judges must consider social issues (e.g., mental illness, drug addiction) in lieu of providing a sentence. Offenders are either sentenced to a government treatment center in conjunction, or instead of, a punitive measure such as imprisonment. Ultimately, the judge determines if the defendant is legally responsible for their actions, for if they are, retribution is one of the main purposes of the court.

From our new data, this factor is supported. An interviewee from Brazil stated that legislation requires social reintegration with punishment. Although this applies to all offenders, more often minor offenders receive rehabilitation over adults. A similar pattern was found in Italy, as our interviewee stated that juvenile offenders are rarely punished but are instead entrusted to social services. These services provide some form of educational program to the juveniles but are not considered to be special courts. In reality, the interviewee stated, that rehabilitation is already a focus, but due to such high recidivism rates in Italy, PSCs in their precise definition might be a necessity. In Moldova, if an offender is determined to have a mental illness, they must receive medical treatment instead of punishment. If the status of the offender is up for debate, then the approach is to administer sentences with complementary treatment. Part of the sentence can be suspended if they consent to the treatment, which some legal professionals in the United States might not agree with. For example, offering lighter sentences in agreement for treatment can be viewed as coercive because the offender has to agree that they are guilty in some form (Brank & Haby, 2013; Nolan, 2009). These rehabilitation alternatives in Moldova are also considered due to jail crowding. In support of this, an interviewee from Russia stated that every judge is required to sentence those who received a drug charge to treatment but cannot control whether they actually go to treatment. In all, the new data supports Miller's (2020) factor.

A judge's role

The next factor in Miller's (2020) typology centers on the role of judges. Much like in the United States, new data supports that, in many countries, a judge's purpose is to adjudicate the outcomes or consequences for wrongdoing. In China, the role of judges is as a punisher, and as a result judges strive to be an "iron face who is impartial and incorruptible." From a cultural perspective, our interviewee mentioned that from early on, in China, persons are raised with "tiger parents." Parents in China enforce the notion that a price must be paid for any form of wrongdoing. Many stories that children are told growing up reinforce the idea that punishment is equitable to justice, and this perspective is heavily embedded in their approach to the legal system. Our interviewee describes it as a "harmonious coexistence between bloody penalties and enthusiastic applause."

Under this reason falls the idea that judges might not feel qualified to address drug use or mental health issues (Nolan, 2009). For instance, American law schools do not provide education for legal professionals, which would be the tools required to establish a PSC. In Russia, the law specifies that judges are not allowed to address anything beyond legal issues. Therefore, according to our interviewee, it is inferred that judges cannot become experts in topics such as mental illness or drug abuse. Furthermore, a judge cannot be mandated to get such degrees that would allow them to understand such social issues. Instead, judges are only allowed to contact health professionals or psychologists for perspective. Likewise, in Italy, our interviewee stated that their constitution has a stipulation in which it explicitly bans the appointment of "extraordinary or special judges." Finally, as mentioned in conjunction with the lack of resources argument (factor 1), many countries argued that it would not be possible due to finances and high caseload to train judges to be specialized in social issue topics (e.g., drug addiction, domestic abuse).

Miller (2020) posited that some judges might fear they would appear as activists (Nolan, 2009), creating a situation in which they would be criticized for any effort to generate social change. Miller (2020) provides an example from an interviewee who stated that, in Columbia, when a court ordered Congress to solve a social issue regarding the displacement of citizens, this was considered extremely controversial. To step out of their main role as a judge that only delivers sentences to create a PSC would risk being deemed what is known as an "entrepreneurial judge." An entrepreneurial judge can focus on their special interests to ultimately move and shape the law (McIntosh & Cates, 1997). Miller (2020) found that some judges do not have the power to do so, such as in France. Our new data highly supports this factor; for example, in Brazil, judges have very limited autonomy, so they would not have the power to establish PSCs. Sweden is similar, as our interviewee stated that judges do not have the authority to determine a sentence, and it is the role of the Parole and Probation institution to rehabilitate any offenders. In opposition, judges in Nigeria have a large amount of autonomy according to an interviewee but are only recently becoming daring in their sentences to encourage rehabilitation. Otherwise, despite their discretion, judges do not offer forms of rehabilitation efforts through their sentences.

A related aspect of this factor is the belief that social issues are addressed by Congress or other lawmakers rather than the courts. Miller (2020) provided an example from Columbia, in which a mayor—rather than judges—opened a rehabilitation center for drug addiction. Almost every person who provided reasons as to why their country has not adopted a PSC stated that either the government, Congress, or other form of lawmakers in their country have authority above and beyond judges. Therefore, the lawmakers would have to introduce some form of rehabilitative efforts or initiation to develop PSCs.

Another perspective revealed in the Miller (2020) study is that the role judges play in the criminal justice system should not mix with the social services system. The new data supports this perspective; the interviewee from Italy stated that rehabilitation is entrusted to social services, and that these structures are explicitly and purposefully separated. According to our interviewee from China, judges are seen as "robots," supporting the sentiment that judges are supposed to assume the role of referee and nothing more. Moreover, an interviewee from Nigeria used the exact same metaphor to describe judges—as "robots." In India, judges are not encouraged to delve into what drove an offender to commit the crime, but only to follow what is strictly prescribed under legislation. Judges in Brazil are to strictly adhere to promoting general deterrence through punitiveness, not to help or rehabilitate.

In the context of the overall typology, the role of judges found the most support compared to other factors. Whether citing judges' role in the legal system, fear of how judges might be perceived for stepping outside their role, the role that lawmakers play over judges in instituting social change, or the belief that social care systems should not intertwine with the criminal justice system were widely supported by the new data.

A devotion to bigger issues

The final factor of the Miller (2020) typology to be considered is broader issues, such that the country does not have the time nor resources to dedicate to PSCs. Miller (2020) cited that in France, there is acknowledgment that PSCs would be useful in addressing social issues, but more pressing issues are demanding the legal system's attention. From the current data, one interviewee from Egypt cited that the country is currently dealing with much larger criminal issues, including homeland security and terrorism. In Nigeria, due to "other matters" that are currently filling judges' dockets, the courts do not have time to dedicate to other social issues in the country. In Ghana, political vigilantes are currently the focus of concern for the country, as other social issues have remained in the background.

Two interviewees from Columbia indicated that the country is dealing with an unprecedented amount of poverty, homelessness, and starvation, among other social issues affecting citizens that currently demand attention. Furthermore, one of the interviewees stated that because Columbia is one of the largest producers of drugs in the world, this topic has to be approached with caution. As a result of such a tumultuous relationship, Columbia does not focus on rehabilitation but instead directs attention toward regulating production. In recent years, Turkey has been facing political turmoil that demands attention; for example, the interviewee stated that stigmatized groups (e.g., LGBTQ+, minorities) are becoming more marginalized. The interviewee stated that, because of major political corruption, it would not be possible to implement PSCs. In the context of the overall typology, countries facing broader and more pressing issues as a factor is well-supported by the new data.

A community's demands

The newest addition to the typology involves community demand. In other words, the community itself has no desire or actively protests the adoption of PSCs. Such reasonings center around moral, social, or religious beliefs that a community might hold. These reasonings are based on community sentiment. Community sentiment, defined in this context, are the collective or shared attitudes or opinions of certain countries (Miller & Chamberlain, 2015). Community sentiment has long played a role in shaping the direction of legal legislation and reform in the United States (Chamberlain & Shelton, 2015; Sigillo & Sicafuse, 2015). Similarly, community sentiment can determine the adoption of PSCs amongst a multitude of countries.

One common theme found amongst the new data was the idea that vengeance and punishment are perceived to be more suitable for dealing with offenders than rehabilitation. These reasons can vary from religious or historical background to public trust residing in the fact that courts punish offenders. In Columbia, an interviewee stated that as a result of a violent colonial past and a largely Catholic following, the community abides by violence to solve issues, such that vengeance is the endorsed mode of resolution. Likewise, due to such a large Muslim population, Turkey has adopted a very punitive approach when it comes to offenders. Specifically, political authority is derived through Muslim values of obedience to authority. Similarly, when asked what Nigeria's overall philosophy toward criminality was, an interviewee responded with an "eye for an eye." Answering the same question, an interviewee from Egypt responded that punishment and deterrence were the main philosophies when handling criminal activity. In sum, it seems to be that one common community sentiment is focused on punishment, but some of that sentiment is derived from religious values.

In an extension of this relationship, punishment can be heavily intertwined with public trust. In Italy, although not an explicit sentiment, public trust is gained through the promise that offenders are prosecuted. Further, Italy delegates punishments disproportionate to the crime committed, as it seems to be a widely held belief that this is the way to deter crime. Another interviewee from Columbia shares a similar sentiment, stating that legal procedures hold more public trust than political negotiations for determining the course of action for an offender. The legal procedures are viewed as impartial and objective, which garners community trust.

Community sentiment can also be related to cultural values, particularly what values are instilled into a person throughout their lifetime. In China, it is considered a waste to rehabilitate offenders as this approach is considered too soft on crime. Furthermore, our interviewee stated that community sentiment views punishment as tangible and rehabilitation as a "fairy tale," and the community prefers the tangible option. In other words, because the idea that punishment equals justice is a deeply embedded community sentiment, any other form of consequence (e.g., rehabilitation) is seen as an unrealistic consequence.

Deep cultural values can appear not just in how punishment is perceived, but how those who might receive help are perceived. In Israel, the community sentiment toward their Palestinian neighbors is considered to be a main reason why PSCs have not been introduced. From an early age, both Israelis and Palestinians have been taught to believe that the other is an enemy, or just that, an "other." The tension between these two groups has been long withstanding, beginning at the end of the nineteenth century and continuing long into 2022 (Center for Preventive Action, 2022). For such reasons, continued violence in the form of missile threats, bombings, stabbings have led to a general distrust between the neighboring groups. The interviewee posited that Israelis feel that the occupation of Palestine is essential to protect themselves from Palestinians and hypothesize that Palestinians might feel they need to protect themselves through any means necessary against the occupation. Due to such a strained relationship, institutions in Israel reflect these values, and this might explain why PSCs have not yet been established. Israeli courts have jurisdiction over Palestinians, so PSCs would help rehabilitate Palestinians as well. As a result of the societal divide, Israel has not adopted PSCs.

Community demands can also consist of the general disbelief that PSCs are not effective for the issues at hand. PSCs have faced some scrutiny because of little empirical, rigorous assessment of their effectiveness (Collins, 2021). For example, evaluations of drug courts in the United States have evidenced mixed effectiveness in drug courts. Some evaluations reported little to no impact on recidivism rates, and one resulted in an increase in recidivism rates (Latessa & Reitler, 2015).

This notion of negative community sentiment toward PSCs was a common theme that emerged in the new data that was not present in Miller's (2020) typology. One interviewee from Indonesia mentioned that adopting PSCs has been disputed due to beliefs that they are ineffective. Our interviewee from China mentioned that PSCs act like an "armchair strategist," because they are full of ideas but do not actually fix the issues. This belief has also been interrelated to beliefs that they are "rewarding" rather than helpful (Brazil), or that if offenders did not seek treatment before the crime, they would not seek it/need it after the fact (Sweden).

Community demands are a proposed addition to Miller's (2020) typology because community sentiment is an important predictor in determining how the court carries out what each respective crime defines as "justice." In the United States, PSCs are relatively flexible in the power given to local practice to ensure that local culture and issues are incorporated. Yet, some are calling for the standardization of PSC practices, which could interfere with community sentiment (Casey & Rottman, 2005). Community sentiment is thus crucial in the decision of whether to implement PSCs.

Summary and Future Directions

All of these factors, taken individually or in conjunction, can influence whether a country decides to adopt PSCs. These factors share common themes regarding ability, community sentiment, and the unique composition of society. Ability refers to the variety of resources available (or unavailable) to a country. PSCs require the motivation and participation of judges, offenders, and treatment providers to be established and maintained. These legal actors need access to empirically validated treatments, locations, and the technology to administer such treatments, fiscal support, and living accommodations. As previously mentioned, although they are intended to reduce costs once in practice, the costs to establish PSCs are relatively high (Nolan, 2001). The country would have to be at a stage of development legally and economically to dedicate the time, focus, and resources to direct attention to the social issues PSCs are intended to mitigate.

Throughout the chapter, we have found support that ability plays a large role in whether a country adopts PSCs. Some countries cited fiscal resources; some countries just do not have the finances to dedicate toward establishing PSCs. Resources can come in the form of personnel, clientele, and treatment centers as well. Most countries have cited that due to such a high caseload it would not be feasible to stretch their time or the legal system any further to establish PSCs. Others cited the training required for legal personnel, or just not enough personnel to be employed at PSCs. Fewer countries cited a lack of clientele or treatment centers available to help offenders, but these factors still play a major role in the adoption of PSCs.

Community sentiment involves the general attitudes or opinions a society holds collectively. For example, the legal system in the United States was built on the idea that the public can influence it (e.g., lawmakers are voted in and are representative of the people). Many of the interviewees mentioned that community sentiment in their countries is incompatible with the values of a PSC. Some countries' religious values, for example, rest on the idea that vengeance is necessary when handling offenders. Other countries put their trust in the legal system because they deliver punishment and the legal system is viewed as an objective but punitive entity. Additionally, some countries have deeply embedded the idea that punishment is equitable to justice into their culture. From a different perspective, others might view those who are being helped by PSCs negatively, therefore lacking a desire to establish PSCs. Finally, another common theme found in community sentiment is just an overall, general skepticism in PSCs. This can manifest in opinions that PSCs are not useful, or just downright unnecessary, when it comes to solving the country's complex social issues.

Community sentiment can also apply to how a country perceives the role of the judge and the magnitude of other social issues in their country. The judge's role might be viewed as not powerful enough to create PSCs or stretched too thin to dedicate time toward other social issues. In contrast, others view the judge as a powerful executioner, and the community relies on that view to be salient to deter crime. When it comes to major issues taking the forefront of a country's attention, some countries are dealing with impoverished conditions, overwhelming violence, or political discourse that need all the possible resources dedicated to that cause.

The differential and unique composition of society plays a major role in determining the adoption of PSCs. In fact, this is one of the largest debates amongst cultural psychologists. Essentially, the question is: is it better to study a culture as a single unit, without referring to other groups as a point of comparison, or is it more beneficial to search for the underlying idealistic differences between cultures (Miyamoto & Eggen, 2013)? In the context of answering why PSCs are adopted or not, both perspectives are required. It is important to know the meanings the culture attaches to terms like offender, crime, rehabilitation, punishment to understand why their specific country has not adopted PSCs. However, discovering embedded differences between cultures can lead to generating a typology much like in this chapter. The purpose of this typology is to create an accessible and comprehensible list of factors that help explain why some countries have not adopted PSCs.

The countries mentioned throughout this chapter do not necessarily lack PSCs. For example, in India, the Special and Fast Track courts exist to deal with prevailing numbers of motor vehicle accidents in the country. These courts are considered "special courts" in India but are not designated to initiate any form of social change. More specifically, these courts are designed to help reduce caseloads that would normally be placed upon the main court system. Such courts do not attempt to reduce the number of motor vehicle accidents or educate offenders. Many countries mentioned in this chapter have some form of court to deal with a special interest or specific social issues, but the target goal is not rehabilitation.

Ideally, it would be beneficial to further empirically investigate each country's legal system to understand why PSCs have been adopted. The interviews provided throughout this article are anecdotal; therefore, empirical investigation, either through the form of census data or observational work, could further confirm or provide counterevidence to the typology set out by Miller (2020). Furthermore, it might be useful to compare and contrast this chapter with the preceding chapter to attempt a cost–benefit analysis; that is, to empirically investigate whether persons would more strongly support reasons to adopt PSCs compared to the disadvantages or hurdles that come from established them. This is not to say that this chapter takes any personal stance upon the utility of PSCs. Instead, it provides a brief overview as to why some countries have not yet adopted the rehabilitative model.

PSCs have been backed by laudatory data to prove their usefulness in the United States (Collins, 2021; see also Chapter 5 this volume). However, this usefulness does not always successfully translate into other domains. The countries in this chapter are unique in their beliefs, abilities, composition, sentiments, and values, and this fact is not to be understated. Furthermore, this latter fact is not to be perceived as negative. The PSC is a rehabilitative model that might not always be viewed as benefiting those who the country views as worth benefiting, the model might be too costly fiscally, or it just might not align with the overall community sentiment of that country. Therefore, this is not to say that the country is incapable, nor is the institution of the PSC incapable. Rather, this is to say that both entities have goals that might be discordant, and these perspectives might become dynamic or static with time. According to community sentiment, the people influence the legislation, and this ultimately determines whether a PSC is adopted.

SECTION 5
PROBLEM-SOLVING COURTS
Looking to the Future by Looking at the Past

11

The Benefits (Pros) and Drawbacks (Cons) of Problem-Solving Courts

A Scientific Understanding of Variations in Perspectives across Societies

Problem-Solving Courts, Society, and Progress

Problem-solving courts (PSCs) generally have the goal of finding solutions to crime problems, hence the name (see Wood et al., 2018). As with many programs, including specialty court programs, there are benefits and drawbacks. This chapter discusses the pros and cons of PSCs, identifying the pros and cons related to science and societal variations.

A driving motivation behind PSCs is that they are innovative ways to more effectively deal with societal problems either directly or indirectly related to crime (Kaplan et al., 2018). Although the ultimate goal might have been to reduce recidivism, PSCs often strive for other goals related to the health and well-being of their participants. However, PSCs initially were touted as successful in idea only and quickly became popular. Only after they were widely adopted did the scientific community begin to study their effectiveness and success in meeting their goals. From this growing body of research, new conclusions were reached, and new policy recommendations were developed. As with any new and popular program, increased attention also exposed potential drawbacks to PSCs and negative outcomes for the participants. These ranged from legal concerns to negative effects on participant well-being.

The purpose of this chapter is to synthesize and summarize the scientific consensus in research on the overall influence and impact of PSCs on society and legal discourse. Both the benefits (pros) and drawbacks (cons) will be identified to provide a coherent picture of the status of the research on PSCs. Some countries are concerned with ethical and legal issues that are not applicable to other countries. Thus, pros and cons are not universal and have

Society, Science, and Problem-Solving Courts. Monica K. Miller, Mia A. Holbrook, Logan A. Yelderman, and Kylie Kulak, Oxford University Press. © Oxford University Press 2025. DOI: 10.1093/oso/9780190059804.003.0011

societal undertones. These pros and cons, and differences across courts, are discussed more thoroughly below. While no final answer is provided to the question of whether or not PSCs are effective, several themes are identified and potential indicators of the benefits of PSCs are outlined to aid in future research investigations.

Benefits (Pros) of Problem-Solving Courts

The first, and potentially the most significant, benefit of PSCs is the ability of the courts to be effective in solving the problems they set out to solve (Boldt, 2017). This typically involves the reduction in general recidivism and reoffending in the specific behavior addressed by the court. For example, prostitution courts try to reduce general crime and incidences of prostitution, and drug courts try to reduce general crime and drug use. Mental health courts (MHCs) try to reduce crime and treat mental illness, and community courts try to reduce crime and restore community bonds and interpersonal trust. Although many participants go through the courts and report positive outcomes or experiences, the overall effectiveness of PSCs remains a scientific question, one with a complex answer (see Chapters 5 and 6).

The perceived effectiveness of PSCs was initially based on the success and effectiveness of the drug court (Castellano, 2011). Adult drug courts have received a significant amount of scholarship and seem to suggest robust results in reducing crime and drug use (Casey & Rottman, 2005; Marlowe, 2010; Shaffer, 2011; see Chapter 6 of this text). In fact, it is possible that much of the excitement and support for drug courts was a result of an increased focus on the scientific study of drug court effectiveness (e.g., Downey & Roman, 2010). It is also possible that the excitement preceded the increased scientific attention. Nevertheless, the focus shifted from recalled experiences to demonstrable changes based on data and evidence. Drug courts received extensive attention from the scientific community assessing recidivism, drug use, and cost-effectiveness. The novel application of scientific rigor, including meta-analytic studies, enhanced the confidence in drug courts, which might have spilled over into other PSCs (see Chapter 5). Moreover, more advanced scientific approaches to understanding drug court effectiveness led to more nuanced conclusions (Marlowe, 2010; NADCP, 1997).

Drug courts extended to juveniles upon the development of juvenile drug courts. However, the research into drug court effectiveness hit a snag when applied to juveniles. Juvenile drug courts were not as effective as adult drug courts, which seemed to perplex the field. In a unique turn of events, four meta-analyses and one multi-site outcome study were published over the course of about five years (Mitchell et al., 2012; Stein et al., 2013, 2015; Sullivan et al., 2016; Tanner-Smith et al., 2016). It is quite rare in most fields to have such a high number of meta-analyses on the same topic in such a short amount of time. It is possible that the field wanted juvenile drug courts to be effective, so they kept trying to re-analyze their effectiveness with these meta-analyses. As recently as 2022, another multi-site study emerged, again assessing the outcomes of juvenile drug courts across 10 sites. In this study, juvenile drug courts provided small to moderate benefits in the reduction of substance use and recidivism and increased access to mental health services. However, these findings likely depended on the use of evidence-based practices and adherence to the guidelines for best practices (Belenko et al., 2022). Investigations into various explanations as to if and why juvenile drug courts perform worse than adult courts became necessary (Mei et al., 2019; Wilson et al., 2019). In sum, the importance of effectiveness as the main benefit of PSCs has catalyzed research to provide conclusive evidence, especially if the existing evidence was unclear. This shows how critical the effectiveness benefit is to the legal system and research community.

Drug courts were not the only PSC to receive attention from the scientific community regarding effectiveness, although drug courts might be the only type of PSC to receive enough evidence to meet the threshold of "conclusive effectiveness" (e.g., Lowenkamp et al., 2005; Marlowe, 2010, 2011). MHCs have also received increased scientific attention. MHC studies have reported a generally positive effect in reducing recidivism, and MHCs are considered a better option than many other mental health-based early release programs (Black, 2020; Fox et al., 2021; Han, 2020; Loong et al., 2019; Yuan & Capriotti, 2019). As with many PSCs, after the emergence of drug courts, the growth of MHCs likely outpaced the research into their effectiveness (Hughes & Peak, 2012). This provided an opportunity to assess their effectiveness and examine their processes and related outcomes but provided little opportunity to make major contributions because the outcomes of this research lagged behind the establishment of these courts across the country and into more global expansion. Any effect of research would be minimal because the momentum for MHCs was premised on their potential effectiveness rather than their demonstrated effectiveness. However, research has continued in MHCs and several studies have begun to involve MHCs in other countries, such as Australia and Canada (Davidson et al., 2016; Davis et al., 2015; Lim & Day, 2016). As with drug courts, an increase in scientific attention paid to MHCs has led to the emergence of some nuances in their effectiveness. For example, MHCs might be more effective for participants with certain demographic backgrounds, lower risk profiles, and stronger program adherence (Linhorst et al., 2015; Simonsson et al., 2020).

Other PSCs also lack research on overall effectiveness, despite explicit calls for such investigations. For example, in veterans' treatment courts (VTCs), there has been some research in program and participant needs and program completions and terminations, but there remains a need for more research into their effectiveness (Baldwin & Brooke, 2019; Johnson et al., 2016; Lucas & Hanrahan, 2016). Many of these specialty courts, like community courts and prostitution courts, grew much more rapidly than did research and scientific attention. Although this was the case, research has been attempting to catch up and remains the same today. Barriers in developing and executing rigorous enough designs to establish court effectiveness likely play a role in which courts receive scientific attention and which do not. It is possible that there is a self-selection bias with some of these types of courts as well. However, neither of these changes the need for more research to better evaluate the benefits of PSCs.

A second benefit of PSCs is the enhanced opportunities and expanded roles for the legal officials, primarily the judges and attorneys. PSCs provide more latitude in judicial discretion and allow judges to engage more proactively in planning and supervising participants' behavioral changes and treatment progress (Hora & Stalcup, 2008; King, 2011). Judges and court teams adapt to participants' cases as they progress and evolve because of their continued involvement in the cases, an opportunity absent in traditional court programs or settings (Hueston, 2021). Moreover, with increased judges' involvement and discretion, participants might become more satisfied with the service from the court program, which could lead to increased compliance (see Kennedy, 2012). This is especially true for courts that provide and value input from the participants when making program decisions that affect that participant. For attorneys, PSCs, especially community courts, can provide defense attorneys more opportunities for their clients (i.e., the court participants) when compared to traditional settings (Adler & Taylor, 2012).

A third benefit of PSCs is the translation of societal goals to participants' goals through a dynamic and interactive court program. PSCs, such as community courts in Canada, can contribute to the accomplishment of national public health goals (Garcia et al., 2019). In addition to public safety, offender restoration, and crime prevention, PSCs play a moralizing role in the community by being more compassionate toward offenders; reducing the stigma associated with juvenile delinquency, like in Ohio Community Courts; and addressing racism, like in Canadian Indigenous Community Courts (Beck et al., 2006; Douds & Hummer, 2019; EagleWoman, 2019; Hueston, 2021; Steinberg, 2018). PSCs can help prioritize, and even compel, treatment; help correct injustices; and reach populations of offenders that get overlooked or undertreated by traditional settings (Steinberg, 2018).

A fourth benefit of PSCs is that they can also be considered new and additional treatment options for offenders with unique needs (see Kaplan et al., 2018), such as VTCs for offenders with combat history and combat related treatment needs (Douds & Hummer, 2019; Kieckhaefer & Luna, 2020). PSCs can be especially helpful when catching treatment needs early and when providing services to youth (e.g., Beck et al., 2006).

Other benefits of PSCs include procedural fairness through procedural justice, effective incentives and sanction that could reduce reoffending, and the application of the Risk-Need-Responsivity model (Bowen & Whitehead, 2016; DeMatteo et al., 2019). Judges might also receive benefits from job satisfaction, reducing burnout (Kaplan et al., 2018). Overall, PSCs can provide more flexible roles for judges and attorneys, more treatment options for offenders, and a way to help accomplish societal goals.

Risks (Cons) of Problem-Solving Courts

Ideally, PSCs have only positive outcomes, or at the very least neutral outcomes, but this is not the case. As with many programs, there are risks and costs associated with PSCs, and many researchers and participants identify these "cons," when comparing them to the "pros" of PSCs. Plainly stated, not all PSCs have happy endings for all participants (e.g., D'Emic, 2014).

The first risk of PSCs is the potential for forced treatment to undermine its own effectiveness. Several types of PSCs have a "treatment" aspect to them, such as MHCs and drug courts (this is beyond our scope but see DeMatteo et al., 2019). This treatment is typically carried out by an independent treatment provider but, because it is a part of the court program, it might be seen as required rather than voluntary (Matejkowski et al., 2020). This is especially true for post-adjudication PSC models (Hora, 2002). The perception of forced treatment might undermine the effectiveness of the treatment or the participant's compliance with the program because the treatment aspect of the program might be viewed as an extension of the court and any distrust or perceived illegitimacy associated with the court might transfer to the treatment provider as well (see Boldt, 2009). The relationship between the treatment provider and the participant is built on trust, which impacts the effectiveness of the treatment. Any perception that the treatment provider is an arm of the criminal justice system or is tasked with legal supervision of the participant can degrade the trust of the participant and render the treatment services ineffective. Thus, the distinct roles of the court and the treatment provider should be made clear to the participants and be perceived as non-coercive.

The second risk is that PSCs might threaten or deny due process to offenders by acting as team-driven plea deals (Adler & Taylor, 2012). PSCs deny due process by engaging in net-widening, increasing restrictions and supervision, limiting freedoms, and increasing the chance a participant will be caught violating the program terms (Gal & Dancig-Rosenberg, 2020). This is especially problematic if the offenses targeted by PSCs occur disproportionately among poor, immigrant, and minority populations (Das, 2008; Steinberg & Albertson, 2016). PSCs might also deny due process by reducing or limiting the role and capacities of the defense council or compromising the defense's perspective on the client as a result of being part of a team with the judge and prosecution (Kluger et al., 2002; Steinberg & Albertson, 2016). Not all court teams might include defense counsel, and this would be particularly consequential in any pre-adjudication programs. The constitutionality challenges in the United States differ from other countries, though, such as Australia, where there are not the same individual rights guaranteed and protected at the federal level despite jurisdiction but that the constitutional rights of the people are found at the jurisdiction level. Thus, the constitutionality of certain aspects of PSCs might differ depending on the country (Schaefer & Beriman, 2019). The subversion of constitutional rights might decrease the overall perceived legitimacy and authority of the court and decrease public support for PSC programs (see Chapter 3 for a full discussion).

The third risk related to PSCs is the unfair treatment of victims. Because criminal offenses involve victims, and PSCs involve elements of therapeutic jurisprudence and restorative justice (see Chapter 3 for a full discussion), it is critical to identify and understand the role of the victims in the PSCs. However, it appears that there is significant criticism that PSCs have not figured out the role of the victim in relation to the role of the participant/offender. VTCs have been considered to neglect victims while domestic violence courts have been considered to focus too much on victims (Das, 2008; Douds & Shultz, 2021). Neglecting victims could impede the progress of the participant by reducing the weight placed on the wrongness of their crimes. Placing too much emphasis on the victim might shift resources, time, and effort away from the participant, which could slow down or thwart any rehabilitation efforts for the participant. As PSCs adopt restorative justice approaches and move forward with including victims in the court program and treatment plan for the participant, they will need to refine the specific role of the victim to be sure the program is still geared toward the participant's rehabilitation while acknowledging how involving the victim can help with that process.

The fourth risk is the instability of structure and resources to meet the needs of the participants. For example, MHCs face the problem of underserving their participants. Although MHCs mandate mental health treatment, the effectiveness likely depends on available community resources (Warnke, 2019). Courts that rely on community resources can only be effective to the extent that their community can provide treatment and opportunities for re-integration for the participants. MHCs are also often not expansive enough; for example, they often do not include treatment for traumatic brain injuries (Wagner, 2020). This could be a problem of magnitude and scope in that mental health is such a vast field with an extremely large array of disorders and illnesses that the possibility that a court could include the resources to handle all mental health cases is very low. Even with a focus on mental health treatment, it is possible that other related needs, such as criminogenic needs, are largely neglected (Edwards et al., 2020). Thus, one issue with PSCs, and especially MHCs, is that the needs of the population served by the court are much more extensive than the services provided by the court.

The fifth risk is the perception of manipulation in treatment courts. Many PSCs specialize in specific crimes (e.g., drug courts and domestic violence courts), specific treatment needs (MHCs) or specific crime goals, such as promoting community safety and trust in the courts (e.g., community courts). However, VTCs do not fit these descriptions. VTCs establish a unique military bond with the participants, which is used to suggest an enhanced sense of understanding of the participants and to incorporate targeted care based on their military experience. This likely increases perceptions of court legitimacy and buy-in from the participants (Gallagher & Ashford, 2021; Smith, 2012). Although this seems like a good tactic and potentially a thoughtful approach, when paired with data showing ineffectiveness of VTCs (Smith, 2012) and potentially increased supervision, this tactic might appear deceitful to those who feel obligated to a specialty court (due to military status) but then receive ineffective treatment. Therefore, people who fought for the protection and safety of their country might overly trust and rely on court programs that promise to take care of them as a way to show appreciation for their sacrifices but fail to meet their needs.

The sixth risk is that PSCs might provide numerous opportunities to negatively label participants and reiterate failure. In some courts, any offense or violation is considered a failure (Porter et al., 2010). This type of labeling might reduce self-efficacy or decrease motivation to comply with program requirements. Additionally, participants often attend court hearings with the judge regularly and discuss successes and failures, which might make the failures more salient. Such exchanges with the judge could cause anxiety and anticipated anxiety in future hearings, potentially impacting the participant's progress (see Chapter 4 for a full discussion).

The final risk of PSCs is that PSCs often provide inappropriate programming for their participants. For example, applying the drug court model to other PSCs assumes the different types of offenses and population are the same, which we know is inaccurate. Moreover, the adult drug court model was applied to juveniles, upon the inception of juvenile drug treatment courts, and created a mismatch between the needs of the youth and the type of services provided by the model. Along these same lines, when the program is appropriate but the court team does not adhere to the program guidelines and procedures, best practices, or evidence-based practices, the effectiveness of the court can dramatically decline (Blair et al., 2015; Warnke, 2019).

Overall, PSCs have many potential benefits and many potential costs. The extent to which these courts are beneficial to society is still up for debate. Both Petrila (2013) and Linhorst and Dirks-Linhorst (2015) make an excellent point about MHCs in that any one MHC might be effective, but the pressing question is whether or not there are enough (effective) MHCs to curb mental illness and reduce mental health related criminal offenses and recidivism at the societal level. This same idea can be applied to any PSC. Are there enough drug courts to curb drug related crimes? Are domestic violence courts reducing domestic violence in their jurisdictions? Are prostitution courts reducing prostitution, and are VTCs lowering veteran crime rates?

It is important to note that a change in a single person's life might be justification enough for some, but because it is society that is investing in these courts, change at the societal level should be of high priority in the evaluation of these courts. The application of scientific methods and analyses can help answer these questions.

Science and Problem-Solving Courts' Effectiveness

This section examines the role of science in the evaluations and perceptions of the PSCs' risks and benefits. The implementation of PSCs really gained traction at a critical juncture with science and technology. This is possibly one of the factors that spurred the research community's interest in the effectiveness of court programs, alongside the rise in the demand and push for evidence-based programs and treatments.

Computer technology was growing more sophisticated, and the internet began to provide new opportunities. When drug courts took off, there was an initial research interest into their effectiveness and how well they could address the problems of drugs and crime. Computing technology allowed researchers to apply advanced sophisticated statistical analyses and the internet provided a platform by which to inform broader society of the results of these court assessments, which eventually spread globally (see Miller, 2020). PSCs were implemented in England, Australia, Canada, and Ireland (King, 2011). The growth of PSCs has been paralleled by a growth in scientific interest in the effectiveness and impact of these PSCs. In some countries, the scientific evidence of the court's effectiveness in the United States encouraged the adoption of similar courts, such as several pilot PSCs in Ireland (O'Hare, 2018). As numerous countries adopt PSCs, there will be a greater and more detailed picture generated regarding the effectiveness of these courts; however, in many countries (e.g., China), there is simply not enough research on PSCs to determine their effectiveness (Li & Liu, 2019). As more scientific attention is paid to these courts, more evidence will surface as to whether or not they are working and effective in reducing recidivism, rehabilitating offenders, and improving societies.

Science still has a place in PSCs beyond general effectiveness. Science has been used to establish evidence-based practices and evidence-based treatments. Science has also produced social scientific theories and hypotheses from which PSCs are developed (e.g., Wiener et al., 2010).

The scientific method and program evaluation methods have also created frameworks by which courts can analyze their own data and progress and track changes and improvements. Additionally, scientific methods, such as meta-analyses, have enabled a broader look at larger scale effects of PSCs. Social science and survey methods have also allowed participants to voice their thoughts and feelings about these courts through anonymous questionnaires.

Scientific research also has another role in PSCs, which is to help these courts eliminate preventative failures. As pointed out by Berman and Fox (2016), most criminal justice systems, such as police departments and courts, do not have the ability to make decisions and set up policies and initiatives that are likely to end in failure because when failures occur in these arenas, people's lives are at stake. Scientists and researchers are better able to engage in work that might be likely to end in failure, often through tightly controlled experimental designs or low impact and low risk field studies. Moreover, it is difficult for PSCs to collect and analyze data on their program. Many state and local agencies require some data, but it is often related to general outcomes and not tied to a scientific study or research questions. Social scientists and evaluators can work with courts and conduct scientific studies related to the PSC programs (see DeMatteo et al., 2019). This can be done in several ways, and a few are discussed below.

First, science can be used at the aggregate, like with multi-site studies and meta-analyses, to compare PSCs to the alternative traditional criminal justice programs. In this case, scientific research can provide data-driven answers to questions about reducing recidivism, improving the physical or mental health of the participants, and increasing school engagement or employment post-program. These types of studies can give the public a bird's eye view of the broader policy and program "idea." In addition to outcome focused studies, cost–benefit studies can also be conducted at an aggregate level. This helps inform the public about what costs are associated with PSCs and it allows the public to then determine if the rewards are worth it (assuming outcomes are made known to the public).

Second, scientific research can be applied to assess individual program improvements. Researchers can assess changes in policies and procedures by assessing before and after implementation. Researchers can also assess incremental changes, such as adding certain incentives or sanctions. Using science to guide data collection and data analysis, courts can understand how their program procedures impact specific outcomes in which they are interested. For example, courts could use scientific research to assess the impact of a new incentive policy on graduation or completion rates. This approach can help courts tailor their program services and goals to the population they serve.

Third, scientific research can observe and analyze very detailed or isolated phenomena outside of a court in a tightly controlled environment. The information discovered in this research can then be used by the courts to amend and revise their programs. For example, courts often use punishment as a deterrent and motivator. However, as a result of experimental research, courts have begun adopting more incentive-based motivation techniques. This was made possible by researchers conducting tightly controlled experiments on behavioral compliance motivations and behavior modifications, which the courts, of course, could not conduct themselves. However, this research informed PSCs as to how they might increase motivation among participants by using attractive incentives rather than (or in addition to) severe punishment.

The relationship between science and criminal justice will continue to evolve and the role of science in PSCs will be parallel to that evolution. PSCs will likely integrate scientific research more as time goes on and will develop around scientific understanding, research results, and suggested applications; however, courts have to collect data on their team, participants, and programs, which many do not (see Yelderman, 2016). Researchers and practitioners can use science to weigh the benefits and costs of PSCs to help determine whether or not they are worthwhile endeavors or if focus and attention should be paid to alternative policies and programs.

Society and Problem-Solving Courts' Effectiveness

Societies differ in how they view, interpret, and punish crime. Six of these differences are included in the Social Mind-set (SMS) model (see Chapter 8 for a full discussion), and they all shape policies and responses to criminal behavior (Miller & Westbrook, 2021). People from different countries have different social mind-sets that they apply to criminal behavior. This comes from differences in culture, history, experience, and attitudes. These culminate in leadership and authority figures, who then draft and shape policy responses to crime. This leads to a seemingly different response to seemingly similar problems. Applying the SMS model, PSCs are responses that emerge from the integration of a country's major historical and social events, economy and legal system, culture, inclusion of scientific research in major political and governmental decisions, justice orientation and principles, and explanations for crime attributions (Miller & Westbrook, 2021). Because countries differ across the six factors, so do their responses. Also, because of these six factors, countries that implement the same policy response might have different success rates of those policies, such as with PSCs.

Although science can be used to determine if a court is engaging in statistically significant changes, it is important that these changes also translate into observable changes. A great litmus test for the effectiveness of a court is if the public starts to notice changes. This might be people noticing that homelessness is decreasing in their area, that fewer youth seem to have drug problems, that there is less observable prostitution, and so on. It might take a large, dramatic change for the community as a whole to pick up on these changes, but the courts and public media can help. Courts can celebrate graduations and success stories publicly, news media can promote stories about the success of these courts, and social media can be used to generate excitement and knowledge about the positive trends created by these types of courts, specifically the extent to which they are effective and are helping people. Word of mouth can be a great way for friends and families to share the benefits of these courts regarding their loved ones.

Some courts, like drug courts, have used celebrities to promote awareness and support for their courts (Satterberg & Daugaard, 2019). Such tactics can generate positive attitudes toward the courts, support, and provide examples of major success. However, with celebrities, this comes with a risk that any relapse will be made publicly available (more so than with others) and could indicate the failure of the court program. Moreover, any court's effectiveness could be undermined by negative perceptions of the court's authority or legitimacy (see Chapter 3).

The public pays taxes that support these programs, and communities often include numerous stakeholders who dedicate much time and resources. Community and public trust, support, and overall sentiment are critical components of starting and sustaining PSCs. After all, they are called "problem-solving courts" because they claim to solve the problems of individuals and communities, so their ability to do so should be observable by whom they serve.

The success of PSCs might differ across societies because of differences in public support, but also because of differences in culture and societal structure. Nolan (2009) articulates this very clearly: "Embedded in American problem-solving courts are cultural assumptions that significantly challenge long-held understandings of the meaning and practice of justice—assumptions that when transplanted . . . may significantly challenge or alter the legal cultures of importing countries" (2009, p. 4). Essentially, PSCs are a product of their culture, and deviations from American culture might jeopardize the ability for PSCs to succeed or thrive to the extent they do in the United States. This, of course, might be truer for some courts over others, but it does reflect the importance placed on culture and society.

The success of PSCs also depends, in part, on the number of other legal options there are for offenders. For example, societies with many diversionary options and alternatives to traditional incarceration or traditional criminal justice might find less excitement and success than societies in which PSCs are the only alternative (see Collins, 2019a, 2019b). Moreover, PSCs require resources, stakeholders, and partners, and if societies do not have these supports and structures, then the PSCs might fail due to the lack of infrastructure. This is critical for courts like community courts in which the integration of community stakeholders and service providers is fundamental to the operation of the court. In this way, community resources dictate the establishment of the courts, and any lessening of those resources would be detrimental to the success of the court. Societies and cultures that struggle to provide community resources might not consider the community court model, and if they do, expect lower success rates. For example, US courts tend to rely on the ability to use and leverage community resources, which provides an advantage or environment conducive to community court success. Australian courts are largely successful because they have strong ties to local and regional resources, particularly health resources (Hughes & Shanahan, 2019).

One of the most popular successes of PSCs in the United States is the drug court, which has been adopted in other countries. However, countries like Ireland and Brazil have not seen the same benefits and effectiveness of these courts, which is often attributed to different contributing factors specific to the country or culture (Collins, 2019a; Guilherme, 2019). This includes social structure, economic structure, and political structure.

The judge also plays a large role; therefore, societal differences in judges' roles would shape the operation and outcomes of PSCs. In the United States, the judge has significant oversight and latitude in decision-making in PSCs. Judges can mandate treatment, make decisions about medication, and dictate supervision requirements (Csete, 2019). Judicial roles and the legal allowance of judicial discernment impact the outcome, especially if the outcomes are strongly tied to program fidelity requiring less variability and more rigid practices. Judges that stray from the program might jeopardize the evidence-based outcomes on which the program was initially founded.

Conclusions

PSCs will be evaluated based on what they can provide to the client and greater society compared to what they cost in time and money and client behavior. This essentially boils down to an assessment of whether or not the clients are better off after the program than when they started. However, this assessment might be too simplistic because with stakeholders and tax dollars involved, the change from before to after the program likely needs to be quite substantial to justify the funding and effort put into these court programs. In contrast, the clients and their families might put emphasis on the importance of saving just one life, as each life is valuable. While both of these are likely true and largely supported by public sentiment, specific success in reaching these goals can be studied using scientific research methods.

Scientific research in PSCs can help address some of these specific questions by examining the magnitude of change in clients' behaviors and the relative community, societal, and economic impact. Currently, it appears that the benefits posed to clients involve improvements in the biopsychosocial realm (e.g., reduced recidivism and drug use) and drawbacks involve threats to freedom, coercion, financial cost, and stigmatization. The fundamental cost–benefit analysis of PSCs involves a balance of personal well-being in exchange for freedom and financial resources.

The scientific community has had, and continues to play, a pivotal role in providing answers to the question of whether or not PSCs are effective. This is done by identifying the benefits (pros) of PSCs by analyzing data on completion, recidivism, treatment, and so forth. This is also done by identifying the drawbacks (cons) of implementing PSCs. The scientific community is not the only group with input on PSCs' effectiveness, but society also has a stake in these programs, specifically the communities they serve. In this case, communities are not as data driven as researchers, but instead evaluate the general positive or negative perceived impact these courts have on the individuals they serve and the community, and often the community evaluates the general purpose of these programs to gauge their own support, which can include program costs as well. However, there is hope that the courts will continue to improve these programs as they collaborate with researchers and apply scientific methods to study and understand what makes them successful and what aspects of each program contributes to enhancing the lives of the clients and society.

CONCLUSION

12

Society, Science, and Problem-Solving Courts

Yesterday, Today, and Tomorrow

Concluding Remarks about Science and Society

Some social scientists believe the world is becoming more "Americanized" or "Westernized" through globalization; this is in part because Western societies are sometimes perceived as more advanced (e.g., stronger economies, democratic governments; Chiu et al., 2011). Yet there is still great variability across countries, particularly in terms of culture, legal procedures, and governmental structures. Societies continue to change over time, and because law is a reflection of culture (and vice versa; see Chapter 7), the law and court system will also change. Problem-solving courts (PSCs) are but one example of a legal system that has developed and evolved in some societies, such as the United States, but not others.

Science and technology also provide avenues for changes in law. New types of crimes, such as white-collar crimes and cybercrimes, give rise to the need for new laws. New court cases that incorporate research and data lead to new rulings on various issues. Legal systems such as PSCs require various types of technology, ranging from online systems that track a person's therapy and drug tests to computers that calculate statistics to determine whether the program is effective (see Chapters 5 and 6).

Both science and society provide workable foundations to explain differences in PSCs within the United States and abroad. This chapter draws conclusions about how science and society have affected the development (or not) of PSCs in the past, resulting in the courts of today. It also will make some predictions about how science and society will affect the PSCs of tomorrow. This includes issues of diversity, establishing quality evaluations, and expansion versus contraction.

Society, Science, and Problem-Solving Courts. Monica K. Miller, Mia A. Holbrook, Logan A. Yelderman, and Kylie Kulak, Oxford University Press. © Oxford University Press 2025. DOI: 10.1093/oso/9780190059804.003.0012

Science: Past and future

Science plays many roles in the development (or not) of PSCs. For purposes of this book, science includes social sciences (e.g., sociology, political science, psychology, criminal justice, culture), medical science (e.g., drug testing, mental health testing and treatment), and technology (e.g., ankle monitors, internet). PSCs are evaluated scientifically to test whether they are producing the intended outcomes.

PSCs are an innovative, science-based way to protect the well-being of both vulnerable populations and society as a whole. A common theme throughout the chapters considers the role of science and technology in the development (or not) of PSCs as they are today. Indeed, the Social Mindset (SMS) model discussed in Chapter 8 specifically proposes that availability of science and technology can influence whether PSCs are adopted. Interviews in Chapter 9 discussed how scientific advances in medicine have contributed to the development of PSCs, particularly drug courts. Chapter 9 also highlighted how advances in technology have led to the development and maintenance of PSCs by increasing contact (e.g., email) amongst participants and professionals. Similarly, science likely will play a role in the future of PSCs.

Science and technology have been essential in the history of PSCs. These courts would not have developed as they have without technology and science. This includes social science, behavioral science, medical science, and evaluation methods and statistics. Science and technology allow judges to act as case workers to monitor participants' progress regarding mental health counseling, drug tests, and/or employment and to respond to changes in participants' behaviors and attitudes. For instance, addiction research can inform judges as to the best way to manage setbacks (e.g., failed drug test). Electronic monitoring can ensure that participants only go to approved locations (e.g., home, work, counseling center) to help hold participants accountable and to ensure that the participants are receiving the best version of the program and, thus, maximum positive change. Further, the basis of many PSCa are science-based justice principles, such as procedural justice (PJ): social science research shows that people who are treated fairly and with respect will be more likely to follow the law and have respect for the legal authority's legitimacy (see Chapter 3). Additionally, medical and psychological sciences can help develop new ways to help participants with mental health or addiction issues to prevent recidivism. By applying current practices, such as using brain science and medical disease models, PSC teams can develop the best plans and strategies for treatment and therapy. All these types of science and technology (and many others) combine to make PSCs a reality, and programs based on sound science using reliable technology can produce trust and confidence in their ability to curb problematic behaviors.

Science and technology are both evolving and changing rapidly; therefore, science and technology will continue to shape the *future* of courts. New technological innovations, social and medical research findings, and statistical program evaluations will shape the courts of tomorrow by providing science-based evidence concerning what "works" and what does not "work." Experiments can assess whether or not these courts have an impact on their participants, and meta-analyses are used to determine how substantial this impact is across numerous studies and experiments (as discussed in Chapter 11). These types of methods and techniques are shaping the narrative as to whether PSCs provide a benefit to the community and which aspects of these courts likely contribute to their success. Yet the influence of science and technology will likely not be uniform world-wide, as access and use of science and technology is not uniform—PSCs differ by culture, country, and society. Finally, legal authorities in some countries might find that technology is lacking (see Chapter 10). For example, basic web-based programs and communication systems allow judges to communicate with therapists, employers, and legal actors who monitor participants. Drug tests and mental health tests and treatments also must be available to carry out such programs; thus, as they become more available, more courts might be able to develop in the future in societies where they do not currently exist.

Technology also allows courts to be more adaptable to unforeseen events. The most prominent and recent example is the COVID-19 pandemic. By integrating technology in courts, judges, participants, and legal teams were able to still meet and discuss each case while staying physically distant and adhering to the Centers for Disease Control and Prevention's (CDC) guidelines, managing the potential spread of the virus, and quarantining if contracting the virus. Through email, telephone, and virtual interactions, court programs can adapt to many challenges.

There are several ways in which PSCs can benefit from future advances in science and technology. First, PSCs should rely on new advances in science. Sometimes this means that PSCs can incorporate new findings that are not necessarily specific to PSCs but still applicable. For instance, Kanani et al. (2024) propose a three-step process to identify how the legal system should address substance use as a predictor of recidivism. Specifically, substance use is commonly believed to be related to crime and thus is used as a risk factor in risk assessment instruments. However, not all substances have the same strength of relationship to crime. Thus, the authors offer a framework that helps clinicians better assess a participant's future risk by considering the type of substance used by the participant. Although Kanani et al. (2024) did not apply their three-step process to PSCs, this is a feasible use of the model. Jaymes Fairfax-Columbo (one of the authors) notes that the framework could help determine which offenders are appropriate for a drug court (Personal communication, January 2, 2024). For example, an offender who committed a crime to further their substance use (e.g., a burglary from a car) might be better fit for a drug court as compared to an offender who commits a crime with a less clear connection to their drug use or as compared to an offender whose substance use leads to repeated violent crime (to which punishment that includes treatment is more appropriate.). Fairfax-Columbo also notes that the framework could also determine how best to intervene with a participant in a drug court. For instance, a person who uses substances to cope with other problems (e.g., homelessness or mental health issues) might not be a good fit for a drug court because the drug use is secondary to the other problems and is not a direct cause of the crime (Personal communication, January 2, 2024). In sum, the model proposed by Kanani et al. (2024) has not been used specifically in the context of PSCs but such an application would be a useful tool for judges who must determine which offenders should be included in a PSC. In this way, reliance on science is one of the ways PSCs can continue to improve in the future.

Second, the PSCs of the future should rely on the justice principles and psychology that are supported in rigorous research. For instance, PJ is the notion that the way in which a dispute or legal case is handled is important in shaping a person's perception of fairness. In these cases, the authority and legitimacy of the legal actors or offices directly impacts their ability to enforce laws and whether or not the person will comply with the law. For instance, an offender who offends because of an addiction might feel that a drug court sentence including rehabilitative drug treatment is fairer than a traditional prison sentence without rehabilitation; as a result, the offender may be more compliant with those court proceedings. Social science research largely supports these notions (as discussed in Chapter 3). An evaluation by Miller et al. (2020) found that PSCs most commonly *used* justice principles of PJ and therapeutic jurisprudence (TJ), but the justice principles most often associated with successful court evaluations were community sentiment and adversarial process. Based on our own analyses in Chapter 6, we suggest that the use of TJ is also associated with successful court evaluations. Future PSC implementations should consider the justice principles of TJ, community sentiment, and adversarial process, within reasonable application, for that court.

Because PSCs help accomplish goals for the participant *and* for the community, new courts will need to gain community support, and psychologists can help with this as well. Social scientists from many backgrounds have noted the importance of gaining community support for legal (and non-legal) endeavors. Some PSCs were formed specifically to address community sentiment, but all programs should pay close attention to sentiment. The sentiment of various communities (the general population, judges, lawmakers) is important because it affects perceived legitimacy of the legal system (Miller et al., 2015). These principles are the foundation of only some PSCs, which often vary by society, and social science research largely supports the benefit of applying these principles in the criminal justice system, particularly through PSCs (as discussed in Chapter 3).

Finally, and perhaps most critically, PSCs should regularly conduct scientific evaluations to help them establish whether or not they are meeting their goals. If PSCs are trying to reduce recidivism and increase employment, then evaluations can help determine if that outcome actually occurred. This might suggest that PSCs either include a team member who is able to conduct these evaluations or team up with researchers to help them with such evaluations (Christensen et al., 2022; Summers & Shdaimah, 2010). Chapter 5 and 6 could be critical to new courts. Examining the assessments of PSCs across the United States and other nations (see Chapter 5) uncovers both similarities and distinctions in their methodologies, results, and obstacles encountered by these specialized judicial initiatives. As each type of PSC possesses distinct objectives, tactics, and results, evaluations need to be structured accordingly. However, due to the commonalities in strategies and goals among various PSCs, many assessments employ comparable benchmarks (as discussed in Chapter 6).

The scientific methods of the evaluations of various PSCs can rely on this information to know what is most likely to work. This, however, is reliant on culture because what works in one society is not necessarily going to work in another society. However, cross-cultural comparison in research could help provide evidence as to when programs and practices might translate across cultures and when they might not.

Society: Past and future

Society and culture have shaped the past development of courts, which is evident from Chapters 9 and 10. For instance, Chapter 9 discusses how, in the United States, gambling has become a serious addiction issue, generating the creation of problem gambling courts (Song, 2022). Chapter 9 also discusses how cultural definitions of marital rape have changed in Argentina, becoming a legal, rather than dismissed, issue. These types of changes move issues from outside to inside the legal context, creating a potential need for new laws and programs.

Chapter 10 discusses examples that explain why PSCs have not been developed in some countries, such as a cultural belief in Sweden that a PSC would unfairly provide special treatment to offenders. Additionally, perceptions of offenders might be partially dependent on prison populations as well. For example, the US prison population (percentage of the national population) is about four to five times higher than in Sweden. Thus, the need for reform, rehabilitation, and justice might differ as a result of cultural and political differences and differences in punishment goals.

Another example of societal influence in Italy involves interviewees (in Chapter 10) who report that defendants who enter a PSC might be negatively stigmatized and stereotyped within their society. Thus, PSCs do not facilitate growth and reintegration, an element crucial to restorative justice (RJ) (see Chapter 3), but instead cause bias and prejudice and lower the chance for successful societal reintegration. These are but a few examples of how society and culture has shaped the adoption or development (or lack thereof) of PSCs.

Society and culture are also likely to affect the future of PSCs as well. This book cannot offer "best practices" because every country would identify different practices that would be "best" based on their own culture (see DeMatteo et al., 2019, for some general best practices for various court types). However, legal professionals can glean from this book a plan to make innovative PSCs a reality in their country in the future—if they deem that such courts are appropriate for their society. There are a number of considerations that relate to the future of PSCs in various societies.

First, Chapter 7 discusses potential culturally informed practices courts might use when sentencing and rehabilitating defendants, such as considering a defendants' country of origin, language proficiency, or current living conditions. For instance, they might learn about the medical science related to the link between mental health and crime and the evaluation science that demonstrates that mental health courts (MHCs) can reduce recidivism. Legal authorities can also discover social science findings concerning psychological attributions that might hinder the adoption of courts. While people in some countries make strong personal attributions (e.g., crime is a result of personality), others make strong situational attributions (e.g., crime is a result of social factors such as poverty). Social science can help authorities change attributions to get buy-in from the public and various legal and health groups whose participation is essential.

Second, in the future, PSCs should test some of the assumptions of Chapters 7 and 8 in this book. While Chapter 7 provides a discussion of how societies around the world differ from each other, Chapter 8 offers an explanation of why, using the SMS model. This general social-science-based model suggests how six factors (e.g., a society's wealth, high-publicity events, access to science) affect whether a society pays attention to a social issue and acts to address it. The SMS Model explains why societies differ in both what they consider to be a crime and what they consider to be the proper response to that crime (e.g., helping or imprisoning offenders). Although the model can be applied to an array of topics, the chapter in this section applies the model to PSCs. These have not been tested however, so future scientists can test whether these cultural influences do, in fact, influence the adoption of PSCs.

Third, while society and culture can shape PSCs, there is also the fundamental question of whether or not PSCs begin to shape society. If each PSC is effective at the local level, and if there are enough PSCs in a given state, province, region, or country, then there should be a sizable and noticeable macro-level effect of the combined implementation of PSCs on overall crime rates. Researchers should have this goal in mind, whether it is through large-scale longitudinal studies, meta-analyses, or comparative analyses. Determining if PSCs make a ripple in country-level crime is absolutely critical to the future of any scientific understanding of the effectiveness of PSCs.

Chapter 10 identifies some barriers for things that are essential to making courts feasible. Structurally, countries that have not adopted PSCs either do not have the resources available to handle the case loads, or do not have enough cases to implement a PSC. Further, some of these countries have social issues that are their primary focus at the moment, whether it be poverty, homelessness, or general instability. Finally, some countries just do not have the community demands or community sentiment to support a PSC; some countries' values or beliefs oppose PSCs.

In sum, societal factors influence whether the society has PSCs. One major value that seems to be held among countries that do not have PSCs is that they believe PSCs might bring stigma upon defendants or that rehabilitation is an unfair consequence for a criminal act. Other societies will never have PSCs because nearly everyone in their country (e.g., Spain) receives rehabilitation and as long as rehabilitation is a right, they do not need "special" courts. Although PSCs have been around for about 35 years, the rigorous evaluation of them has lagged behind. As research involving PSCs continues to grow, especially in countries outside of the United States, there will be a greater understanding as to what makes them effective, reliable, publicly accepted, and worthwhile (i.e., cost-effective). From this, best practices, model courts, and programming recommendations will become available and better suited for various types of courts across different countries and cultures.

The future of problem-solving courts

In addition to the contributions to science and society, this book offers many insights into the possible future of PSCs (see also DeMatteo et al., 2019). Probably the most critical, and immediate, area of need is the implementation of structured rigorous program evaluations. Results of these evaluations will determine if specific courts are meeting their goals and serving the participants, as well as if the courts should be expanded or contracted. Moreover, these evaluations, when taken together, can provide a great picture and indication of the overall effectiveness of specific types of PSCs, which is critical in the general discussion about the efficacy of PSCs to meet their goals.

An important question for the future of PSCs is whether there is a growing need for them or if that need is slowly contracting. While there was an initial boon in PSCs, at their conception, the growth will likely be reconsidered as more research is made available. This will also play a part in determining the role of PSCs in the future. For example, should PSCs remain separate individual courts, or should the lessons learned from PSCs be "taken to scale" and implemented throughout all courts and criminal justice programs (e.g., Sanchez & Miller, 2009). The role of PSCs in the greater criminal justice landscape will evolve as more is learned from future research and evaluations.

Further, PSCs should consider issues of diversity in developing future programming. Some courts apply a one-size-fits-all approach which might be tailored to a particular demographic and not be equally effective for other demographics. Although evaluations can help detect these disparities, PSCs will only benefit from this information if they adopt a more tailored approach using treatments, resources, and responses to meet the specific needs of the participants. Finally, there are a number of issues (e.g., violation of due process rights) that all PSCs should consider going forward. Each of these future considerations are discussed in more detail below.

Evaluations are needed

Perhaps the most important action item involving the future of PSCs concerns scientific evaluations of their effectiveness and costs (see also Chapter 5 and 6 for more about evaluations). Existing evaluations are incomplete and have distinct flaws (e.g., only measuring short-term recidivism rates as outcomes; see e.g., Wood et al., 2018), but more comprehensive and rigorous evaluations could shed light on the future of PSCs. Now that PSCs have existed for a few decades, some of their advantages are more clear: (1) the expertise that a PSC can bring can increase the quality and consistencies of rulings, (2) PSCs can reduce overcrowded case dockets, (3) PSCs can promote judges' satisfaction with their jobs, (4) PSCs could be cost-effective over time, and (5) PSCs might have benefits for participants and their families (Wood et al., 2018). On the other hand, there is now a clearer understanding of the disadvantages of PSCs: (1) PSCs might be coercive or violate rights, (2) PSCs could lead judges to experience burnout or vicarious trauma, and (3) PSCs have costs above the traditional legal system (Wood et al., 2018). These advantages and disadvantages should be operationalized and weighed to determine their feasibility in the future (see Chapter 11 for more on the pros and cons of PSCs) . Each society could weigh the pros and cons differently, resulting in different outcomes across states or nations. These scientific and economic evaluations will ultimately determine whether a particular society decides to expand or contract their PSC courts.

Expansion versus contraction

An important part of this conclusion discusses the future expansion and contraction of PSCs. Many researchers, judges, and experts believe they "should" either expand or contract (see Kaplan et al., 2018). In just a few decades, PSCs have expanded dramatically. Although it is a well-intentioned effort to offer help to those experiencing social issues, it is not a given that PSCs should be taken to scale and widely offered, for many reasons (see, generally, Chapter 10 for reasons other countries do not have PSCs).

First, there is no uniform delivery or even definition of a PSC, which might limit their effectiveness. In the expansion that has already occurred, PSCs have deviated from the initial drug court model in many ways. PSCs have expanded beyond providing services for a discrete group of people (e.g., participants with mental health issues). There are now "hybrid" courts that handle participants with *both* mental health and drug use issues. Courts have also expanded to focus on the type of person, rather than the type of social issue. For instance, there are courts specifically for veterans (e.g., in the United States) or illegal immigrants (e.g., in Italy). Other PSCs focus on educating participants but do not have the characteristics of PSC courts. For instance, animal courts educate people who have abused their pets or who have kept dangerous pets, yet there is no specific rehabilitation program or monitoring. There is no set of principles or best-practices for all PSCs, and many types of PSCs do not even have a best-practices model for their type. If PSCs do not have best practices based on research, and if they get too watered down, this could have negative effects (Kaplan et al., 2018). This was essentially the outcome when adult drug court practices were applied to juvenile drug courts (Mei et al., 2019).

Second, there are some instances in which expansion might not be appropriate simply because there is not enough research as to whether they work, how they best work, or for whom they best work. For instance, there is a dispute as to whether DWI/DUI courts should be used for first-time offenders or reserved for second- or third-time offenders. Similarly, some courts have sentenced men who solicit prostitutes to "john's school" to educate them about the social ills of prostitution. These courts might be ineffective or have unintended behavioral/psychological consequences.

In some cases, courts develop guiding principles or practices to try to streamline the court model with the hope of universal positive effects for those jurisdictions that implement PSCs. Although the application of any PSC might depend on the jurisdiction's resources and community, an evidence-based model might help close the gap in different outcomes across courts. For example, drug courts and juvenile drug courts have had guiding principles, and courts that tended to stray away from these principles tended to fare worse (Blair et al., 2015).

Third, there is also concern that having too many PSCs will dramatically change the court systems in ways that are not necessarily beneficial. One concern is that having too many PSCs will turn the court system into a set of PSCs with expert judges instead of the adversarial system that protects people's rights. On the other hand, if judges are not experts in the areas of their PSC (e.g., homelessness, prostitution, drug use), they might not be able to facilitate the program well. Thus, finding a balance in offender protections and judicial expertise and discretion is critical for the future of PSCs.

Finally, many resources are needed to expand courts to deal with social issues, and expansion might not be feasible in some cases because of the lack of resources. This includes buy-in from law enforcement, the court systems, and the public. In some countries, it also requires legislative action, heavy resources, and restructuring of the justice system. In many cases, it requires development of more extensive social services and community networks. Also, education services are needed for judges who will be charged with administering such courts. Other resources include technology, medical advancement, and accessible social science, which are critical in the expansion of such courts.

In sum, there is much debate as to whether PSCs should be expanded or contracted—or remain virtually the same. This is an issue that will be debated in the future of PSCs. A second issue, discussed next, is the inclusion of diversity issues in PSCs.

Diversity in problem-solving courts

Another special issue in going forward is for PSCs to consider issues of diversity. Are the treatments and court operations "one size fits all"? Do they "work" better for some (White men) but not others (minority women)? Would PSCs work better if they considered the unique needs of diverse groups? Scientific research is needed to help address these questions.

Diversity issues in PSCs can manifest in various ways and might impact the effectiveness of these programs. As with most criminal justice programs, diversity is an ongoing effort in the context of PSCs. PSCs are more likely than traditional courts to positively serve diverse populations because there is a focus on individualized justice. Recognizing the unique needs of individuals from various backgrounds is often a crucial part of the PSC process. Therefore, most courts approach participants with specific considerations, such as personalized needs and cultural and social concerns.

PSCs also emphasize community involvement and continuing education. Educating the community about the purpose and benefits of PSCs can help transparency about the process and encourage all community members to be well-informed about their processes. In addition to a focus on community, most PSC courts have a multi-faceted staff that requires more detailed and recurring training. Often, those training include specialized ethical training and cultural competency (Holbrook, 2019). Training for court personnel on topics of individualized justice, cultural competency, diversity, and inclusion is essential. These types of training can enhance the understanding of the community being served, work to reduce biases, and improve interactions with individuals and the community.

Although PSCs might be better equipped to approach diversity issues, they are not problem-free. Whereas these are positive steps toward ensuring equity in the realm of PSCs, issues still need to be addressed. While training is offered to PSC staff, there needs to be a higher focus on cultural sensitivity and the population being served. Lack of cultural sensitivity and competence among court personnel might result in misunderstandings and miscommunications with participants from diverse backgrounds, dissuading future participation or community investment. Ensuring that training is tailored to reduce diversity issues and enhance cultural competency is necessary for the future of PSCs.

Another problem with diversity and PSCs includes inequalities in access. Certain demographic groups might face barriers to accessing PSC programs, leading to disparities in participation rates. PSC programs are more involved, as opposed to the traditional court process. Therefore, there are natural barriers present that need to be accounted for to reduce inequities. A straightforward solution addresses logistical obstacles, such as transportation or language barriers. Ensuring equal access is necessary for the future of PSCs.

Finally, implicit bias in the courtroom workgroup is a well-researched phenomenon in the traditional court system. These same problems of implicit bias also occur within the PSC environment (Collins, 2021). Just as in the traditional system, PSC judges and court personnel might unknowingly hold implicit biases that could affect decision-making and the administration of justice. Ongoing training is crucial to recognize and actively reduce implicit bias to mitigate these issues.

Areas for improvement

Although there are many positives to PSC programs and their impact on their communities, there are also many areas for improvement and change. By actively addressing these issues, PSCs can better fulfill their mission of providing fair and effective justice for all participants. PSCs face many barriers related to social mind-sets, economics, ethics, and politics that could prevent their implementation or hasten their contraction (Wood et al., 2018).

First, numerous courts collect data but never analyze the outcomes (Yelderman, 2016). They simply enter the required data into the required database but do not have the resources or ability to analyze their data. Others assess the data but do not understand the implications of the data or do not know how to interpret the data. In some cases, the courts are not able to develop questions that would guide and drive data collection. This is because the courts often lack the time to devote to such a task due to their strenuous workloads, or they lack the expertise to think in this way (e.g., hiring a research specialist or data consultant). Often the gap between court data and science is having a person dedicated to using what is or can be collected to draft a few questions to guide the analyses of court outcomes.

Second, some courts might violate basic ethics (for reviews, see DeMatteo et al., 2019; Kaplan et al., 2018; Wood et al., 2018). For instance, many courts do not allow participants to have an attorney, and some do not provide hearings and other processes that protect participants' due process rights. Participants could ultimately serve more time (e.g., if they have a drug relapse and receive punishment) than they would have served for the original crime (e.g., misdemeanor drug possession) in a traditional court; this is sometimes called "net-widening" (Atkin-Plunk, 2021). Further, punishing drug addiction (a medical condition) could be seen as unethical (see Kaplan et al., 2018). Another concern is that courts might be unethical because the choice between going to jail or participating in a PSC might be coercive rather than an ethical free choice—the participant might feel that they have to participate in the PSC to avoid imprisonment. Lastly, there are issues with consent and confidentiality when courts and therapy providers share private and health information. (see DeMatteo et al., 2019)

There are a number of legal concerns about PSCs, as well. First, PSCs in the United States could violate Fourth Amendment rights because participants waive their rights to be free from searches (e.g., clothing searches). Second, PSCs could violate the US First Amendment rights to be free from government forcing someone to engage in religion (e.g., if a judge orders Alcoholics Anonymous, which has a religious component). Finally, PSCs could violate equal protection if two similarly situated participants are treated differently (e.g., if there is a PSC in one county but not the next, or if the court sets eligibility criteria which means one participant gets a PSC, but another does not based on specific court criteria).

Third, and finally, more attention is needed from lawmakers, courts, and research scientists. PSCs cost money and they must be beneficial for the state or country to incur the cost. Science can help provide that foundational, necessary information to make the argument for why PSCs should be adopted. This is also true for courts that wish to apply for grants. However, without the scientific understanding of courts, how they operate, and if they work, that argument and justification for the existence and expansion of PSCs is difficult to make.

Rethinking the role of problem-solving courts

Another special issue going forward is (re)defining the role of the PSC in society, such as whether or not courts should be developed in the first place or modified to better fit the society and culture. Courts were not necessarily developed with psychology or justice principles in mind initially. Now that courts are in many countries, and there is some science on what "works," PSCs might be modified to include elements of effectiveness or best practices. As previously noted, courts might be contracted or eliminated if they are not working or if the community (i.e., the public or the legal community) decides that it is not the courts' role to help (as is the case in many countries, see Chapter 10). In many countries, traditional courts are tasked with helping offenders. Thus, there is no need for a specialty court or a PSC because they would be viewed as redundant with the traditional court system. This is the approach taken in many European courts—there are no "special helping" courts because "normal" courts "help." However, this is largely dependent on society. For example, it is less likely that traditional courts and PSCs are viewed as the same in the United States where retribution is favored over rehabilitation and thus the prison population is high. Instead, a traditional court is considered harsh, and PSCs are diversion programs in which offenders sidestep the strictness of the punishment oriented traditional court in favor of a more just rehabilitative court. Also, US tribal courts, while not technically a "problem-solving" court like drug courts, include judges that adopt RJ and the "helping" philosophies of the PSCs (Clarren, 2017). Therefore, tribal court models might be more beneficial for some societies over others. The success of any particular model in any particular country is a topic for future scientific research, which is severely needed.

Conclusion

PSCs have developed out of a fundamental desire to help restore people and rebuild communities. They have required new approaches to understanding the role of judges; the ethical reach of legal supervision; and the balance between punishment, rehabilitation, and community safety. PSCs provide unique avenues that empower the courts, judges, and the community to help shape the future of offenders. With the aid of research and technological advancement, PSCs have evolved and been adapted to meet the specific needs of countries and their citizens. The past, present, and future of PSCs lies at the intersection of science (psychology, justice philosophies, and technology) and society, which are intertwined in many ways. It is through science that the effectiveness and potential benefits of PSCs are determined, but it is through society overall that fit and support can be established. Only with a supportive society can science be used to develop, revise, and fine-tune PSCs to help them reach their goals.

Not all societies have adopted PSCs. This might be due to a lack of science and/or technology, the rejection of a particular punishment goal or justice principle, or a lack of resources (see Chapters 9 and 10). Shaped by culture and reformed through science, PSCs have carved out a novel way to address crime and criminal offenders. As with many things, it is critical to look backward to make good decisions moving forward. Expansion of PSCs should be informed by careful scientific evaluations of existing courts, rigorous research reports inclusive of various court types, and increased research attention over time to ensure the reliability and validity of results. Programs need to test whether they are making positive changes for the participants, the courts, and society in general. Such thoughtful considerations will help ensure that PSCs are reaching their goals, are cost effective, and provide positive behavioral change for participants; after all, the reason PSCs exist is to enhance the lives of those who are participating.

Additionally, PSCs will only succeed if they are well understood and well supported by the communities they serve. While some countries are eliminating some or all of their PSCs, other countries are still adding new PSCs (see e.g., Atkin-Plunk, 2021). Science and society likely will play a role in the future of PSCs. It is only through the continued pursuit of scientific research, the openness to change and revised current programs, and the careful consideration of cultural and societal barriers that PSCs will be successfully evaluated and implemented in the future.

References

Aboriginal Justice Advisory Committee. (2000). Discussion paper: Circle sentencing involving Aboriginal communities in the sentencing process. Aboriginal Justice Advisory Committee.

Abram, K. M., & Teplin, L. A. (1991). Co-occurring disorders among mentally ill jail detainees: Implications for public policy. *American Psychologist 46*(10), 1036–1045. https://doi.org/10.1037/0003-066X.46.10.1036

Acierno, R., Hernandez, M. A., Amstadter, A. B., Resnick, H. S., Steve, K., Muzzy, W., & Kilpatrick, D. G. (2010). Prevalence and correlates of emotional, physical, sexual, and financial abuse and potential neglect in the United States: The national elder mistreatment study. *American Journal of Public Health 100*(2), 292–297. https://doi.org/10.2105/AJPH.2009.163089

Adcock, C. F. (2009). The collateral anti-therapeutic effects of the death penalty. *Florida Coastal Law Review 11*, 289. https://doi.org/10.2139/ssrn.1462850

Adler, J., & Taylor, B. (2012). Minding the elephant criminal defense practice in community courts. *Judges' Journal 51*(2), 10–15. https://www.innovatingjustice.org/publications/minding-elephant-criminal-defense-practice-community-courts

Adolphe, A., Van Golde, C., & Blaszczynski, A. (2019). Examining the potential for therapeutic jurisprudence in cases of gambling-related criminal offending in Australia. *Current Issues in Criminal Justice 31*(2), 236–254. https://doi.org/10.1080/10345329.2019.1603071

Agnew-Pauley, W. (2019). Diversion in the criminal justice system: Examining interventions for drug-involved offenders. In J. Collins, W. Agnew-Pauley, & A. Soderholm (Eds.), *Rethinking drug courts: International experiences of US Policy Export* (pp. 123–147). London Publishing Partnership.

Albonetti, C. A., & Hepburn, J. R. (1997). Probation revocation: A proportional hazards model of the conditioning effects of social disadvantage. *Social Problems 44*(1), 124–138. https://doi.org/10.1525/sp.1997.44.1.03x0216h

Almquist, L., & Dodd, E. (2009). *Mental health courts: A guide to research-informed policy and practice.* Council of State Governments Justice Center. https://www.ojp.gov/ncjrs/virtual-library/abstracts/mental-health-courts-guide-research-informed-policy-and-practice

AM, A. F., Payne, J., Gelb, K., Morgan, M. A., & Makkai, T. (2016). Queensland drug and specialist courts review: Final Report. Queenslands Courts. https://www.courts.qld.gov.au/__data/assets/pdf_file/0004/514714/dc-rpt-dscr-final-full-report.pdf

Amaral, S., Dahl, G., Endl-Geyer, V., Hener, T., & Rainer, H. (2023). Arrests are effective in breaking the cycle of domestic violence. Vox EU. March 17. https://cepr.org/voxeu/columns/arrests-are-effective-breaking-cycle-domestic-violence#:~:text=Our%20main%20result%20is%20that,51%25%20reduction%20in%20repeat%20offenses.

American Bar Association (ABA). (2006). *Homelessness courts: Taking the courts to the streets.* Commission on Homelessness & Poverty.

American Medical Association (AMA). (1992). American Medical Association diagnostic and treatment guidelines on domestic violence. *Archives of Family Medicine 1*(1), 39–47. https://doi.org/10.1001/archfami.1.1.39

American Psychiatric Association (APA). (2022). *Diagnostic and statistical manual of mental disorders* (5th ed., text rev.). APA. https://doi.org/10.1176/appi.books.9780890425787

Ammann, J. J. (2000). Addressing quality of life crimes in our cities: Criminalization, community courts, and community compassion. *St. Louis University Law Journal 44*(3), 811–820.

Andrews, D. A., & Bonta, J. (1998). *The psychology of criminal conduct* (2nd ed.). LexisNexis.

Andrews, D. A., & Bonta, J. (2006). *The psychology of criminal conduct* (4th ed.). LexisNexis.

Andrews, D. A., Bonta, J., & Wormith, J. S. (2006). The recent past and near future of risk and/or need assessment. *Crime & Delinquency 52*(1), 7–27. https://doi.org/10.1177/0011128705281756

Angel, C. M., Sherman, L. W., Strang, H., Ariel, B., Bennett, S., Inkpen, N., Keane, A., & Richmond, T. S. (2014). Short-term effects of restorative justice conferences on post traumatic stress symptoms among robbery and burglary victims: A randomized controlled trial. *Journal of Experimental Criminology 10*(3), 291–307. https://doi.org/10.1007/s11292-014-9200-0

Animals & Society Institute. (2020). Animal court. https://www.animalsandsociety.org/

Armstrong, M. M., Miller, M. K., & Griffin, T. W. (2015). An examination of sex offender registration and notification laws: Can community sentiment lead to ineffective laws? In M. K. Miller, J. A. Blumenthal, & J. Chamberlain (Eds.), *Handbook of community sentiment* (pp. 239–251). Springer.

Aseline, E. D., & João Lobo Antunes, M. (2021). Tribal healing to wellness courts. In E. M. Ahlin & A. S. Douds (Eds.), *Talking problem-solving courts to scale: Diverse applications of the specialty court model* (pp. 195–210). Lexington Books.

Ashford, J. (2004). Treating substance abusing parents: A study of the Pima County family drug court approach. *Juvenile and Family Court Journal 55*(4), 27–37. https://doi.org/10.1111/j.1755-6988.2004.tb00171.x

Atkin-Plunk, C. (2021). Drug courts: The beginning of the movement. In E. M. Ahlin & A. S. Douds (Eds.), *Talking problem-solving courts to scale: Diverse applications of the specialty court model* (pp. 5–30). Lexington Books.

Atkin-Plunk, C. A., Peck, J. H., & Armstrong, G. S. (2019). Do race and ethnicity matter? An examination of racial/ethnic differences in perceptions of procedural justice and recidivism among problem-solving court clients. *Race and Justice 9*(2), 151–179.

Atkinson, H. G., Curnin, K. J., & Hanson, N. C. (2016). U.S. state laws addressing human trafficking: Education of and mandatory reporting by health care providers and other professionals. *Journal of Human Trafficking 2*(2), 111–138. https://doi.org/10.1080/23322705.2016.1175885

ATSIC. (1997). Outcomes statement for the Ministerial Summit on Indigenous Deaths in custody. *Indigenous Law Bulletin 4*(5), 15. http://classic.austlii.edu.au/au/journals/IndigLawB/1997/79.html

Audette, A. P., & Weaver, C. L. (2015). Faith in the court: Religious out-groups and the perceived legitimacy of judicial decisions. *Law & Society Review 49*(4), 999–1022. https://doi.org/10.1111/lasr.12167

AUDIT. (n.d.). Alcohol Use Disorders Identification Test—About AUDIT. Auditscreen.org

Austin, J., & Juergen, D. (1999). Standards for batterer programs: A review and analysis. *Journal of Interpersonal Violence 14*(2), 152–168. https://doi.org/10.1177/088626099014002004

Australian Bureau of Statistics. (2003). Yearbook Australia 2003: Crime and justice—Indigenous prisoners. Australia Now. https://www.abs.gov.au/ausstats/abs@.nsf/0/68ABB1D86BC6E0BCCA256CAE0018EF4F?opendocument

Ayoub, L. H., & Pooler, T. (2015). Coming home to Harlem: A randomized controlled trial of the Harlem Parole Reentry Court. Center For Court Innovation. https://www.ojp.gov/ncjrs/virtual-library/abstracts/coming-home-harlem-randomized-controlled-trial-harlem-parole

Baba, S. (2018). Canadian developments in alternative sentencing: Mental health courts (Part 2). *McGill Journal of Law and Health*. https://mjlh.mcgill.ca/2018/02/06/canadian-developments-in-alternative-sentencing-mental-health-courts-part-2/

Babb, B. (2013). Unified family courts: An interdisciplinary framework and a problem-solving approach. In R. L. Wiener & E. M. Brank (Eds.), *Problem-solving courts: Social science and legal perspectives* (pp. 65–82). Springer. https://doi.org/10.1007/978-1-4614-7403-6_5

Babcock, J. C., & Steiner, R. (1999). The relationship between treatment, incarceration, and recidivism of battering: A program evaluation of Seattle's coordinated community response to domestic violence. *Journal of Family Psychology 13*(1), 46–59. https://doi.org/10.1037/0893-3200.13.1.46

Bakht, N. (2005). Problem solving courts as agents of change. *Criminal Law Quarterly 50*(3), 224–254. https://heinonline.org/HOL/P?h=hein.journals/clwqrty50&i=240

Bala, N., Lindsay, R. C. L., & McNamara, E. (2000). Testimonial aids for children: The Canadian experience with closed circuit television, screens and videotapes. *Criminal Law Quarterly (Toronto) 44*(4), 461–486.

Baldwin, J. M., & Brooke, E. J. (2019). Pausing in the wake of rapid adoption: A call to critically examine the veterans treatment court concept. *Journal of Offender Rehabilitation 58*(1), 1–29. https://doi.org/10.1080/10509674.2018.1549181

Banks, P., Conger, J., & Cram, J. M. (2014). Elder protection courts: Judicial perspective, holistic approach. *Experience 24*(1), 12–30. https://heinonline-org/HOL/P?h=hein.journals/experien24&i=14

Barnes, C. D., Brown, R. P., & Osterman, L. L. (2012). Don't tread on me: masculine honor ideology in the U.S. and militant responses to terrorism. *Personality & Social Psychology Bulletin 38*(8), 1018–1029. https://doi.org/10.1177/0146167212443383

Bath, E. P., Godoy, S. M., Morris, T. C., Hammond, I., Mondal, S., Goitom, S., Farabee, D., & Barnert, E. S. (2020). A specialty court for U.S. Youth impacted by commercial sexual exploitation. *Child Abuse & Neglect 100*, 104041. https://doi.org/10.1016/j.chiabu.2019.104041

Baumeister, R. F., Vohs, K. D., Nathan DeWall, C., & Zhang, L. (2007). How emotion shapes behavior: Feedback, anticipation, and reflection, rather than direct causation. *Personality and Social Psychology Review 11*(2), 167–203. https://doi.org/10.1177/1088868307301033

Beck, V. S., Ramsey, R. J., Lipps, J. T. R., & Travis III, L. F. (2006). Juvenile diversion: An outcome study of the Hamilton County, Ohio unofficial juvenile community courts. *Juvenile and Family Court Journal 57*(2), 1–10. https://doi.org/10.1111/j.1755-6988.2006.tb00117.x

Belasco, A. (2014). The cost of Iraq, Afghanistan, and other global war on terror operations since 9/11. Policy File. Federation of American Scientists. https://sgp.fas.org/crs/natsec/RL33110.pdf

Belenko, S. R. (1998). Research on drug courts: A critical review. *National Drug Court Institute Review*, 10–55. https://ntcrc.org/wp-content/uploads/2020/06/DCRVolume1-1_Research_on_Drug_Courts_A_Critical_Review.pdf

Belenko, S. (2001). Research on drug courts: A critical review, 2001 update. National Center on Addiction and Substance Abuse, Columbia University. https://www.ojp.gov/ncjrs/virtual-library/abstracts/research-drug-courts-critical-review-2001-update

Belenko, S., Dembo, R., Knight, D. K., Elkington, K. S., Wasserman, G. A., Robertson, A. A., Welsh, W. N., Schmeidler, J., Joe, G. W., & Wiley, T. (2022). Using structured implementation interventions to improve referral to substance use treatment among justice-involved youth: Findings from a multisite cluster randomized trial. *Journal of Substance Abuse Treatment 140*, 108829. https://doi.org/10.1016/j.jsat.2022.108829

Behnken, M. P., Bort, A., & Borbon, M. (2017). Race and gender recidivism differences among juvenile mental health court graduates. *Juvenile and Family Court Journal 68*(2), 19–31. https://doi.org/10.1111/jfcj.12092

Benesh, S. C. (2006). Understanding public confidence in American courts. *The Journal of Politics 68*(3), 697–707.

Bentley, P., & Bakht, N. (2004). Problem solving courts as agents of change. *Journal of the Commonwealth Magistrates' and Judges' Association 15*(3), 7–15.

Berenson, S. (2010). The movement toward veterans courts. *Journal of Poverty Law and Policy 44*(2), 37–42. https://heinonline.org/HOL/P?h=hein.journals/clear44&i=39

Berman, G. (2000). What is a traditional judge anyway? Problem-solving in the state courts. *Judicature 84*(2), 78–85. https://heinonline-org.unr.idm.oclc.org/HOL/P?h=hein.journals/judica84&i=80

Berman, G. (2011). Try Again, Fail Again, Fail Better: Lessons from Community Courts – Interview with Greg Berman. [Interview]. https://www.ojp.gov/library/publications/try-again-fail-again-fail-better-lessons-community-courts-interview-greg

Berman, G., & Feinblatt, J. (2001). Problem-solving courts: A brief primer. *Law & Policy* 23(2), 125–140. https://doi.org/10.1111/1467-9930.00107

Berman, G., & Feinblatt, J. (2005). *Good courts: The case for problem-solving justice.* The New Press.

Berman, G., & Fox, A. (2005). Justice in Red Hook. *Justice System Journal 26*(1), 77–90. https://doi.org/10.1080/0098261X.2005.10767739

Berman, G., & Fox, A. (2016). *Trial and error in criminal justice reform: Learning from failure.* Rowman & Littlefield.

Berman, G., Lippman, J., Haynes, C. J., Indelman, A., Blake, P., Armer, J., & Tapia, A. (2003). Red Hook Community Justice Center.

Bicchieri, C., & Funcke, A. (2018). Norm change: Trendsetters and social structure. *Social Research: An International Quarterly 85*(1), 1–21. https://doi.org/10.1353/sor.2018.0002

Bicchieri, C., & McNally, P. (2018). Shrieking sirens: Schemata, scripts, and social norms. How change occurs. *Social Philosophy and Policy 35*(1), 23–53. https://doi.org/10.1017/S0265052518000079

Bicchieri, C., Muldoon, R., & Sontuoso, A. (2018). Social norms. *The Stanford encyclopedia of philosophy.*

Black, C. (2020). Mental-health courts: Expanding the model in an era of criminal justice reform. *Washington University Journal of Law and Policy 63*, 299–323. https://openscholarship.wustl.edu/law_journal_law_policy/vol63/iss1/15

Blair, L., Sullivan, C., Latessa, E., & Sullivan, C. J. (2015). Juvenile drug courts: A process, outcome, and impact evaluation. *Juvenile Justice Bulletin*, 1–9. https://ojjdp.ojp.gov/sites/g/files/xyckuh176/files/pubs/248406.pdf

Blakey, J. M., Mueller, D. J., & Richie, M. (2017). Strengths and challenges of a prostitution court model. *Justice System Journal 38*(4), 364–379. https://doi.org/10.1080/0098261X.2017.1327335

Blatier, C. (1998). The specialized jurisdiction in France: a better chance for minors. *International Journal of Law, Policy and the Family 12*(2), 146–160.

Bloom, B., & Tavrow, P. (2018). Are primary care clinicians serving low-income patients more likely to screen for domestic violence? *Journal of Community and Preventive Medicine 1*(2), 1–8. https://doi.org/10.33309/2638-7719.010201

Blue-Howells, J. H., Clark, S. C., van den Berk-Clark, C., & McGuire, J. F. (2013). The U.S. Department of Veterans Affairs Justice programs and the sequential intercept model: Case examples in national dissemination of intervention for justice-involved veterans. *Psychological Services 10*(1), 48–53. https://doi.org/10.1037/a0029652

Blumer, H. (1971). Social problems as collective behavior. *Social Problems 18*(3), 298–306. https://doi.org/10.2307/799797

Blumer, H. (1973). A note on symbolic interactionism: Reply to Huber. *American Sociological Review 38*, 797–798.

Boehnlein, J. K., Schaefer, M. N., & Bloom, J. D. (2005). Cultural considerations in the criminal law: The sentencing process. *Journal of the American Academy of Psychiatry and the Law 33*(3), 335–341. https://pubmed.ncbi.nlm.nih.gov/16186197/

Boldt, R. C. (2009). A circumspect look at problem-solving courts. In P. C. Higgins and M. B. Mackinem (Eds.), *Problem-solving courts: Justice for the twenty-first century* (pp. 13–32). Praeger.

Boldt, R. C. (2017). Problem-solving courts. In E. Luna (Ed.), *Reforming criminal justice: Volume 3, pretrial and trial processes* (pp. 273–304). Sandra Day O'Connor College of Law, Arizona State University. https://law.asu.edu/sites/default/files/pdf/academy_for_justice/13_Reforming-Criminal-Justice_Vol_3_Problem-Solving-Courts.pdf

Boles, S. M., Young, N. K., Moore, T., & DiPirro-Beard, S. (2007). The Sacramento Dependency drug court: Development and outcomes. *Child Maltreatment 12*(2), 161–171. https://doi.org/10.1177/1077559507300643

Boothroyd, R., Mercado, C. Poythress, N., & Petrila, J. (2005). Clinical outcomes of defendants in mental health court. *Psychiatric Services 56*(7), 829–834. https://doi.org/10.1176/appi.ps.56.7.829

Borders, B. (2015). Veterans imprisoned by the violent shadows of military war time: The expansion of the insanity defense to include post-traumatic stress disorder. *The Journal of Legal Medicine 36*(1), 73–99. https://doi.org/10.1080/01947648.2015.1049923

Bottoms, A., & Tankebe, J. (2012). Beyond procedural justice: A dialogic approach to legitimacy in criminal justice. *Journal of Criminal Law and Criminology (1973–) 102*(1), 119–170. http://www.jstor.org/stable/23145787

Boudon, R. (1996). The cognitivist model: A generalized rational-choice model. *Rationality and Society 8*(2), 123–150. https://doi.org/10.1177/104346396008002001

Bouffard, J. A., & Richardson, K. A. (2007). The effectiveness of drug court programming for specific kinds of offenders: Methamphetamine and DWI offenders versus other drug-involved offenders. *Criminal Justice Policy Review 18*(3), 274–293.

Bowen, P., Qasim, A., & Tetenbaum, L. (2013). *A snapshot of domestic violence courts.* Center for Court Innovation.

Bowen, P., & Whitehead, S. (2016). Problem-solving courts: An evidence review. Centre for Justice Innovation. https://justiceinnovation.org/publications/problem-solving-courts-evidence-review

Bowman-Perrott, L., Burke, M. D., de Marin, S., Zhang, N., & Davis, H. (2015). A meta-analysis of single-case research on behavior contracts: Effects on behavioral and academic outcomes among children and youth. *Behavior Modification 39*(2), 247–269. https://doi.org/10.1177/0145445514551383

Bozza, J. A. (2011). Seeing the forest through the trees: thinking critically about mental health courts. *Chapman Journal of Criminal Justice 2*, 165–190.

Braithwaite, J. (1989). *Crime, shame and reintegration.* Cambridge University Press.

Braithwaite, J. (1998). Restorative justice. In M. Tony (Ed.), *The handbook of crime and punishment* (pp. 323–344). Oxford University Press.

Braithwaite, J. (1999). Restorative justice: Assessing optimistic and pessimistic accounts. *Crime and Justice 25*, 1–127. http://www.jstor.org/stable/1147608.

Braithwaite, J. (2002). Setting standards for restorative justice. *British Journal of Criminology 42*(3), 563–577. https://doi.org/10.1093/bjc/42.3.563

Brank, E. M., Carsten Kucera, S., & Hays, S. A. (2005). Parental responsibility statutes: An organization and policy implications. *Journal of Law and Family Studies 7*(1), 1–155.

Brank, E., & Haby, J. A. (2013). The intended and unintended consequences of problem-solving courts. In R. L. Wiener & E. Brank (Eds.), *Problem-solving courts: Social science and legal perspectives* (pp. 239–241). Springer.

Breckenridge, J., Winfree, L., Maupin, J., & Clason, D. (2000). Drunk drivers, DWI "drug court" treatment, and recidivism: Who fails? *Justice Research and Policy 2*(1), 87–106. https://doi.org/10.3818/JRP.2.1.2000.87

Briggs, D., & Auty, K. (2003). Koori Court Victoria— Magistrates' Court (Koori Court) Act 2002. Paper presented at Australian and New Zealand Society of Criminology Conference, Sydney, October.

Britton, P., Ilgen, M. A., Rudd, D. M., & Conner, K. R. (2012). Warning signs for suicide within a week of healthcare contact in Veteran decedents. *Psychiatry Research 200*(2–3), 395–399. https://doi.org/10.1016/j.psychres.2012.06.036

Brook, J., Akin, B. A., Lloyd, M. H., & Yan, Y. (2015). Family drug court, targeted parent training and family reunification: Did this enhanced service strategy make A difference?: Family drug court, targeted parent training. *Juvenile & Family Court Journal 66*(2), 35–52. https://doi.org/10.1111/jfcj.12028

Brown, R. (2010). Associations with substance abuse treatment completion among drug court participants. *Substance Use & Misuse 45*(12), 1874–1891. https://doi.org/10.3109/10826081003682099

Bruns, E. J., Pullmann, M. D., Weathers, E. S., Wirschem, M. L., & Murphy, J. K. (2012). Effects of a multidisciplinary family treatment drug court on child and family outcomes: Results of a quasi-experimental study. *Child Maltreatment 17*(3), 218–230. https://doi.org/10.1177/1077559512454216

Buck, T. L. (2017). *A proposed review of recidivism rates and technologies in Minnesota's Sixth District DWI court's pilot SBIRT program* [Doctoral dissertation, College of St. Scholastica].

Buenaventura, M. (2018). *Treatment not custody: Process and impact evaluation of the Santa Sonica homeless community court* [Doctoral dissertation, Pardee RAND Graduate School].

Bullard, C. E., & Thrasher, R. (2016). Evaluating mental health court by impact on jurisdictional crime rates. *Criminal Justice Policy Review 27*(3), 227–246. https://doi.org/10.1177/0887403414562420

Bureau of Indian Affairs. (n.d.). Tribal Court System. U.S. Department of the Interior. https://www.bia.gov/CFRCourts/tribal-justice-support-directorate

Bureau of Justice Assistance. (2010). Prisoner Reentry Program. Bureau of Justice Assistance. https://bja.ojp.gov/funding/awards/2010-dd-bx-0684

Burger, J. M. (2009). Replicating Milgram: Would people still obey today? *American Psychologist 64*(1), 1–11. https://doi.org/10.1037/a0010932

Burgess, R. L., & Akers, R. L. (1966). A differential association-reinforcement theory of criminal behavior. *Social Problems 14*(2), 128–147. https://doi.org/10.2307/798612

Burns, S. L., & Peyrot, M. (2003). Tough love: Nurturing and coercing responsibility and recovery in California drug courts. *Social Problems 50*(3), 416–438. https://doi.org/10.1525/sp.2003.50.3.416

Burton, M. (2006). Judicial monitoring of compliance: Introducing "problem solving" approaches to domestic violence courts in England and Wales. *International Journal of Law, Policy and the Family 20*(3), 366–378. https://doi.org/10.1093/lawfam/ebl017

Butts, J. (2001). Introduction: Problem-solving courts. *Law & Policy 23*(2), 121–124.

Cacciatore, M. A., Browning, N., Scheufele, D. A., Brossard, D., Xenos, M. A., & Corley, E. A. (2018). Opposing ends of the spectrum: Exploring trust in scientific and religious authorities. *Public Understanding of Science 27*(1), 11–28. https://doi.org/10.1177/0963 66251666109

Calathes, W. (1990). Gun control in a developing nation: The Gun Court Act of Jamaica. *International Journal of Comparative and Applied Criminal Justice 14*(1–2), 317–344. https://doi.org/10.1080/01924036.1990.9688948

Calabrese, A. (2002). Neighborhood justice: The red hook community justice center. *Judges J 41*, 7–13.

Caldeira, G. A., & Gibson, J. L. (1995). The legitimacy of the Court of Justice in the European Union: Models of institutional support. *American Political Science Review 89*(2), 356–376.

Calinescu, T., & Adminaite, D. (2018). Progress in reducing drink driving in Europe. European Transport Safety Council.

Cameron, L., & Thorsborne, M. (2001). Restorative justice and school discipline: Mutually exclusive. In H. B. Strang & J. Braithwaite, *Restorative justice and civil society* (pp. 180–194). Cambridge Press.

Canada. (2012). National action plan to combat human trafficking. Government of Canada. https://www.publicsafety.gc.ca/cnt/rsrcs/pblctns/ntnl-ctn-pln-cmbt/index-en.aspx

Canada, K. E., & Gunn, A. J. (2013). What factors work in mental health court? A consumer perspective. *Journal of Offender Rehabilitation 52*(5), 311–337.

Canadian Department of Justice. (n.d.). Federal child support guidelines: A comprehensive review—Volume 1—Children come first: A report to Parliament reviewing the provisions and operation of the federal child support guidelines. https://www.justice.gc.ca/eng/rp-pr/fl-lf/child-enfant/rp/v1/v1_1.html

Carey, S., Allen, T., Einspruch, E., & Mackin, J. (2015). Using behavioral triage in court-supervised treatment of DUI offenders. *Alcoholism Treatment Quarterly 33*(1), 44–63.

Carey, S., Fuller, B., & Kissick, K. (2008). Michigan DUI courts outcome evaluation: Final report. NPC Research.

Carlson, A. (2009). The family in America: Retrospective and prospective. *Family in America: A Journal of Public Policy 23*(3), 1–13.

Carlson, K. P. (2004). Child abuse or parent abuse? *Pediatrics 113*(1 Pt 1), 181–182. https://doi.org/10.1542/peds.113.1.181

Carroll, J. S., & Payne, J. W. (1977). Crime seriousness, recidivism risk, and causal attributions in judgments of prison term by students and experts. *Journal of Applied Psychology 62*(5), 595–602. https://doi.org/10.1037/0021-9010.62.5.595

Casey, P. M., & Rottman, D. B. (2005). Problem-solving courts: Models and trends. *Justice System Journal 26*(1), 35–56. https://doi.org/10.1080/0098261X.2005.10767737

Casey, T. (2004). When good intentions are not enough: Problem-solving courts and the impending crisis of legitimacy. *SMUL Review 57*, 1459.

Cassetty, J. (1978). *Child support and public policy*. Lexington Books.

Castellano, U. (2011). Problem-solving courts: Theory and practice. *Sociology Compass 5*(11), 957–967.

Castellano, U. (2017). The politics of benchcraft: The role of judges in mental health courts. *Law & Social Inquiry 42*(2), 398–422.

Cavanaugh, J. M. (2011). Helping those who serve: Veteran's treatment courts foster rehabilitation and reduce recidivism for offending combat veterans. *New England Law Review 45*, 463–487.

Cavanaugh, M. R., & Franklin, T. W. (2012). Do DWI courts work? An empirical evaluation of a Texas DWI court. *Journal of Offender Rehabilitation 51*(4), 257–274.

Center for Court Innovation. (2015). Responding to sex trafficking in your jurisdiction: A planning toolkit. Human Trafficking and the State Courts Collaborative.

Center for Disease Control. (2021). History of the Surgeon General's Reports on Smoking and Health. October. www.cdc.gov

Center for Preventive Action. (2022). Israeli–Palestinian conflict. Global Conflict Tracker. October 27. https://cfr.org/global-conflict-tracker/conflict/israeli-palestinian-conflict

Center for Substance Abuse Treatment (CSAT). (2004). Substance abuse treatment and family therapy. Substance Abuse and Mental Health Services Administration. http://www.ncbi.nlm.nih.gov/books/NBK64269/

Centre for Public Health Excellence. (2010). *Methods for the development of NICE public health guidance* (3rd ed.). Centre for Public Health Excellence.

Chamberlain, J., & Miller, M. K. (2009). Evidence of secondary traumatic stress, safety concerns, and burnout among a homogeneous group of judges in a single jurisdiction. *Journal of the American Academy of Psychiatry and the Law Online 37*(2), 214–224.

Chamberlain, J., & Shelton, H. D. E. (2015). Methods and measures used in gauging community sentiment. In M. Miller, J. Blumenthal, & J. Chamberlain (Eds.), *Handbook of community sentiment* (pp. 43–54). Springer. https://doi.org/10.1007/978-1-4939-1899-7_2

Chase, D. J., & Hora, P. F. (2000). Implications of therapeutic jurisprudence for judicial satisfaction. *Court Review 37*(1), 12–20.

Chase-Lansdale, P. L., & Brooks-Gunn, J. (1995). *Escape from poverty: What makes a difference for children?* Cambridge University Press.

Children's Defense Fund. (2009). *Protect children, not guns 2009*. Children's Defense Fund.

Chiu, C., Gries, P., Torelli, C. J., & Cheng, S. Y. Y. (2011). Toward a social psychology of globalization. *Journal of Social Issues 67*(4), 663–676. doi:10.1111/j.1540-4560.2011.017721.x

Choi, S. (2012). Family drug courts in child welfare. *Child and Adolescent Social Work Journal 29*, 447–461.

Christensen, E., Blomquist, M., Dixon, T. (2022). Judicial—Academic Partnerships for Juvenile Drug Treatment Courts. A Technical Assistance Bulletin. National Council of Juvenile and Family Court Judges. https://www.ncjfcj.org/wp-content/uploads/2023/08/Judicial---Academic-Partnerships-for-JDTCs_Final2.pdf

Christy, A., Poythress, N. G., Boothroyd, R. A., Petrila, J., & Mehra, S. (2005). Evaluating the efficiency and community safety goals of the Broward County mental health court. *Behavioral Sciences & the Law 23*(2), 227–243. https://doi.org/10.1176/appi.ps.56.7.829

Chuang, E., Moore, K. A., Barrett, B., & Young, M. S. (2012). Effect of an integrated family dependency treatment court on child welfare reunification, time to permanency and re-entry rates. *Children and Youth Services Review 34*, 1896–1902.

Cialdini, R. B., Kallgren, C. A., & Reno, R. R. (1991). A focus theory of normative conduct: A theoretical refinement and reevaluation of the role of norms in human behavior. *Advances in Experimental Social Psychology 24*, 201–234. https://doi.org/10.1016/S0065-2601(08)60330-5

Cialdini, R. B., Reno, R. R., & Kallgren, C. A. (1990). A focus theory of normative conduct: Recycling the concept of norms to reduce littering in public places. *Journal of Personality and Social Psychology 58*(6), 1015–1026. https://doi.org/10.1037/0022-3514.58.6.1015

Circle sentencing—Involving Aboriginal Communities in the sentencing process. (2001). Discussion Paper. Aboriginal Justice Advisory Council of New South Wales.

Cissner, A. B., & Thomforde Hauser, R. (2021). Seeking safety and accountability through domestic violence courts. In E. M. Ahlin & A. S. Douds (Eds.), *Talking problem-solving courts to scale: Diverse applications of the specialty court model* (pp. 215–238). Lexington Books.

Clark, S., McGuire, J., & Blue-Howells, J. (2010). Development of veterans treatment courts: Local and legislative initiatives. *Drug Court Review 7*(1), 171–208.

Claro, H. G., Oliveira, M. A. F. D., Titus, J. C., Fernandes, I. F. D. A. L., Pinho, P. H., & Tarifa, R. R. (2015). Drug use, mental health and problems related to crime and violence: Cross-sectional study. *Revista Latino-Americana de Enfermagem 23*(6), 1173–1180. https://doi.org/10.1590/0104-1169.0478.2663

Clarren, R. (2017). Native American peacemaking courts offer a model for reform. *Investigate West*. November 30. https://www.invw.org/2017/11/30/native-american-judge-shows-peacemaking-courts-offer-a-model-for-reform/

Clear, T. R., & Karp, D. R. (1998). The community justice movement. In D. R. Karp (Ed.), *Community justice: An emerging field* (pp. 3–28). Rowman & Littlefield Publishers.

Cobb, S. (1976). Social support as a moderator of life stress. *Psychosomatic Medicine 38*(5), 300–314. https://doi.org/10.1097/00006842-197609000-00003

Cochran, J. C. (2014). Breaches in the wall: Imprisonment, social support, and recidivism. *Journal of Research in Crime and Delinquency 51*(2), 200–229. https://doi.org/10.1177/0022427813497963

Cochran, J. K., Paquette Boots, D., & Chamlin, M. B. (2012). Political identity and support for capital punishment: A test of attribution theory. *Journal of Crime and Justice 29*(1), 45–79. https://doi.org/10.1080/0735648X.2006.9721217.

Cohen, D. (1998). Culture, social organization, and patterns of violence. *Journal of Personality and Social Psychology 75*(2), 408–419. https://doi.org/10.1037//0022-3514.75.2.408

Cohen, D., & Nisbett, R. E. (1994). Self-protection and the culture of honor: Explaining Southern violence. *Personality and Social Psychology Bulletin 20*(5), 551–567. https://doi.org/10.1177/0146167294205012

Cohen, D., & Nisbett, R. E. (1997). Field experiments examining the culture of honor: The role of institutions in perpetuating norms about violence. *Personality and Social Psychology Bulletin 23*(11), 1188–1199. https://doi.org/10.1177/01461672972311006

Cohen, R. L. (2016). Restorative justice. In C. Sabbagh & M. Schmitt (Eds.), *Handbook of social justice theory and research* (pp. 257–272). Springer.

Collins, E. (2021). The problem of problem-solving courts. *UC Davis Law Review 54*(3), 1573–1629. https://doi.org/10.2139/ssrn.3492003

Collins, J. (2019a). Explaining the failure of drug courts in the United Kingdom. In J. Collins, W. Agnew-Pauley, & A. Soderholm (Eds.), *Rethinking drug courts: International experiences of US Policy Export* (pp. 99–122). London Publishing Partnership.

Collins, J. (2019b). The Irish experience: Policy transfer from US drug courts. In J. Collins, W. Agnew-Pauley, & A. Soderholm (Eds.), *Rethinking drug courts: International experiences of US Policy Export* (pp. 51–74). London Publishing Partnership.

Colvin, M. (2000). *Crime and coercion: An integrated theory of chronic criminality*. Springer.

Colvin, M., Cullen, F. T., & Ven, T. V. (2002). Coercion, social support, and crime: An emerging theoretical consensus. *Criminology 40*(1), 19–42.

Coker, D. (2001). Crime control and feminist law reform in domestic violence law: A critical review. *Buffalo Criminal Law Review 4*(2), 801–860. https://doi.org/10.1525/nclr.2001.4.2.801

Connor, T. (2021). Community courts: Restoring the community one case at a time. In E. M. Ahlin & A. S. Douds (Eds.), *Talking problem-solving courts to scale: Diverse applications of the specialty court model* (pp. 141–162). Lexington Books.

Cosden, M., Ellens, J., Schnell, L., & Yamini-Diouf, Y. (2005). Efficacy of a mental health treatment court with assertive com-munity treatment. *Behavioral Sciences and the Law 23*(2), 199–214.

Council of State Governments Justice Center. (2008). *A guide to the role of crime victims in mental health courts*. Council of State Governments.

Craig, R. L., Felix, H. C., Walker, J. F., & Phillips, M. M. (2010). Public health professionals as policy entrepreneurs: Arkansas's childhood obesity policy experience. *American Journal of Public Health 100*(11), 2047–2052. https://doi.org/10.2105/AJPH.2009.183939

Criminal Justice Alliance. (2015). Fairness in the courts: The best we can do. [Address by Lord Neuberger]. https://criminaljusticealliance.org/wp-content/uploads/The-Best-We-Can-Do-Lord-Neuberger-at-the-CJA-100415.pdf

Crowe, E., & Higgins, E. T. (1997). Regulatory focus and strategic inclinations: Promotion and prevention in decision-making. *Organizational Behavior and Human Decision Processes 69*(2), 117–132.

Csete, J. (2019). Drug courts in the United States: Punishment for "patients"? In J. Collins, W. Agnew-Pauley, & A. Soderholm (Eds.), *Rethinking drug courts: International experiences of US Policy Export* (pp. 1–20). London Publishing Partnership.

CSG Justice Center. (2021). Mental health courts. Justice Center, The Council of State Governments. https://csgjusticecenter.org/projects/mental-health-courts/

Cullen, F. T. (1994). Social support as an organizing concept for criminology: Presidential address to the Academy of Criminal Justice Sciences. *Justice Quarterly 11*(4), 527–559. https://doi.org/10.1080/07418829400092421

Cullen, F. T., Jonson, C. L., & Mears, D. P. (2016). Reinventing community corrections. *Crime and Justice 46*(1), 27–93. https://doi.org/10.1086/688457

Cullen, F. T., Wright, J. P., & Chamlin, M. B. (1999). Social support and social reform: A progressive crime control agenda. *Crime & Delinquency 45*(2), 188–207. https://doi.org/10.1177/0011128799045002000

Cunneen, C. (2001). *Conflict, politics and crime: Aboriginal communities and the police*. Allen & Unwin. https://doi.org/10.4324/9781003115243

D'Emic, M. J. (2014). Mental health courts: Bridging two worlds. *Touro Law Review 31*(3), 369–376.

Dalke, I. (2020). Courting the community: Legitimacy and punishment in a community court. *Contemporary Sociology 49*(6), 547–548. https://doi.org/10.1177/0094306120963121cc

Daly, K. (2007). The limits of restorative justice. In K. Daly (Ed.), *Handbook of restorative justice* (pp. 134–145). Routledge.

Daly, K. (2017). Restorative justice: The real story. In K. Daly (Ed.), *Restorative Justice* (pp. 85–109). Routledge.

Daly, K., & Hayes, H. (2001). Restorative justice and conferencing in Australia. In *Trends & issues in Crime and Criminal Justice, 186*. Australian Institute of Criminology. https://www.aic.gov.au/publications/tandi/tandi186

Damen, T. G., van Leeuwen, M. L., Dijksterhuis, A., & van Baaren, R. B. (2014). Authority defied: Need for cognitive closure influences regulatory control when resisting authority. *Journal of Personality 82*(4), 310–316. https://doi.org/10.1111/jopy.12058

Dang Vang v. Vang Xiong X. Toyed. 944 F.2d 476 (9th Cir. 1991)

Darnell, A. J., & Schuler, M. S. (2015). Quasi-experimental study of Functional Family Therapy effectiveness for juvenile justice aftercare in a racially and ethnically diverse community sample. *Children and Youth Services Review 50*, 75–82.

Das, A. (2008). Immigrants and problem-solving courts. *Criminal Justice Review 33*(3), 308–328.

Davidson, F., Heffernan, E., Greenberg, D., Butler, T., & Burgess, P. (2016). A critical review of mental health court liaison services in Australia: A first national survey. *Psychiatry, Psychology and Law 23*(6), 908–921.

Davis, K. M. (2014). A program evaluation of Toronto's mental health court for youth.

Davis, K. M., Peterson-Badali, M., Weagant, B., & Skilling, T. A. (2015). A process evaluation of Toronto's first youth mental health court. *Canadian Journal of Criminology and Criminal Justice 57*(2), 159–188.

Dawson, M., & Dinovitzer, R. (2001). Victim cooperation and the prosecution of domestic violence in a specialized court. *Justice Quarterly 18*(3), 593–622.

DeMatteo, D., Heilbrun, K., Thornewill, A., & Arnold, S. (2019). *Problem-solving courts and the criminal justice system*. Oxford University Press.

DeMatteo, D., Marlowe, D. B., Festinger, D. S., & Arabia, P. L. (2009). Outcome trajectories in drug court: Do all participants have serious drug problems? *Criminal Justice and Behavior 36*(4), 354–368.

Denver Trial Lawyers. (2018, January 9). *What makes the U.S. court system unique worldwide.* https://www.denvertriallawyers.com/blog/2018/january/what-makes-the-u-s-court-system-unique-worldwide/

Department of Justice Canada. (2008). *Aboriginal courtwork program. Summative evaluation. Final report.* Department of Justice Canada.

Department of Justice Canada. (2013). *Gladue Practices in the Provinces and Territories.* Research and Statistics Division.

Department of Justice Canada. (2018). Indigenous courtwork program. Government of Canada. https://www.justice.gc.ca/eng/fund-fina/gov-gouv/acp-apc/index.html

Desai, K. (2013). Legal strategies in the fight to end human trafficking. *HLRe: Off the Record 3*(2), 33–60.

Deschenes, E. P., Turner, S., & Greenwood, P. W. (1995). Drug court or probation?: An experimental evaluation of Maricopa County's drug court. *Justice System Journal 18*(1), 55–73.

Dirks-Linhorst, P. A., Kondrat, D., Linhorst, D. M., & Morani, N. (2013). Factors associated with mental health court nonparticipation and negative termination. *Justice Quarterly 30*(4), 681–710. doi: 10.1080/07418825.2011.615756

Dirks-Linhorst, P. A., & Linhorst, D. M. (2012). Recidivism outcomes for suburban mental health court defendants. *American Journal of Criminal Justice 37*, 76–91.

Ditton, P. (1999). *Special report: Mental health and treatment of inmates and probationers.* Washington, DC: US Department of Justice.

Dollar, C. B., Ray, B., Hudson, M. K., & Hood, B. J. (2018). Examining changes in procedural justice and their influence on problem-solving court outcomes. *Behavioral Sciences & the Law 36*(1), 32–45.

Dong, X., & Simon, M. A. (2013). Elder abuse as a risk factor for hospitalization in older persons. *JAMA Internal Medicine 173*(10), 911–917. https://doi.org/10.1001/jamainternmed.2013.238

Dorf, M. C., & Fagan, J. A. (2003). Problem-solving courts: From innovation to institutionalization. *American Criminal Law Review 40*, 1501.

Doris, J. M., Stitch, S., and Walmsley, L. (2020). Empirical approaches to altruism. In E. N. Zalta (Ed.), *The Stanford Encyclopedia of Philosophy*. Springer.

Douds, A. S., Ahlin, E. M., Howard, D., & Stigerwalt, S. (2017). Varieties of veterans' courts: A statewide assessment of veterans' treatment court components. *Criminal Justice Policy Review 28*(8), 740–769. https://doi.org/10.1177/0887403415620633

Douds, A. S., & Hummer, D. (2019). When a veterans' treatment court fails: Lessons learned from a qualitative evaluation. *Victims & Offenders 14*(3), 322–343. https://doi.org/10.1080/15564886.2019.1595248

Douds, A. S., & Shultz, H. (2021). Are victims' rights honored in veterans courts? A statewide assessment of law on the books versus law in action. *Victims & Offenders 16*(6), 912–930. https://doi.org/10.1080/15564886.2021.1912871

Douds, A. S., Warburton, E. R., & Cassidy, K. A. (2021). Restoring humanity through human trafficking courts? In E. M. Ahlin & A. S. Douds (Eds.), *Talking problem-solving courts to scale: Diverse applications of the specialty court model* (pp. 239–266). Lexington Books.

Douglas, J. M., & Guidry, S. R. (2013). *Report on the Texas legislature, 83rd session: An urban perspective.* Earl Carl Institute for Legal and Social Policy.

Downing, J. A. (2002). Individualized behavior contracts. *Intervention in School and Clinic 37*(3), 168–172. https://doi.org/10.1177/105345120203700306

Downey, P. M., & Roman, J. (2010). *A Bayesian meta-analysis of drug court cost-effectiveness.* The Urban Institute, The District of Columbia Crime Policy Institute. www.ndcrc.org

Driscoll, D. T. (2018). Solving the problem of problem-solving justice: Rebalancing federal court investment in reentry and pretrial diversion programs. *Minnesota Law Review 102*, 1381–1412. https://scholarship.law.umn.edu/mlr/105

Drug Strategies. (1997). *Cutting crime: Drug courts in action.* Drug Strategies.

Duffy, J. (2011). Problem-solving courts, therapeutic jurisprudence and the Constitution: If two is company, is three a crowd? *Melbourne University Law Review 35*(2), 394–425.

Dunford, D., & Haag, A. (2020). A review on the effectiveness of Canadian and American mental health courts. *International Journal of Risk and Recovery 3*(2), 28–42. https://doi.org/10.15173/ijrr.v3i2.4112

Dweck, C. S., Chiu, C. Y., & Hong, Y. Y. (1995). Implicit theories and their role in judgments and reactions: A word from two perspectives. *Psychological Inquiry 6*(4), 267–285. https://doi.org/10.1207/s15327965pli0604_1

EagleWoman, A. (2019). Envisioning Indigenous community courts to realize justice in Canada for First Nations. *Alberta Law Review 56*, 669. https://doi.org/10.29173/alr2516

Eckberg, D. A. (2001). *Hennepin county community justice project: Summary report of short-term evaluation.* Hennepin County District Court Research Department.

Eckenroth, D. (2015). Wealthy "justice": The role wealth plays in sentencing and in the affluenza defense. *New England Journal on Criminal and Civil Confinement 41*(2), 443–462.

Edgemon, A. K., Rapp, J. T., Coon, J. C., Cruz-Khalili, A., Brogan, K. M., & Richling, S. M. (2021). Using behavior contracts to improve behavior of children and adolescents in multiple settings. *Behavioral Interventions 36*(1), 271–288. https://doi.org/10.1002/bin.1757

Edwards, J. L. P., & Ray, J. J. A. (2005). Judicial perspectives on family drug treatment courts. *Juvenile & Family Court Journal 56*(3), 1–27. https://doi.org/10.1111/j.1755-6988.2005.tb00106.x

Edwards, E. R., Sissoko, D. R., Abrams, D., Samost, D., La Gamma, S., & Geraci, J. (2020). Connecting mental health court participants with services: Process, challenges, and recommendations. *Psychology, Public Policy, and Law 26*(4), 463–475. https://doi.org/10.1037/law0000236

Elbogen, E. B., Johnson, S. C., Newton, V. M., Straits-Troster, K., Vasterling, J., Wagner, H. R., & Beckham, J. C. (2012). Criminal justice involvement, trauma, and negative affect in Iraq and Afghanistan war era veterans. *Journal of Consulting and Clinical Psychology 80*(6), 1097–1102. https://doi.org/10.1037/a0029967

Elek, J. (2019). Judicial perspectives on emotion, emotion management, and judicial excellence in the USA. *Judicial Perspectives on Emotion, Emotion Management, and Judicial Excellence in the USA (March 26, 2019).* Forthcoming, Oñati Socio-Legal Series. https://doi. org/10.35295/osls. iisl/0000-0000-0000-1033

Ellsworth, P. C., & Scherer, K. R. (2003). Appraisal processes in emotion. In R. J. Davidson (Ed.), *Handbook of Affective Sciences* (pp. 572–595). Oxford University Press.

Erez, E., Ibarra, P., Bales, W., & Gur, O. (2012). GPS monitoring technologies and domestic violence: An evaluation study. NCJRS. https://www.ncjrs.gov/pdffiles1/nij/grants/238910.pdf

Espinal, N. (2023). How the shelter court gives San Bernardino County's homeless a clean slate. *The Sun*. December 14. https://www.sbsun.com/2023/12/14/how-the-shelter-court-gives-san-bernardino-countys-homeless-a-clean-slate/

Estes, C. (2024). Phoenix launches new court for unsheltered people. https://www.kjzz.org/2024-01-16/content-1868473-phoenix-launches-new-court-unsheltered-people

ETSC. (2018). Alcohol interlocks and drink driving rehabilitation in the EU—Guidelines for Member States. European Transport Safety Council.

Fairfax-Columbo, J. (2024). Personal communication. January 2.

Fallows, J. (2020, March 18). 2020 time capsule #5: The 'Chinese virus.' *The Atlantic*. https://www.theatlantic.com/notes/2020/03/2020-time-capsule-5- the-chinese-virus/608260/

Fanarraga, I., & Koetzle, D. (2021). Mental health courts: Policy and practice. In E. M. Ahlin & A. S. Douds (Eds.), *Talking problem-solving courts to scale: Diverse applications of the specialty court model* (pp. 31–52). Lexington Books.

Farole Jr., D. J., Puffett, N., Rempel, M., & Byrne, F. (2005). Applying problem-solving principles in mainstream courts: Lessons for state courts. *Justice System Journal 26*(1), 57–75. https://doi.org/10.1080/0098261X.2005.10767738

Farrington, D. P., Gottfredson, D. C., Sherman, L. W., & Welsh, B. C. (2002). The Maryland scientific methods scale. In L. W. Sherman, D. P. Farrington, B. C. Welsh, & D. L. MacKenzie (Eds.), *Evidence-based crime prevention* (pp. 13–21). Routledge.

Feder, L., & Wilson, D. B. (2005). A meta-analytic review of court-mandated batterer intervention programs: Can courts affect abusers' behavior? *Journal of Experimental Criminology 1*, 265–262. https://doi.org/10.1007/s11292-005-1179-0

Federal Bureau of Investigation. (2013). *Crime in the United States, 2012*. Unified Crime Report. U.S. Department of Justice.

Fell, J. C., Tippetts, A. S., & Langston, E. A. (2011). An evaluation of the three Georgia DUI courts (No. DOT HS 811 450). United States National Highway Traffic Safety Administration. https://doi.org/10.21949/1525776

Fessinger, M., Hazen, K., Bahm, J., Cole-Mossman, J., Heideman, R., & Brank, E. (2020). Mandatory, fast, and fair: Case outcomes and procedural justice in a family drug court. *Journal of Experimental Criminology 16*, 49–77.

Finn, P., & Newlyn, A. K. (1993). *Miami's "drug court:" A different approach*. National Institute of Justice.

Fisler, C. (2015). When research challenges policy and practice: Toward a new understanding of mental health courts. *Judges Journal 54*, 8.

Flanagan, T. J., McGarrell, E. F., & Brown, E. J. (1985). Public perceptions of the criminal courts: The role of demographic and related attitudinal variables. *Journal of Research in Crime and Delinquency 22*(1), 66–82.

Florey, K. (2013). Beyond uniqueness: Reimaging the tribal courts' jurisdiction. *California Law Review 101*(6), 1499–1564.

Ford, S. (2012). A social psychology model of the perceived legitimacy of international criminal courts: Implications for the success of transitional justice mechanisms. *Vanderbilt Journal of Transnational Law 45*, 405.

Fortson, R., & Carbaugh, J. A. (2014). Survey of tribal court effectiveness studies. *Alaska Justice Forum 31*(3–4), 15–20.

Fox, B., Miley, L. N., Kortright, K. E., & Wetsman, R. J. (2021). Assessing the effect of mental health courts on adult and juvenile recidivism: A meta-analysis. *American Journal of Criminal Justice 46*, 644–664.

Franco, C. (2011). Drug courts: Background, effectiveness and policy issues for Congress. *Journal of Current Issues in Crime, Law and Enforcement 4*(1/2), 19–50.

Franke, N. D., & Shdaimah, C. (2022). "I have different goals than you, we can't be a team": Navigating the tensions of a courtroom workgroup in a prostitution diversion program. *Ethics and Social Welfare 16*(2), 193–205.

Franklin, T. W. (2010). Community influence on prosecutorial dismissals: A multilevel analysis of case-and county-level factors. *Journal of Criminal Justice 38*(4), 693–701.

Freedman, M. H. (1998). Our constitutionalized adversary system. *Chapman Law Review 1*, 57–90.

Freeman, K. (2003). Health and well-being outcomes for drug-dependent offenders on the NSW Drug Court program. *Drug and Alcohol Review 22*(4), 409–416. https://doi.org/10.1080/09595230310001613921

Freeman-Wilson, K., & Huddleston, C. W. (1999). DWI/drug courts: Defining a national strategy. National Drug Court Institute. http://www.nadcp.org/learn/about-nadcp/national-drug-court-institute

Friedman, M. J. (2006). Posttraumatic stress disorder among military returnees from Afghanistan and Iraq. *American Journal of Psychiatry 163*(4), 586–593. https://doi.org/10.1176/ajp.2006.163.4.586

Friedman, M., & Savage, L. J. (1948). The utility analysis of choices involving risk. *Journal of Political Economy 56*(4), 279–304. https://www.jstor.org/stable/1826045

Friedmann, R. R. (1992). *Community policing: Comparative perspectives and prospects.* Palgrave Macmillan.

Frink, D. D., & Ferris, G. R. (1998). Accountability, impression management, and goal setting in the performance evaluation process. *Human Relations 51*(10), 1259–1283. https://doi.org/10.1023/A:1016938030748

Fronius, T., Persson, H., Guckenburg, S., Hurley, N., & Petrosino, A. (2016). Restorative justice in US Schools: A research review. WestEd Justice & Prevention Research Center. https://www.wested.org/wp-content/uploads/2019/04/resource-restorative-justice-in-u-s-schools-an-updated-research-review.pdf

Fulham, L., Blais, J. Rugge, T., & Schultheis, E. A. (2023). The effectiveness of restorative justice programs: A meta-analysis of recidivism and other relevant outcomes. *Criminology & Criminal Justice*. Advance online publication. https://doi.org/10.1177/17488958231215228

Funk, P. (2005). Governmental action, social norms, and criminal behavior. *Journal of Institutional and Theoretical Economics (JITE)/Zeitschrift für die gesamte Staatswissenschaft 161*(3), 522–535. https://www.jstor.org/stable/40752536

Gal, T. (2020). Restorative justice myopia. *International Journal of Restorative Justice 3*(3), 341–355. https://doi.org/10.5553/IJRJ.000051

Gal, T., & Dancig-Rosenberg, Hadar. (2017). Characterizing community courts. *Behavioral Sciences & the Law 35*(5–6), 523–539. https://doi.org/10.1002/bsl.2310

Gal, T., & Dancig-Rosenberg, H. (2020). "I am starting to believe in the word 'justice'": Lessons from an ethnographic study on community courts. *American Journal of Comparative Law 68*(2), 376–411. https://doi.org/10.1093/ajcl/avaa017

Gallagher, J. M., & Ashford, J. B. (2021). Perceptions of legal legitimacy in veterans treatment courts: A test of a modified version of procedural justice theory. *Law and Human Behavior 45*(2), 152–164. https://doi.org/10.1037/lhb0000441

Gant, F., & Grabosky, P. N. (2000). *The promise of crime prevention.* Australian Institute of Criminology.

Gant, F., & Grabosky, P. N., & Australian Institute of Criminology. (2000). *The promise of crime prevention/Frances Gant and Peter Grabosky*. Australian Institute of Criminology.

Garcia, R. A., Kenyon, K. H., Brolan, C. E., Coughlin, J., & Guedes, D. D. (2019). Court as a health intervention to advance Canada's achievement of the sustainable development goals: A multi-pronged analysis of Vancouver's downtown community court. *Globalization and Health 15*(1), 1–14. https://doi.org/10.1186/s12992-019-0511-9

Gatowski, S. I., Dobbin, S. A., & Summers, A. (2013). Exploring the value-added of specialized problem-solving courts for dependency cases. In R. L. Wiener & E. M. Brank (Eds.), *Problem-solving courts: Social science and legal perspectives* (pp. 33–53). Springer. https://doi.org/10.1007/978-1-4614-7403-6_3

Gavin, P., & Sabbagh, M. (2019). Developing community courts with restorative justice in Ireland. *British Journal of Community Justice 15*(2), 19–40.

Gelfand, M. J., Nishii, L. H., & Raver, J. L. (2006). On the nature and importance of cultural tightness-looseness. *Journal of Applied Psychology 91*(6), 1225–1244. https://doi.org/10.1037/0021-9010.91.6.1225

Gendreau, P., Little, T., & Goggin, C. (1996). A meta-analysis of the predictors of adult offender recidivism: What works! *Criminology 34*(4), 575–607. https://doi.org/10.1111/j.1745-9125.1996.tb01220.x

Gendreau, P., Smith, P., & French, S. (2006). The theory of effective correctional intervention: Empirical status and future directions. In F. Cullen & M. Coleman (Eds.), *Taking stock: The status of criminology theory* (pp. 419–446). Transaction Press.

Gervey, B. M., Chiu, C.-y., Hong, Y.-y., & Dweck, C. S. (1999). Differential use of person information in decisions about guilt versus innocence: The role of implicit theories. *Personality and Social Psychology Bulletin 25*(1), 17–27. https://doi.org/10.1177/0146167299025001002

Gibbs, J. (1968). Crime, punishment, and deterrence. *Southwestern Social Science Quarterly 48*(4), 515–530. http://www.jstor.org/stable/42867909

Gibbs, J. (1975). *Crime, punishment and deterrence.* Elsevier.

Gilbert, D. T., & Wilson, T. D. (2000). Miswanting: Some problems in the forecasting of future affective states. In J. P. Forgas (Ed.), *Feeling and thinking: The role of affect in social cognition* (pp. 178–197). Cambridge University Press.

Global Overview of Sex Offender Registration and Notification Systems | Office of Justice Programs (ojp.gov). (2014).

Goldkamp, J. S. (1999). Challenges for research and innovation: When is a drug court not a drug court? In W. C. Terry (Ed.), *The early drug courts: Case studies in judicial innovation* (pp. 166–177). Sage Publications.

Goldkamp, J. S., & Weiland, D. (1993). Assessing the impact of Dade County's Felony Drug Court. National Institute of Justice. https://www.ojp.gov/pdffiles1/nij/145302.pdf

Goodale, G., Callahan, L., & Steadman, H. J. (2013). Law & psychiatry: What can we say about mental health courts today? *Psychiatric Services 64*(4), 298–300. https://doi.org/10.1176/appi.ps.201300049

Goodey, J. (1994). Fear of crime: What can children tell us? *International Review of Victimology 3*(3), 195–210. https://doi-org.unr.idm.oclc.org/10.1177/026975809400300302

Goodman, G. S., Tobey, A. E., Batterman-Faunce, J. M., Orcutt, H., Thomas, S., Shapiro, C., & Sachsenmaier, T. (1998). Face-to-face confrontation: Effects of closed-circuit technology on children's eyewitness testimony and jurors' decisions. *Law and Human Behavior 22*(2), 165–203. https://doi.org/10.1023/A:1025742119977

Goldthorpe, J. H. (1998). Rational action theory for sociology. *British Journal of Sociology 49*(2), 167–192. https://doi.org/10.2307/591308

Gondolf, E. W. (2000). Mandatory court review and batterer program compliance. *Journal of Interpersonal Violence 15*(4), 428–437. https://doi.org/10.1177/088626000015004006

Gover, A. R., Brank, E. M., & MacDonald, J. M. (2007). A specialized domestic violence court in South Carolina: An example of procedural justice for victims and defendants. *Violence Against Women 13*(6), 603–626. https://doi.org/10.1177/1077801207301553

Grassian, S. (2006). Psychiatric effects of solitary confinement. *Washington University Journal of Law & Policy 22*(1), 325–383.

Graveline, F. J. (2012). Idle no more: Enough is enough! *Canadian Social Work Review/Revue Canadienne de Service Social* 29(2), 293–300. http://www.jstor.org/stable/43486286

Gravett, B. (2015). Countering human trafficking: The UK's efforts. *Migration and the Security Sector Paper Series.* DCAF. https://www.dcaf.ch/sites/default/files/publications/documents/1511DCAF-MSS-GravettTHB-UK.pdf

Green, B., Furrer, C., Worcel, S., Burrus, S., & Finigan, M. (2007). How effective are family treatment drug courts? Outcomes from a four-site national study. *Child Maltreatment 12*(1), 43–59. https://doi.org/10.1177/1077559506296317

Greenberg, G. A., & Rosenheck, R. A. (2008). Jail incarceration, homelessness, and mental health: A national study. *Psychiatric services (Washington, D.C.) 59*(2), 170–177.

Grier, W. H., & Cobbs, P.M. (1968). *Black rage.* Basic Books. https://doi.org/10.1177/10443 8946911

Griffin, T., & Miller, M. K. (2008). Child abduction, AMBER alert, and crime control theater. *Criminal Justice Review 33*(2), 159–176. https://doi.org/10.1177/0734016808316778

Grommon, E., Hipple, N. K., & Ray, B. (2016). An outcome evaluation of the Indianapolis community court. *Criminal Justice Policy Review 28*(3), 220–237. https://doi.org/10.1177/0887403415573774

Grommon, E., Rydberg, J., & Carter, J. (2017). Does GPS supervision of intimate partner violence defendants reduce pretrial misconduct? Evidence from a quasi-experimental study. *Journal of Experimental Criminology 13*(4), 483–504. https://doi.org/10.1007/s11292-017-9304-4

Grosfeld, E., Scheepers, D., & Cuyvers, A. (2022). Value alignment and public perceived legitimacy of the European Union and the Court of Justice. *Frontiers in Psychology 12*, 785892.

Gross, E. K. (1999). An Evaluation/Assessment of Navajo Peacemaking. Report prepared under Grant No. 97-IJ-CX-0039 awarded by the National Institute of Justice, Office of Justice Programs, U.S. Department of Justice. Northern Arizona University. (https://www.ncjrs.gov/pdffiles1/nij/grants/187675.pdf).

Gruber, A., Cohen, A., & Mogulescu, K. (2016). Penal welfare and the new human trafficking intervention courts. *Florida Law Review 68*(5), 1333–1402. https://scholarship.law.ufl.edu/flr/vol68/iss5/3

Grzyb, T., Doliński, D., Trojanowski, J., & Bar-Tal, Y. (2018). Cognitive structuring and obedience toward authority. *Personality and Individual Differences 133*, 115–120. https://doi.org/10.1016/j.paid.2017.08.032

Guenaga, A. (2011). Improving the odds: Changing the perception of problem gambling and supporting the growth of problem gambling courts. *UNLV Gaming Law Journal 1*(2), 133–154. https://scholars.law.unlv.edu/glj/vol2/iss1/7

Guilherme Mendes de Paiva, L. (2019). Drug policy, therapeutic jurisprudence and criminal justice in Brazil. In J. Collins, W. Agnew-Pauley, & A. Soderholm (Eds.), *Rethinking drug courts: International experiences of US Policy Export* (pp. 75–98). London Publishing Partnership.

Guerra, V. M., Giner-Sorolla, R., & Vasiljevic, M. (2013). The importance of honor concerns across eight countries. *Group Processes & Intergroup Relations 16*(3), 298–318. https://doi.org/10.1177/1368430212463451

Hagan, J., & McCarthy, B. (1997). *Mean streets: Youth crime and homelessness.* Cambridge University Press.

Haidt, J. (2001). The emotional dog and its rational tail: A social intuitionist approach to moral judgment. *Psychological Review 108*(4), 814–834. https://doi.org/10.1037/0033-295X.108.4.814

Haidt, J. (2007). The new synthesis in moral psychology. *Science 316*(5827), 998–1002.

Haidt, J. (2024). *The anxious generation: How the great rewiring of childhood is causing an epidemic of mental illness.* Penguin Press.

Hakuta, J., Soroushian, V., & Kralstein, D. (2008). *Do community courts transform the justice response to misdemeanor crime? Testing the impact of the midtown community court.* Center for Court Innovation.

Haldane, D. (1989). Culture clash or animal cruelty? Two Cambodian refugees face trial after killing dog for food. *Los Angeles Times.* March 13. https://www.latimes.com/archives/la-xpm-1989-03-13-me-495-story.html

Hamilton, Z. (2010). *Do reentry courts reduce recidivism? Results from the Harlem Parole Reentry Court.* Center for Court Innovation.

Han, S., Riddell, J. R., & Piquero, A. R. (2023). Anti-Asian American hate crimes spike during the early stages of the COVID-19 pandemic. *Journal of Interpersonal Violence 38*(3–4), 3513–3533. https://doi.org/10.1177/08862605221107056

Han, W. (2020). Effect of behavioral health services and neighborhood disadvantages on recidivism: A comparison of mental health court and traditional court participants. *Journal of Experimental Criminology 16*(1), 119–140. https://doi.org/10.1007/s11292-019-09402-0

Haney, C. (2018). The psychological effects of solitary confinement: A systematic critique. *Crime and Justice 47*(1), 365–416. https://doi.org/10.1086/696041

Hanson, R. K., & Bussière, M. T. (1998). Predicting relapse: A meta-analysis of sexual offender recidivism studies. *Journal of Consulting and Clinical Psychology 66*(2), 348–362. https://doi.org/10.1037/0022-006X.66.2.348

Harrell, A., Castro, J., Newmark, L., & Visher, C. (2007). Final report on the evaluation of the Judicial Oversight Demonstration: Executive summary. *Final report for National Institute of Justice*. Grant 99-WT.

Harrington, J. R., & Gelfand, M. J. (2014). Tightness–looseness across the 50 United States. *Proceedings of the National Academy of Sciences 111*(22), 7990–7995. https://doi.org/10.1073/pnas.1317937111

Harris, P. (2020). *Black rage confronts the law*. New York University Press. https://doi.org/10.18574/nyu/9780814744765.003.0006

Harrison, L. D., & Scarpitti, F. R. (2002). Introduction: Progress and issues in drug treatment courts. *Substance Use & Misuse 3*(12), 1441–1467. https://doi.org/10.1081/ja-120014418

Hartley, R. D., & Baldwin, J. M. (2019). Waging war on recidivism among justice-involved veterans: An impact evaluation of a large urban veterans treatment court. *Criminal Justice Policy Review 30*(1), 52–78. https://api.semanticscholar.org/CorpusID:75464969

Haselhuhn, M. P., Schweitzer, M. E., & Wood, A. M. (2010). How implicit beliefs influence trust recovery. *Psychological Science 21*(5), 645–648.

Hassoun Ayoub, L., & Rempel, M. (2021). Reentry courts. In E. M. Ahlin & A. S. Douds (Eds.), *Talking problem-solving courts to scale: Diverse applications of the specialty court model* (pp. 73–90). Lexington Books.

Hawkins, M. D. (2009–2010). Coming home: Accommodating the special needs of military veterans to the criminal justice system. *Ohio State Journal of Criminal Law 7*, 563–574.

Hayes, H., & Daly, K. (2003). Youth justice conferencing and re-offending. *Justice Quarterly 20*(4), 725–764. https://doi.org/10.1080/07418820300095681

Heaney, C. A., & Israel, B. A. (2008). Social networks and social support. In K. Glanz, B. K. Rimer, & K. Viswanath (Eds.), *Health behavior and health education: Theory, research, and practice* (pp. 189–210). Jossey-Bass.

Heck, C., & Roussell, A. (2007). State administration of drug courts: Exploring issues of authority, funding, and legitimacy. *Criminal Justice Policy Review 18*(4), 418–433. https://doi.org/10.1177/08874034073056

Heine, S. J. (2010). Cultural psychology. In S. T. Fiske, D. T. Gilbert, & G. Lindzey (Eds.), *Handbook of social psychology* (Vol. 2, 5th ed., pp. 1423–1464). Wiley.

Henggeler, S. W., McCart, M. R., Cunningham, P. B., & Chapman, J. E. (2012). Enhancing the effectiveness of juvenile drug courts by integrating evidence-based practices. *Journal of Consulting and Clinical Psychology 80*(2), 264–275. https://doi.org/10.1037/a0027147

Hennick, E. E. (2017). *The homeless court in Salt Lake City, Utah: Access to justice and mercy for a disenfranchised population*. [Doctoral dissertation, University of Utah].

Herzog-Evans, M. (2016). "What on earth can this possibly mean?" French reentry courts and experts' risk assessment. *International Journal of Law and Psychiatry 44*, 98–108. https://doi.org/10.1016/j.ijlp.2015.08.036

Hiday, V. A., & Ray, B. (2010). Arrests two years after exiting a well-established mental health court. *Psychiatric Services 61*(5), 463–468. https://doi.org/10.1176/ps.2010.61.5.463

Higgins, E. T. (1998). Promotion and prevention: Regulatory focus as a motivational principle. In M. P. Zanna (Ed.), *Advances in experimental social psychology* (Vol. 30, pp. 1–46). Academic Press.

Higgins, E. T., Shah, J., & Friedman, R. (1997). Emotional responses to goal attainment: Strength of regulatory focus as moderator. *Journal of Personality and Social Psychology 72*(3), 515–525. https://doi.org/10.1037/0022-3514.72.3.515

Hiller, M., Belenko, S., Taxman, F., Young, D., Perdoni, M., & Shaum, C. (2010). Measuring drug court structure and operations: Key components and beyond. *Criminal Justice and Behavior 37*(9), 933–950. https://doi.org/10.1177/0093854810373727

Hinds, L., & Murphy, K. (2007). Public satisfaction with police: Using procedural justice to improve police legitimacy. *Australian and New Zealand Journal of Criminology 40*(1), 27–42. https://doi.org/10.1375/acri.40.1.27

Hinshaw, C. (2005). Taking a gamble: Applying therapeutic jurisprudence to compulsive gambling and establishing gambling treatment courts. *Gaming Law Review 9*(4), 333–342. https://doi.org/10.1089/glr.2005.9.333

Holbrook, M. A. (2019). *Quality of life: Assessing the multi-faceted world of community court* [Doctoral Dissertation, Washington State University].

Holcomb, J. B., McMullin, N. R., Pearse, L., Caruso, J., Wade, C. E., Oetjen-Gerdes, L., Champion, H. R., Lawnick, M., Farr, W., Rodriguez, S., & Butler, F. K. (2007). Causes of death in U.S. Special Operations Forces in the global war on terrorism: 2001–2004. *Annals of Surgery 245*(6), 986–991. https://doi.org/10.1097/01.sla.0000259433.03754.98

Holloway, S. D. (1988). Concepts of ability and effort in Japan and the United States. *Review of Educational Research*, 58, 327–345.

Honardoost, M. Z., & Ahlin, E. M. (2021). Juvenile dependency courts: Goals and challenges of the Adoption and Safe Families Act of 1997. In E. M. Ahlin & A. S. Douds (Eds.), *Talking problem-solving courts to scale: Diverse applications of the specialty court model* (pp. 121–140). Lexington Books.

Hora, P. (2002). A dozen years of drug treatment courts: Uncovering our theoretical foundation and the construction of a mainstream paradigm. *Substance Use & Misuse 37*(12–13), 1469–1488.

Hora, P., Schma, G., & Rosenthal, J. T. (1999). Therapeutic jurisprudence and the drug treatment court movement: Revolutionizing the criminal justice system's response to drug abuse and crime in America. *Notre Dame Law Review 74*(2), 439–538.

Hora, P. F., & Stalcup, T. (2008). Drug treatment courts in the twenty-first century: The evolution of the revolution in problem-solving courts. *Georgia Law Review 42*(3), 717–776.

Hough, M., Jackson, J., Bradford, B., Tilley, N., & Sidebottom, A. (2017). Policing, procedural justice and prevention. In N. Tilley & A Sidebottom (Eds.), *Handbook of crime prevention and community safety* (pp. 274–293). Routledge.

House, J. S. (1981). *Work stress and social support.* Addison-Wesley.

House, J. S., Landis, K. R., & Umberson, D. (1988). Social relationships and health. *Science 241*(4865), 540–545.

Houser, K., & Belenko, S. (2015). Disciplinary responses to misconduct among female prison inmates with mental illness, substance use disorders, and co-occurring disorders. *Psychiatric Rehabilitation Journal 38*(1), 24–34. https://www.nytimes.com/2022/11/30/us/homeless-policies-new-york-world.html

Howerton, M. (2023, June 16). *10 years ago, 'affluenza' teen Ethan Couch killed four and injured several others in drunk-driving crash.* ABC8. https://www.wfaa.com/article/news/local/ethan-couch-affluenza-10-years-since-deadly-drunk-driving-crash/287-a8ea72a1-592e-49dd-a097-fd1bb80e237e

Huang, N., Zuo, S., Wang, F., Cai, P., & Wang, F. (2017). The dark side of malleability: Incremental theory promotes immoral behaviors. *Frontiers in Psychology 8*, 1341. https://doi.org/10.3389/fpsyg.2017.01341

Huddleston, C. W., Marlowe, D. B., & Casebolt, R. (2008). *Painting the current picture: A national report card on drug courts and other problem-solving courts in the United States.* National Drug Court Institute.

Huddleston, W., & Marlowe, D. B. (2011). *Painting the current picture: A national report card on drug courts and other problem-solving court programs in the United States.* National Drug Court Institute. https://www.ndci.org/wp-content/uploads/PCP%20Report%20FINAL.PDF

Huecker, M. R., King, K. C., Jordan, G. A., & Smock, W. (2023). Domestic violence. In W. B. Ackley et al. (Ed.), *StatPearls.* StatPearls Publishing. https://www.ncbi.nlm.nih.gov/books/NBK499891/

Hueston, J. H. (2021). The compassionate court: Reforming the justice system inside and outside. *Court Review 57*(2), 108–118. http://aja.ncsc.dni.us/publications/court-review.html

Hughes, C., & Shanahan, M. (2019). Drug courts in Australia. In J. Collins, W. Agnew-Pauley, & A. Soderholm (Eds.), *Rethinking drug courts: International experiences of US Policy Export* (pp. 21–50). London Publishing Partnership.

Hughes, S., & Peak, T. (2012). Evaluating mental health courts as an ideal mental health intervention. *Best Practices in Mental Health: An International Journal 8*(2), 20–37.

Isaac, N., & Enos, P. (2001). *Documenting domestic violence: How health care providers can help victims.* National Institute of Justice.

Jacobson, I. G., Ryan, M. A., Hooper, T. I., Smith, T. C., Amoroso, P. J., Boyko, E. J., Gackstetter, G. D., Wells, T. S., & Bell, N. S. (2008). Alcohol use and alcohol-related problems before and after military combat deployment. *Journal of the American Medical Association 300*(6), 663–675. https://doi.org/10.1001/jama.300.6.663

Jensen, E. L., & Mosher, C. (2006). Adult drug courts: Emergence, growth, outcome evaluations, and the need for continuum of care. *Idaho Law Review 42*(2), 443–470.

Jervis, R. (1979). Deterrence theory revisited. *World Politics 31*(2), 289–324. https://doi.org/10.2307/2009945

Jervis, R. (1989). Rational deterrence: Theory and evidence. *World Politics 41*(2), 183–207. https://doi.org/10.2307/2010407

Jeung, R., Kulkarni, M. P., & Choi, C. (2020, April 1). Epidemic of hate: Asian xenophobia amid coronavirus. *Los Angeles Times.* Retrieved from https://www.latimes.com/opinion/story/2020-04-01/coronavirus-anti-asian-discrimination-threats

Ji, L. J., Nisbett, R. E., & Su, Y. (2001). Culture, change, and prediction. *Psychological Science 12,* 450–456.

Johnson, R. S., Stolar, A. G., McGuire, J. F., Clark, S., Coonan, L. A., Hausknecht, P., & Graham, D. P. (2016). US veterans' court programs: An inventory and analysis of national survey data. *Community Mental Health Journal 52*(2), 180–186. https://doi.org/10.1007/s10597-015-9972-3

Johnston, E. L. (2012). Theorizing mental health courts. *Washington University Law Review 89,* 519. http://scholarship.law.ufl.edu/facultypub/182

Johnstone, G., & Van Ness, D. W. (2007). The meaning of restorative justice. In Johnstone and Van Ness (Eds.), *Handbook of restorative justice* (pp. 5–23). Routledge.

Johnstone, G., & Van Ness, D. W. (2013). The meaning of restorative justice. In G. Johnstone and D. W. Van Ness (Eds.), *Handbook of restorative justice* (pp. 5–23). Willan.

Johnstone, Q. (2001). The Hartford Community Court experiment: An experiment that has succeeded. *Connecticut Law Review 34,* 123–156. http://hdl.handle.net/20.500.13051/1178

Jones, B. J. (2000). Role of Indian tribal courts in the justice system. Sisseton-Wahpeton Sioux Tribal Court. http://www.nrc4tribes.org/files/Role%20of%20Indian%20Tribal%20Courts-BJ%20Jones.pdf

Jones, R. K. (2005). *Final report: Evaluation of the DUI Court program in Maricopa County, Arizona.* Mid-America Research Institute, Inc. of New England.

Jonson, C. L., & Cullen, F. T. (2015). Prisoner reentry programs. *Crime and Justice 44*(1), 517–575.

Kahneman, D. (2011). *Thinking fast and slow.* Farrar, Straus and Giroux.

Kahneman, D., & Tversky, A. (1979). Prospect theory: An analysis of decision under risk. *Econometrica 47*(2), 263–291. https://doi.org/10.2307/1914185

Kaiser, K. A., & Holtfreter, K. (2016). An integrated theory of specialized court programs: Using procedural justice and therapeutic jurisprudence to promote offender compliance and rehabilitation. *Criminal Justice and Behavior 43*(1), 45–62. https://doi.org/10.1177/0093854815609642

Kaiser, K. A., & Rhodes, K. (2019). A drug court by any other name? An analysis of problem-solving court programs. *Law and Human Behavior 43*(3), 278–289. https://doi.org/10.1037/lhb0000325

Kammrath, L. K., & Peetz, J. (2012). You promised you'd change: How incremental and entity theorists react to a romantic partner's promised change attempts. *Journal of Experimental Social Psychology 48*(2), 570–574. https://doi.org/10.1016/j.jesp.2011.10.015

Kanani, H., Fairfax-Columbo, J., & DeMatteo, D. (2024). Considering nuance in the relationship between substance use and risk: A critical analysis of a one-size-fits-all model. In M. K. Miller, D. DeMatteo, & B. H. Bornstein. (Eds.), *Advances in psychology and law. Vol. 7.* (forthcoming). Springer.

Kao, G., & Joyner, K. (2004). Do race and ethnicity matter among friends? Activities among interracial, interethnic, and intraethnic adolescent friends. *Sociological Quarterly 45*(3), 557–573. https://doi.org/10.1111/j.1533-

Kaplan, T., Miller, M. K., & Wood, E. F. (2018). Looking backwards, looking forward: How the evolution of specialty courts can inform the courts of tomorrow. *Court Review 54*, 14–24.

Karafin, D. (2008). *Community courts across the globe: A survey of goals, performance measures and operations.* Criminal Justice Initiative of Open Society Foundation for South Africa.

Kaeble, D. (2018). Probation and parole in the United States, 2016. *Bureau of Justice Statistics Bulletin.* https://bjs.ojp.gov/content/pub/pdf/ppus16.pdf

Karan, A., Keilitz, S., & Denaro, S. (1999). Domestic violence courts: What are they and how should we manage them. *Juvenile and Family Court Journal 50*, 75–86.

Katz, S. (2009). *Expanding the community court model: Testing community court principles in the Bronx centralized courthouse.* Center for Court Innovation.

Kearney, P. (1990). Law Reform Commission. (1990). *Multiculturalism and the law / The Law Reform Commission ; paper prepared by Pauline Kearney.* Australian Law Reform Commission.

Keilitz, S. (2000). Specialization of domestic violence case management in the courts: B A national survey.

Keilitz, S., Jones, A., & Rubio, D. (2000). *Specialization of domestic violence case management in the courts: Findings from a national survey.* National Center for State Court

Kelley, H. H., & Michela, J. L. (1980). Attribution theory and research. *Annual Review of Psychology 31*(1), 457–501. https://doi.org/10.1146/annurev.ps.31.020180.002325

Kelling, J., & Wilson, J. (1982). Broken windows. *The Atlantic.* March. https://www.theatlantic.com/magazine/archive/1982/03/broken-windows/304465/

Kemmelmeier, M., Burnstein, E., Krumov, K., Genkova, P., Kanagawa, C., Hirshberg, M. S., Erb, H.-P., Wieczorkowska, G., & Noels, K. A. (2003). Individualism, collectivism, and authoritarianism in seven societies. *Journal of Cross-Cultural Psychology 34*(3), 304–322. https://doi.org/10.1177/0022022103034003005

Kendis, B. (2019). Human trafficking and prostitution courts: Problem solving or problematic? *Case Western Law Review 66*(3), 805–841.

Kennedy, K. (2012). Mental health court. *Best Practices in Mental Health 8*(2), 38–46.

Khayesi, J. N. O., & George, G. (2011). When does the socio-cultural context matter? Communal orientation and entrepreneurs' resource accumulation efforts in Africa. *Journal of Occupational and Organizational Psychology 84*(3), 471–492. https://doi.org/10.1111/j.2044-8325.2011.02029.x

Kieckhaefer, J. M., & Luna, S. (2020). Do you think some veterans are receiving a "get out of jail free" card? Examining support for veterans treatment court as a function of mental health and offense type. *Journal of Experimental Criminology 16*, 141–170.

Kilmer, A., &. Emmert, A. (2021). Sex offense courts: A historical and international overview. In E. M. Ahlin & A. S. Douds (Eds.), *Talking problem-solving courts to scale: Diverse applications of the specialty court model* (pp. 267–288). Lexington Books.

King, M. S. (2008). Restorative justice, therapeutic jurisprudence and the rise of emotionally intelligent justice. *The Melbourne University Law Review 32*, 1096–1126.

King, M. S. (2010). Judging, judicial values and judicial conduct in problem-solving courts, indigenous sentencing courts and mainstream courts. *Journal of Judicial Administration 19*(3), 133–159.

King, M. S. (2011). Should problem-solving courts be solution-focused courts. *Revista Jurídica de la Universidad de Puerto Rico 80*, 1005.

Kingdon, J. W. (1984). *Agendas, alternatives, and public policies*. Little Brown.

Kingdon, J. W. (2003). *Agendas, alternatives, and public policies*. Longman Publishing Group.

Klein, K. S. (2016). Truth and legitimacy (in courts). *Loyola University Chicago Law Journal 48*, 1–79.

Kluger, J., Murrell, P., Tauber, J., Zeidman, S., Calabrese, A., & Hendricks, S. (2002). The impact of problem solving on the lawyer's role and ethics. *Fordham Urban Law Journal 29*(5), 1892–1924. https://ir.lawnet.fordham.edu/ulj/vol29/iss5/13

Knauff, W. S. (2007). Herbert Blumer's theory of collective definition and the battle over same-sex marriage. *Journal of Human Behavior in the Social Environment 14*(3), 19–43. https://doi.org/10.1300/J137v14n03_02

Knudsen, K. J., & Wingenfeld, S. (2016). A specialized treatment court for veterans with trauma exposure: Implications for the field. *Community Mental Health Journal 52*(2), 127–135.

Koetzle, D., Listwan, S. J., Guastaferro, W. P., & Kobus, K. (2015). Treating high-risk offenders in the community: The potential of drug courts. *International Journal of Offender Therapy and Comparative Criminology 59*(5), 449–465. https://doi.org/10.1177/0306624X13515635

Kohlberg, L. (1974). Education, moral development and faith. *Journal of Moral Education 4*(1), 5–16.

Kohlberg, L., & Hersh, R. H. (1977). Moral development: A review of the theory. *Theory Into Practice 16*(2), 53–59.

Kopelovich, S., Yanos, P., Pratt, C., & Koerner, J. (2013). Procedural justice in mental health courts: Judicial practices, participant perceptions, and outcomes related to mental health recovery. *International Journal of Law and Psychiatry 36*(2), 113–120.

Korobkin, R. B., & Ulen, T. S. (2000). Law and behavioral science: Removing the rationality assumption from law and economics. *California Law Review 88*, 1051.

Koshan, J. (2018). Specialized domestic violence courts in Canada and the United States: Key factors in prioritising safety for women and children. *Journal of Social Welfare and Family Law 40*(4), 515–532. https://doi.org/10.1080/09649069.2018.1519656

Kotabe, H. P., Righetti, F., & Hofmann, W. (2019). How anticipated emotions guide self-control judgments. *Frontiers in Psychology 10*, 1614. https://doi.org/10.3389/fpsyg.2019.01614

Kratcoski, P. C., & Edelbacher, M. M. (2009). Juvenile justice in Austria and the United States: Similarities and differences. *International Journal of Police Science & Management 11*(2), 203–216. https://doi.org/10.1350/ijps.2009.11.2.124

Krebs, C. P., Lindquist, C. H., Koetse, W., & Lattimore, P. K. (2007). Assessing the long-term impact of drug court participation on recidivism with generalized estimating equations. *Drug and alcohol dependence 91*(1), 57–68. https://doi.org/10.1016/j.drugalcdep.2007.05.011

Kruglanski, A. W., Ellenberg, M., Szumowska, E., Molinario, E., Speckhard, A., Leander, N. P., Pierro, A., Di Cicco, G., & Bushman, B. J. (2023). Frustration-aggression hypothesis reconsidered: The role of significance quest. *Aggressive Behavior 49*(5), 445–468. https://doi.org/10.1002/ab.22092

Kruglanski, A. W., Webster, D. M., & Klem, A. (1993). Motivated resistance and openness to persuasion in the presence or absence of prior information. *Journal of Personality and Social Psychology 65*(5), 861–876. https://doi.org/10.1037/0022-3514.65.5.861

Kubiak, S. P., Sobeck, J., & Rose, I. (2005). "It's not a gap, it's a gulf." *Best Practices in Mental Health 1*(2), 19–33.

Kugler, M. B., Funk, F., Braun, J., & Gollwitzer, M. (2013). Differences in punitiveness across three cultures: A test of American exceptionalism in justice attitudes. *Journal of Criminal Law & Criminology 103*(4), 1071–1114. https://doi.org/0091-4169/13/10304-1071

Kulig, T. C., & Butler, L. C. (2019). From "whores" to "victims": The rise and status of sex trafficking courts, victims, and offenders. *Victims and Offenders 14*(3), 299–321. https://doi.org/10.1080/15564886.2019.1595242

La Prairie, C., Gliksman, L., Erickson, P. G., Wall, R., & Newton-Taylor, B. (2002). Drug treatment courts—A viable option for Canada? Sentencing issues and preliminary findings from the Toronto court. *Substance Use & Misuse 37*(12), 1529–1566.

LaCayo, R. (1993). The "cultural" defense. *Time*. December 2. https://time.com/archive/6724365/the-cultural-defense/

Labriola, M., Bradley, S., O'Sullivan, C., Rempel, M., & Moore, S. (2009). *A national portrait of domestic violence courts*. Center for Court Innovation.

Landsman, S. (1984). *The adversary system: A description and defense*. American Enterprise Institute for Public Policy Research.

Lang, C. (2013). Locating the civil rights movement: An essay on the deep south, midwest, and border south in Black freedom studies. *Journal of Social History 47*(2), 371–400. http://www.jstor.org/stable/43305919

Lang, J. (2011). *What is a community court? How the model is being adapted across the United States*. U.S. Department of Justice, Office of Justice Programs, Bureau of Justice Assistance.

Lanterman, J. L. (2020). Restorative justice practices and challenges in the United States. In C. C. Spohn & P. K. Brennan (Eds.), *Handbook on sentencing policies and practices in the 21st century* (pp. 360–377). Routledge.

Lanza-Kaduce, L., Akers, R., Krohn, M., & Radosevich, M. (1984). Cessation of alcohol and drug use among adolescents: A social learning model. *Deviant Behavior 5*, 79–96. https://doi.org/10.1080/01639625.1984.9967633

Lapham, S. C., Kapitula, L. R., C'de Baca, J., & McMillan, G. P. (2006). Impaired-driving recidivism among repeat offenders following an intensive court-based intervention. *Accident Analysis & Prevention 38*(1), 162–169. https://doi.org/10.1016/j.aap.2005.08.009

Latessa, E. J., & Reitler, A. K. (2015). What works in reducing recidivism and how does it relate to drug courts? *Ohio Northern University Law Review 41*(2), 757–790.

Latimer, J., Dowden, C., & Muise, D. (2005). The effectiveness of restorative justice practices: A meta-analysis. *Prison Journal 85*(2), 127–144. https://doi.org/10.1177/0032885505276969

Laux, K. (2019). Gambling addiction: Increasing the effectiveness and popularity of problem gambling diversion in Nevada courts. *UNLV Gaming Law Journal 9*, 247.

Lee, C. G., Cheesman, F., Rottman, D., Swaner, R., Lambson, S., Rempel, M., & Curtis, R. (2013). *A comprehensive evaluation of the Red Hook Community Justice Center*. National Center for State Courts.

Lee, H. M. C. (2012). Fatherhood in the child support system: An innovative problem-solving approach to an old problem: Fatherhood in the child support system. *Family Court Review 50*(1), 59–70.

Leith, S. A., Ward, C. L., Giacomin, M., Landau, E. S., Ehrlinger, J., & Wilson, A. E. (2014). Changing theories of change: Strategic shifting in implicit theory endorsement. *Journal of Personality and Social Psychology 107*(4), 597–620. https://doi.org/10.1037/a0037699

Lempinen, E., & Brice, A. (2022). Berkeley voices: How Roe v. Wade radically changed American culture. *Berkeley News*. June 29. https://news.berkeley.edu/2022/06/29/kristin-luker-on-roe-v-wade

Leon, C. S., & Shdaimah, C. S. (2012). JUSTifying scrutiny: State power in prostitution diversion programs. *Journal of Poverty 16*(3), 250–273.

Leone, N. (2020). *A comparative analysis of the politics of gun control legislation in the United States and Australia*. [Honors thesis, College of the Holy Cross].

Levy, S. R., Stroessner, S. J., & Dweck, C. S. (1998). Stereotype formation and endorsement: The role of implicit theories. *Journal of Personality and Social Psychology 74*(6), 1421–1436. https://doi.org/10.1037/0022-3514.74.6.1421

Li, S. D., & Liu, T. H. (2019). Problem-solving courts in China: Background, development, and current status. *Victims & Offenders 14*(3), 360–374. https://doi.org/10.1080/15564886.2019.1595246

Liggins, D. L. (1999). Urban Survival Syndrome: Novel concept or recognized defense. *The American Journal of Trial Advocacy 23*(1), 215–235.

Liles, B. D., Blacker, D. M., Landini, J. L., & Urquiza, A. J. (2016). A California multidisciplinary juvenile court: Serving sexually exploited and at-risk youth. *Behavioral Sciences and the Law 34*, 234–245.

Lim, L., & Day, A. (2014). Mental health diversion courts: A two year recidivism study of a South Australian mental health court program. *Behavioral Sciences & the Law 32*(4), 539–551.

Lim, L., & Day, A. (2016). Mental health diversion courts: A prospective study of reoffending and clinical outcomes of an Australian mental health court program. *Journal of Offender Rehabilitation 55*(4), 254–270. https://doi.org/10.1080/10509674.2016.1159639

Lind, E. A., Tyler, T. R., & Huo, Y. J. (1997). Procedural context and culture: Variation in the antecedents of procedural justice judgments. *Journal of Personality and Social Psychology 73*(4), 767–780. https://doi.org/10.1037/0022-3514.73.4.767

Lindquist, C., Lattimore, P., Willison, J. B., Steffey, D., Stahl, M. H., Scaggs, S., Welsh- Loveman, J., & Eisenstat, J. (2018). *Cross-site evaluation of the Bureau of Justice assistance FY 2011 Second Chance Act Adult Offender Reentry Demonstration Projects: Final report.* National Institute of Justice.

Linhorst, D. M., & Dirks-Linhorst, P. (2015). Mental health courts: Development, outcomes, and future challenges. *Judges Journal 54*(2), 22–27.

Linhorst, D. M., Kondrat, D., & Dirks-Linhorst, P. A. (2015). Rearrests during mental health court supervision: Predicting rearrest and its association with final court disposition and postcourt rearrests. *Journal of Offender Rehabilitation 54*(7), 486–501. https://doi.org/10.1080/10509674.2015.1076105

Listwan, S., Cullen, T., & Latessa, L. (2006). How to prevent prisoner re-entry programs from failing: Insights from evidence-based corrections. *Federal Probation 70*(3), 19–25.

Lloyd, M. H. (2015). Family drug courts: Conceptual frameworks, empirical evidence, and implications for social work. *Families in Society 96*(1), 49–57. https://doi.org/10.1606/1044-3894.2015.96.7

Loeber, R., & Stouthamer-Loeber, M. (1986). Family factors as correlates and predictors of juvenile conduct problems and delinquency. *Crime and Justice 7*, 29–149. https://doi.org/10.1086/449112

Loong, D., Bonato, S., Barnsley, J., & Dewa, C. S. (2019). The effectiveness of mental health courts in reducing recidivism and police contact: A systematic review. *Community Mental Health Journal 55*(7), 1073–1098. https://doi.org/10.1007/s10597-019-00421-9

Lopez, C. (2018). Homeless courts. NCSC. http://www.ncsc.org/sitecore/content/microsites/trends/home/Monthly-Trends-Articles/2017/Homeless-Courts.aspx

Lowder, E. M., Desmarais, S. L., & Baucom, D. J. (2016). Recidivism following mental health court exit: Between and within-group comparisons. *Law and Human Behavior 40*(2), 118.

Lowder, E. M., Rade, C. B., & Desmarais, S. L. (2018). Effectiveness of mental health courts in reducing recidivism: A meta-analysis. *Psychiatric Services 69*(1), 15–22. https://doi.org/10.1176/appi.ps.201700107

Lowenkamp, C. T., Holsinger, A. M., & Latessa, E. J. (2005). Are drug courts effective: A meta-analytic review. *Journal of Community Correction 28*, 5–10.

Lowenkamp, C. T., & Latessa, E. J. (2005). Increasing the effectiveness of correctional programming through the risk principle: Identifying offenders for residential placement. *Criminology and Public Policy 4*(2), 263–290. https://doi.org/10.1111/j.1745-9133.2005.00021.x

Lucas, P. A., & Hanrahan, K. J. (2016). No soldier left behind: The veterans court solution. *International Journal of Law and Psychiatry 45*, 52–59. https://doi.org/10.1016/j.ijlp.2016.02.010

Lutze, F. E., & Van Wormer, J. G. (2007). The nexus between drug and alcohol treatment program integrity and drug court effectiveness: Policy recommendations for pursuing success. *Criminal Justice Policy Review 18*(3), 226–245. http://journals.sagepub.com/doi/10.1177/0887403406302327

MacDonald, J. M., Morral, A. R., Raymond, B., & Eibner, C. (2007). The efficacy of the Rio Hondo DUI court: A 2-year field experiment. *Evaluation Review 31*(1), 4–23. https://doi.org/10.1177/0193841X06287189

Mackenzie, G., Spiranovic, C., Warner, K., Stobbs, N., Gelb, K., Indermaur, D., Roberts, L., Broadhurst, R., & Bouhours, T. (2012). Sentencing and public confidence: Results from a national Australian survey on public opinions towards sentencing. *Australian and New Zealand Journal of Criminology 45*(1), 45–65. https://doi.org/10.1177/0004865811431328

Mackin, J., Lucas, L., Lambarth, C., Waller, M., Allen, T., Carey, S., & Finigan, M. (2009). *Ann Arundel and Howard County DWI court programs: Outcome and cost evaluation.* NPC Research.

Makkai, T., & Veraar, K. (2003). Final report on the South East Queensland drug court. Australian Institute of Criminology. https://www.aic.gov.au/publications/tbp/tbp6

Manning, P. (1984). Community policing. *American Journal of Police 3*(2), 205–227.

Marchetti, E., & Daly, K. (2004). *Indigenous courts and justice practices in Australia.* Australian Institute of Criminology.

Marcus, M. (1992). Above the fray or into the breach: The judge's role in New York's adversarial system of criminal justice. *Brooklyn Law Review 57*, 1193–1219.

Marcus, R. L. (2002). Reform through rulemaking. *Washington University Law Quarterly 80*(3), 901–944.

Marder, I., & Wexler, D. B. (2021). Mainstreaming restorative justice and therapeutic jurisprudence through higher education. *University of Baltimore Law Review 50*, 399–424. https://ssrn.com/abstract=3653411

Marinos, V., & Whittingham, L. (2019). The role of therapeutic jurisprudence to support persons with intellectual and developmental disabilities in the courtroom: Reflections from Ontario, Canada. *International Journal of Law and Psychiatry 63*, 18–25.

Markus, H. R., & Kitayama, S. (1991). Culture and the self: Implications for cognition, emotion, and motivation. *Psychological Review 98*, 224–253.

Marlowe, D. B. (2002). Effective strategies for intervening with drug abusing offenders. *Villanova Law Review 47*(4), 989–1026.

Marlowe, D. B. (2010). *Research update on adult drug courts.* National Association of Drug Court Professionals. www.ndci.org

Marlowe, D. B. (2011). The verdict on drug courts and other problem-solving courts. *Chapman Journal of Criminal Justice 2*(1), 53–92.

Marlowe, D. B., & Carey, S. M. (2012). *Research update on family drug courts.* National Association of Drug Court Professionals. www.ndci.org

Marlowe, D. B., Festinger, D. S., Arabia, P. L., Dugosh, K. L., Benasutti, K. M., & Croft, J. R. (2009). Adaptive interventions may optimize outcomes in drug courts: A pilot study. *Current Psychiatry Reports 11*(5), 370–376. https://doi.org/10.1007/s11920-009-0056-3

Marlowe, D. B., Hardin, C. D., & Fox, C. L. (2016). *Painting the current picture: A national report on drug courts and other problem-solving courts in the United States.* Technical report. National Drug Court Institute (NADCP).

Marlowe, D. B., & Kirby, K. C. (1999). Effective use of sanctions in drug courts: Lessons from behavioral research. *National Drug Court Institute Review 2*(1), 1–31.

Maron, D. F. (2009). Drug courts appeal to democrats and republicans. *Newsweek.* October 6. https://www.newsweek.com/drug-courts-appeal-democrats-and-republicans-81225

Marques, P., & Voas, R. (2013). Are we near a limit or can we get more safety from vehicle alcohol interlocks? *Addiction 108*(4), 657–658. https://doi.org/10.1111/add.12002

Marshall, C. D. (2020). Restorative justice. In P. Babie & R. Sarre (Eds.), *Religion matters: The contemporary relevance of religion* (pp. 101–117). Springer.

Marshall, T. F. (1999). *Restorative justice: An overview.* Home Office.

Martin, A. (2017). The EU and Common Child Support Laws. August 18. http://www.childsupportlaws.co.uk/eu-common-child-support-laws.html

Martin-Buck, F. P. (2016). Driving safety: An empirical analysis of ridesharing's impact on drunk driving and alcohol-related crime. *Semantic Scholar*, 5672970.

Martino, A., Sitran, A., & Rosa, C. (2014). *Technical development and employment of alcohol interlocks in road safety policy.* European Parliament's Committee on Transport and Tourism.

Maruna, S., & LeBel, T. P. (2003). Welcome home? Examining the "reentry court" concept from a strengths-based perspective. *Western Criminology Review 4*(2), 91–107.

Matejkowski, J., Han, W., & Conrad, A. (2020). Voluntariness of treatment, mental health service utilization, and quality of life among mental health court participants. *Psychology, Public Policy, and Law 26*(2), 185–197. https://doi.org/10.1037/law0000227

Matsumoto, D. (2007). Culture, context, and behavior. *Journal of Personality 75*(6), 1285–1320. https://doi.org/10.1111/j.1467-6494.2007.00476.x

Maxwell, G., & Morris, A. (2001). Family group conferences and re-offending. In A. Morris & G. Maxwell (Eds.), *Restorative justice for juveniles: Conferencing, mediation and circles* (pp. 243–263). Hart Publishing.

McCaffrey, B. (2013). Opening comments. Presented at the Veterans' Court Conference, Washington, DC, December 2.

McGarrell, E. F. (2001). Restorative justice conferences as an early response to young offenders. U.S. Department of Justice, Office of Juvenile Justice and Delinquency Prevention. https://ojp.gov/ncjrs/virtual-library/abstracts/restorative-justice-conferences-early-response-young-offenders-1

McIntosh, W. V., & Cates, C. L. (1997). *Judicial entrepreneurship: The role of the judge in the marketplace of ideas.* Greenwood Press.

McIvor, G. (2009). Therapeutic jurisprudence and procedural justice in Scottish drug courts. *Criminology & Criminal Justice: An International Journal 9*(1), 29–49. https://doi.org/10.1177/1748895808099179

McKenna, K. (2007). *Evaluation of the north Liverpool community justice centre.* UK Ministry of Justice.

McIvor, G. (2004). *Reconviction following drug treatment and testing orders.* Scottish Executive Social Research.

McNamara, L. (2000). Indigenous community participation in the sentencing of criminal offenders. *Indigenous Law Bulletin 5*(4), 5–10. https://classic.austlii.edu.au/au/journals/IndigLawB/2000/72.html

McNeeley, S. (2018). A long-term follow-up of the Minnesota high risk revocation reduction reentry program. *Journal of Experimental Criminology 14*(4), 439–461. https://doi.org/10.1007/s11292-018-9330-x

McNiel, D., & Binder, R. (2007). Effectiveness of a mental health court in reducing criminal recidivism and violence. *American Journal of Psychiatry 164*, 1395–1403. https://doi.org/10.1176/appi.ajp.2007.06101664

Meesmann, U., & Rossi, M. (2015). *Drinking and Driving: Learning from Good Practices Abroad.* Belgian Road Safety Institute—Knowledge Centre Road Safety.

Mei, X., van Wormer, J. G., Lu, R., Abboud, M. J., & Lutze, F. E. (2019). Validating drug court collaboration instrument: Differences in model adherence between adult and juvenile drug courts. *International Journal of Offender Therapy and Comparative Criminology 63*(11), 1990–2017. https://doi.org/10.1177/0306624X19836547

Meierhoefer, B. (2011). Judge-involved supervision programs in the federal courts: Summary of findings from the survey of chief United States probation officers. *Federal Probation 75*(2), 37–47. https://www.uscourts.gov/sites/default/files/75_2_7_0.pdf

Menkel-Meadow, C. (2007). Restorative justice: What is it and does it work? *Annual Review Law & Social Science 3*, 161–187. https://doi.org/10.1146/annurev.lawsocsci.2.081805.110005

Meredith, T. (2007). *Georgia's DUI Court programs reduce recidivism.* Applied Research Services, Inc.

Mezey, N. (2001). Law as culture. *Yale Journal of Law & the Humanities 13*(1), 35–68.

Michaels, J. A., & Douds, A. S. (2021). A trifecta of challenges for veterans treatment courts. In E. M. Ahlin & A. S. Douds (Eds.), *Talking problem-solving courts to scale: Diverse applications of the specialty court model* (pp. 163–194). Lexington Books.

Milano, V. (2017). The European court of human rights' case law on human trafficking in light of L.E. v. Greece: A disturbing setback? *Human Rights Law Review 17*(4), 701–727. https://doi.org/10.1093/hrlr/ngx031

Milgram, S. (1974). The dilemma of obedience. *Phi Delta Kappan 55*(9), 603–606. https://www.jstor.org/stable/20297701

Miller, M. K. (2019). A qualitative analysis and eleven-factor typology of factors encouraging or discouraging the development of problem solving courts in various countries. *Journal of Experimental Criminology 16*, 79–100. https://doi.org/10.1007/s11292-019-09368-z

Miller, M. K. (2020). A qualitative analysis and eleven-factor typology of hypothesized factors encouraging or discouraging the development of problem-solving courts in various countries. *Journal of Experimental Criminology 16*(1), 79–100. https://doi.org/10.1007/s11292-019-09368-z

Miller, M. K., Block, L. M., & DeVault, A. (2020). Problem-solving courts in the United States and around the world: History, evaluation, and recommendations. In M. Miller & B. Bornstein (Eds.), *Advances in Psychology and Law* (Vol. 5, pp. 301–371). https://doi.org/10.1007/978-3-030-54678-6_9

Miller, M. K., Blumenthal, J. A., & Chamberlain, J. (Eds.). (2015). *Handbook of community sentiment.* Springer.

Miller, M. K., & Chamberlain, J. (2015). "There ought to be a law!": Understanding community sentiment. In M. Miller, J. Blumenthal, & J. Chamberlain (Eds.), *Handbook of community sentiment* (pp. 3–28). Springer. https://doi.org/10.1007/978-1-4939-1899-7_1

Miller, M. K., Jami, W. A., & Anderson, L. A. (2020). When culture and law collide: The role of cultural differences in court decisions. *Charleston Law Review 14*, 339–371.

Miller, M. K., & Westbrook, A. (2021). The Social Mind-set Model potentially explains varying societies' responses to social and criminal behavior. *Oñati Socio-Legal Series 11*, S404–S424.

Miller, P., Curtis, A., Sonderlund, A., Day, A., & Droste, N. (2015). Effectiveness of interventions for convicted DUI offenders in reducing recidivism: A systematic review of peer-reviewed scientific literature. *American Journal of Drug and Alcohol Abuse 41*(1), 16–29. https://doi.org/10.3109/00952990.2014.966199

Miller, S. L. (2011). *After the crime: The power of restorative justice dialogues between victims and violent offenders.* New York University Press.

Miller, V. (2013). Cultural differences can affect crime, justice in Eastern Iowa. *The Gazette.* February 14. https://www.thegazette.com/news/cultural-differences-can-affect-crime-justice-in-eastern-iowa/

Miller, J. L., & Johnson, D. C. (2009). *Problem solving courts: A measure of justice.* Rowman & Littlefield.

Miner-Romanoff, K. (2015). An evaluation study of a criminal justice reform specialty court—CATCH Court: Changing actions to change habits. Franklin University. https://dam.assets.ohio.gov/image/upload/ocjs.ohio.gov/occs/CATCH%20FULL%20REPORT%20for%20Court%20CL%205.30.15.pdf

Ministry of Justice. (2015). Annual report and accounts. https://assets.publishing.service.gov.uk/government/uploads/system/uploads/attachment_data/file/434016/moj-annual-report-and-accounts-2014-15.pdf

Mirchandani, R. (2008). Beyond therapy: Problem-solving courts and the deliberative democratic state. *Law & Social Inquiry 33*(4), 853–893. https://www.jstor.org/stable/30234201

Mitchell, R. E., & Hodson, C. A. (1986). Coping and social support among battered women: An ecological perspective. In S. E. Hobfoll, (Ed.), *Stress, social support, and women* (pp. 153–169). Hemisphere.

Mitchell, O., Wilson, D. B., Eggers, A., & MacKenzie, D. L. (2012). Assessing the effectiveness of drug courts on recidivism: A meta-analytic review of traditional and non-traditional drug courts. *Journal of Criminal Justice 40*(1), 60–71. https://doi.org/10.1016/j.jcrimjus.2011.11.009

Miyamoto, Y., & Eggen, A. (2013). Cultural perspectives. In J. Delamater & A. Ward (Eds.), *Handbook of social psychology* (2nd ed., pp. 595–624). Springer.

Monroe, K. R., & Maher, K. H. (1995). Psychology and rational actor theory. *Political Psychology 16*(1), 1–21. https://doi.org/10.2307/3791447

Moore, M., & Hiday, V. (2006). Mental health court outcomes: A comparison of re-arrest and re-arrest severity between mental health court and traditional court participants. *Law and Human Behavior 30*, 659–674. https://doi.org/10.1007/s10979-006-9061-9

Moore, K., Sharp, A., Alitz, P., Yampolskaya, S., Kleinman, M., Carlson, M., & Argerious, A. (2020). Reconsidering success for an integrated family dependency treatment court. *Children and Youth Services Review 114*, 105037. https://doi.org/10.1016/j.childyouth.2020.105037

Moss, J. C. (2019). The politics of drug courts. *Graduate Theses, Dissertations, and Problem Reports*, 7426. https://researchrepository.wvu.edu/etd/7426

Mouttapa, M., Huang, T. T., Shakib, S., Sussman, S., & Unger, J. B. (2003). Authority-related conformity as a protective factor against adolescent health risk behaviors. *Journal of Adolescent Health 33*(5), 320–321. https://doi.org/10.1016/s1054-139x(03)00252-0

Mueller, D., (2012). Treatment courts and court-affiliated diversion projects for prostitution in the United States: A report from the Prostitution Alternatives Round Table of the Chicago Coalition for the Homeless. Paper presented at the 9th International Human Trafficking, Prostitution, and Sex Work Conference, Toledo, OH.

Mujuzi, J. D. (2016). Victim participation in the criminal justice system in the European Union through private prosecutions: Issues emerging from jurisprudence of the European Court of Human Rights. *European Journal of Crime, Criminal Law, and Criminal Justice 24*, 107–134. http://dx.doi.org/10.1163/15718174-24032088

Muñoz Chamorro, C. D. (2021). The indigenous participation as a pathway to decoloniality in a developing world: A reading from the constitutional jurisprudence in Colombia. *Revista de la Facultad de Derecho y Ciencias Políticas 51*(135), 303–325.

Murphy, E., Miller, M. K., Cunius, M. K., & Kruger, S. A. (2024). Individual differences are more influential than group differences in perceptions of the court' role in addressing social issues [Manuscript submitted for publication]. Interdisciplinary Social Psychology, University of Nevada.

Murray, S., & May, S. (2018). Envisioning a community justice centre for Western Australia? Feasibility, challenges, and opportunities. *University of Western Australia Law Review 43*(1), 221–239.

National Association of Drug Court Professionals. (1997). *Defining drug courts: The key components.* Office of Justice Programs, U.S. Department of Justice.

National Association of Drug Court Professionals. (2013). *Adult drug court best practice standards, vol. 1.* National Association of Drug Court Professionals.

National Association of Drug Court Professionals. (2018). *Adult drug court best practice standards, vol. 1.* National Association of Drug Court Professionals.

National Center for Fathering (NCF). (n.d.). *Our history.* National Center for Fathering. https://fathers.com/about-ncf/our-history/

National Center for Statistics and Analysis. (2015). *The economic and societal impact of motor vehicle crashes, 2010* (Revised). U.S. Department of Transportation.

National Center on Elder Abuse. (2017). *Decision-making ability and risk of elder mistreatment (Research brief).* National Center on Elder Abuse.

National Committee for the Prevention of Elder Abuse, Virginia Tech, & Metlife Mature Market Institute. (2011). The MetLife study of elder financial abuse: Crimes of occasion, desperation, and predation against America's elders. https://ltcombudsman.org/uploads/files/issues/mmi-elder-financial-abuse.pdf

National Crime Council. (2007). *Problem solving justice: The case for community courts in Ireland.* Stationery Office.

National Institute of Justice. (2020). Problem-solving courts. February, 20. https://docs.google.com/document/d/1gO82w1148kc7_nttS2EYQaLFKm9UBWtV/edit

NDCRC. (2012). *Frequently asked questions.* National Drug Court Resource Center, Bureau of Justice Assistance.

Nedim, U. (2015). Should we have specialist courts for war veterans? Sydney Criminal Lawyers. https://www.sydneycriminallawyers.com.au/blog/should-we-have-specialist-courts-for-war-veterans/

Nesheim, Neil. (2010). Evaluating restorative justice in Alaska: The Kake Circle. Institute for Court Management, Court Executive Development Program. http:/cdm16501.contentdm.oclc.org/cdm/ ref/collection/famct/id/293

Newmark, L., Rempel, M., Diffily, K., & Kane, K. M. (2004). *Specialized felony domestic violence courts: Lessons on implementation and impacts from the Kings County experience.* Center for Justice Innovation.

New York Times. (2022). https://www.nytimes.com/2024/04/27/business/affordable-housing-religious-organizations.html

New Mexico Courts. (n.d.). Pre-adjudication animal welfare Court. https://metro.nmcourts.gov/services-programs/pre-adjudication-animal-welfare-court/

NHTSA. (2007). *Traffic safety facts: 2007 data.* National Center for Statistics and Analysis.

NHTSA. (2012). *Traffic safety facts: 2012 data.* National Center for Statistics and Analysis.

Nisbett, R. E., & Cohen, D. (1996). *Culture of honor: The psychology of violence in the South.* Westview Press.

Nobles, M. R. (2008). *Evaluating Philadelphia's gun court: Implications for crime reduction and specialized jurisprudence.* [Doctoral dissertation, University of Florida].

Nolan Jr., J. L. (2001). *Reinventing justice: The American drug court movement.* Princeton University Press.

Nolan Jr., J. L. (2003). Redefining criminal courts: Problem-solving and the meaning of justice. *American Criminal Law Review 40*(4), 1541–1565.

Nolan Jr., J. L. (2009). *Legal accents, legal borrowing: The international problem-solving court movement.* Princeton University Press.

Nolan Jr., J. L. (2010). Harm reduction and the American difference: Drug treatment and problem-solving courts in comparative perspective. *Journal of Health Care Law & Policy 13*(1). https://digitalcommons.law.umaryland.edu/jhclp/vol13/iss1/4/

Nolan Jr., J. L. (2012). Problem-solving courts: An international comparison. In J. Petersilia & K. R. Reitz (Eds.), *The Oxford handbook of sentencing and corrections* (pp. 150–172). Oxford University Press.

Nolan Jr., J. L. (2017). *Drug courts: In theory and in practice.* Routledge.

Nored, L. S., & Carlan, P. E. (2008). Success of drug court programs: Examination of the perceptions of drug court personnel. *Criminal Justice Review 33*(3), 329–342. https://doi.org/10.1177/0734016808322050

Nugent, W., Umbreit, M., Wiinamaki, L., & Paddock, J. (2001). Participation in victim–offender mediation and reoffender: Successful replication? *Research in Social Work Practice 11*(1), 5–23. https://doi.org/10.1177/104973150101100101

Nugent-Borakove, M. E. (2009). *Seattle municipal community court: Outcome evaluation final report.* Justice Management Institute.

Nunn, G. A. (2017). Introduction: Perceived legitimacy and the state judiciary. *Vanderbilt Law Review 70*(6), 1813–1817. https://scholarship.law.vanderbilt.edu/vlr/vol70/iss6/8

Office of Child Support Enforcement. (2020). *Administration for Children and Families*. Office of Child Support Enforcement.

O'Hare, G. (2018). Problem-solving justice and problem-solving courts: What Northern Ireland can learn from the US experience of mental health courts. *Irish Probation Journal 15*, 148–160.

O'Hear, M. M. (2009). Rethinking drug courts: Restorative justice as a response to racial injustice. *Stanford Law & Policy Review 20*, 463–500.

Office for Victims of Crime. (n.d.). *Human trafficking task force e-guide*. Training and Technical Assistance Center, Office of Justice Programs. https://www.ovcttac.gov/taskforceguide/eguide/

Office of Juvenile Justice and Delinquency Prevention. (1999). 100th anniversary of the juvenile court, 1899–1999. *Juvenile Justice—United States. Office of Juvenile Justice and Delinquency Prevention 6*(2), 1–40.

Office of Juvenile Justice and Delinquency Prevention. (2002). *Juvenile Gun Court - Birmingham, AL*. U.S. Department of Justice.

Office of Public Affairs. (2022). Federal judges sentence three men convicted of racially motivated hate crimes in connection with the killing of Ahmaud Arbery in Georgia. August 8. United States Department of Justice. https://www.justice.gov/opa/pr/federal-judge-sentences-three-men-convicted-racially-motivated-hate-crimes-connection-killing

Palermo, G. B. (2010). The Nevada mental health courts. *International Journal of Law and Psychiatry 33*(4), 214–219.

Palmer, N. (2010). The essential role of social work in addressing victims and survivors of trafficking. *ILSA Journal of International & Comparative Law 17*(1), 43–58. https://nsuworks.nova.edu/ilsajournal/vol17/iss1/3

Pao, M. (2015). How America's child support system failed to keep up with the times. *NPR*. https://www.npr.org/2015/11/19/456632896/how-u-s-parents-racked-up-113-billion-in-child-support-debt

Patronek, G. J. (1999). Hoarding of animals: An under-recognized public health problem in a difficult-to-study population. *Public Health Reports 114*(1), 81–87. https://doi.org/10.1093/phr/114.1.81

Payne, J. (2005). *Final report on the North Queensland Drug Court* (NCJ No. 211421). Australian Institute of Criminology.

Pennell, S., Kerry, N., & San Diego Association of Governments. (2001). San Diego Homeless Court Program: A Process and Impact Evaluation. http://www.courts.ca.gov/documents/2001SANDAGHomelessCourtEvaluation.pdf.

People v. Aphaylath. (1986). 117 A.D.2d 981 (N.Y. App. Div.).

People v. Wu. (1991). 286 Cal.Rptr. 868 (C.A.).

Perlin, M. L. (2024). "I hope the final judgments' fair": Alternative jurisprudence, legal decision-making, and justice. In M. K. Miller, L. A. Yelderman, M. T. Huss, & J. A. Cantone (Eds.), *The Cambridge handbook of psychology and legal decision-making* (pp. 17–31). Cambridge University Press.

Perlin, M. L. (2018). Who will judge the many when the game is through: Considering the profound differences between mental health courts and traditional involuntary civil commitment courts. *Seattle University Law Review 41*, 937–962.

Petrila, J. (2013). Mental health courts may work, but does it matter if they do? In R. L. Wiener & E. Brank (Eds.), *Problem-solving courts: Social science and legal perspectives* (pp. 133–137). Springer.

Petrucci, C. (2021). DWI courts. In E. M. Ahlin & A. S. Douds (Eds.), *Talking problem-solving courts to scale: Diverse applications of the specialty court model* (pp. 53–72). Lexington Books.

Petty, R. E., & Cacioppo, J. T. (1996). *Attitudes and persuasion: Classic and contemporary approaches*. Westview Press.

Pitesa, M., & Thau, S. (2013). Masters of the universe: How power and accountability influence self-serving decisions under moral hazard. *Journal of Applied Psychology 98*(3), 550–558. https://doi.org/10.1037/a0031697

Plaks, J. E., Stroessner, S. J., Dweck, C. S., & Sherman, J. W. (2001). Person theories and attention allocation: Preferences for stereotypic versus counterstereotypic information. *Journal of Personality and Social Psychology 80*(6), 876–893. https://doi.org/10.1037/0022-3514.80.6.876

Popovic, J. (2002). Judicial officers: Complementing conventional law and changing the culture of the judiciary. *Law Context: A Socio-Legal Journal 20*(2), 121–136.

Porter, R., Rempel, M., & Mansky, A. (2010). *What makes a court problem solving? Universal performance indicators for problem-solving justice.* Center for Court Innovation.

Poulson, B. (2003). A third voice: A review of empirical research on the psychological outcomes of restorative justice. *Utah Law Review 15*(9), 167–203.

Pratto, F., Stallworth, L. M., Sidanius, J., & Siers, B. (1997). The gender gap in occupational role attainment: A social dominance approach. *Journal of Personality and Social Psychology 72*(1), 37–53. https://doi.org/10.1037/0022-3514.72.1.37

Public Safety Canada. (2004). *Canadian National Crime Prevention Strategy: 2004–2007 Annual report.* Public Safety Canada.

Raaijmakers, Q. A. W., Engels, R. C. M. E., & Van Hoof, A. (2005). Delinquency and moral reasoning in adolescence and young adulthood. *International Journal of Behavioral Development 29*(3), 247–258. https://doi.org/10.1177/01650250544000035

Rabinovich-Einy, O. (2015). The legitimacy crisis and the future of courts. *Cardozo Journal of Conflict Resolution 17*, 23–75. https://api.semanticscholar.org/CorpusID:8165052

Rahman, K. (2018). Overview of corruption and anti-corruption in Ghana. September 11. U4 Anti-Corruption Resource Centre. https://knowledgehub.transparency.org/assets/uploads/helpdesk/overview-of-corruption-and-anti-corruption-in-ghana-2018.pdf

Ray, B., & Dollar, C. B. (2014). Exploring stigmatization and stigma management in mental health court: Assessing modified labeling theory in a new context. *Sociological Forum 29*(3), 720–735. https://doi.org/10.1111/socf.12111

Reagan, K. (2024). New "community court" allows Phoenix's homeless population to avoid incarceration. *KPNX.* January 8. https://www.12news.com/article/news/local/valley/new-community-court-allows-phoenix-homeless-population-avoid-incarceration/75-5370090e-91f8-46a4-9eca-c29570ca3712

Redlich, A. D. (2013). The past, present, and future of mental health courts. In R. L. Wiener & E. Brank (Eds.), *Problem-solving courts: Social science and legal perspectives* (pp. 147–161). Springer.

Redlich, A. D., Steadman, H. J., Monahan, J., Robbins, P. C., & Petrila, J. (2006). Patterns of practice in mental health courts: A national survey. *Law and Human Behavior 30*(3), 347–362. https://doi.org/10.1007/s10979-006-9036-x

Reısıg, J. A., & Mıller, M. K. (2009). How the social construction of "child abuse" affect immigrant parents: Policy changes that protect children and families. *International Journal of Social Inquiry 2*(1), 17–37.

Reno, J., Marcus, D., Leary, M., & Gist, N. (2000). *Keeping illegal activity out of rental property: A police guide for establishing landlord training programs.* Bureau of Justice Assistance, U.S. Department of Justice, Office of Justice Programs.

Rest, J. R. (Ed.). (1994). *Moral development in the professions: Psychology and applied ethics.* Psychology Press.

Richard, R., Van Der Pligt, J., & De Vries, N. (1996). Anticipated affect and behavioral choice. *Basic and Applied Social Psychology 18*(2), 111–129. https://doi.org/10.1207/s15324834basp1802_1

Ridgel, M. S., Engberg, M. D., Greenberg, S., Turner, C. D., & Dembosky, J.W. (2007). *Justice, treatment, and cost: An evaluation of the fiscal impact of Allegheny County Mental Health Court.* RAND Corporation.

Riley, B. J., Baigent, M., Harris, S., Larsen, A., Nye, T., & Battersby, M. (2018). Extinction of gambling cue-reactivity: A pilot study in a problem gambling treatment setting. *Journal of Addiction & Recovery 2*, 1010.

Rizzo, M. S. (2020). *Post-incarceration reentry outcome: The impact of reentry court participation*. Drexel University.

Robertson, A. M., Garfein, R. S.,Wagner, K. D., Mehta, S. R., Magis-Rodriguez, C., Cuevas-Mota, J., Moreno-Zuniga, P. G., Strathdee, S. A., Proyecto El Cuete IV, & STAHR II. (2014). Evaluating the impact of Mexico's drug policy reforms on people who inject drugs in Tijuana, B.C., Mexico, and San Diego, CA, United States: A binational mixed methods research agenda. *Harm Reduction Journal 11*(4). https://doi.org/10.1186/1477-7517-11-4.

Robinson, S. M., & Adinoff, B. (2016). The classification of substance use disorders: Historical, contextual, and conceptual considerations. *Behavioral Sciences 6*(3), 18. https://doi.org/10.3390/bs6030018

Rodriguez, N. (2007). Restorative justice at work: Examining the impact of restorative justice resolutions on juvenile recidivism. *Crime & Delinquency 53*(3), 355–379. https://doi.org/10.1177/0011128705285983

Rodriguez, N., & Webb, V. J. (2007). Probation violations, revocations, and imprisonment: The decisions of probation officers, prosecutors, and judges pre- and post-mandatory drug treatment. *Criminal Justice Policy Review 18*(1), 3–30. https://doi.org/10.1177/0887403406292956

Roe-Sepowitz, D. E., Hickle, K. E., Loubert, M. P., & Egan, T. (2011). Adult prostitution recidivism: Risk factors and impact of a diversion program. *Journal of Offender Rehabilitation 50*(5), 272–285. https://doi.org/10.1080/10509674.2011.574205

Rogers, K. (2006). Promoting paradigm of collaboration in an adversarial legal system: An integrated problem-solving perspective for shifting prevailing attitudes from competition to cooperation within the legal profession. *Barry Law Review 6*, 137–162.

Roots, K. (2013). Trafficking or pimping: An analysis of Canada's human trafficking legislation and its implications. *Canadian Journal of Law & Society 28*(1), 21–42. https://doi.org/10.1017/cls.2012.4

Roots, K., & De Shalit, A. (2015). Evidence that evidence doesn't matter: The case of human trafficking in Canada. *Atlantis 37*(2), 65–80.

Rose, D. R., & Clear, T. R. (1998). Incarceration, social capital, and crime: Implications for social disorganization theory. *Criminology 36*(3), 441–480. https://doi.org/10.1111/j.1745-9125.1998.tb01255.x

Ross, K. (2019). Report reveals increase in criminal & civil human trafficking suits brought against hotel chains in 2019. Human Trafficking Institute. https://traffickinginstitute.org/report-reveals-increase-in-criminal-civil-human-trafficking-suits-brought-against-hotel-chains-in-2019/

Ross, K. (2020). Federal report finds U.S. federal courts handled 606 human trafficking cases in 2019. *Human Trafficking Institute*. https://www.traffickinginstitute.org/federal-report-finds-u-s-federal-courts-handled-606-criminal-human-trafficking-cases-in-2019/

Ross, L. (1977). The intuitive psychologist and his shortcomings: Distortions in the attribution process. In Leonard Berkowitz (Ed.), *Advances in experimental social psychology* (Vol. 10, pp. 173–220). Academic Press.

Ross, R. (2011). Because there won't be a next time: Why justice court is an inappropriate forum for domestic violence cases. *Journal of Law & Family Studies 13*(2), 329–344.

Ross, S., Halsey, M., Bamford, D., Cameron, N., & King, A. (2009). *Evaluation of the neighbourhood justice centre, city of Yarra. Final report*. University of Melbourne.

Rottman, D. B. (2007). Adhere to procedural fairness in the justice system. *Criminology & Public Policy 6*(4), 835–842. https://doi.org/10.1111/j.1745-9133.2007.00478.x

Rottman, D., & Casey, P. (1999). Therapeutic jurisprudence and the emergence of problem-solving courts. *National Institute of Justice Journal 240*, 12–19.

Rottman, D., & Casey, P. (2000). Therapeutic jurisprudence & the emergence of problem-solving courts. *Alternatives to Incarceration* 6(2), 27–30.

Rowden, E. (2018). Distributed courts and legitimacy: What do we lose when we lose the courthouse? *Law, Culture, and the Humanities 14*(2), 263–281.

Ruggeri, A. (2009). New courts give troubled veterans a second chance: The system can better take account of a veteran's physical and emotional condition. April 3. *U.S. News & World Report.* http://www.usnews.com/news/national/articles/2009/04/03/new-courts-give-troubled-veterans-a-second-chance

Russell, R. T. (2009). *Veterans treatment courts developing throughout the nation: Improving outcomes and services in a tight economy.* Eric County Court.

Saint-Germain, M. A., & Calamia, R. A. (1996). Three strikes and you're in: A streams and windows model of incremental policy change. *Journal of Criminal Justice 24*(1), 57–70. https://doi.org/10.1016/0047-2352(95)00052-6

Salazar, L. F., Baker, C. K., Price, A. W., & Carlin, K. (2003). Moving beyond the individual: Examining the effects of domestic violence policies on social norms. *American Journal of Community Psychology 32*(3-4), 253–264.

Salsi, G., Mazzotti, M. C., Carosielli, G., Ingravallo, F., & Pelotti, S. (2015). Elder abuse awareness in Italy: Analysis of reports to the prosecutor office of bologna. *Aging Clinical and Experimental Research 27*(3), 359–363. https://doi.org/10.1007/s40520-014-0277-0

Samuels, H. G. (2004). Review to consider the merits of establishing a Specialist Gun Court in New South Wales. New South Wales Parliament. https://www.parliament.nsw.gov.au/tp/files/29428/Review%20on%20Gun%20Court.pdf

Sanchez, M. H., & Miller, M. K. (2009). Using therapeutic jurisprudence to design a special treatment court to address illegal prostitution. In M. K. Miller (Ed.), *Contemporary perspectives on legal regulation of sexual behavior: Psycho-legal research and analysis* (pp. 63–76). Nova.

Sarteschi, C., Vaughn, M., & Kim, K. (2011). Assessing the effectiveness of mental health courts: A Quantitative review. *Journal of Criminal Justice 39*(1), 12–20. https://doi.org/10.1016/j.jcrimjus.2010.11.003

Satterberg, D., & Daugaard, L. (2019). Connections, not convictions: Prosecution of people with substance use disorder in the age of America's behavioral health crisis. *UCLA Criminal Justice Law Review 3*(1), 137–152. https://escholarship.org/uc/item/36c7c07m

Saum, C. A., & Hiller, M. L. (2009). Should violent offenders be excluded from drug court participation? An examination of the recidivism of violent and nonviolent drug court participants. *Criminal Justice Review 33*(3), 291–307.

Schaffer, D. (2011). Looking inside the black box of drug courts: A meta-analytic review. *Justice Quarterly 28*(3), 492–521. https://doi.org/10.1080/07418825.2010.525222

Schaefer, L., & Beriman, M. (2019). Problem-solving courts in Australia: A review of problems and solutions. *Victims & Offenders 14*(3), 344–359. https://doi.org/10.1080/15564886.2019.1595245

Schepard, A. I., & Bozzomo, J. W. (2003). Efficiency, therapeutic justice, mediation, and evaluation: Reflections on a survey of unified family courts. *Family Law Quarterly 37*(3), 333–359. https://scholarlycommons.law.hofstra.edu/faculty_scholarship/502

Schiller, W. L., Pearce, J., & Jones, L. R. (2019). *Individualizing responses to motivate behavior change in youth: A four-pronged approach.* National Council of Juvenile and Family Court Judges.

Schma, W. G., & Rosenthal, J. T. (1997). Therapeutic jurisprudence and the drug court movement: Revolutionizing the criminal justice system's response to drug abuse and crime in America. *Notre Dame Law Review 74*, 439–454.

Schneider, R. D. (2010). Mental health courts and diversion programs: A global survey. *International Journal of Law and Psychiatry 33*(4), 201–206. https://doi.org/10.1016/j.ijlp.2010.07.001

Schomerus, G., Lucht, M., Holzinger, A., Matschinger, H., Carta, M. G., & Angermeyer, M. C. (2011). The stigma of alcohol dependence compared with other mental disorders: A review of population studies. *Alcohol and Alcoholism 46*(2), 105–112. https://doi.org/10.1093/alcalc/agq089

Schultz, P. W., & Tabanico, J. J. (2009). Criminal beware: A social norms perspective on posting public warning signs. *Criminology 47*(4), 1201–1222.

Schweig, S., Malangone, D., & Goodman, M. (2012). *Prostitution diversion programs.* Center for Court Innovation.

Scott, J. (2000). Rational choice theory. *Understanding Contemporary Society: Theories of the Present 129*, 126–138.

Shaffer, D. K. (2011). Looking inside the black box of drug courts: A meta-analytic review. *Justice Quarterly 28*(3), 493–521.

Shannon, L., Himes, M., Nash, S., & Neweel, J. (2021). Opioid intervention courts. In E. M. Ahlin & A. S. Douds (Eds.), *Talking problem-solving courts to scale: Diverse applications of the specialty court model* (pp. 289–310). Lexington Books.

Shaver, A. W. (2013). Gender issues in problem-solving courts. In R. L. Wiener & E. Brank (Eds.), *Problem-solving courts: Social science and legal perspectives* (pp. 133–130). Springer.

Shdaimah, C. S., & Wiechelt, S. A. (2012). Converging on empathy: Perspectives on Baltimore city's specialized prostitution diversion program. *Women & Criminal Justice 22*(2), 156–173.

Sheeran, P., & Orbell, S. (1999). Implementation intentions and repeated behaviour: Augmenting the predictive validity of the theory of planned behaviour. *European Journal of Social Psychology 29*(2–3), 349–369. https://doi.org/10.1002/(SICI)1099-0992(199903/05)29:2/3<349::AID-EJSP931>3.0.CO;2-Y

Sheppard, D., & Kelly, P. (2002). *Juvenile gun courts: Promoting accountability and providing treatment.* Office of Juvenile Justice and Delinquency Prevention.

Sherman, L. L., Strang, H. H., Barnes, G. G., Bennett, S. S., Angel, C. C., Newbury-Birch, D., Jones, D. J., & Gill, C. E. (2007). *Restorative justice: The evidence.* The Smith Institute.

Sherman, L., Strang, H. H., & Woods, D. (2000). *Recidivism patterns in the Canberra reintegrative shaming experiments.* Australian National University, Centre for Restorative Justice, Research School of Social Sciences.

Sherman, L. W. (2001). Reducing gun violence: What works, what doesn't, what's promising. *Criminal Justice 1*(1), 11–25. https://doi.org/10.1177/1466802501001001002

Sherman, L. L., & Strang, H. H. (2007). *Restorative justice: The evidence.* The Smith Institute.

Sherman, L. W., Strang, H., Barnes, G., Woods, D. J., Bennet, S., Inkpen, N., Newbury-Birch, D., Rossner, M., Angel, C., Mearns, M., & Slothower, M. (2015a). Twelve experiments in restorative justice: The Jerry Lee program of randomized trials of restorative justice conferences. *Journal of Experimental Criminology 11*(4), 501–540. https://doi.org/10.1007/s11292-015-9247-6

Sherman, L. W., Strang, H., Mayo-Wilson, E., Woods, D. J., & Ariel, B. (2015). Are restorative justice conferences effective in reducing repeat offending? Findings from a Campbell systematic review. *Journal of Quantitative Criminology 31*(1), 1–24. https://doi.org/10.1007/s10940-014-9222-9

Sigillo, A. E., & Sicafuse, L. L. (2015). The influence of media and community sentiment on policy decision-making. In M. Miller, J. Blumenthal, & J. Chamberlain (Eds.), *Handbook of community sentiment* (pp. 29–42). Springer. https://doi.org/10.1007/978-1-4939-1899-7_2

Simpson, J. (2012). *Will child support court increase the frequency and amount of child support paid by non-custodial parents?* [Thesis, University of Nevada, Reno].

Simmons, P. L. (1999). Solving the nation's drug problem: Drug courts signal a move toward therapeutic jurisprudence. *Gonzaga Law Review 35*(2), 237–265.

Simonsson, P., Farwell, M. M., & Solomon, P. L. (2020). Judicial perspectives on mental health courts: The role of psychiatric disorder and violence risk. *International Journal of Law and Psychiatry 70*(9), 101562. https://doi.org/10.1016/j.ijlp.2020.101562

Skeem, J., & Lowenkamp, C. (2020). Using algorithms to address trade-offs inherent in predicting recidivism. *Behavioral Sciences & the Law 38*(3), 259–278. https://doi.org/10.1002/bsl.2465

Skitka, L. J., Bauman, C. W., & Lytle, B. L. (2009). Limits on legitimacy: Moral and religious convictions as constraints on deference to authority. *Journal of Personality and Social Psychology 97*(4), 567–578. https://doi.org/10.1037/a0015998

Skrzypiec, G., Wundersitz, J., & McRostie, H. (2004). *Magistrates court diversion program: An analysis of post-program offending.* Office of Crime Statistics and Research.

Slattery, M., Dugger, M. T., Lamb, T. A., & Williams, L. (2013). Catch, treat, and release: Veteran treatment courts address the challenges of returning home. *Substance Use & Misuse 48*(10), 922–932. https://doi.org/10.3109/10826084.2013.797468

Slinger, E., & Roesch, R. (2010). Problem-solving courts in Canada: A review and a call for empirically-based evaluation methods. *International Journal of Law and Psychiatry 33*(4), 258–264. https://doi.org/10.1016/j.ijlp.2010.06.008

Smee, D. E., McGuire, J., Garrick, T., Sreenivasan, S., Dow, D., & Woehl, D. (2013). Critical concerns in Iraq/Afghanistan war veteran-forensic interface: Veterans treatment court as diversion in rural communities. *Journal of the American Academy of Psychiatry and the Law 41*(2), 256–262.

Smith, G., & Simpson, R. (2014). Gambling addiction defence on trial: Canadian expert witness perspectives. *International Journal of Criminology and Sociology 3*, 319–326. https://doi.org/10.6000/1929-4409.2014.03.27

Smith, J. W. (2012). The Anchorage, Alaska veterans court and recidivism: July 6, 2004–December 31, 2010. *Alaska Law Review 29*(1), 93–164.

Smith, P., Gendreau, P., & Swartz, K. (2009). Validating the principles of effective intervention: A systematic review of the contributions of meta-analysis to the field of corrections. *Victims and Offenders 4*(2), 148–169. https://doi.org/10.1080/15564880802612581

Smith, P. C., Schmidt, S. M., Allensworth-Davies, D., & Saitz, R. (2010). "Primary care validation of a single-question alcohol screening test": Erratum. *Journal of General Internal Medicine 25*(4), 375. https://doi.org/10.1007/s11606-010-1255-7

Smith, P. S. (2006). The effects of solitary confinement on prison inmates: A brief history and review of the literature. *Crime and Justice 34*(1), 441–528. https://doi.org/10.1086/500626

Sneirson, J. F. (1995). Black rage and the criminal law: Principled approach to polarized debate. *University of Pennsylvania Law Review 143*(6), 2251–2288. https://doi.org/10.2307/3312591

Solicitor, P. N., & Barrister, J. F. (2011). Is there a need for a specialist Veteran's Courts in the UK? *InsideTime.* https://insidetime.org/is-there-a-need-for-a-specialist-veterans-courts-in-the-uk-4/

Solum, L. B. (2004). Procedural justice. *Southern California Law Review 78*(1), 181–322.

Somers, J. M., Currie, L., Moniruzzaman, A., Eiboff, F., & Patterson, M. (2012). Drug treatment court of Vancouver: An empirical evaluation of recidivism. *International Journal of Drug Policy 23*(5), 393–400. https://doi.org/10.1016/j.drugpo.2012.01.011

Song, F. (2022). Problem gambling diversion programs: A review of implementations and challenges. *UNLV Gaming Law Journal 12*(2), 227–238.

Spinak, J. M. (2008). Romancing the court. *Family Court Review 46*(2), 258–274.

Staddon, J. E., & Cerutti, D. T. (2003). Operant conditioning. *Annual Review of Psychology 54*(1), 115–144. https://doi.org/10.1146/annurev.psych.54.101601.145124

State v. Kargar. (1996). 679 A.2d 81 (M.E.).

Steadman, H. J., Davidson, S., & Brown, C. (2001). Mental health courts. *Psychiatric Services 52*, 457–458.

Steadman, H. J., Redlich, A. D., Griffin, P., Petrila, J., & Monahan, J. (2005). From referral to disposition: Case processing in seven mental health courts. *Behavioral Sciences & the Law 23*(2), 215–226. https://doi.org/10.1002/bsl.641

Steadman, H. J., Redlich, A., Callahan, L., Robbins, P. C., & Vesselinov, R. (2011). Effect of mental health courts on arrests and jail days: A multisite study. *Archives of General Psychiatry 68*(2), 167–172. http://doi:10.1001/archgenpsychiatry.2010.134

Stein, D. M., Deberard, S., & Homan, K. (2013). Predicting success and failure in juvenile drug treatment court: A meta-analytic review. *Journal of Substance Abuse Treatment 44*(2), 159–168. https://doi.org/10.1080/1067828X.2013.764371

Stein, D. M., Homan, K. J., & DeBerard, S. (2015). The effectiveness of juvenile treatment drug courts: A meta-analytic review of literature. *Journal of Child & Adolescent Substance Abuse 24*(2), 80–93.

Steinberg, J. K. (2018). A theory of civil problem-solving courts. *New York University Law Review 93*(6), 1579–1632.

Steinberg, R., & Albertson, S. (2016). Broken windows policing and community courts: An unholy alliance. *Cardozo Law Review 37*(3), 995–1024.

Steinberg, L., & Scott, E. S. (2003). Less guilty by reason of adolescence: Developmental immaturity, diminished responsibility, and the juvenile death penalty. *American Psychologist 58*(12), 1009–1018. https://doi.org/10.1037/0003-066X.58.12.1009

Steps to Justice. (2019). What is a Gladue or Indigenous Peoples Court? Steps to Justice. https://stepstojustice.ca/questions/criminal-law/what-gladue-or-indigenous-peoples-court/

Stinchcomb, J. B. (2010). Drug courts: Conceptual foundation, empirical findings, and policy implications. *Drugs: Education, Prevention, & Policy 17*(2), 148–167. https://doi.org/10.3109/09687630802286901

Stork, H. (1993). *Les rituels du coucher de l'enfant. Variations culturelles[titolo in inglese]*. ESF.

Sullivan, C. J., Blair, L., Latessa, E., & Sullivan, C. C. (2016). Juvenile drug courts and recidivism: Results from a multisite outcome study. *Justice Quarterly 33*(2), 291–318. https://doi.org/10.1080/07418825.2014.908937

Sullivan, D., & Tifft, L. (2001). *Restorative justice: Healing the foundations of our everyday lives*. Willow Tree Press.

Summers, A., & Shdaimah, C. S. (2010). Creating judicial-academic partnerships: An effective way to leverage resources for evaluation. National Council of Juvenile and Family Court Judges. https://www.ncjfcj.org/wp-content/uploads/2012/03/JudicialAcademciBrief-R.pdf

Sviridoff, M., Rottman, D. B., Ostrom, B., & Curtis, R. (2000). *Dispensing justice locally: The implementation and effects of the Midtown community court*. Routledge.

Sviridoff, M., Rottman, D. B., Weidner, R., Cheesman, F., Curtis, R., Hansen, R., & Ostrom, B. (2002). *Dispensing justice locally: The impacts, costs and benefits of the Midtown community court*. U.S. Department of Justice, Office of Justice Programs, National Institute of Justice.

Sward, E. E. (1989). Values, ideology, and the evolution of the adversary system. *Indiana Law Journal 64*(2), 301–356. https://www.repository.law.indiana.edu/ilj/vol64/iss2/4

Tam, K.-P., Shu, T.-M., Ng, H. K.-S., & Tong, Y.-Y. (2013). Belief about immutability of moral character and punitiveness toward criminal offenders. *Journal of Applied Social Psychology 43*(3), 603–611. https://doi.org/10.1111/j.1559-1816.2013.01041.x

Tamarit, J., & Luque, E. (2016). Can restorative justice satisfy victims' needs? Evaluation of the Catalan victim-offender mediation programme. *Restorative Justice 4*(1), 68–85. https://doi.org/10.1080/ 20504721.2015.1110887

Tamir, M., John, O. P., Srivastava, S., & Gross, J. J. (2007). Implicit theories of emotion: Affective and social outcomes across a major life transition. *Journal of Personality and Social Psychology 92*(4), 731–744. http://dx.doi.org/10.1037/0022-3514.92.4.731

Tankebe, J. (2009). Policing, procedural fairness and public behaviour: A review and critique. *International Journal of Police Science & Management 11*(1), 8–19. https://doi.org/10.1350/ijps.2009.11.1.105

Tanner-Smith, E. E., Lipsey, M. W., & Wilson, D. B. (2016). Juvenile drug court effects on recidivism and drug use: A systematic review and meta-analysis. *Journal of Experimental Criminology 12*, 477–513. https://doi.org/10.1007/s11292-016-9274-y

Taylor, C. J. (2017). Program evaluation of the Federal Reentry Court in the Eastern District of Pennsylvania: Report on program effectiveness for the first 265 Reentry Court participants. Research report prepared for the Federal Probation Department and US District Court, Eastern District of Pennsylvania. https://digitalcommons.lasalle.edu/cgi/viewcontent.cgi?article=1009&context=soc_crj_faculty

Taylor, C. J. (2020). Mentee and mentor perceptions of a mentoring court for high-risk probationers. *Probation Journal 67*(3), 214–227. https://doi.org/10.1177/02645505209391

Taylor-Dunn, H. (2016). The impact of victim advocacy on the prosecution of domestic violence offences: Lessons from a realistic evaluation. *Criminology & Criminal Justice 16*(1), 21–39. https://doi.org/10.1177/174889581559958

Terry, W. C. (1999). *The early drug courts: Case studies in judicial innovation.* Sage Publications.

The Supreme Court of Ohio. (2017). The judiciary's response to the opioid epidemic. August https://www.supremecourt.ohio.gov/docs/JCS/specDockets/resources/JudResponseOpioid.pdf

Thibaut, J., & Walker, L. (1975). *Procedural justice: A psychological analysis.* Erlbaum.

Thibaut, J., Walker, L., LaTour, S., & Houlden, P. (1974). Procedural justice as fairness. *Stanford Law Review 26*(6), 1271–1289. https://doi.org/10.2307/1227990

Thorsborne, M., & Blood, P. (2005). The challenge of culture change: Embedding restorative practice in schools. Paper presented at the Sixth International Conference on Conferencing, Circles and other Restorative Practices, Sydney, Australia.

Tiger, R. (2011). Drug courts and the logic of coerced treatment. *Sociological Forum 26*(1), 169–182. http://www.jstor.org/stable/23027286

Tomporowski, B., Buck, M., Bargen, C., & Binder, V. (2011). Reflections on the past, present, and future of restorative justice in Canada. *Alberta Law Review 48*(4), 815–829. https://canlii.ca/t/2941

Town of Amherst. (2018). Treatment Courts. https://www.amherst.ny.us/content/departments.php?dept_id=dept_21&menu_id=menu_05

Triandis, H. C., & Marin, G. (1983). Etic plus emic versus pseudoetic: A test of a basic assumption of contemporary cross-cultural psychology. *Journal of Cross-Cultural Psychology 14*(4), 489–500. https://doi.org/10.1177/0022002183014004007

Tribal-State Judicial Consortium. (n.d.). What do we do? Judicial Branch of New Mexico. https://tribalstate.nmcourts.gov

Triplett, R., & Payne, B. (2004). Problem solving as reinforcement in adolescent drug use: Implications for theory and policy. *Journal of Criminal Justice 32*(6), 617–630. https://doi.org/10.1016/j.jcrimjus.2004.08.012

Troeger, K. C., & Douds, A. S. (2021). Creating a home base for treatment in homeless courts. In E. M. Ahlin & A. S. Douds (Eds.), *Talking problem-solving courts to scale: Diverse applications of the specialty court model* (pp. 91–116). Lexington Books.

Trupin, E., Richards, H., Wertheimer, D. M., & Bruschi, C. (2001). *City of Seattle Municipal Court: Mental health court, evaluation report.* Seattle Municipal Court, Seattle Mental Health Court.

Tsai, B. (2000). The trend toward specialized domestic violence courts: Improvements on an effective innovation. *Fordham Law Review 64*(4), 1285–1327. https://ir.lawnet.fordham.edu/flr/vol68/iss4/8

Tsai, J., Finlay, A., Flatley, B., Kasprow, W. J., & Clark, S. (2018). A national study of veterans treatment court participants: Who benefits and who recidivates. *Administration and Policy in Mental Health 45*(2), 236–244. https://doi.org/10.1007/s10488-017-0816-z

Tutty, L., & Koshan, J. (2013). Calgary's specialized domestic violence court: An evaluation of a unique model. *Alberta Law Review 50*(4), 731–755.https://doi.org/10.29173/alr74

Tyler, T. R. (1987). Procedural justice research. *Social Justice Research 1*(1), 41–65. https://doi.org/10.1007/BF01049383

Tyler, T. R. (1988). What is procedural justice-criteria used by citizens to assess the fairness of legal procedures. *Law & Society Review 22*(1), 103–135. https://doi.org/10.2307/3053563

Tyler, T. R. (1989). The psychology of procedural justice: A test of the group-value model. *Journal of Personality and Social Psychology 57*(5), 830–838. https://doi.org/10.1037/0022-3514.57.5.830

Tyler, T. R. (1990). Justice, self-interest, and the legitimacy of legal and political authority. In J. J. Mansbridge (Ed.), *Beyond self-interest* (pp. 171–179). University of Chicago Press.

Tyler, T. R. (2003). Procedural justice, legitimacy, and the effective rule of law. *Crime and Justice 30*, 283–357. https://www.jstor.org/stable/1147701

Tyler, T. R. (2004). Enhancing police legitimacy. *The Annals of the American Academy of Political and Social Science 593*(1), 84–99. https://doi.org/10.1177/0002716203262627

Tyler, T. R. (2006). Psychological perspectives on legitimacy and legitimation. *Annual Review Psychology 57*, 375–400. https://doi.org/10.1146/annurev.psych.57.102904.190038

Tyler, T. (2022). *Advanced introduction to law and psychology*. Edward Elgar Publishing.

Tyler, T. R., Goff, P. A., & MacCoun, R. J. (2015). The impact of psychological science on policing in the United States: Procedural justice, legitimacy, and effective law enforcement. *Psychological Science in the Public Interest 16*(3), 75–109. https://doi.org/10.1177/1529100615617791

Tyler, T. R., & Jackson, J. (2014). Popular legitimacy and the exercise of legal authority: Motivating compliance, cooperation, and engagement. *Psychology, Public Policy, and Law 20*(1), 78–95. https://doi.org/10.1037/a0034514

Tyler, T., & Jackson, J. (2013). Future challenges in the study of legitimacy and criminal justice. Public Law Working Paper, No. 264. Yale Law School. http://dx.doi.org/10.2139/ssrn.2141322

Tyler, T., & Lind, A. (2002). Procedural justice. In J. Sanders & V. Hamilton (Eds.), *Handbook of justice research and law* (pp. 65–92). Kluwer.

Tyler, T. R., & Sevier, J. (2013). How do the courts create popular legitimacy-the role of establishing the truth, punishing justly, and/or acting through just procedures. *Albany Law Review 77*, 1095–1137.

Umbreit, M. (1998). Restorative justice through victim-offender mediation: A multi-site assessment. *Western Criminology Review 1*(1), 1–29. https://www.ojp.gov/ncjrs/virtual-library/abstracts/restorative-justice-through-victim-offender-mediation-multi-site

UNICEF. (2016). Female genital mutilation and child marriage in Sudan—are there any changes taking place? https://www.unicef.org/sudan/media/1071/file

United States Department of Justice (2021, April 28). *Three Georgia men charged with federal hate crimes and attempted kidnapping in connection with the death of Ahmaud Arbery.* https://www.justice.gov/opa/pr/three-georgia-men-charged-federal-hate-crimes-and-attempted-kidnapping-connection-death

United States Government Accountability Office. (2005). *Adult drug courts: Evidence indicates recidivism reductions and mixed results for other outcomes* (GAO-05-219). Report to Congressional Committees. https://www.gao.gov/products/GAO-05-219

Updegrove, A. H., & Muftic, L. R. (2019). Childhood polyvictimization, adult violent victimization, and trauma symptomatology: An exploratory study of prostitution diversion program participants. *Journal of Family Violence 34*, 733–743. https://doi.org/10.1007/s10896-018-0015-

U.S. Department of Health and Human Services. (2001). *Adoption and foster care analysis and reporting system: Fact sheet.* U.S. Department of Health and Human Services.

U.S. Department of Justice. (1997). *Defining drug courts: The key components.* Drug Courts Resource Series. U.S. Department of Justice.

U.S. Department of Justice. (2013). Justice department selects three domestic violence courts to serve as resources to specialized courts nationwide. Department of Justice, Office of Public Affairs. https://www.justice.gov/opa/pr/justice-department-selects-three-domestic-violence-courts-serve-resources-specialized-courts

U.S. Department of Justice. (2020). *Drug courts.* U.S. Department of Justice, Office of Justice Programs.

U.S. Department of Veterans Affairs. (2015). Health benefits. http://www.va.gov/healthbenefits/apply/veterans.asp

U.S. Department of Veteran's Affairs. (2017). *Veterans Court Inventory Update.* Office of Public Affairs.

U.S. Sentencing Commission. (2010). The Sentencing Reform Act of 1984: Principal features. U.S. Sentencing Commission. https://www.ussc.gov/research/research-and-publications/simplification-draft-paper-2

Vachuska, K. F. (2020, March 29). Initial effects of the coronavirus pandemic on racial prejudice in the United States: Evidence from google trends. https://doi.org/10.31235/osf.io/bgpk3

Van de Veen, S. L. (2004). Some Canadian problem-solving court processes. *Canadian Bar Review 83*(1), 91–158. https://canlii.ca/t/2cjc

Van Ness, D. (2005, February). Restorative justice in prisons. In *Symposium on Restorative Justice and Peace in Colombia, Cali, Kolumbija* (Vol. 9, p. 12).

Van Ness, D. W. (2016). *An overview of restorative justice around the world.* Eleventh United Nations Congress on Crime Prevention and Criminal Justice.

Van Wormer, J. (2010). *Understanding operational dynamics of drug courts.* [Doctoral dissertation, Washington State University].

Vance, S. E. (2011). Judge-involved supervision in the federal system: Background and research. *Federal Probation 80*(1), 15–23.

Vermunt, R. (2014). Doing good to self and others: Some ideas about the antecedents, processes, and consequences of fair resource allocation. *Social Justice Research 27*, 504–517. https://doi-org.unr.idm.oclc.org/10.1007/s11211-014-0224-4

Vermunt, R., & Steensma, H. (2016). Procedural Justice. In C. Sabbagh & M. Schmitt (Eds.), *Handbook of social justice theory and research* (pp. 219–236). Springer.

Victorian Department of Justice (VDOJ). (1999). *Victorian Aboriginal Justice Agreement.* Victorian Department of Justice.

Visher, C. A., Harrell, A., Newmark, L., & Yahner, J. (2008). Reducing intimate partner violence: An evaluation of a comprehensive justice system-community collaboration. *Criminology and Public Policy 7*(4), 495–523. https://doi.org/10.1111/j.1745-9133.2008.00524.x

Volokh, E. (2015). Statutory rape laws and ages of consent in the U.S. *Washington Post.* May 1. https://www.washingtonpost.com/news/volokh-conspiracy/wp/2015/05/01/statutory-rape-laws-in-the-u-s/

Wagner, A. R. (2020). The criminally damaged brain and the need to expand mental health courts: A look at the traumatized mind, unfortunate criminal consequences, and the divergent paths of prison or treatment. *Nova Law Review 44*(3), 403–440.

Wahab, S. (2005). Navigating mixed-theory programs: Lessons learned from a prostitution-diversion project. *Affilia 20*(2), 203–221. https://doi.org/10.1177/0886109905274571

Wahab, S. (2006). Evaluating the usefulness of a prostitution diversion project. *Qualitative Social Work 5*(1), 67–92. https://doi.org/10.1177/1473325006061539

Wales, H. W., Hiday, V. A., & Ray, B. (2010). Procedural justice and the mental health court judge's role in reducing recidivism. *International Journal of Law and Psychiatry 33*(4), 265–271. https://doi.org/10.1016/j.ijlp.2010.06.009

Wallace, D. (2011). The promise of DWI court: What does it mean and why should prosecutors care? *Chapman Journal of Criminal Justice 2*(1), 101–128.

Walters, G. D., & Bolger, P. C. (2019). Procedural justice perceptions, legitimacy beliefs, and compliance with the law: A meta-analysis. *Journal of Experimental Criminology 15*(3), 341–372. https://doi.org/10.1007/s11292-018-9338-2

Wang, X., Zhang, H., & Bull, R. (2023). Understanding perceived legitimacy of correctional officers among male juvenile offenders in China: From a system perspective. *International Journal of Law, Crime and Justice 73*, 100596. 100596.https://doi.org/10.1016/j.ijlcj.2023.100596

Warnke, A. (2019). Mental health courts: The silver bullet made of rubber. *Kansas Journal of Law & Public Policy 29*(2), 256–276.

Warren, R. K. (2000). Public trust and procedural justice. *Court Review 37*(3), 12.

Warren-Kigenyi, N., & Coleman, H. (2014). *DWI recidivism in the United States: An examination of state-level driver data and the effect of look-back period on recidivism prevalence.* Traffic Safety Facts, U.S. Department of Transportation.

Watts, J., & Weinrath, M. (2017). The Winnipeg mental health court: Preliminary findings on program implementation and criminal justice outcomes. *Canadian Journal of Community Mental Health 36*(1), 67–82. https://doi.org/10.7870/cjcmh-2017-005

Weibull, J. W., & Villa, E. (2005). Crime, punishment and social norms (No. 610). SSE/EFI Working Paper Series in Economics and Finance.

Weidner, R., & Davis, C. (2000). *Benefits and costs of the Hennepin county community court: A preliminary analysis.* Institute on Criminal Justice, University of Minnesota Law School.

Wellford, C. F., Pepper, J. V., Petrie, C. V., National Research Council, Division of Behavioral and Social Sciences and Education, Committee on Law and Justice, and Committee to Improve Research Information and Data on Firearms. (2005). *Firearms and violence: A critical review.* National Academies Press. https://doi.org/10.17226/10881

Wenzel, M. (2004). The social side of sanctions: Personal and social norms as moderators of deterrence. *Law and Human Behavior 28*(5), 547–567. https://doi.org/10.1023/B:LAHU.0000046433.57588.71

Wexler, D. B. (1992). Putting mental health into mental health law: Therapeutic jurisprudence. *Law and Human Behavior 16*(1), 27–38.https://doi.org/10.1007/BF02351047

Wexler, D. B. (2000). Therapeutic jurisprudence: An overview. *Thomas M. Cooley Law Review 17*(1), 125.

Wexler, D. B., & Winick, B. J. (2008). Therapeutic Jurisprudence. In *Principles of Addiction Medicine*, 4th Edition.

Whitmer, G. (1979). From hospitals to jails: The fate of California's deinstitutionalized mentally ill. *American Journal of Orthopsychiatry 50*(1), 65–75. https://doi.org/10.1111/j.1939-0025.1980.tb03263.x

WHO Regional Office for Europe. (2017). *Status report on alcohol and health.* World Health Organization.

Whonnock, K. (2008). *Aboriginal Courts in Canada.* The Scow Institute.

Widra, E., & Herring, T. (2021). *States of incarceration: The global context 2021.* September. Prison Policy Initiative. https://www.prisonpolicy.org/global/2021.html

Wiechelt, S. A., & Shdaimah, C. S. (2011). Trauma and substance abuse among women in prostitution: Implications for a specialized diversion program. *Journal of Forensic Social Work 1*(2), 159–184. https://doi.org/10.1080/1936928X.2011.598843

Wiener, R. L., & E. M. Brank (Eds.). (2013). *Problem-solving courts: Social science and legal perspectives.* Springer.

Wiener, R. L., & Georges, L. (2013). Social psychology and problem-solving courts: Judicial roles and decision making. In R. L. Wiener and E. M. Brank (Eds.), *Problem solving courts* (pp. 1–20). Springer.

Wiener, R. L., Winick, B. J., Georges, L. S., & Castro, A. (2010). A testable theory of problem-solving courts: Avoiding past empirical and legal failures. *International Journal of Law and Psychiatry 33*(5–6), 417–427. https://doi.org/10.1016/j.ijlp.2010.09.012

Williamson, E., Dutch, N. M., & Clawson, H. J. (2009). National symposium on the health needs of human trafficking victims: Post-symposium brief. U.S. Department of Health and Human Services. https://aspe.hhs.gov/system/files/pdf/75841/ib.pdf

Wilson, D. B., Mitchell, O., & MacKenzie, D. L. (2006). A systematic review of drug court effects on recidivism. *Journal of Experimental Criminology 2*(4), 459–487. https://doi.org/10.1007/s11292-006-9019-4

Wilson, R., Cortoni, F., & McWhinnie, A. (2013). Circles of support & accountability: A Canadian National outcomes of findings. *Sexual Abuse 21*(4), 412–430. https://doi.org/10.1177/1079063209347724

Wilson, D. B., Olaghere, A., & Kimbrell, C. S. (2019). Implementing juvenile drug treatment courts: A meta-aggregation of process evaluations. *Journal of Research in Crime and Delinquency 56*(4), 605–645. https://doi.org/10.1177/002242781982663

Wilson, T. D., Wheatley, T., Meyers, J. M., Gilbert, D. T., & Axsom, D. (2000). Focalism: A source of durability bias in affective forecasting. *Journal of Personality and Social Psychology 78*(5), 821–836. https://doi.org/10.1037//0022-3514.78.5.821

Wingrove, T., Korpas, A. L., & Weisz, V. (2011). Why were millions of people not obeying the law? Motivational influences on non-compliance with the law in the case of music piracy. *Psychology, Crime & Law 17*(3), 261–276. https://doi.org/10.1080/10683160903179526

Winick, B. J. (2003). Therapeutic jurisprudence and problem-solving courts. *Fordham Urban Law Journal 30*(3), 1055–1103. https://ir.lawnet.fordham.edu/ulj/vol30/iss3/14

Wolf, R. V. (2005). California's collaborative justice courts: Building a problem-solving judiciary. Center for Court Innovation, Judicial Council of California and Administrative Office of the Courts. http://www.courts.ca.gov/documents/California_Story.pdf

Wolf, R. V. (2007). *Principles of problem-solving justice.* Bureau of Justice Assistance.

Wolf, R. V. (2011). Reentry courts, looking ahead: A conversation about strategies for offender reintegration. Center for Court Innovation. https://www.courtinnovation.org/sites/default/files/documents/Reentry_Courts.pdf

Wolff, N. (2002). Courts as therapeutic agents: Thinking past the novelty of mental health courts. *Journal of the American Academy of Psychiatry and the Law Online 30*(3), 431–437.

Wolff, N. (2013). Domestic violence courts: The case of lady justice meets the serpents of the caduceus. In R. Wiener, & E. Brank (Eds.), *Problem solving courts.* New York, NY: Springer. https://doi.org/10.1007/978-1-4614-7403-6_6

Wolff, N., Fabrikent, N., & Belenko, S. (2011). Mental health courts and their selection processes: Modeling variation for consistency. *Law and Human Behavior 35*(5), 402–412. https://doi.org/10.1007/s10979-010-9250-4

Wolfe, E., Guydish, J., & Termondt, J. (2002). A drug court outcome evaluation comparing arrests in a two year follow-up period. *Journal of Drug Issues 32*(4), 1155–1172.

Wood, E. F., Miller, M. K., & Kaplan, T. (2018). Specialty courts: Time for a thorough assessment. *Mississippi College Law Review 36*(3), 332–349.

Worcel, S., Furrer, C., Green, B., Burrus, S., & Finigan, M. (2008). Effects of family treatment drug courts on substance abuse and child welfare outcomes. *Child Abuse Review 17*, 427–443. https://doi.org/10.1002/car.1045

World Population Review. (2023). Countries where prostitution is legal. https://worldpopulationreview.com/country-rankings/countries-where-prostitution-is-legal

Yamada, D. C. (2021). Therapeutic jurisprudence: Foundations, expansion, and assessment. *University of Miami Law Review 75*(3), 660. https://repository.law.miami.edu/umlr/vol75/iss3/3

Yap, M. B., & Devilly, G. J. (2004). The role of perceived social support in crime victimization. *Clinical Psychology Review 24*(1), 1–14. https://doi.org/10.1016/j.cpr.2003.09.007

Yelderman, L. A. (2016). An assessment of juvenile drug courts' knowledge of evidence-based practices, data collection, and the use of AA/NA. *Juvenile and Family Court Journal 67*(1), 33–48. https://doi.org/10.1111/jfcj.12055

Yelderman, L. A. (2017). Mentoring programs in juvenile treatment drug courts: Understanding the difficulties of applying best practices. *Journal of Applied Juvenile Justice Services*, 28–49. https://irp.cdn-website.com/45a58767/files/uploaded/2017-Mentoring%20Programs%20%28Yelderman%29.pdf

Young, N. K., & Marlowe, D. B. (2014). *Matching service to need: Exploring what high-risk high-need means for family drug courts* [National Webinar]. Children and Family Futures.

Yount, K. M., & Li, L. (2010). Domestic violence against married women in Egypt. *Sex Roles: A Journal of Research 63*(5–6), 332–347. https://doi.org/10.1007/s11199-010-9793-3

Yuan, Y., & Capriotti, M. R. (2019). The impact of mental health court: A Sacramento case study. *Behavioral Sciences & the Law 37*(4), 452–467.https://doi.org/10.1002/bsl.2421

Zehr, H. (1995). Justice paradigm shift: Values and visions in the reform process. *Mediation Quarterly 12*, 207–216.

Zhang, S., Huang, H., Wu, Q., Li, Y., & Liu, M. (2019). The impacts of family treatment drug court on child welfare core outcomes: A meta-analysis. *Child Abuse & Neglect 88*, 1–14. https://doi.org/10.1016/j.chiabu.2018.10.014

Zhao, Y. (2002). Cultural divide over parental discipline. *New York Times.* May 29. https://www.nytimes.com/2002/05/29/nyregion/cultural-divide-over-parental-discipline.html.

Zhao, M., & Zhang, Y. (2019). Parental childcare support, sibship status and mothers' second-child plans in urban China. *Demographic Research 41*(47), 1315–1346. https://doi.org/10.4054/DemRes.2019.41.47

Zhu, X. D., & Liu, J. (2020). Education in and after Covid-19: Immediate responses and long-term visions. *Postdigital Science and Education*, 1–5. https://doi.org/10.1007/s42438-020-00126-3

Zimring, F. E., & Hawking, G. J. (1973). *Deterrence: The legal threat in crime control.* University of Chicago Press.

Zozula, C. (2019). *Courting the community court: Legitimacy and punishment in a community court.* Temple University Press.

Zweig, J. M., Rossman, S. B., Roman, J. K., Markman, J. A., Lagerson, E., & Schafer, C. (2011). *The multi-site adult drug court evaluation: What's happening with drug courts? A portrait of adult drug courts in 2004. Vol. 2.* National Institute of Justice.

Index

For the benefit of digital users, indexed terms that span two pages (e.g., 52–53) may, on occasion, appear on only one of those pages.

Note: Figures are indicated by an italic *f* following the page number.